QBASIC
Beginners Book

QBASIC Beginners Book

Ian Sinclair

Bruce Smith Books

QBASIC Beginners Book

ISBN: 1-873308-21-3 First Edition: September 1993.

Editors: Peter Fitzpatrick and Mark Webb.

Typesetting: Bruce Smith Books Ltd.

Cover design: Jude at *Wire Design Studio*

Internal design: Steve Prickett/*image*MAKERS.

Bruce Smith Books is an imprint of Bruce Smith Books Limited.

Published by: Bruce Smith Books Limited, PO Box 382, St. Albans, Herts, AL2 3JD. Telephone: (0923) 894355, Fax: (0923) 894366.

Registered in England No. 2695164.
Registered Office: 51 Quarry Street, Guildford, Surrey, GU1 3UA.

Printed and bound in the UK by Bell & Bain.

The Author

With over 150 books on computer-related subjects under his belt since 1972, Ian Sinclair brings a wealth of both writing and technical experience to his work. Born in 1932 and educated at St Andrews university, he worked in radar display systems before moving into lecturing and then writing full-time.

Ian lives in the heart of glorious Suffolk and writes full-time, accompanied by the sounds of Classic FM.

Contents

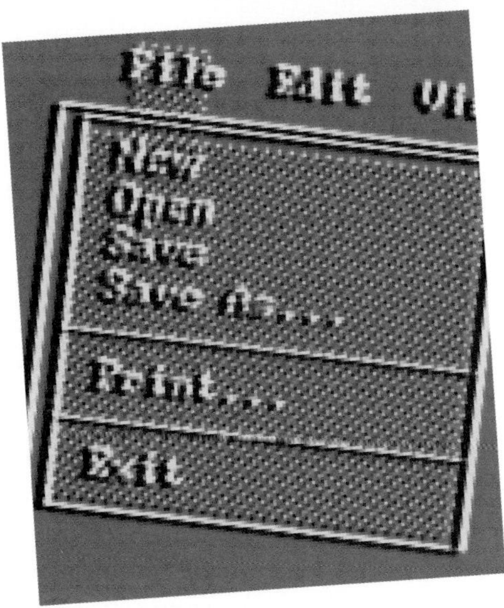

Preface

BASIC is a language that has existed in many more than the legendary 57 varieties but now, some thirty years after its creation, we seem at last to have accepted it as the universal computer language. Though academics have always rejected the use of BASIC as a satisfactory language (satisfactory for academics that is), the fact remains that it is one of the few languages in which nearly everything of a computing nature can be done.

Many other famous languages have weak spots such as a poor handling of memory or an inability to handle strings easily. The more modern versions of BASIC allow the user to do, in reasonably simple ways, actions that are difficult and convoluted in other languages. In addition, BASIC programs are almost always easier to read than others. For these reasons, every small computer has a version of BASIC, and many users have taken advantage of this to create programs for themselves.

The feature that has always attracted users to BASIC is that it allows programming to be learned by examples that are truly short, without the need for several lines of preliminary material. This is unusual among programming languages, and it appeals to anyone whose typing skills are not yet fully developed. It also makes a book of this nature considerably more compact, since much more can be learned from a large number of short examples than from a few long ones.

Of the versions of BASIC that are available for the PC compatible machines, two are generally provided along with the MS-DOS operating system. One is GW-BASIC, which is almost identical to the BASICA provided with the IBM PC machine. The other, introduced along with MS-DOS 5.0, is QBASIC, an offshoot from the outstandingly successful Microsoft QuickBasic. GW-BASIC looks rather old-fashioned by now, retaining all the features of versions of BASIC from the past, but QBASIC is a thoroughly modern interpreted BASIC which deserves a high position in any list of languages suitable for learning programming methods. There is, however, no introduction to the language included in the MS-DOS 5.0 manuals and the Help system is of little assistance to anyone not familiar with a modern version of BASIC.

This book is designed both as an introduction and a more advanced tutorial to the many features of QBASIC programming. Programming, after all, is one of the features for which a computer is intended. Owning a computer and not programming it for yourself is like buying a Ferrari and getting someone else to drive it – while you pay for the petrol. If you have never programmed a computer for yourself, this book will show you how to get started. If you have some experience of earlier makes of computers, then this book will open a new world of business-biased programming to you. QBASIC is very much aimed at the user who has serious business applications in mind, but has a range of the graphics and colour commands that allow very interesting screen displays to be achieved, for either business or pleasure. Only the commands that require a knowledge of the design and organisation of the PC machine have been treated briefly, others are dealt with in detail with examples where relevant.

Every program which appears in this book, and every example of programming commands, has been tested on QBASIC, using a 386 machine with a VGA display. All programs are based on the major release QBASIC 1.0 but are compatible with minor revisions such as 1.1.

Nothing has been copied untested from the Help pages, and where a command has operated in a way that is not obvious from description, I have pointed out the differences. Where menus permit selection by using the mouse, I have emphasised mouse methods, because it is likely that most users of a PC machine will by now be using a mouse, and this method of selection is far less laborious than the methods based on cursor keys.

This book is Volume One of a two volume set. This volume concentrates on the essentials, for the beginner, of learning QBASIC. Volume Two – Complete A to Z Guide – provides a handy reference, with examples, for every QBASIC command.

Ian Sinclair

Note: The key which is variously marked as RETURN, ENTER, or with the hooked arrow ←┘ is referred to throughout as ENTER in this book. Please be aware that some program examples show lines that have had to be split up to fit the page width. These would normally be typed without a break, taking a new line only for each new command word (in capital letters).

Development of BASIC

Learning to program

A surprising number of computer users have, at some stage or other, written some simple programs in BASIC, yet don't fully understand what programming is about. It's obviously impossible to deal with everything that is known about programming in the space of this book because people have been programming computers for a long time now, and so much is known. What we can do, however, is to outline a methodical approach which will be very useful to you, and to demonstrate it in each section of this book. As far as possible, then, each example in this book is part of a process that leads up to useful programs and also provides you with routines that you can use in your own programs.

At the risk of antagonising the reviewers who believe that every computer owner is already an expert, we need to start by asking what we expect a computer to do. The short answer is that it's a machine which can organise information for you. Give it a set of names and addresses, and it will store them, arrange them into alphabetical order, produce the address for a name that you type, and so on. Give it a list of names and payments to a club, and it will give you a list of who paid how much and who still owes what. Give it a load of numbers in answer to questions about your earnings and expenses, and it will show you your correct tax code.

These actions, however, are not so much carried out by the computer as by the instructions of the program that it is running.

You may have bought the machine along with a printer in order to run business programs, like spreadsheets, databases and wordprocessors as many owners do. Programs like these are designed by professionals, using much larger computers, so you can't really hope to come up with a new and earth-shattering business program all on your own with a small machine.

What you can do, though, is to use the machine for your own unique purposes, things that no-one has thought it worthwhile to provide a ready made program for. You might want to keep track of the members of your rugby club, or the purchases from your mail-order catalogue. You might want to devise educational games for your own children, or quizzes which are suited to their particular needs. You might want to run a local camera club, keep track of shares on the Stock Exchange, keep an analysis of what your car costs, or check your income tax – the list is endless. Whatever your own interest, whether it's tracing your ancestors or cataloguing the works of a long-dead writer, you'll need a program.

Of course, if you intend to use the computer as you use a washing machine, running only programs which came with the machine or which you can buy, then the manual which comes with the machine will serve most of your needs. The program is what we call the software of the machine. Without a suitable program, the computer can do nothing. The machine itself is the brainless bit, the clever part is the program. So how do you go about writing a program?

It isn't as difficult as you might think. The reason is that there has been a lot of progress in this respect in the last twenty years. Once upon a time, computers were big machines which had to be programmed by skilled people who understood the number code system (called machine-code) that the computer used – and each computer used its own machine code system. As time went on, programming languages were invented. A programming language is a way of instructing a computer by using command words which are English words. Even before microcomputers were dreamed of, there were several of these programming languages, but the most important one for us is BASIC.

BASIC is short for Beginners All-purpose Symbolic Instruction Code. It was invented at Dartmouth College, USA, as a way of teaching computer programming. Since then it has spread like wildfire to become the programming language that is used for each and every personal or home computer. It's still a good language for beginners in the sense that it's easy to learn, but it has also developed into a language that gives you a lot of control over your computer. There's more about the development of BASIC and other programming languages later in this chapter.

Now the reasonable question to ask at this point is: why should you program the computer for yourself when, for a few thousand pounds, you could have as many professionally written programs as you might need? The figure of a few thousand pounds is one good reason in itself if you are a home user, though for business purposes this might be chicken-feed. The one single overwhelming answer to this question is that only by programming for yourself do you get exactly what you want. Suppose, for example, you run a small mail-order catalogue group, and you want to keep tabs on who has ordered what, how much has been paid and when delivery is made. Now there isn't a commercial program to do just exactly this, as far as I know. You could buy a set of business programs such as spreadsheets and databases and accounts packages, but you'll be overwhelmed by them. They all need a lot of learning to use and they all do very much more than you need.

A business accounts program, for example, keeps a dozen ledgers going, has entries for aged debtors, bought ledger and all sorts of other accountancy terms, and you spend most of your time trying to work out which bits are needed and what you are supposed to enter into each of them. Since you can't dispense with any of them, though, you have to try to use them all, just as if you were running a medium-scale business. By spending just a fraction of that time and a lot less money on learning to program for yourself, you could have your own program, tailored to your own needs and doing what you need of it. Remember that when you buy a program written by someone else, the program is in charge, and it decides how you have to proceed.

When you write your own program, you are in charge, and you decide what the program produces. If you don't need VAT paperwork, the program doesn't produce it or ask you for your VAT registration number each time you start using it. If you want printed receipts, your program provides them. If you need a list of customers in alphabetical order, your program can be made to give that, or a list in order of how much they owe you – it's all up to you to decide what you want and arrange for it to be supplied. Control, then, is the main reason for wanting to program.

There's another reason, which has nothing to do with business but a lot to do with curiosity. You can use a computer as you might use a car, putting up with its odd little ways, but never doing anything to understand them. Using a computer in this way is never entirely satisfying – you always feel that the machine will have the last word. Just as by understanding what makes a car tick (or run smoothly as the case may be) you can drive it better and avoid breakdowns, you can also, by learning more about the computer become able to make better use of it.

In addition, programming is a very considerable aid to thinking. When you learn to program, you also learn to break a problem down into manageable pieces, and work on the pieces. If you are programming for some business reason, you'll learn a lot more about your business from writing the program than you imagined possible. If you program for a hobby reason, then both your hobby and your computing will come on in leaps and bounds. You don't have to start at Professor level to get a lot from programming – just watch a class of eight-year olds at work with a computer. At the other end of the scale, there is no such thing as being too old to get to grips with programming, nor is anything that we term a physical disability any form of handicap.

Programming languages

A computer program is a set of instructions, and a programming language is concerned with how these instructions are written. When you use a computer, as distinct from programming it, you use direct commands. Each command, like the DIR and COPY of your MS-DOS operating system, is set into action by typing its name and then pressing the ENTER key. Systems such as Windows are only roundabout methods of issuing these same commands, allowing you to pick from commands whose names are already printed.

In a program, the words of command are written in the sequence in which we want them to be carried out, but they are not carried out until we issue a command word or press a key that starts the sequence running. The difference is important. A direct command is carried out by typing the name, then pressing ENTER. If you want to repeat the command, you have to go through all of these steps again. A program, by contrast, can consist of a number of separate steps, written once, and which can be executed as many times as you like just by using one command, RUN or, in the case of QBASIC, by pressing the SHIFT and F5 keys together – written as SHIFT-F5. The words or codes that are used to mean instructions in a program are what make up the programming language, along with the way that the words must be used, which is the syntax of the language.

Language development

To start with, we have to look at programming languages generally. At the bottom of the heap of programming level comes machine code, writing directly in the number-codes which are what the machine works with. Machine code programming is tedious, error-prone and very difficult to check. The only reasons for using it are that it's the only way to program a completely new microprocessor for which nothing is written, because of its speed, the small amount of memory that is needed, and because of the control that it gives you.

There are always features of a machine that can be controlled only by machine code. No language like BASIC or PASCAL or C can ever cope with every possibility and if you want to have your screen scrolling sideways, or to run an unusual disk system, or to use a non-standard printer, you might need machine code to write the routines. There is such a continuing need for machine code that we need a programming language, assembler language, in order to write machine code with less tedium and fewer bugs. Assembler language, then, comes slightly higher up the scale compared to machine code, because it's easier to write, but it still produces the fastest running instructions – machine code.

What about the other end of the scale? There's one high-level language, COBOL, which looks almost like a set of instructions in English when you read a program written in this language. When you write programs in a language of this type, you don't expect to have to worry about the details of the machine. You aren't interested in what microprocessor it uses (on a mainframe computer, you don't even have a microprocessor). You don't need to know ASCII codes, or routine addresses in RAM, or any of the things that constantly occupy the minds of assembly language programmers. You simply write your program lines, run them on the machine, and sit back like anyone else until the program crashes. The language processor (a compiler) converts the instructions of your program into machine code, this machine code is recorded, and from then on the computer executes the machine code each time you need it. The name *high-level* is a good one – you are so far above the ground level of machine code that you hardly know there's a machine there. Needless to say, the language is the same no matter which machine you happen to be programming.

Between the heights of COBOL, FORTRAN and ALGOL, the three classic programming languages, and the ground level of machine code, there are languages at all sorts of intermediate levels. The fundamental problem is that high level languages are powerful but inefficient. They allow you to turn your problem-solving methods into programs that run smoothly, but at a great cost in memory space and speed. Most of them are compiled languages, meaning that the lines of instructions are converted by a compiler program into faster-running machine-code, and this code is then recorded as your working program. They can be cumbersome, using lines and lines of program which can take all day to compile. At the other end, machine code is very compact, very fast and very efficient, but sheer hell to write and debug in any quantity.

The reason that we have such a large number of programming languages is that we are constantly trying to get a better balance of these different virtues. What we want is a high-level language that makes it easy to express our solutions, is very compact both in statement length and use of memory, and which translates into a few bytes of machine code as would be given by an assembler. There's no such language, and probably never will be, but some come nearer than others, and some are a better solution for some kinds of problems.

The problem that BASIC was originally devised to solve was the problem of teaching the older language FORTRAN. Beginners All-purpose Symbolic Instruction Code is exactly what it originally was – a simple language intended to serve as an introduction to programming, and modelled on one of the great original computer languages, FORTRAN. The advantage of the original BASIC was that it was simple to learn, but close enough to the methods of FORTRAN to make the conversion easy. BASIC could be made in interpreter form, and using an incredibly small amount of memory (as little as 4 K). The use of an interpreter system meant that mistakes could be easily and quickly found and corrected.

The interpreter system is one that runs a program in BASIC by converting each instruction to machine code and running that instruction, rather than by converting the whole program. This allows each BASIC instruction to be interrupted, so that when a mistake is found it can be corrected and the program run again, rather than using the tedious process of recompiling the whole program. There are, however, compiled BASICs like Microsoft Quick BASIC and BASIC-7, and Borland's Turbo-BASIC, which will produce COM or EXE programs and which are used for writing commercial software. Finally, BASIC can also be written in code that takes up only a small amount of memory. It was for precisely these reasons that when microcomputers became available, they featured BASIC as their programming language.

Since then, BASIC has developed a long way, and it's no longer just a language for beginners. As the language grew, it acquired more features from other languages and without losing its simplicity, soon became a language in its own right, not just a path to an almost-forgotten FORTRAN.

Because of the intensive use of BASIC versions on small computers, the language became a general purpose one, good for all kinds of programs whether your interests were in accounts, science, engineering, text editing or whatever. Other languages tended to remain specialised, good for only one or two selected purposes, while BASIC grew to fit the needs of a much wider band of users. Nowadays, more people can program in BASIC than in any other language, and they don't necessarily learn it so that they can learn another language. After all, you don't learn English so that you can later learn Icelandic (sorry, Magnus).

Interpreting and compiling

Computing languages like BASIC can be arranged in two ways. One of these ways is called interpreted and the other compiled. The QBASIC of MS-DOS 5.0 is of the interpreted type. This means that the instructions which you have typed are held in the memory of the computer as a set of code numbers. When you run a program written in QBASIC, the QBASIC program must be present in the memory, and it will interpret each code number for an instruction and make it work. That means that the machine has to find what the code means, and then act on it. Acting on it means that the machine has to locate another set of coded instructions in its memory, and use these to direct the microprocessor, the 8086, 80286, 80386 or 80486, which is at the heart of the computer.

A language which uses interpretation is slow, because each command has to be looked up, in turn, as the computer comes to it. A compiler, by contrast, does the looking up once just after the program has been written. The instructions are then turned directly into the microprocessor codes. When a compiled program runs, then, there is no looking up to do, and the speed can be very much greater. In addition, a compiled BASIC program can be run like any of the programs that have COM or EXE extension names, just by typing its name. You don't have to have BASIC loaded in to run such programs. Many of the programs that are shown in the directory listing of disks that you buy as ending with EXE or COM are of this type, though many of them will have been compiled from other languages, such as C or PASCAL.

For learning the language from scratch, however, an interpreter is much better, because it allows you to alter the program when an error occurs, and try again. This sort of thing is never easy with a compiled program, which is why compilers are mainly used by professionals. As time goes on, however, you may feel that you need to use a faster-running language. The great advantage of the PC computer is that you have the choice. Both QBASIC and its stable-mate QuickBASIC share an almost identical set of command words, so that a program written for QBASIC can be compiled by QuickBASIC when you want to make the change.

QBASIC is unusually well-equipped for finding out where a fault exists in a program (see Chapter 17). This makes it very suitable for learning the crafts of programming, and the fact that you can later convert your QBASIC programs into compiled COM or EXE programs is an additional incentive. Start then with Chapter Two in your discovery of what QBASIC has to offer, and try for yourself each of the examples, because it is only by typing and running examples that they will have any real meaning for you.

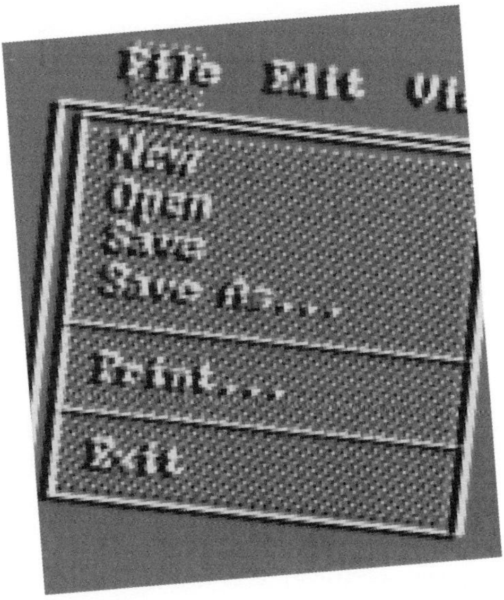

Principles

Basics of BASIC

The BASIC language is built like any other language, with vocabulary and syntax. The vocabulary is the words used to form instructions and the syntax is the way in which they are used. Like any other language, BASIC has rules which you have to learn. What makes it so much easier for you to learn is that the command words are mainly English-looking words, and the rules are simple. In addition, your interpreter will tell you when you have disobeyed the rules, sometimes even before you try to run the program you have written.

To learn about BASIC, then, you have to learn what a number of words mean. There are about 240 of these words in QBASIC, the meaning of many of them is fairly obvious and only a fairly small number are commonly used. In addition, you have to learn the correct way to use each word. This is where you really come up against the brainless machine part of computing. The computer can make use of a command which uses the correct word in the correct way. If you spell the word wrongly, use it in the wrong way, or use the wrong word, the machine can't do anything – so it stops. When it does this, a message will appear on the screen to tell you what happened. This is called an *error message*, and from what it says, you should be able to find what went wrong. In fact, the error message is more usually sent from the program that is currently running (such as the BASIC interpreter), but the point is that what you use as a command has to be acceptable.

If that sounds simple, it's because it is simple, which is why it needs to be learned. Suppose you had a foreign friend who understood only about two hundred words of English. How would you make him understand, using only the words he knows, that you want him to do something like arrange words in alphabetical order or find how many members of the dominoes club have paid their subscriptions? The answer is that you have to break up these complicated actions into a lot of simple steps. You then have to describe each step in the words that your two–hundred-word friend understands.

There's one big difference here, though. A human who knows a couple of hundred words of a language will pick up other words very quickly. A computer doesn't have this ability. Every instruction has to be made out of these important command words, the *keywords* as we call them. A program consists of an arrangement of these keywords in such a way that something useful is done. A program might be educational, amusing, for business or leisure, working with words or with numbers, whatever you want it to be. Whatever it is, though, it still has to make use of these keywords, because that's all that it can use. You can't type instructions like "Who ordered a dozen spob-tackers?" or "What will my payments be if I pay back one fifth of the mortgage next month?". These are questions for humans with human brains, not for computers until a human writes a program. Computers have memory. They can store information and they can store instructions. They can't think what a new instruction might mean, though, which is why we have to write programs.

Data types

The computer works with data, items of information, but its ability to work with such data is severely limited because the machine itself can deal internally only with numbers. Whatever else the computer is expected to deal with must be capable of being converted into number form, and what we refer to as different data types are in fact different ways of converting data into numbers that can be stored. The simplest data type is the single character, any one of the keys on the keyboard. Each of these is represented by a code number in the range between 32 (the space) and 126 (the ~ tilde sign) – the code 127 is a small triangle which is not on the keyboard. In addition, another set of characters can be obtained from codes 128 to 255 and most PC users know that these characters can be put on to the screen by holding down the Alt key and typing the number on the numeric keypad at the right hand side of the keyboard.

These codes for characters are called ASCII or ANSI codes (the ASCII set is the 32 to 127 set, the ANSI set includes the ASCII set and also the 128 to 255 set). Each of them uses a number in the range 0 to 255, which is as much as one unit of memory, one byte, can store. The memory consists of miniature electrical switches which can be either on or off, one of two possible states, so that numbers have to be stored as powers of 2, binary numbers. A number such as 57, for example, is stored as 32 + 16 + 8 + 1, which needs only four switches, because each switch in a set of eight deals with a different power of two, Figure 2.1.

128	64	32	16	8	4	2	1	Powers of two.
1	0	0	0	1	1	0	1	Binary example.
128				8	4		1	Values.
			= 141					Equivalent.

Figure 2.1. How a set of 1 or 0 switches can encode a binary number when each switch represents a different power of two.

When we want to store words, it is undesirable to store each character of a word in a different part of the memory. Consecutive characters in a word or phrase are stored one following the other in the memory, forming a data type called a *string*. When a string is stored in the memory it is usual to have one byte of memory allocated for each character, plus extra bytes to keep a record of the number of bytes used in the string and where it starts – this makes it easier for the machine to count out the number of bytes. QBASIC, like most versions of BASIC, uses the string data type for words, but does not have a separate system for characters – a character is just a very short string.

Strangely enough, numbers are more difficult to deal with because of the use of binary counting, and there are two important number types. The integer type is a whole number, with no fractions. Any whole number can be coded into binary if you use sufficient bytes. If you use one byte, you can code only the numbers 0 to 255, but if you use two bytes, you can keep one byte, the most significant byte, to carry over each 256, so that the number 257 would be coded as a 1 in the most significant byte and a 1 in the less significant byte, Figure 2.2.

High byte	Low byte	Equivalent
0	25	25
1	256	256
1	47	303
2	85	597
25	66	6466
122	13	31245

Figure 2.2. Using two bytes to represent larger integer numbers – one complication is the way that negative numbers are represented.

Using two bytes allows a range of 0 to 65535 (which is 256 x 256 - 1), and the more bytes you can use the larger the range of numbers you can deal with. Integers can be positive or negative, and the difference is dealt with by using half of the possible range of binary codes for positive numbers and the other half for negative numbers.

Integer numbers, however, are not so useful for work that involves calculations that can result in fractions, particularly divisions. A different method therefore has to be used for numbers, variously called *real* or *floating-point* numbers, in which a decimal fraction is part of the number. This system requires the number to be stored in two parts, not whole number and fraction as you might think, but a more elaborate coding which is very similar to the Standard number system for ordinary numbers, noted in more detail in Appendix A.

The essence of this system as applied to binary numbers is that part of the coding involves a binary fraction. Now a binary fraction works out exactly for numbers like 0.5 (which is 1/2, binary 0.1) or 0.25 (which is 1/4, binary 0.01), or any number that is the inverse of a power of 2 (such as 1/128), or any number that is the sum of these, like .75 (which is in denary 0.5 + 0.25). For other fractions, the conversion is inexact, no matter how many bytes you use for storage, though the greater the number of bytes you use, the more precise the results will be. In addition, because the method of storing these floating-point numbers is so much more elaborate, the machine takes longer to work with them.

QBASIC allows the use of the string type along with a large range of number types (integer, long integer, float single and float double). In addition, you can create your own data types which consist of a mixture of existing data types. For example, you might want a data type called TODAY which consisted of a Date (as a string), a Note (a string), some money income (single-precision), some money outgoing (single precision) and the day number for the year (integer). You could then use this type as if it were one of the established data types.

Pictures and sound

The coding of words and numbers accounts for a large part of computing, but for a lot of programming it is necessary to code pictures, and some applications require the coding of sound. The ordinary tasks of displaying numbers and words on the screen are taken care of by the operating system of the computer, and what we are concerned with here is how pictures and sound are stored so that the operating system can work with them.

A picture, ignoring the details of the monitor display, is a set of dots on a screen. For a monochrome monitor, these dots can be black, white, or any of a set of shades between black and white. For a colour monitor, the dots can be of different colours and of different brightnesses, so that more information has to be stored. The coding system must therefore store a set of numbers, dealing with all the dots of a full screen (or a portion of screen) in order, using a number code to express both brightness and colour.

This allows the programming language to create pictures by specifying the brightness and colour of each dot in a full screen or a window, which, however, is very long-winded, particularly if the screen display you want to create is just a few thin lines. Provision is made, therefore, for storing instructions rather than screen dots, each instruction creating some element like a line or a circle. This is the fundamental difference between drawing and painting programs – the painting programs work with individual dots; the drawing programs with elements like lines and circles.

Sound is a vibration in the air, and each pitch of sound corresponds to a definite number of vibrations per second, mainly in the range of 100 per second (a very low note) to 8,000 per second (a very high note). Each pitch can therefore be coded simply as a number. Using this system can produce notes, but these sound nothing like the sound of any musical instrument (or even like some unmusical instruments), because musical instruments do not create notes of a constant level – the loudness varies between the start and finish of each note, and each note consists of a mixture of tones of different pitch as well. For more realistic sound, then, several numbers have to be stored for each note to express the mixture of pitches and the way that the loudness level (amplitude) varies while the note is sounding.

Program elements

Given the various data types that can be used, we now need to look at how a programming language works with these data types. The first two names to become acquainted with are constants and variables.

A constant is a data item that remains fixed throughout the duration of a program, and which can be represented in the program by a name. We could for example, use the name JOBLOT to represent the phrase "A unique collection of items of historical interest, eminently collectable". We could also apply this to a number, using VATRATE to mean 0.175, or PISIZE to mean 3.1416. We could also use a name to represent a picture or a sound.

Why use a name? The answer is simple, and it carries a clue to the usefulness of the system. In the course of a program, you might have to use a quantity, a phrase like "of unique historical interest" or a number line 0.175, many times, possibly hundreds of times. Now if at any stage you decided to alter the phrase to "of specialised interest" or the number, heaven and European Community forbid, to 0.20, you would have a lot of alteration to do in a program. If, however, the phrase is represented by the constant JOBLOT, there will be one line, and only one line, in which this word is equated (assigned) with the phrase. Change this line, and you change the meaning of JOBLOT for every point in the program where it is used. Likewise, change the value of VATRATE from 0.175 to 0.2 and you have adjusted the whole program for a new VAT rate by one simple action.

The constant is useful, but the variable is even more useful. A variable is, like a constant, a name that can be used for some phrase or number. The difference is that the variable will change in value. At one point in the program, the name FIRST might mean Zachary; later in the program it might mean Aaron, so that the name is fixed but the meaning varies. This allows, just to give one example, a set of actions to be applied to a phrase or number represented by a variable name, then the name used for something else and the same actions carried out all over again. Once again, this saves effort, because if we used a constant for each phrase or number, the action commands would have to be written separately for each one. By using a variable, the action commands remain the same and only the value assigned to the variable is changed. Early versions of BASIC provided for the use of variables for constant quantities as well – after all, a constant is just a variable that does not change.

A variable name can be applied to any form of data. QBASIC uses two systems, one for compatibility with old-style BASICs, the other compatible with more modern languages. In the older system, a plain name represents a single-precision number, and any other data type is signalled by a special name ending. For example, a-name would be a variable for a single-precision number, but a-name$ would be a name for a string variable.

The more modern system is to define each variable name and to state in the definition what type it is. This allows any of the standard types to be used, and it also allows for any user-defined type, as noted earlier in this chapter. All names used in this system are plain, with no special ending characters.

In the past, some versions of BASIC required the use of the word LET to assign a value to a variable, such as LET a$="Name", but this has not been in general use for many years. QBASIC will recognise the word (in case it occurs in an old program) but it is not needed.

Global and local

Constants and variables can be described as *global* and *local*. When a program consists, as it should, of a set of small pieces which are used in turn, these pieces can be almost totally self-contained. Any variables that they use are for internal use only, and simply do not exist in the rest of the program. Such variables are called local.

By contrast, traditional versions of BASIC have always used global variables – any variable created in any part of the program can be used in any other part. This can be convenient, but it can lead to considerable confusion when two portions of program alter the value of a variable unwittingly. QBASIC allows you to use either the older style or the modern one as you choose. Constants are always global.

Static and dynamic

Variables can be *static* or *dynamic*. This is not of primary importance when you start to dabble in BASIC, but it can be important later when you try to do more ambitious things. A static variable has its value stored in a piece of memory that is reserved for variables, and this piece of memory is reserved throughout the time that the program is running. By contrast, a dynamic variable is stored in a temporary piece of memory which is wiped clean when the variable is no longer in use. This type of memory is used for local variables, and is also used for some arrays, see later.

Functions

A programming language needs to consist of more than just a few data types, along with provision for constants and variables. In the course of a program, some actions have to be carried out on the data that is stored in the form of constants and variables, and it would be very time-consuming if everything had to be designed from scratch each time.

Programming languages therefore contain a set of functions, with each function carrying out an action on a number or a string. This way, the program can be written by calling up one function after another rather than by working with the data directly. When you use a calculator to find the LOG of 23, for example, you do not expect to have to go through several hundred steps of calculation – pressing the LOG key on the calculator calls up the actions that carry out the whole set of steps.

Functions of a programming language can be numerical, allowing you to find the logarithm of a number or its square root, or they can be string functions, allowing you to find the number of characters in a string, or to find if a specified word occurs in the string. These are just examples taken at random to show the scope of functions.

Each function normally acts on data that is stored in the form of a variable, so that the function consists of two parts, the name of the function and the name of the variable – this last part is usually called the *argument* of the function, and is usually enclosed within brackets so that the computer can pick it out. Most functions are meaningless if no argument is present, so that an error message is delivered if a function has no argument. The argument is the way that is used to pass the variable value to the function.

There are some tasks you might want to use in a program of your own for which there is no ready-made function. This problem is solved by using some form of *procedure*. A procedure is a home-made function, written like a miniature program to deal with data in the form of variables, and also delivering its results as variables (perhaps by altering the values of the original variables). The action of supplying a procedure with the variable(s) that it needs is called *passing variables* to the procedure, and it is normally done in the same way, by enclosing the variable name or names in brackets.

Program structure

The structure of a program means the way that it carries out its actions by calling up functions and procedures in order of use until all of the processing has been done. This needs some organisation, because the order in which actions are carried out needs to be correct, and the most satisfactory method of arranging a program is to design it as a set of main steps, with each main step consisting of a number of smaller steps, Figure 2.3. This allows each step, large or small, to be designed in the same way and it often allows each step to be tested separately. In addition, some steps may be standard ones that can be used over and over again in different programs.

Main 1	**Minor 1**	**Minor 2**	**Minor 3**	
Main 2	**Minor 4**	**Minor 5**		
Main 3	**Minor 6**	**Minor 7**	**Minor 8**	**Minor 9**
Main 4	**Minor 10**	**Minor 11**		
END				

Figure 2.3. A program normally consists of a set of main *steps which can be divided into* minor *steps.*

A program with a clear structure is easier to write, easier to modify and easier to correct if anything goes wrong. Early versions of BASIC were criticised on the grounds that it was too easy for a programmer to make untidy poorly-organised programs. It was always possible to write well-structured programs in BASIC, but you had to be really determined. Modern versions of BASIC encourage good programming methods in the way that languages like Pascal do, and when you see BASIC being criticised as a language it is generally by someone who has not used BASIC since 1979.

Once such a program is designed, it has to be typed, using an *editor.* An editor is a simple form of wordprocessor, which stores the instruction list that you type in the form of ASCII codes in a file. You can look at this file on screen or print it, it's called a *listing.* It has no effect until you have QBASIC running and you open the file and run the instructions. The interpreter part of QBASIC then carries out the instructions in order. If there is a problem, the action halts and an error-message appears, requiring you to return to the editor, alter the program and either continue or start running again. This makes the editor the first part of QBASIC that you need to become closely acquainted with.

Starting QBASIC

1. For users of the MS-DOS 5 or MS-DOS 6 DOSSHELL, QBASIC can be put on the Programs list in a group, so that it can be started by double-clicking the mouse on the name QBASIC.
2. If you do not use DOSSHELL, the simplest way is to create a Batch file. Suppose, for example, that QBASIC is in a directory called C:\BASIC. The batch file lines might read as:

```
CD C:\BASIC
QBASIC
CD\
```

and this would be recorded under the filename QB.BAT, and placed in a directory called BATS. The AUTOEXEC.BAT file of the computer should contain a PATH statement, and that statement should include BATS; so that the BATS file can be found automatically. You can then run QBASIC by typing QB when the computer is running.

3. The long hard way is to remember the directory name, and type a direct command to MS-DOS such as:

```
\BASIC\QBASIC
```

Whichever way you start, the Opening screen of QBASIC appears shortly after you have issued the starting commands.

note ***You can use the Editor of QBASIC itself to create a batch file.***

QBASIC add-ons

There are several add-on parts (parameters and switches) that can be used following the QBASIC command:

1. You can follow QBASIC with a file path and name for a BASIC program file that you want to be loaded into QBASIC as it starts.
2. You can use /b to force the display to be in black and white, even if you use a colour monitor.
3. Using /editor will start up the MS-DOS Editor.
4. For any user of a CGA screen, /g will provide a better display.
5. Using /h will force QBASIC to make use of as many screen lines as your display can handle.
6. The addition /mbf converts some of the number filing functions to modern standards – see Appendix B.
7. Using /nohi allows you to obtain better displays on a monitor that does not allow high-intensity video.
8. The /run addition, followed by a path and filename, will run the BASIC program (not just load it) that is named in the command.

Using the Editor

Program instructions

To type program instructions requires the use of the editor screen of QBASIC. When you start QBASIC, the EDIT screen looks as in Figure 3.1, offering you some initial Help in the shape of the Survival Guide.

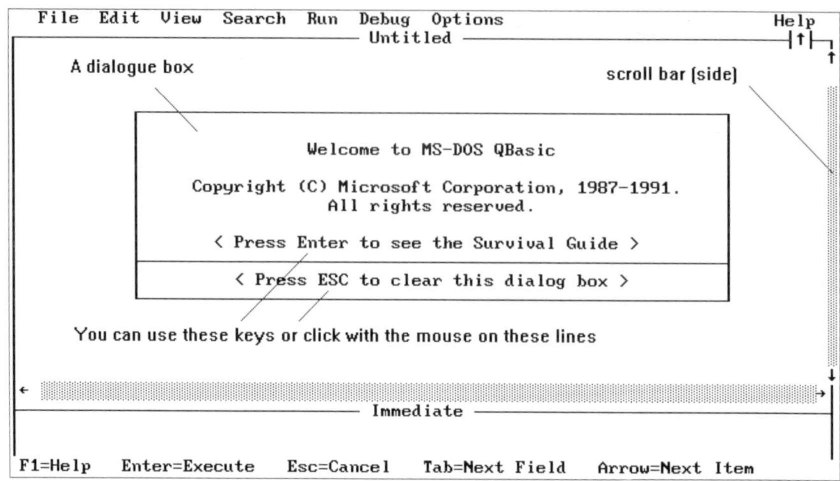

Figure 3.1. The appearance of the EDIT screen when you start QBASIC.

The screen below, Figure 3.2, indicates the ways of using the menus, but does not mention until later the most obvious way that is open to most users – the mouse.

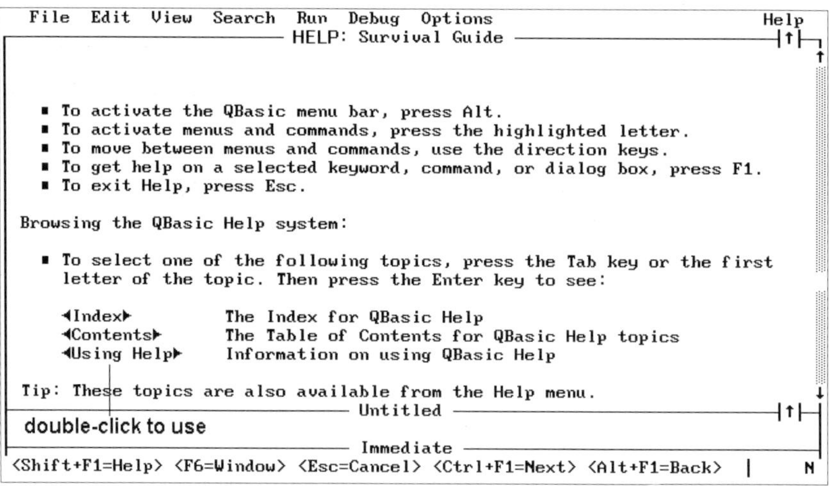

Figure 3.2. The Survival Guide screen with its advice.

If you are using the cursor keys, the menu bar at the top of the screen is activated by pressing the Alt key. With this bar highlighted, you can press the highlighted letter of each menu to activate the menu. You can then move to a command using the cursor keys and start the command using the ENTER key. Pressing F1 will summon help on whatever you have selected, and pressing the Esc key will return you from Help to the main screen.

The editor also understands WordStar commands (using the Ctrl key along with letter keys) so that if you are a seasoned WordStar user you can keep using the commands that are familiar to you.

There are three important mouse actions, clicking, double-clicking and dragging.

The clicking action is the most common one. For example, to open the File menu, you would move the mouse to place the cursor on the word File in the menu at the top of the screen, and quickly press and release the lefthand mouse button. This is called *clicking on the File*.

- Double-clicking is used to select items in the Help section. The mouse cursor is moved to the menu item and the mouse button is clicked twice in quick succession. This is used to select a Help action from the Contents list, such as:

  <— Editing keys —>

  by double-clicking between the arrowheads.

- Dragging is used to select a portion of text. If the cursor is placed at the start of a piece of text, the mouse button held down, and the mouse moves with the button still held down, the text will be marked (it will change colour) until the button is released.

All of these actions use the lefthand mouse button – the righthand button is not normally used in QBASIC, though other programs make use of it.

- Any menu can be opened by clicking on it with the mouse, and each item in a menu can be selected by clicking on its name with the mouse.

The main program is started when you press the Esc key on the first screen. This provides a blank screen, Figure 3.3, with the words 'Untitled' at the top and 'Immediate' near the bottom. There is an important difference between these two.

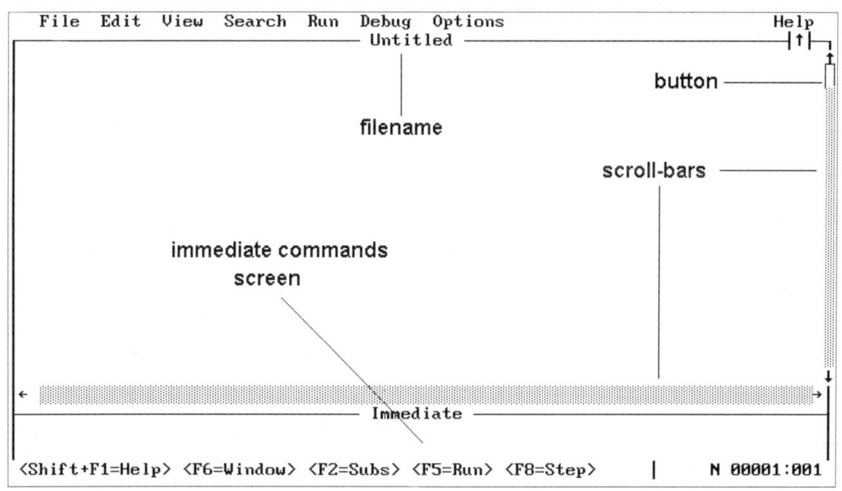

Figure 3.3. The main editing screen, allowing you to switch between Untitled and Immediate (you can also switch to Help and Output).

- The Immediate screen accepts any commands you type and executes them when you press the ENTER key.
- The Untitled screen allows you to type in a program. When you press ENTER, any keywords in a line will be converted to capital (uppercase) letters, but the commands are not obeyed.

There are two other screens in addition. There is a Help screen which will display whatever Help topic you select to view, and there is an Output screen, which displays the results of running a BASIC program. When a BASIC program is running, only the Output screen is used. You can switch to and from the Output screen by using the F4 key and between the other screens by using the F6 key.

Make yourself a keyboard template to remind yourself of these F-key actions – they are listed in the Help section of QBASIC.

Whatever you type in the window that starts off as Untitled is taken to be a BASIC program that you will later save, providing a filename. Such a program is arranged into sets of instructions, usually referred to as lines. This is slightly misleading in that a program *line* may take up several lines on the edit screen window or on paper. What marks a program line is that it is ended by pressing the ENTER key. The order in which these lines of instructions will be carried out is the order in which they appear on the Edit screen. If you want to insert a new line somewhere, then the editing methods summarised below will allow this to be done, so that you can have second thoughts.

When you have typed a program, it can be saved on disk, When you opt to save it in this way you will be asked to supply a filename, of which you need only type the main part of up to eight characters. The editor adds the extension letters of BAS if you forget them, so that if you type TEST1, the program will be recorded as TEST1.BAS. If you type TEST1.BAS it will be saved using this name.

You don't *have* to use the extension letters of BAS, but since these letters are the standard extension for BASIC programs it makes sense to do so.

QBASIC differences

If you have ever used an older version of BASIC, you will doubtless wonder what happened to line numbers. On older versions, BASIC has to be written with each program line numbered. This is because such a number is the only way that the machine can distinguish between a direct command and a program line. BASIC instructions written *without* a line number are commands and instructions *with* a line number are program instructions or statements. This scheme is not needed for QBASIC, because the separation between direct commands and BASIC program lines is made by your selection of Immediate or Untitled editing window in the editor. You can type line numbers if you want to and, if you are copying a long program from a magazine, it can be a useful way of checking that you haven't missed anything. It's important to note, however, that the line numbers have no real meaning in QBASIC.

In other versions of BASIC, for example, you can type a line that starts with the number 50, and this line will be placed between line 40 and line 60 no matter where or when you typed it. This does *not* work in QBASIC. A line is placed where you put it when you edit, and if you want a line to be put between two others, you either make a space and type it there or use the Cut and Paste actions of the editor to shift it there. The act of putting in a line number has absolutely no effect on where a line ends up in the program. If you have previously used BASIC on another machine, I strongly advise you to follow what has been done in this book and to dispense with line numbers. That way, you will not be confused by your earlier experience. If this is your first taste of BASIC, then by programming in this way you are learning good habits that will be helpful if you move to any other programming language, like C, Pascal or Modula-2.

That aside, the other differences between QBASIC and earlier dialects of BASIC are in size and features. QBASIC is a very big BASIC, with a huge number of commands, more than can be catered for in full detail in just one book. This means that there is a lot more to learn but, by way of compensation, you can make much more effective use of the language. This book deals with both the elements, getting you started with this very rich version of BASIC, and the more advanced topics, such as graphics and data filing as well. If you have had little or no experience with QBASIC at a reasonably simple level, you should leave Chapters 17 onwards until you feel you are ready for them.

We shall deal with typing in programs in the following chapter, when we start on programming itself but, for the moment, it is important to get to grips with the editor as a way of working with the text of a program. The easiest way to get some experience is to load in one of the existing demonstration programs, and to use it to become familiar with the editing commands. Providing you do not save this program back to the disk there is no prospect of damaging the program. You can use the shortest of the programs, REMLINE.BAS for this purpose.

Before you use REMLINE.BAS for editing practice, make the file read-only. If you are using MS-DOS 5 or 6, start DOSSHELL, place the cursor on REMLINE.BAS and click to highlight the name. Then select Attributes from the File menu, and click on Read-only. This makes it impossible to change the file by saving an altered copy.

What follows assumes that QBASIC and its demonstration files have been placed in a directory called BASIC. If you have used a different directory name (possibly you have QBASIC in the MS-DOS directory) you will need to ensure for yourself that you are using the correct directory.

Editing

Editing means changing something that has already appeared on the screen, and the first requirement is to have something on the editing screen. To load the example, REMLINE.BAS:

1. Click on the File menu option, Figure 3.4 (or press Alt and then F). This shows the options of New, Open, Save, Save As, Print and Exit.

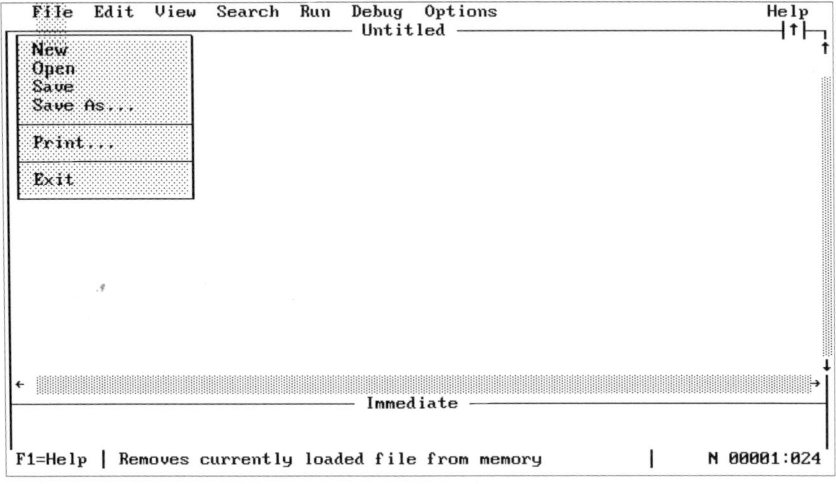

Figure 3.4. The File menu as it appears in the editor.

2. Click on Open (or press the O key). You will see the menu of BAS files, Figure 3.5. If the files are in another directory you can use the Dirs/Drives box to alter directory (by clicking on the drive letter, subdirectory name, or the .. entry which means one directory back from the BASIC directory)

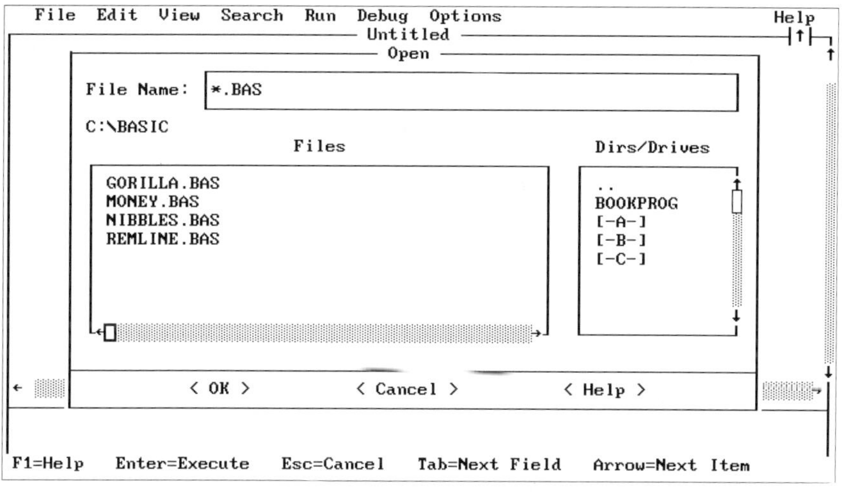

Figure 3.5. The file listing obtained from the Open command.

note From now on, an action such as Selecting file and then Open will be typed as File – Open.

3. In this example, click on the name REMLINE.BAS. If you get a message about a loaded file not saved, press the N key (unless you actually have a file that you want to save).

4. The program appears:

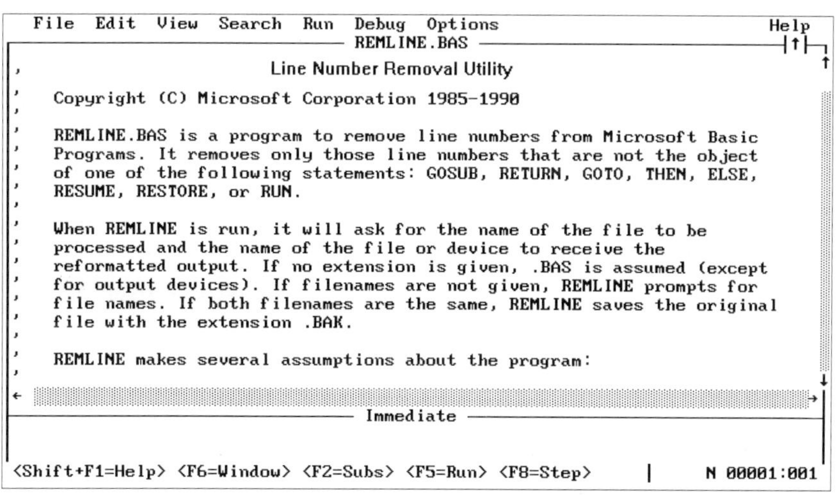

Figure 3.6. The start of the REMLINE.BAS program as it is seen on the screen.

The first part of the program consists entirely of reminders that form no part of the program. They are used to remind you of what the program does and how to use it, and because each line on the screen starts with the single-quote character (') the interpreter ignores these lines and goes straight to the first command line.

Cursor and scrolling movement

With this program in place, we can look first at how to move around the text. By far the simplest method is to use the mouse. When you are using a mouse you will see two cursors, the large block mouse cursor and the small bright flashing line, the editing cursor. All typing and deleting actions start at the editing cursor.

1. You can move the mouse cursor to any point on the screen and click to place the editing cursor at that point.
2. Clicking on the arrow at the foot of the scroll-bar moves down the text by one line (the text, in fact, all moves up the screen by one line).
3. Clicking on the scroll-bar below the button moves down the text by one screen page (18 lines).
4. Clicking on the arrow at the top of the scroll-bar moves up the text by one line.
5. Clicking on the scroll-bar above the button moves up the text by one screen page.
6. If any text is wider than the screen you can use the scroll-bar at the foot of the screen in the same way – click on the arrow to move by one column, or on either side of the button to move by one screen width.

The use of the mouse like this is by far the simplest way of looking at different parts of the text, but if you have no mouse or prefer to use the keyboard, the keys are summarised in Table 3.1.

Movement	Keys
Character Left	Left Arrow
Character right	Right Arrow
Word left	Ctrl+Left Arrow
Word right	Ctrl+Right Arrow
Line up	Up Arrow
Line down	Down Arrow
First indentation level of current line	Home
Beginning of next line	Ctrl+Enter
End of line	End
Move to next window	F6
Increase size of active window	Alt+Plus
Decrease size of active window	Alt+Minus

Table 3.1. The keys that can be used for cursor movement instead of the mouse.

note There are separate key methods for moving the cursor and for scrolling the screen. The use of the Bookmark command is another convenient way of finding portions of a long text.

Bookmarking allows up to four invisible code markers to be placed into text so that you can locate any part of the text easily. To create a bookmark you press the Ctrl and K keys together, release them, and then press a number key in the range 0 to 3. To find a bookmark again, press the Ctrl and Q keys together, release them, and then type the same number key as you used when you created the bookmark.

You can practice moving the editing cursor around and switching between the screens before you try out the commands that alter the text.

Text alteration

You can delete the character that is under the cursor by using the Delete key, or the character to the left of the cursor by using the DEL-left key (usually labelled with a left-pointing arrow and placed just above the ENTER key). Note that the Home key will place the cursor at the left of a line, and the End key will place it on the last character of the line. You can delete more than one character in sequence by holding either DEL key down, and this allows you to correct a short line by deleting and retyping.

Block actions

The editor of QBASIC contains many of the actions of a wordprocessor, and one of the most important is block editing. A block of text is a marked portion, and the marking is usually done by using colour inversion, exchanging foreground and background colours.

The simplest marking method uses the mouse. Taking the REMLINE.BAS example again, the marking can be done using the mouse as follows:

1. Place the mouse cursor at the start of the text and press the (lefthand) button.
2. Holding the button down, move the mouse so that its cursor moves down over the lines of the program. Each line will be changed to inverse colour as this is done.
3. When you have reached the end of the third section, release the button. This will leave a section marked, Figure 3.7, with the foreground and background colours reversed.

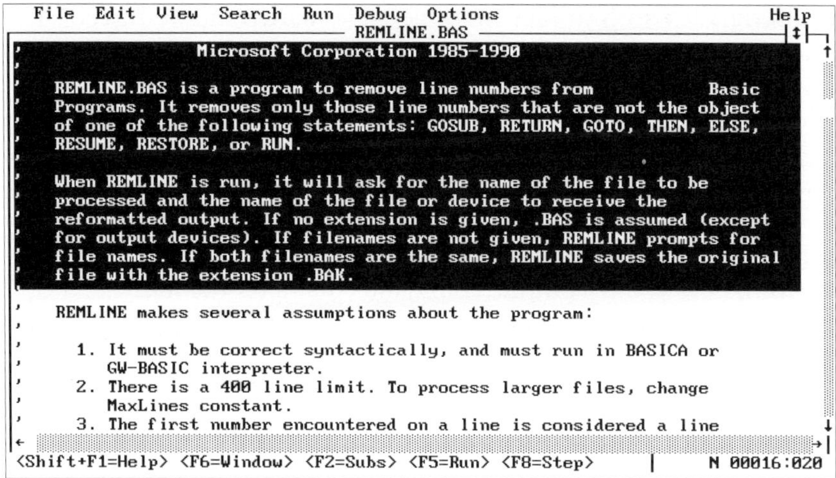

Figure 3.7. A block of text marked by the editor.

4. You can now make use of the commands of the Edit menu, in particular of Cut, Copy, Paste and Clear:

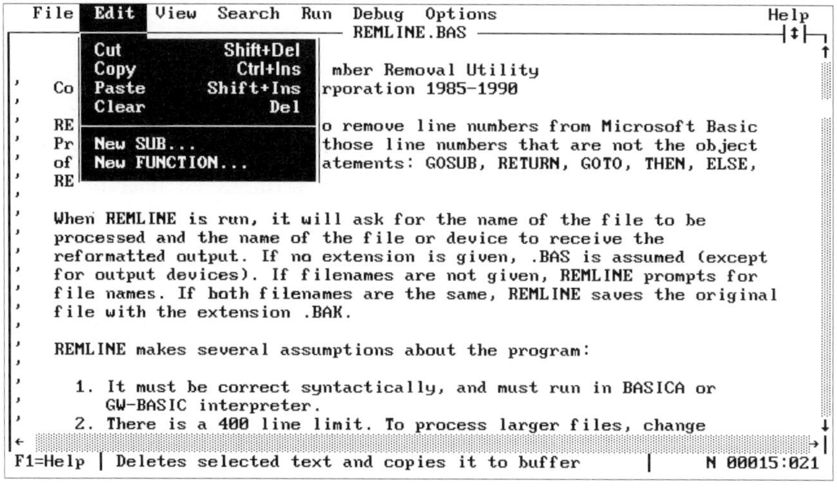

Figure 3.8. Selecting from the Edit menu for Cut, Copy and Paste.

The Cut command will have the effect of making the marked portion of text disappear. You can then move the cursor to another part of the text and select Paste. This will place the Cut piece of text into the position of the cursor.

The other option, Copy, leaves the original marked text as it is, but allows a copy to be made by moving the cursor and using the Paste command. The Clear command deletes the marked portion.

tip Always use Cut to remove text, because this allows you to replace it later, provided you do not Cut any other text subsequently.

- Marking can also be done by using key strokes, as in Table 3.1. This, however, is usually a clumsier method than the use of the mouse.
- You can remove the marking of a piece of text (without moving the text) by clicking on any other part of the text.
- Marking by using the mouse is not confined to the lines that you can see on the screen. If you drag the mouse to the bottom scroll-bar, the text will scroll, allowing you to mark all of the text if you want. If you mark too far, you can move the mouse in the opposite direction, unmarking part of the text. The marking is not fixed until the mouse button is released.
- The other two options of the Edit menu, labelled as NewSUB and NewFUNCTION, are more specialised and will be covered in Chapter 12 onwards.

The other menus

The menus other than File and Edit are of less interest initially, but there are some items that you may find useful even fairly early in editing work. The Run and Debug menus, in particular, are of use only when you are using and writing programs – you can use the Run menu to try out any of the demonstration programs. The View menu contains the items Split and Subs. Of these, Split allows the screen to be split into separate windows, each showing different views. For example, if you have been using Help and also looking at REMLINE.BAS, using Split will allow both to be visible at the same time:

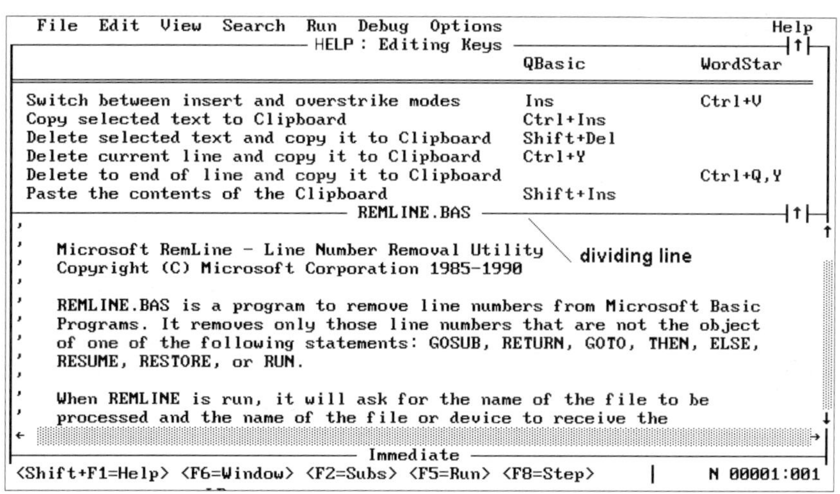

Figure 3.9. Using a split screen display to see a program and some Help at the same time.

- The border between these windows can be moved. In the example, dragging the title of REMLINE.BAS up or down with the mouse will move the dividing line so as to show more or less of this window.

- Split views like this can be very useful if you need, for example, to keep a particular piece of Help in view while you work on a text file.
- Note that the word RUN can be typed as a command in the Immediate window, and will cause whatever program is currently loaded to run. You can also use RUN as a statement in a program, making another program (whose name must be specified) run in place of the program that contained the RUN statement.

The Subs item allows other parts of a text file to be examined. As Chapter Two pointed out, a good program is designed in sections that are variously called *subroutines*, *procedures* or *functions*, all of which are called into action by a main program. When you look at the program REMLINE.BAS you can only see the main program and not the subroutines. This avoids confusion, and concentrates your attention on the main piece of text. To see the subroutines, click on the Subs option of the View menu.

This brings up the view shown in Figure 3.10. This lists the subroutines by name and, by double-clicking on any one of the names, you can examine and edit that subroutine. This allows you to work on sections of a long program without any distractions from the rest of the program.

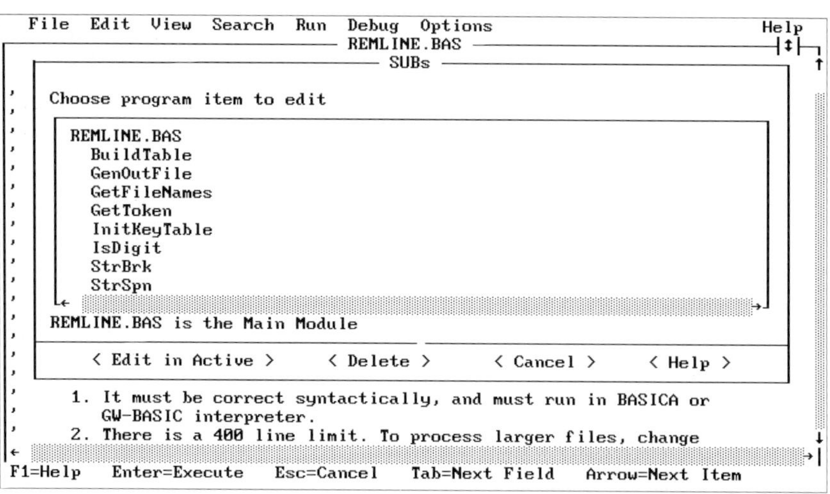

Figure 3.10. A subroutine listing so that you can pick which part of the program to edit. This is used only for the advanced SUB type of subroutine, not for the older GOSUB type.

- If you want to see both the main program and a subroutine you can split the screen as described earlier.

To return from a subroutine which is on display in this way, use View Subs again and double-click on REMLINE.BAS again.

The Search menu is used, like the corresponding action of a wordprocessor, to search for words or phrases, and also to change them. When you use Search Find, the Find dialogue box appears, Figure 3.11. You can type a word or phrase in the box (the text will scroll if you need more space than the box allows), and when the <OK> is clicked, the find action will look for the word or phrase.

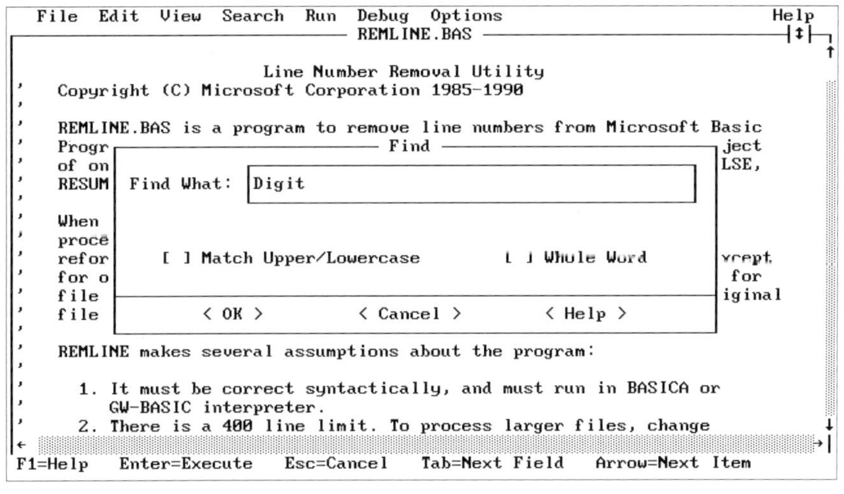
File Edit View Search Run Debug Options Help
REMLINE.BAS
Line Number Removal Utility
' Copyright (C) Microsoft Corporation 1985-1990
' REMLINE.BAS is a program to remove line numbers from Microsoft Basic
Find
Find What: Digit
[ ] Match Upper/Lowercase
< OK > < Cancel > < Help >
' REMLINE makes several assumptions about the program:
' 1. It must be correct syntactically, and must run in BASICA or
' GW-BASIC interpreter.
' 2. There is a 400 line limit. To process larger files, change
F1=Help Enter=Execute Esc=Cancel Tab=Next Field Arrow=Next Item

Figure 3.11. Using the Find action to look for a word or phrase. This can be very useful for ensuring that any change is applied to the whole program.

- This Find action extends to the whole program, including all the subroutines, not just the visible main program.The options of Find are to match upper or lower case and to look for whole words only. If you click on the Match option (which puts a cross in the box) then, for example, looking for `Digit' will not find `digit'. If you click on the Whole Word option, looking for `Digit' will not find `IntDigit'. Both of these examples would be found if the boxes are allowed to remain unticked.

The Change option of Search uses a larger dialogue box in which you specify the word or phrase you want to find, and the replacement word or phrase you want to use. An additional option in this box is to Find and Verify or to Change All. When you select the Find & Verify box, each change is notified for your approval, but when you use Change All, the whole action is automatic.

tip

Always use Find & Verify unless you are certain that the changes do not need to be checked.

The Options menu contains Display, Help path and Syntax checking. Of these, the Help path is needed only if you have decided, for some reason, to put the QBASIC.HLP file in a separate directory, not along with the main QBASIC.EXE program. Syntax checking appears in the list with a dot next to the name, indicating that it is selected. Clicking on this line will remove the dot, clicking again will reinstate it. Syntax checking should be left on, because it makes programming simpler by removing some forms of errors before a program is run.

The Display option, Figure 3.12, allows you to select the colours you want to use for normal text, the current statement (command), and breakpoint lines (explained later). There are 16 colours that you can use for background or foreground in each option, and the defaults are acceptable whether you are using a colour monitor or not. If you do make changes, use contrasting background and foreground colours so that you can see the text easily.

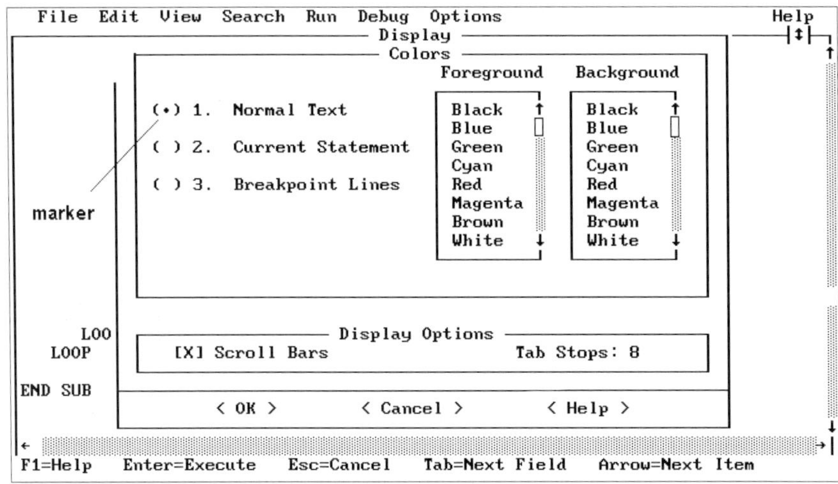

Figure 3.12. The Display option, allowing you to choose colours.

The other options of visible scroll-bars and the use of eight Tab stops, are sensible and do not need to be changed.

Loading and saving

Typing program instructions into the computer would be of little use if we could not save the programs on disk and recall them for later use. Practically all varieties of interpreted BASIC use the word LOAD to mean reading a program from a disk, and SAVE to mean recording a program on disk, and these words are used by QBASIC by selecting them from the Files menu of the editor screen.

If you still have the REMLINE.BAS program loaded, click on the File – New option, and answer No to the question about saving the file (if you have made the file read-only, as recommended, you cannot save the version in the computer's memory). The editing screen will now bear the name `Untitled' again.

Now type the test program shown in Table 3.2. Notice that if you typed rem in lower-case (small) letters these will have been converted into upper-case (capital) letters each time you press the ENTER key.

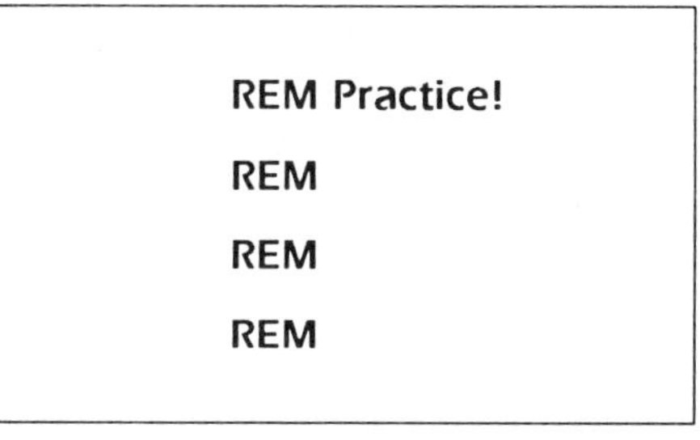
REM Practice!
REM
REM
REM

Table 3.2. A test program to check that you can save and load.

All BASIC instruction words are converted in this way, and it's good practice always to type in lower case so that you can check for misspellings simply by looking to see if the words appear in upper case or not when you look at the text.

This is not much of a program – rem means REMINDER, and is ignored by either an interpreter or a compiler – it's used to start a reminder line so that you know what your program is supposed to do at this point. The REM keyword is equivalent to the use of the apostrophe (') in this respect and anything following REM on a line will be ignored.

With the four lines typed in, select File – Save, which brings up the SAVE form:

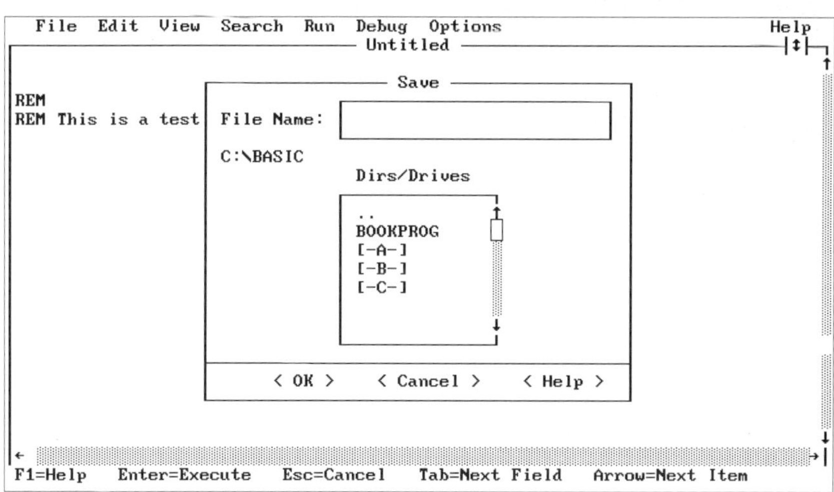

Figure 3.13. The SAVE form which allows you to pick drive and/or directory and type a filename.

You can choose a drive letter or other directory if required. If you do not, the file will be saved to the same directory as QBASIC itself. The name should consist of up to eight characters, it must start with a letter and must not use any of the following:

*** + = [ ] ; : , . / ?**

or include a space, a tab character or the ENTER key character.

When you click on <OK> or press the ENTER key, the program file is saved like any other piece of text.

The SAVE AS option allows you to save an existing file under another name. You might, for example, have loaded in an existing program and modified to make it suitable for another purpose. By using SAVE AS, you can save this modified program using another filename. If you simply use SAVE, the modified program is saved, replacing the original, which might not be what you want.

The Load command loads the text back into the QBASIC editor ready to edit or run, and the New command will clear the text editor ready for you to type a new program. Finally, Exit allows you to end QBASIC and return to MS-DOS or to DOSSHELL.

As you become more acquainted with the editor you will appreciate how useful it is and how easily programs written in other BASIC versions can be adapted by using the editor. In addition, when you come to use the more advanced features of QBASIC, you will see how the editor helps in allowing you to pick out SUBs and functions, see later.

Getting Outputs

Direct and program modes

There are two ways in which you can use a BASIC interpreter. One way is called *direct mode*, and is available in QBASIC by using the Immediate screen (double-click on 'Immediate') but not on the Untitled editing screen. Direct mode means that you type in a command, press the ENTER key and the command is carried out at once. This can be useful, but the more important way of using the interpreter is in program mode.

In program mode the interpreter is issued with a set of instructions, with a guide to the order in which they are to be carried out. This set of instructions is the *program*. The difference is important, because the instructions of a program can be repeated as many times as you like with very little effort on your part. A direct command, by contrast, will be repeated only if you type the whole command again, and then press ENTER. The set of command words that can be used, along with the rules for using them, make up what is called a *programming language*, which in this case is BASIC.

note: Strictly speaking, a command means a keyword used in Immediate mode, and a statement means a keyword used in a program. The two are often interchanged.

Let's now take a look at the difference between a direct command and a program statement in QBASIC. If you want the interpreter to carry out the direct command to add two numbers, 1.6 and 3.2, then you have to move the cursor to the Immediate window (click on the word immediate, or use the F6 key until this name is highlighted) and type:

```
print 1.6 + 3.2
```

and then press ENTER.

You have to start with print (or PRINT or its abbreviation ?), because an interpreter is a dumb machine, and it obeys only a few preset instructions. Unless you use the word 'print', the interpreter has no way of telling that what you want is to see the answer on the screen. It doesn't recognise instructions like GIVE ME or WHAT IS, only a few words (about 240 of them) that we call its *reserved words, keywords* or *instruction words*. PRINT is one of these words. So that you can recognise these reserved words more easily in this book, they are printed in upper-case (capital) letters from now on. You know by now, however, that you can type them in either upper-case or lower-case. You will always see them converted to upper-case each time you end a program line with the ENTER key.

Always type keywords in lower-case – this checks for correct spelling because they are converted to upper-case only if correctly spelled. It is undesirable to use ? for PRINT – a bad habit.

When you press the ENTER key after typing PRINT 1.6 + 3.2 the screen changes to a blank which shows the answer, 4.8, at the top lefthand corner. This is the View, Output or Results screen, and the message 'Press any key to continue' indicates how to get back to the Immediate and editing screens.

Results on the View screen stay on that screen – they are not erased by switching back to the Editing or Immediate screens. To clear the View screen type CLS in the Immediate screen. You can also use CLS as the first instruction of each program.

A program in QBASIC does not work in the same way. A program is typed in, using the Edit screen which will show the name Untitled until you save the text, and the statements or instructions of the program are not carried out when you press the ENTER key. Instead, the instructions are stored in the memory, ready to be carried out as and when you want. The interpreter needs some way of recognising the difference between your direct commands and your program instructions. With QBASIC this is done by using the two different screens and from now on, most of the work will be done using the Edit screen.

The PRINT statement, then, is the way that we get the interpreter to provide information output to us. With very few exceptions, all use of the interpreter involves three things: inputs, processes, and outputs. The hard part about programming is not learning the language of BASIC, it's learning how to get what you want from these three actions. For the moment, we'll leave inputs aside, and concentrate on outputs and a bit of processing.

Processing means doing whatever we want to do with numbers or words. It can be as simple as adding two numbers, or as complicated as putting a set of names and addresses into alphabetical order by surname. It can mean producing shapes and colours on the screen, and moving them about. It can mean producing sound, either sound effects or music, to go with the screen displays. In short it means any of the actions that make an interpreter so interesting and useful.

Let's start programming, then, with the arithmetic actions of add, subtract, multiply and divide. Interpreters aren't used all that much for calculation, but it's useful to be able to carry out calculations now and again. In addition, you are much more likely to recognise the sort of instructions that use numbers than the ones which are used to work with words. Figure 4.1 shows a four-line program which will print some arithmetic results. The process here consists of four bits of arithmetic, each with an output.

```
PRINT 5.6 + 6.8
PRINT 9.2 - 4.7
PRINT 5.06 * 6.08
PRINT 7.6 / 1.4
```

Figure 4.1. A four-line arithmetic program using PRINT to output to the View screen.

Take a close look at this, because there's a lot to get used to in these four lines. The star or asterisk symbol in the third line is the symbol that QBASIC uses as a multiply sign. Once again, we can't use the x that you might normally use for writing multiplication because x is a letter. There's no divide sign on the keyboard either, so QBASIC, like all other versions, uses the slash (/) sign in its place. This is the diagonal line which is on the same key as the question mark, not the one which slopes the other way, and which is placed at the lefthand side next to the Z key.

So far, so good. The program is entered by typing it, just as you see it. You must leave a space following PRINT, and if you do not you will see a notice appear:

```
Syntax error
---------------
<OK>  <Help>
```

to bring your attention to this mistake.

- This assumes that you have left Syntax Checking selected in the Options menu of the Editor.

You can type ? in place of PRINT – this and the use of ' for REM are two of the permitted but undesirable abbreviations of QBASIC inherited from older versions. Getting back to the program example, you will have to press the ENTER key when you have completed each instruction line and you should end up with the program looking as it does in the illustration. When you have entered the program by typing it, it's stored in the memory of the interpreter in the form of a set of ASCII codes. You know already how to save the file of instructions to the disk and you need to know now how to make the interpreter carry out the instructions of the program.

- If you miss out spaces and type, for example, 5.06*6.08, the Editor will attend to the spacing when you press the ENTER key. This is another indication of an acceptable entry.

Now to make the program operate, you need another direct command, RUN, and this can be delivered in several ways:

1. You can switch to the Immediate screen, type the word RUN, and press ENTER.
2. You can use the mouse or the keyboard to select the Run menu and then click on Start.
3. You can press the Shift+F5 keys together.

When the program runs, it prints its results in the View screen, so that you should see these figures:

```
12.4
4.5
30.7648
5.428571
```

Figure 4.2. The results as they appear on the View screen.

The last line should give you some idea of how precisely QBASIC can carry out its arithmetic. When you follow the instruction word PRINT with a piece of arithmetic like 5.06*6.08, then what is printed is the result of working out that piece of arithmetic. The program doesn't print the text of 5.06*6.08, just the result of the action.

This program has done two of the main computing actions, process and output, for you. The only input has been the program itself, and we can't alter any of these numbers in the program without altering the program text. Try writing a program of this type for yourself, and see how QBASIC carries out the calculations and displays the answers. All of this is useful, but it's not always handy to get just a set of answers on the screen, especially if you have forgotten what the questions were. QBASIC allows you a way of printing anything that you like on the screen, exactly as you type it, by the use of what is called a *string*. Figure 4.3 illustrates this principle. In each line, some of the typing is enclosed between quotes (inverted commas) and some is not:

```
PRINT "2+2="; 2 + 2
PRINT "2.5*3.5="; 2.5 * 3.5
PRINT "9.4-2.2="; 9.399999 - 2.2
PRINT "27.6/2.2="; 27.6 / 2.2
```

Figure 4.3. Using quote marks to make characters print on the screen exactly as typed.

Enter this short program and run it. Can you see how very differently the computer has treated the instructions? Whatever was enclosed between quotes has been printed exactly as you typed it. Whatever was not between quotes is computed, so that the first line, for example, gives the unsurprising result:

```
2+2=4
```

Now there's nothing automatic about this. If you edit the first line to read:

```
PRINT "2+2="; 5 * 1.5
```

then you'll get the daft reply, when you RUN this, of:

```
2+2= 7.5
```

The computer does as it's told by the program, and that's what you told it to do.

The important point about this example is that it shows how to make a program display what is being done. As before, the statement word PRINT has to be used to make things appear on the screen but, by using quotes, we can make the computer print whatever we want, not just the results of some arithmetic. Try making the computer print some answers for yourself, using this form of program. Note, incidentally, that the lines show, deliberately, combinations of spacing and the use of a semicolon. Where you have the word PRINT followed by a quote ("), then a space is needed and if you omit one the editor will put it in for you when you press the ENTER key. The semicolon followed by another space is also put in for you if you forget.

With all of this accumulated wisdom behind us, we can now start to look at some other printing actions. PRINT, as far as QBASIC is concerned, always means print on to the monitor screen. For activating a paper printer (*hard copy*, it's called), there's a separate instruction LPRINT (dealt with in Chapter 14) and if you want a program listing on paper, the File menu allows this option with its own Print command. These instructions are not useful to you unless you have a printer connected, and if you use them without a printer connected and switched on, the computer will hang up waiting for you to get a printer ready. If you select Print with no printer connected you will get a Device Fault message to remind you, and clicking on <OK> will release you back to the text of the program.

Now try the program in Figure 4.4. When you RUN this program, the words appear on three separate lines. This is because the instruction PRINT doesn't just mean print-on-the-screen. It also means 'take a new line', and start at the lefthand side:

```
PRINT "This is"
PRINT "QBASIC"
PRINT "the new way to program."
```

Figure 4.4. Using the PRINT instruction to place words on the screen in separate lines.

In this example, the words have been placed between quote marks, and they have appeared on the screen just as we typed them, but with no quotemarks showing. This, then, is the sort of programming that is needed when you want to display instructions or other messages on the screen. The real problem, as you'll see when you try it, is of getting the messages to look really neat. Nothing looks worse than printing which has words split, with half of a word on one line and the rest on the next line. Even at this stage, it's possible to make your printing look neat with some care.

Suppose, for example, that you have some long paragraph that you want to type in, using several PRINT lines. Type the PRINT " part, then type the words that you want and continue typing without touching the ENTER key until you reach a position on the screen which is directly underneath the quotemark. If you are in the middle of a word, then erase this word by using the DEL-LEFT key. Now type a second quotemark, and then press ENTER. Start another line now, using PRINT ", and then type the rest of the message in the same way. If you never cross the point where a letter comes directly under a quotemark on the line above, you will never split a word across a line end. Try it.

If you have a large number of PRINT lines, more than 24, the top one will vanish from the screen as each new one is printed. This is called *scrolling*, and one solution is the use of a piece of program that prints only one screen page of 24 or fewer lines at a time, see later.

Now the action of selecting a new line for each PRINT isn't always convenient, and we can change the action by using various punctuation marks and instruction words that we call *print modifiers*. Start this time by acquiring a new habit. Go to the File menu, and select New (you will be asked about saving any existing text). This clears the old program out, but does not clear the View screen, which will clear when you go to the Immediate window and type CLS (ENTER). If you don't use the NEW action, then lines of old programs will get in the way of new ones. Each time you type a line, you simply add it following the last line of any older program that is in the memory, so unless you clear the memory with NEW, there will certainly be confusion.

Now try the program in Figure 4.5. There's a very important difference between Figure 4.5 and Figure 4.4, as you'll see when you RUN it. The effect of a semicolon following the last quote in a line is to prevent the next piece of printing starting on a new line at the lefthand side. When you RUN this program, all of the words appear in one line:

```
PRINT "This is ";
PRINT "QBASIC ";
PRINT "the new way to program."
```

Figure 4.5. The effect of semicolons to prevent a new line from being taken.

It would have been a lot easier just to have one line of program that read:

```
PRINT "This is QBASIC the new way to program"
```

to do this, but there are times when you have to use the semicolon to force two different print items on to the same line. We'll look at that sort of thing later in program examples. Meantime, note also the space between the last letter and the last quote mark in the first two lines. The semicolon doesn't just order the computer to prevent a new line being taken, it also forces it to place one item right up against another. Without the spaces you would have "This isQBASICthe new way to program". Try removing the spaces, and see for yourself.

Row and column output

Neat printing is a matter of arranging your words and numbers into rows and columns, so we'll take a closer look at this particular art now. To start with, we know already that the instruction PRINT will cause a new line to be selected, so the action of this example should not come as too much of a surprise:

```
CLS:PRINT "This is QBASIC"
PRINT: PRINT
PRINT "- ready to work for you"
```

Figure 4.6. Spacing lines with PRINT, in this example using a multi-statement line. The CLS instruction clears the View screen.

The first line contains a novelty, though, in the form of two instructions in one line. The instructions are separated by a colon (:) and you can have several instructions on any one line in this way, taking several screen lines. You can put instructions together in this way almost indefinitely, but it starts to look clumsy and gets very difficult to follow if you overdo it. In a multi-statement line of this type, QBASIC will deal with the different instructions in a left-to-right order.

The instruction CLS should not surprise you either – this clears the screen, and makes the printing start at the top lefthand corner of the View screen. Another point about Figure 4.6 is that the second line causes the lines to be spaced apart. The two PRINT instructions, with nothing to be printed, each cause a blank line to be taken. There are other ways of doing this, as we'll see, but as a simple way of creating a space, it's very handy. Now try for yourself a program which will put words on different lines like this. Remember that you have 24 lines to play with on the full View screen – the 25th line is used for the 'Press any key' message.

Figure 4.7 deals with something that is often very useful, arranging text or numbers into columns. The first line is a PRINT instruction that acts on the numbers 1 and 2:

```
PRINT 1,2
PRINT 1,2,3,4,5
PRINT "one","two"
PRINT "one","two","three"
PRINT "This item is too
long","two"
```

Figure 4.7. How the comma causes words or numbers to be placed into columns each with a fixed starting position.

When these appear on the screen, though, they appear spaced out just as if the screen had been divided into columns. The mark which causes this effect is the comma (do not confuse it with the apostrophe), and the action is completely automatic. As the second line shows, you can get up to five columns in this way on the View screen. Anything that you try to get into a sixth column will actually appear on the first column of the next line down. The action works for words as well as for numbers, as the program illustrates.

When words are being printed in this way, though, you have to remember that the commas must be placed *outside* the quotes. Any commas that are placed inside the quotes will be printed just as they are and won't cause any spacing effect. You will also find that if you attempt to put into a column something that is too large to fit, the long phrase will spill over to the next column, and the next item to be printed will be at the start of the next line. This is illustrated in the fifth line – the first phrase spills over from column 1 into column 2, and the word 'two' is printed starting at the third column .

Commas are useful when we want a simple way of creating several columns, all of the same width. The standard column width is of 15 characters, with a number always starting in the second character position. Using commas in this way gives columns that are all of the same size. A much more flexible method of placing words on the screen exists, however. This makes use of the statement word TAB (short for *tabulate*) to position the cursor anywhere along a line, as Figure 4.8 illustrates.

```
CLS
PRINT TAB(1)"L"; TAB(80)"R"
PRINT TAB(37); "CENTRE"
PRINT TAB(5); "Start here..."
```

Figure 4.8. How TAB is used to position the cursor along the line in a PRINT statement.

The word TAB must be separated from PRINT by a space as shown. For the purpose of using TAB, we need to remember that the full sized View screen is normally divided into a grid of 80 divisions across and up to 25 down. By normally, I mean the situation when you have switched on the computer and done nothing to alter the screen arrangement. The statements which will alter this arrangement are more advanced (the PRINT VIEW statement, Chapter 14).

These screen column and line numbers use a range of 1 to 80 across and 1 to 25 down. The word TAB has to be followed by the number of the column position across the screen, in brackets. If you omit the brackets, the TAB instruction is ignored – the Editor does not pick up this error. In the example, the first line clears the screen, and the second line shows the Left and Right positions on the screen. I have used L and R rather than printing numbers 1 and 76, because the number 76 would have to be printed using TAB(78). A number is always printed with a space in front (to allow for a + or - sign), so the number '76' would take three spaces, TAB positions 78, 79, and 80. The third line then prints the word 'Centre' near the middle of the screen, and we'll look later at how to calculate the correct TAB number for this. The last line simply shows TAB being used to indent a line, which means put a space between the first word and the lefthand side.

Figure 4.9 shows some more secrets of TAB. To TAB across a line, you need to use numbers that lie between 1 and 76 (for a two-digit number), but you can use larger numbers. These will have the effect of getting you to a tab number on the same line. It also shows that you can use an *expression* inside the TAB brackets:

```
CLS:PRINT "Top line"
PRINT TAB(2); "A"
PRINT TAB(5) "TAB(5); ";TAB(3 * 80 + 5); "Where is this?"
```

Figure 4.9. Tabbing with numbers greater than 80.

An expression is a bit of arithmetic that has to be worked out, and in the example, this is 3*80+5. This works out to 233, but it doesn't tab you over to a position 233 columns from the lefthand side, nor does it give you the TAB(5) position three lines down. Instead, it just gives you good old TAB(5). The effect of numbers greater than 80, then, is just to tab as usual to a position that lies between columns 1 and 80.

Centring a word or phrase is done by calculating the correct *across* number for the TAB instruction, and this also can be done in an expression. You have to count up the number of characters that you want to print centred. By characters, I mean letters, digits, spaces and punctuation marks. You then subtract this from 80 and divide the result by 2. Take the whole number part of the answer – forget about any half left over – and this is then the correct number to use with TAB. The expression will have to wait until Chapter 9.

There is another way of spacing out text, using the SPC action. Figure 4.10 shows this in use compared with TAB. The effect of SPC(20) for example is to make 20 spaces, and this is not the same as TAB(20) which goes to the 20th column measured from the lefthand side. SPC is useful if you want a constant spacing between the end of one printed item and the start of another; TAB is better when you want each item to start at a fixed position:

```
CLS
PRINT TAB(2); "BIG"; TAB(20); "BASIC"
PRINT TAB(2); "BIG"; SPC(20); "BASIC"
```

Figure 4.10. Comparing TAB and SPC effects.

Further print placement

TAB has its uses in positioning words or numbers in a PRINT statement line, but we can take much more control over screen position by using the keyword LOCATE. This keyword needs to be followed by one or two numbers. Of these, the first number is a column number, measuring position across the View screen from the lefthand side, and the second is a lines number, measuring the lines down from the top of the screen. Use just one number and the LOCATE statement works just like TAB. If you use both numbers, then they have to be separated by a comma. An important difference between the two is that the numbers for TAB have to be enclosed in brackets.

```
CLS
PRINT "Start position"
LOCATE 6, 12
PRINT "This is here"
```

Figure 4.11. Using LOCATE to position the (invisible) cursor.

Take a look at the example in Figure 4.11. This uses LOCATE to place the invisible cursor at a different spot on the View screen, and then print. LOCATE allows the cursor to be placed anywhere you like, and in any order. This is an important point, because the use of TAB and the comma works only if each position is to the right and/or down as compared to the previous cursor position. LOCATE allows you to print in any order or position – you can print backwards if you like:

```
CLS
PRINT "Start position"
LOCATE 6, 80
PRINT "D"
LOCATE 6, 79
PRINT "N"
LOCATE 6, 78
PRINT "E"
```

Figure 4.12. Printing backwards with LOCATE. If you had a time delay between PRINT lines you would see the effect more clearly.

Armed now with all this ability to get output from the machine, we need to look at how we can put information in – the subject of Chapter Five.

Inputs

Assignment

So far, our computing has been confined to printing numbers and words on the screen, using program lines containing the PRINT keyword, with or without modifications. That's covered two of the main aims of computing, processing and output, but we have to look now at some of the actions that go on before anything is printed. One of these is called *assignment*. Take a look at the program in Figure 5.1. Type it in, run it, and contrast what you see on the screen with what appears in the program. The first line that is printed gives the text on the screen:

```
2 times 23 is 46
```

but the numbers 23 and 46 don't appear in the second line. This is because of the way we have used the letter X as a kind of code for the number 23. The official name for this type of code is a *variable name* or *variable*.

```
CLS
X = 23
PRINT "2 times"X"; is; "2 * X
X = 5
PRINT "X is now"; X
PRINT "and twice X is"; 2 * X
```

Figure 5.1. Assignment in action. The letter X has been used in place of a number.

The second line assigns the variable name X, giving it the value of 23. *Assigns* means that wherever we use X, not enclosed by quotes, the computer will operate with the number 23 instead. Since X is a single character and 23 has two digits, that's a saving of space. It would have been an even greater saving if we had assigned X differently, perhaps as X=2174.3256, for example. The third line then proves that X is taken to be 23, because wherever X appears, not between quotes, 23 is printed, and the expression 2*X is printed as 46. We're not stuck with X as representing 26 for ever, though. The fourth line assigns X as being 5, and the following lines prove that this change has been made.

That's why we call X a *variable* – we can *vary* whatever it is we want it to represent. Until we do change it, though, X stays assigned. Even after you have run the program of Figure 5.1, providing you haven't added new lines or deleted any part of it, you can type PRINT X, and pressing ENTER will show the value of X on the screen. Incidentally, it doesn't matter whether you use X or x, the computer takes these two forms of the letter as being identical for this purpose of assignment.

This very useful way to handle numbers in code form can use a name which *must* start with a letter. You can add to that letter other letters or digits, but not spaces or punctuation marks (apart from the underline symbol '_') so that N, name, and N504 are all names that you can use for number variables, and each can be assigned to a different number. Just to make it even more useful, you can use similar names to represent words and phrases also. The difference is that you have to add a dollar sign ($) to the variable name. If N is a variable name for a number, then N$ (pronounced en-string or en-dollar) is a variable name for a word or phrase. The computer treats these two, N and N$, as being entirely separate and different. The name for a number must not end with the $ sign.

note The more advanced methods of QBASIC allow you to use unmarked names provided that there are lines in the program which *declare* what type of variable each one represents.

There are, as you might expect, some rules to observe. You can pick names which are of up to 40 characters long. If you want to represent a number by the name Total_of_all_entries_so_far then you can do so, because this doesn't break any rules, though it might cause considerable strain to your typing fingers if you had to type it many times over. You have to strike a balance here between something reasonably brief and something that will remind you of what this name is supposed to represent. Older varieties of BASIC allowed you just two characters as a name, and when you wrote a program, you had to keep a list to remind you of what each name represented. QBASIC is much more tolerant in this respect, and the use of names such as Subtotal, Before_VAT, After_tax and so on can make your programs much easier to follow.

There is one very important restriction, however. You cannot and must not use any name that is the name of a reserved word. Words like TAB, LOCATE, PRINT, CIRCLE, LINE, VAL and so on are definitely out as far as variable names are concerned. It's easy to make this mistake, because some keywords are so seldom used that you can easily forget that they are keywords. If you do use a keyword as a variable name, your program will stop at that line with the error message such as:

```
Expected : expression
-------------------------
 <OK>            <Help>
```

to remind you.

note QBASIC treats a name consisting of letters and digits as being the name of an ordinary (floating-point) number. Any name that ends with the dollar sign, such as myname$ or PARTNAME$ is a string variable, and in an assignment made using the = sign (or using READ.DATA, see later), only a number can be assigned to a number variable and only a string can be assigned to a string variable. Chapter 6 deals with other types of number variables.

Constants

QBASIC also allows you to assign a constant. As far as uses are concerned, the differences are not very important, but the use of a constant is more satisfying as far as correct structure is concerned. A constant should be used when the quantity does not vary.

Figure 5.2 shows number constants being assigned and used. The assignment follows the way that a variable is assigned, but with the word CONST as a reminder that a constant is in use. Where a program contains constants, this assignment would be made at the start of the program, so that when you read the text you know at once where the constants are.

```
CLS
CONST VAT = .175
CONST Prof = 0.25
Print "Pre-VAT price is £26; which is £";26 + 26*VAT" after tax
Print "Buying price is £50, selling price is £";50 + 50*Prof
```

Figure 5.2. Using number constants, declared at the start of this short piece of program.

The interpreter treats a constant, as you might expect, as something fixed. If, for example, you put at the end of the example above, another line:

```
CONST VAT = 0.2
```

the effect, when the program was run, would be to produce an error message of:

```
Duplicate definition
--------------------------
<OK>              <Help>
```

to point out the fault. The program would not run until this line was removed.

You can also use CONST along with a string variable, taking care to assign with a string (using quotes). The lines:

```
CONST care$ = "Summer"
PRINT "Begone dull "; care$
CONST bignum$ = "1,000,000"
PRINT "This is a large sum, £";bignum$
```

are valid uses of string constants. Note that when the string consists of a number it has to be enclosed in quotes like any other string, and all you can do with it is print it; you cannot carry out arithmetic (but see Chapter 9).

Reading the data

By making fixed assignments like Start=26 or CONST Pi = 3.1416, we can put data into a program to be used in the program. The reasons for this have already been covered in Chapter 2 and, to remind you, they are:

1. Ease of making changes – one assignment line can be changed instead of changing each point where a quantity is used.
2. Reduced memory use – a floating point number might need eight bytes for storage and by assigning to a constant or a variable, it is stored only once.

Another way of making fixed assignments involves reading items from a list, and it uses two instruction words READ and DATA. The word READ causes the program to select an item from the list and assign the item to a variable name. The list is marked by starting each line of the list with the word DATA. The items of the list can be separated by commas. Each time an item is read from such a list, a *pointer* (or memory position number) is altered so that the next time an item is needed, it will be the next item on the list rather than the one that was read the last time round. The items can be numbers, as illustrated in this chapter, or words, looked at later.

We'll look at this in more detail in the form of examples later, but for the moment we can introduce ourselves to the READ...DATA instructions in a very simple way:

```
CLS
READ prevat
READ taxrate
PRINT "Price is";
PRINT prevat * taxrate
DATA 55,0.175
```

Figure 5.3. A simple example of READ...DATA use, taking two quantities in order from the list.

The second line reads the first item on the list and assigns it to the variable 'prevat' and the next line similarly reads the next number and assigns it to 'taxrate'. The following line then starts to print the result, using a semicolon to keep the printing in the same line while the amount is worked out. The amount is then printed, using the two variables. This is a good example of why it is so useful to be able to keep printing in one line with semicolons. You can print each bit as it is read, and still end up with a complete line. The items in the DATA list are simply read in order, and you must make sure that you place them in the order that you want them.

Using READ and DATA does no more than a set of assignments would do, but does it in a neater looking way. For example, a set of lines such as:

```
A=2
B=6
C=15
D=27
E=0.6
F=7.5
```

can be replaced with:

```
READ A,B,C,D,E,F
```

in the part of the program where this is needed, with the line:

```
DATA 2,6,15,27,0.6,7.5
```

coming anywhere else, either at the start or at the end of the program. You can, for example, write your READ line before you know exactly what you want to assign, and you can even use this as a way of testing several sets of values, because to change values, only the DATA line needs to be edited.

The illustration shows numbers being read from the DATA line, but you could equally easily have used strings, *provided* that a string variable was used for assignment. You cannot assign a string item of data to a number variable, but you can read a data number into a string variable. Having done this, though, the number is in string form – you can print it, but not carry out arithmetic.

The READ...DATA instructions really come into their own when you have a long list of items that are read by repeating a READ step. These would be items that you would need every time that the program was used, rather than the items you would type in as replies. We're not quite ready for that yet, so having introduced the idea, we'll leave it for Chapter Eight.

Keyboard input

So far, everything that has been printed on the screen by a program has had to be placed in the program before it is run, either by direct assignment, or by use of READ...DATA, with the DATA line provided as part of the program. The differences between these two are fairly minor, more a matter of convenience rather than principle; both require the data to be placed within the program. The advantage of READ...DATA is that all the DATA is put into one place, making it easy to check and edit.

Quite a number of types of programs can consist merely of a bit of processing and some output, but with no input apart from whatever was placed in the program. We don't have to be stuck with restrictions like this, however, because the computer allows us another way of putting information, number or name, into a program while it is running. A step of this type is called an *input* and the QBASIC instruction word that is used to cause this to happen is also INPUT.

Figure 5.4 illustrates this with a program that prints your age. Now I don't know your age, so I can't put it into the program beforehand. What happens when you run this is that the words:

```
In what year were you born?
```

are printed on the screen, positioned by the LOCATE instruction in the first program line. On the screen below this you will see a question mark. The computer is now waiting for you to type something, and then press ENTER.

Until the ENTER key is pressed, the program will hang up waiting for you. If you're honest, you will type your year of birth and then press ENTER. When you press ENTER, your year of birth is assigned to the variable 'born'. The program can then continue, so that the question 'What year is this?' is then asked. Once again, you answer by typing the year and pressing ENTER, and the reply is assigned to variable 'nowyear'. In fact, this year could be obtained from the computer's built-in calendar, but that's a refinement that will have to wait for now. The program then prints the age you will be on your birthday this year, assuming that you answered correctly.

```
CLS : LOCATE 3, 5
PRINT "In what year were you born?"
INPUT born: LOCATE 6, 5
PRINT "What year is this?"
INPUT nowyear: LOCATE 9, 5
PRINT "You are"; nowyear - born"; years old this year, then."
END
```

Figure 5.4. Using INPUT to assign a variable with a quantity that you type when the program runs.

You could, of course, have answered 1392 or 1745 or anything else that you pleased for either of these years. The computer has no way of knowing in this program that either of these is not your true year of birth or year now. Now that you can type something that can be assigned to a variable, and then use the variable later, you can use all three of the main computing actions. Could you now, for example, design a program that asked for your annual income, and assigned it, and then asked for your taxcode, and assigned that? Could you then arrange it so that it then cleared the screen, and printed your income after tax (knowing that the amount of tax is taxrate*(income-10*taxcode). You now know all of the commands that are needed.

```
CLS
PRINT "Please give length, width, height.";
INPUT leng, wid, ht
PRINT "Volume is"; leng * wid * ht
END
```

Figure 5.5. Using INPUT with more than one variable. You must type the three numbers separated by commas, then press ENTER.

Figure 5.5 illustrates an INPUT step which uses number variables called 'leng', 'wid' and 'ht' and assigns them all in one line. The same system is used.

When the program hangs up with the question mark appearing, you must type three numbers, separated by commas, and then press the ENTER key. This time, too, the question mark will appear on the same line as the message. This is because there is a semicolon following the PRINT message. The action of pressing ENTER will assign your numbers to variables leng, wid and ht, and allow the program to continue to calculate volume. Note that the variable for length could not be len or long because these are both reserved words, as the Editor would remind you. You cannot enter the three numbers separately by pressing ENTER following typing each number, because this will bring up an error message:

```
Redo from start
```

which allows you to start entry again. Note that this message does *not* mean that you need to start the program again, only the entry of quantities.

This is a simple example of the computer used with input, process and output. The input steps get your numbers and assign them, the process is just multiplication, and the output is the action of printing the product. You could design a program for yourself which added or subtracted or divided numbers to order in this way. When you use a number variable in an INPUT step, then what you have typed when you press ENTER must be a number. If you attempt to enter a word, the computer will refuse to accept it. Some computers stop running at this point, but QBASIC once again brings up the 'Redo from start' message to point out the error and give you another chance of typing a correct entry.

An INPUT can be to a number variable or a string variable, using the same form of the command. The only difference is the variable name which, for a string, has to end with the dollar sign.

The way in which INPUT can be placed in programs can be used to make it look as if the computer is paying some attention to what you type. Figure 5.6 shows an example – but with INPUT used in a different way:

```
CLS
INPUT "Type your annual income, please" ;income
PRINT "With an income of £"income" you probably manage."
```

Figure 5.6. Putting some text into an INPUT statement. The text will be printed before the computer waits for your reply.

This time, there is a phrase following the INPUT instruction. The phrase is placed between quotes, and is followed by a semicolon and then the variable name 'Income'. This line has the same effect as the two lines:

```
PRINT "Type your annual income, please";
INPUT Income
```

and again the question mark appears on the same line as the question, and your reply is also on the same line – unless the length of the name causes letters to spill over on to the next line.

note A point to watch here is that the answer must not contain any comma – if, for example, you type 15,000 this will be taken as being two answers, not one.

There is another type of input statement that can be used to overcome this type of difficulty:

```
LINE INPUT "Type your annual income, please"; cash$
PRINT "You should be able to manage on "£"; cash$
```

Figure 5.7. Using LINE INPUT to accept any form of input – but only for a string variable.

The use of a string variable is the important point here. A number variable cannot accept a comma, but a string variable can, so only a string variable can be used – the Editor will pick this up if you try to use the wrong type of variable name. Using a string variable allows you to print the number that is used in this example, but you cannot perform arithmetic on it – for ways round that problem see Chapter Nine.

Measured input

There is a variant on INPUT in the form of INPUT$, which can be very useful for a variety of purposes, because it allows the number of keystrokes to be counted. This can be particularly useful for 'Press any key' types of reply, or a single-character answer:

```
CLS
PRINT "Please answer y or n"
ans$ = INPUT$(1)
PRINT "You answered "; ans$
REM need that final space!
```

Figure 5.8 Using INPUT$ for a reply of one key only.

Another point about INPUT$ is that it does not display on the screen what is being typed. This makes INPUT$ ideal for entering passwords:

```
CLS
PRINT "Please enter 5-character password"
pass$ = INPUT$(5)
PRINT "Thank you - please
SLEEP 5
PRINT "Password "; pass$; " accepted."
```

Figure 5.9. Using INPUT$ to demonstrate password applications.

This is not, of course, a real password example, just an illustration of why INPUT$ is so useful for this purpose. When you type five characters in this little piece of program, none of the characters will appear on the screen, though they are being assigned to the variable 'pass$'. You cannot get away with the wrong number of characters either – if you enter fewer than five the program will wait as long as it takes for the fifth. If you keep pressing keys in excess of five, the extra keys will be ignored.

The SLEEP action is another useful one which enforces a time delay, for a number of seconds determined by the number that follows the keyword, separated by a space. In this example, SLEEP 5 enforces a five second delay, and then the password is printed.

In a real-life type of passwording action, of course, you would have to type a password which agreed exactly with one that was stored in the program. The programming methods that are needed for this type of action have not been covered yet, but Figure 5.10 shows what is required, and you can come back to it later after you have become more familiar with the DO loop and the IF test.

The program is a DO loop which terminates only when the correct code is entered. As it stands, it can be cracked by pressing Ctrl-Break, but if this key combination is disabled it is not so easy. When the loop starts, bad% has no assignment and will be zero, so that the message is not printed.

The tenth line contains the step a$=INPUT$(5). This means that only five characters can be accepted for this input, and the string of characters will be assigned to a$. The computer hangs up and waits for you when this line runs, but you don't need to press the ENTER key. Immediately you press the fifth key, the entry is complete, but without anything appearing on the screen. In this example, the next line then checks that what you have entered is the correct password. If it is, the main loop ends, and the final message is printed. If not, the variable bad% is assigned so that the first message is printed on the next pass around the loop.

```
CLS
DO : REM Repeats action up to LOOP line
   IF bad% = 1 THEN
      PRINT "Incorrect - access denied - please wait"
   END IF
   FOR n = 1 TO 3000: NEXT
   CLS
   bad% = 1
   PRINT " Please type the 5-letter code"
   a$ = INPUT$(5)
LOOP UNTIL a$ = "qsrbn": REM This is the password
PRINT " Pass, friend"
```

Figure 5.10. Using INPUT$ to specify an input of a specified number of characters, with no need for ENTER, and nothing shown on screen.

INPUT$ is a very useful way of getting an entry of exactly the right number of characters. There's no need to count characters and use a test to detect the entry of the wrong number of characters. An extension to INPUT$ allows entry from disk, but that's too advanced for the moment (such actions are covered in Chapters 18 and 19).

One final point about INPUT$ is that it has to be used in the form:

```
A$ = INPUT$(n)
```

being assigned to a string variable, and with the number of characters enclosed in brackets. The string variable name can be a dummy variable – you are not obliged to use it, and where INPUT$ is used for a 'Press any key' action, the string variable is of no value other than to allow INPUT$ to be used.

The faster read

There is yet another input statement that can assign a key-action into a string variable, INKEY$. Unlike INPUT$, however, INKEY$ does not wait for you to press a key. Instead, its action is to check the keyboard for any key being pressed. If a key is pressed, an ASCII code for that character is assigned to a string variable, the one specified in the INKEY$ lines, and the program continues. If no key is pressed, a blank string is assigned, and the program continues. The key character does not appear on the screen.

The difference between INKEY$ and other input statements is that the machine does not hang about waiting. Checking the keyboard takes only a tiny fraction of a second, and if no key happens to be pressed in that time, INKEY$ returns a blank. If you had an INKEY$ statement in any program of the types that we have been looking at (in place of INPUT, for example), it is most unlikely that there would be any input, because you simply would not have a chance of hitting a key at exactly the right moment.

For that reason, INKEY$ is always used in a piece of program that repeats, a loop. In such a loop, a variable will be assigned using INKEY$, and it is then tested. If it contains a blank, the loop repeats, trying INKEY$ again. If a non-zero ASCII code has been assigned, the loop ends so that you can make use of the variable content, or you can treat it as a dummy variable, simply using INKEY$ as a way of making the computer wait.

Qnote This type of use of INKEY$ is not really necessary in QBASIC because INPUT$ is provided, and there are few occasions where you need to use INKEY$ in a program that you write. It has to be provided to allow you to run programs written for earlier versions of BASIC.

A typical INKEY$ loop is shown in Figure 5.11. This uses the words DO and LOOP UNTIL to start a repetitive action which ends when any string is assigned. The <> sign means not equal, and the "" pair of quotes mean a blank string (there is nothing contained between the quotes). This therefore carries out the test for k$ not being blank, which is the condition that ends the loop:

```
DO
k$ = INKEY$
LOOP UNTIL k$ <> ""
```

Figure 5.11. The form of an INKEY$ loop of the type that is no longer needed in QBASIC.

- The actions of testing are covered in Chapter Seven, and looping in Chapter Eight.

There are still a few actions for which INKEY$ is more suited. You might, for example, want to test for keys being pressed in a longer loop, but without any wait, and two examples of that type of action are shown in Chapter 11.

Finally, there are variants on INPUT and INPUT$ that are used for file reading. These allow inputs of the same forma as INPUT and INPUT$ to be taken from a disk file, using a file channel number in addition to the normal part of the statement. For example, in$ = INPUT$ (5,1) would assign to variable in$ a set of five characters read from a disk whose code number (or channel number) was 1. This type of use is covered in Chapters 18 and 19.

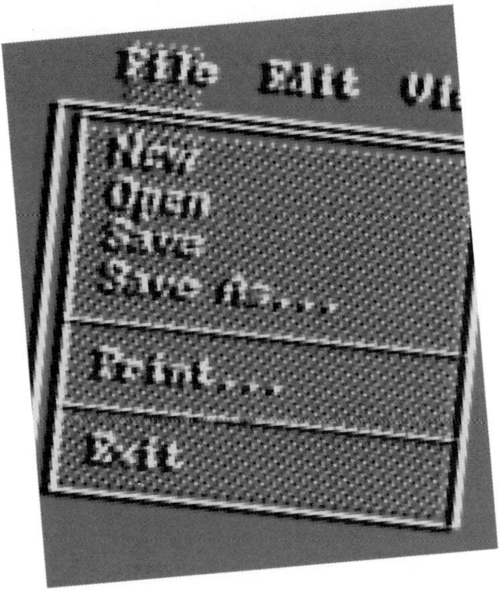

Numbers and Precision

Working with number variables

There's nothing particularly difficult or new about working with number variables, though the idea might be a novelty to you if you never encountered algebra at school. Using variable names, you can type instructions like 'sum * VAT', meaning that whatever number is assigned to variable 'sum' is multiplied by the number (usually 0.175) that has been assigned to variable or CONST VAT. The value of being able to carry out arithmetic on variables in this way is that it allows you to work with any numbers.

For example, if you put into a program the instruction statement:

```
PRINT 40.5 * 0.15
```

then this will print 6.075 every time you run the program. If, however, your instruction is:

```
PRINT sum * VAT
```

what gets printed depends on what has been assigned to 'sum' and 'VAT' and these assignments can be changed during the program. You can, for example, make the computer carry out this action many times, using a whole list of numbers, or using a number that has to be assigned from the keyboard using an INPUT statement. This latter example will be a number that was not put into the program at the time when the program was written, and that's the whole point about programming. You can even make the program read hundreds of numbers from a disk file, and work on these.

Simple arithmetic with variables, then, is typed much as you type simple arithmetic with numbers, using the signs +, -, * and /. This means that you can have lines containing items such as:

```
Sum = First + second
Profit = Gross - expenses
VAT = sell_price * rate
metres = millimetres / 1000
```

The result of such pieces of arithmetic can be printed or, as shown here, assigned to some other variable that will be used later. One complication occurs, however, when the same variable name is used twice. For example, what do we mean by the assignment:

```
Sum = Sum + item ?
```

By the ordinary rules of numbers, this would just be silly, and its meaning hinges on the way that all versions of BASIC use the = sign to mean an assignment, so that the action of Sum = Sum + item means that you add the value of 'Sum' and of 'item', and make this the new value of 'Sum'. No language other than BASIC uses the = sign for both assignment and equality, and it's something that you just have to get used to. Wherever the same variable name appears on each side of the = sign, then the = sign means 'is assigned to', so that statements like A = A * B or C = C - X or D = D / 5 are all examples of this use of the equality sign.

Expressions

An expression is a piece of arithmetic carried out on variable names. We have, in fact been dealing with expressions in the form of statements like Sum = Sum + Item, or Tax = Price * rate. These are very simple expressions, and in most expressions more than one arithmetic action is carried out. We could, for example, have an expression:

```
total = first * rate + second / third
```

which makes use of five variable names. The computer can only make use of this expression if there is a number assigned to each of the variables other than 'total'. If no number has been assigned, then QBASIC will take it that the number zero is assigned. This can lead to an expression giving a false result if a number has not been assigned, and many other languages will not carry out the action of such an expression – the *evaluation* of the expression – if any of the variables has not been assigned.

The next point about expressions is how the value is worked out. In an expression such as A + B * C - D, for example, which of the three arithmetic actions is carried out first? As it happens, expressions, like anything else in computing, follow precise rules, and once you know what the rules are it's not difficult to apply them. The most important rules concern precedence of the arithmetic actions, and once you know about precedence, it's not difficult to find what an expression does. Making up an expression for yourself is another matter, and only practice can help there.

```
1. Anything within brackets
2. Exponentiation such as 2^3
3. Multiplication and Division
4. Addition and Subtraction
```

Figure 6.1. The order of precedence for arithmetic actions.

What this means is that if you have more than one operation in an expression, the operations with higher precedence are always carried out first. If there is no clear precedence, then the order in the expression is simply left to right. For example, if you have the expression:

```
PRINT 5 + 4 * 3 - 6 / 2
```

what do you expect? If everything obeyed a left-to-right order only, the result would be got from 5 + 4 = 9, 9 * 3 = 27, 27 - 6 = 21 and 21 / 2 = 11.5 . It's not like this, though. Because multiplication and division have higher precedence than addition and subtraction, the 4 * 3 = 12 and the 6 / 2 = 3 are worked out first. Having done that, all that is left is of equal precedence, and we get 5 + 12 = 17 and 17 - 3 = 14, which is the answer that the computer will give you. Remember that, in a program, all or most of the quantities would be variables or constants, and to find the numerical answer you would have to find what numbers were assigned to the variables or constants at the time of evaluating the expression. You might, for example, be working with something like Y = K + B * X ^ N. The X ^ N action is carried out first, since the raise-to-a-power action (exponentiation) has highest precedence in this lot, and then the result of this is multiplied by B. Finally, the value of K is added.

One important point to remember is that brackets take precedence over everything else. For example, if you have an expression which boils down to 5 * (4 + 3), then this is not the same as 5 * 4 + 3 (which is 23) but gives 60, because whatever is inside the brackets is worked out first, giving 12 in this case. When there are several sets of nested brackets, meaning brackets inside other brackets, then whatever is innermost has highest precedence. For example, 5 * (4 + (8 - 6 / 2)) gives 45, because the innermost bracket gives 5, adding this to the 4 in the next layer of brackets gives 9, and the result is 5 * 9. For some reason, however, it all looks much more fearsome when used with variables, particularly when there are actions like STR$ and VAL (see Chapter Seven) involved as well.

Types of numbers

The name of a variable can have an ending symbol which determines what type of variable is being used. So far we have used ordinary numbers (short floats) and strings, with the string name being marked out with a dollar sign at the end of the name. There are several other signs that can be used for other forms of numbers, and that's what we need to investigate now.

Remember that QBASIC can also use declaration lines to nominate types for variables, or use statements like DEFINT A – Z.

As noted in Chapter Two, an integer number is a whole number, which can be positive or negative, but which contains no fractions. QBASIC allows you to use short or long integers, the difference being the range of numbers that can be used – as the names suggest, the short integer uses only two bytes of memory, the long integer uses four bytes.

A short integer name can be marked by ending it with the percentage sign, %, so that num%, amount% and count% are all valid short-integer names. The range of a short integer in QBASIC is restricted to any whole number between the limits of -32768 and +32767.

Unlike other number variables, though, integer variables obey very strict rules. The value that is assigned to an integer variable must not contain any fractional part. You can correctly assign quantity% = 5, for example, but not quantity% = 5.5. If you do use quantity% = 5.5, then you will find from using PRINT quantity% that the value which has actually been assigned is 6 and the fraction has been completely ignored. If you had used quantity% = 5.4, the printed value would be 5 – the integer assignment action rounds down anything below the half-way mark, and rounds up anything that is 0.5 or more.

In addition, short integer variables can use only a limited range of values, from -32768 to +32767. If, for example, you try to assign value% = - 32800 or total% = 42000 you will get the message 'Overflow' when the program tries to carry out this command. Overflow means that there isn't enough memory to take the number, because an integer number is restricted to two bytes of memory, less than any other kind of variable.

The name of the integer, however, also takes up memory space, so that if you want to keep your memory requirements low, use short names.

Because so little memory is used for storage, any program which can make use of only short integer variables will run faster and take up less memory than a program which uses the other variable types. If you can be sure that your programs will use only short integer number variables, there are three ways that you can take advantage of this. One is to remember to place the integer mark, %, after each number variable name. Another, which is easier when you are using a large program, is to define all of your integers in advance. You can do this by using DEFINT. For example, if your program starts with:

```
DEFINT J-N
```

then any variable name which starts with J, or with K, L, M, or N, will be an integer. This includes names like NOTE2, JJCM, LOQ, KIM, and so on. It's the first letter that counts here. You can over-ride the action of DEFINT if you like by using one of the other symbols. For example, even if you have used DEFINT J-N, you can still assign a number like K1!=101.76. In this case, K1! is a *single-precision* or *float* number, not an integer.

note

The third method is pre-declaration, demonstrated later.

Integers can be used with any arithmetic action, but it's better to stick to addition, subtraction and multiplication. The reason is that division, along with actions like taking square roots, can give results which can contain fractions. Integer numbers cannot make use of fractions, so something has to give:

```
DEFINT A-Z
PART = 45
QUEST = 12
DEBIT = PART / QUEST
PRINT "Int. division gives 45/12 as"; DEBIT
PRINT "Normal division gives 45/12 as"; PART / QUEST
PRINT" The remainder of 45/12 is"; PART MOD QUEST
END
```

Figure 6.2. Using names defined as integers for integer arithmetic.

The first line defines all variables as short integers, and the following three lines assign integer values to integer variable names. In the fourth line, integer variable DEBIT is assigned with the result of dividing PART by QUEST. Now this result is not an integer, so if it is assigned to an integer variable, the fractional part will be rounded, as the following line shows when the program runs.

The PRINT action, however, is not the same as assignment, and so the correct value is printed in the sixth line. If you use division in a program that makes use of integer variable then you can PRINT the result but you can't be sure that it will be correct if you assign it to an integer variable.

The inability to use fractions, however, does not make integers completely useless for division, because the function MOD (see later) finds out the remainder after a division. The syntax is A MOD B, which gives the remainder after A has been divided by B. This is illustrated in the last line.

It's surprising how many numbers that you deal with are short integers. The most obvious use is in a count, but integers can be used for other calculations. If you have a program which deals with small sums of money, for example, you can convert each amount to pennies and then use an integer variable. The program will not be able to handle a sum of more than 32767 pence, which is £327.67, but this can sometimes be quite useful.

The long integer type of QBASIC allows a range of +2,147,483,647 to -2,147,483,648, using four bytes of storage for each number. This makes it feasible to work with sums of money in long integer form, using pennies and preserving correct arithmetic for normal accounting actions. You must remember, however, that actions such as taking percentages and calculating interest will cause fractions that will be rounded by the action of assigning the result to an integer variable.

If you want a range of names to be long integers, you can use a statement such as:

```
DEFLNG X-Z
```

so that the names XITE, YACHT and ZOO will all be taken as being long integers. As for all other uses of DEF, these name uses can be overridden individually, so that XRAY% would be a short integer, YAHOO$ a string and ZEBRA! a single-precision number.

Note that this override action is not possible if the name has already been assigned with a value.

Floating point number variables

A floating-point, float, or real number variable can be stored in two forms in QBASIC: single-precision and double-precision. As explained in Chapter 2 , these numbers are stored in two parts (mantissa and exponent), of which one part (the mantissa) is always a binary fraction that is seldom precise. A single-precision float number uses four bytes for storage, and its range is from -3.402823E+38 to +3.402823E+38.

Because of the limitations of storage, there also is a lower limit to the size of numbers, which is +2.802597E-45 or -2.802597E-45. The approximations that are inevitable because of the binary fraction system make single-precision numbers accurate to about 6 decimal places.

Single-precision numbers can be marked in the usual set of different ways. One way is to make use of the exclamation mark (!) following each variable name. Names like Added!, BC2X!, and H2! are all valid real number variable names. An alternative is to define a range of variable names as single-precision. This is done by using DEFSNG. For example, DEFSNG A-Z will define all number variables as single-precision, unless some other mark is used following the variable name.

note

This is not normally necessary, because any name that is not followed by a symbol is taken to be that of a single-precision number variable. The ! sign is normally used only when another type is being over-ruled.

```
A = 1 / 11 : B = 7 / 11 - 6 / 11
PRINT A
PRINT B
PRINT A - B
C = 123456789
PRINT C
```

Figure 6.3. The approximations that are involved in storing single-precision numbers.

Figure 6.3 illustrates this, and also shows that numbers which cannot be stored in precise form, like 1/11 and 6/11 and 7/11, will still give the correct answer when added. These numbers are repeating decimals, but the arithmetic actions of single-precision arithmetic round them correctly. It's a different matter for the number 123456789. Though this is well within the limits of size for a single-precision number, it uses too many *significant figures,* so that the PRINT line shows that it is returned as 1.234568E+08, meaning the number 123456800 – the E is used, as in calculators, to mean a power of ten, so that 1.234568E8 means 1.234568 $\times 10^8$ (1 followed by eight zeros).

Numbers of this single-precision kind, then, are perfectly accurate only for values up to 999999 and down to - 999999, six-figure numbers. You can still get accurate results with numbers like 134000000, because the zero's are not significant, they are not the part of the number that is coded into six digits. Similarly, numbers like .00000012 are stored accurately, because once again, the zeros are not part of the number that has to be stored in coded form. These zeros represent a power of ten and it is the rest of the number that is significant.

The QBASIC system ensures that arithmetic which uses single precision numbers will be carried out with good accuracy if the numbers contain six significant figures or less.

Double precision

A variable name which ends with the hashmark (#), or which has been selected, for example by the use of DEFDBL A-Z, is a double-precision variable. A variable of this type needs eight bytes to contain the number value. This allows numbers to be stored precisely up to a maximum of fourteen significant figures. The range of values is from +1.79769313486231E+308 to -1.79769313486231E+308, and the smallest values that can be stored are +4.940656458412465E-324 and -4.940656458412465E-324. Unlike the use of single-precision, which is the default, the use of double-precision has to be a deliberate choice. You would use this only when such accuracy was needed – it seldom is – because the use of double precision arithmetic slows down the action of the computer considerably. As it is, the method that is used for storing either single or double precision numbers is comparatively slow in action compared to the methods that are used for integers. Throughout this book we'll use only as much precision as we need, so you will see the use of the % marks in a lot of the programs in which the default single-precision is not needed. None of the programs here requires double-precision arithmetic.

Handling numbers

The amount of computing that we shall cover in this book will persuade you that computers aren't just about numbers. For some applications, though, the ability to handle numbers is very important. If you want to use your computer to solve scientific or engineering problems, its ability to handle numbers will be very much more important than if you bought it for games, for wordprocessing or even for accounts. It's time, then, to take a brief look at the number abilities of BASIC. In general, if you understand what a mathematical term like Sin or Tan or Exp means, you will have no problems about using these mathematical functions in your programs. If you don't then simply ignore the parts of this section that mention them.

The simplest and most fundamental number action is counting. Counting involves the ideas of incrementing if you are counting up and decrementing if you are counting down. Incrementing a number means adding 1 to it, decrementing means subtracting 1 from it. These actions are programmed in a rather confusing looking way in BASIC:

```
CLS
X% = 5
PRINT "Value of X% is ";X%
X% = X% + 1:PRINT
PRINT "Now after X%=X%+1, X% is";X%
```

Figure 6.4. Incrementing the value of a number stored as a variable.

The value of variable X% is assigned as 5. This is printed, but then the next line increments X%. This is done using the odd-looking instruction X% = X% + 1, meaning that the new value that is assigned to X% is 1 more than its previous value. The rest of the program proves that this action of incrementing the value of X has been carried out.

We could equally well have a line:

```
X% = X% - 1
```

and this would have the effect of making the new value of X% one less than the old value. X% has been decremented this time. We could also use X% = 2 * X% to produce a new value of X equal to double the old value, or X% = X% / 3 to produce a new value of X equal to the old value divided by three.

Number functions

The number functions of BASIC are the statement words that carry out various actions on numbers. So far, we have used the signs +, -, * and /, which are called operators, and we have seen that these obey a strict order of precedence. Number functions are for actions that have a lower precedence, and which are used for a variety of actions that are not simple arithmetic operations. This doesn't make the actions complicated, however, only different. A lot of number functions are used in comparisons, so that you will see them used in expressions that include the signs =, > and <.

The = sign always means *exact* equality, so that 3.99999 is not equal to 4.00000 - the computer does not deal with almost equal quantities. This can cause problems, as we shall see later, because when a number which is not an integer is stored in the memory, it is stored in an approximate form that can cause problems if you want to use the equality sign. The greater-than sign (>) and the less-than sign(<) are used in much the same way as the equality sign, and you can combine the two as <> to mean *not equal to.*

The function ABS is used when you might need to ignore negative signs, because ABS(x) will have the same value whether x is positive or negative. This can be handy if you want to know the difference between two numbers and don't care which is larger. For example, using ABS(x-y) will always give a positive result even if y is greater than x, as Figure 6.5 shows. Note how ABS needs to have an *argument*, meaning that the quantity that ABS is to work on is placed within brackets following the ABS keyword.

```
CLS
x = 45.677
x = 4.674
y = 3.58
z = ABS(y - x)
a = ABS(x - y)
PRINT a, z
```

Figure 6.5. Using ABS to ensure that a subtraction does not produce a negative quantity.

A useful accompaniment to ABS is the SGN function, which is used for testing, because the result of SGN(x) will be -1 if x is negative, 0 if x is 0, and +1 if x is positive. By combining ABS and SGN, you can form routines that will avoid any of the problems that negative or zero values might cause, or you can formulate an answer that is impossible by normal methods.

note The topic of testing is dealt with in Chapter Seven.

This is illustrated in Figure 6.6. The function that is being used is SQR, which stops with an error message if a negative number is used. Now this can be avoided by using ABS, but in some work, you need to use the idea of square roots of negative numbers *(imaginary numbers)*.

No real number has a negative square, so the square root of a negative number cannot be real, but it is very convenient to regard the square root of a negative number as being the product of a real root (of the positive number) and the square root of -1, written as i or j. You can, for example, look on i or j as meaning direction at right angles to the normal, so that 5j means five units along a line at right angles to the X-axis.

```
CLS
FOR j% = 1 TO 5
  READ d%
  PRINT "Square root of"; d%; " is";
  PRINT SQR(ABS(d%));
  IF SGN(d%) = -1 THEN PRINT "j"
  PRINT
NEXT
DATA 3,0,-6,7,-9
```

Figure 6.6. Using SGN and ABS to deal with square roots of negative numbers.

In the listing, some numbers are read in and processed. The square root is found using ABS so that a value can always be obtained, and SGN is used to detect the use of a negative sign and to place a 'j' following the number if the original number was negative.

Using INT and FIX

For a lot of purposes, you need to round numbers. If a calculation of interest payable on an amount of money works out at 355.677892, for example, you cannot possibly pay or receive this amount – it would probably be rounded to 355.68 if you were paying it and to 355.67 if you were receiving it, a financial system called *salami-slicing*. We need to look at the number functions that will chop numbers and can be used for rounding. These functions are INT and FIX and the difference between them is rather subtle.

INT, as the name suggests, takes the integer part of a number, and FIX does so also, but the difference lies in how a negative number is treated:

```
CLS
a = 52.789
b = -52.789
PRINT "Int gives "; INT(a); " and "; INT(b)
PRINT "Fix gives "; FIX(a); " and "; FIX(b)
```

Figure 6.7. The difference between INT and FIX.

When this runs, the first line that is printed displays the numbers 52 and -53 and the second line prints 52 and -52. FIX has simply chopped the fraction from the number, while INT has taken it to the nearest *smaller* whole number. If all your numbers are positive, there is no difference but if you deal with both positive and negative numbers there is a significant difference. The use of INT is more common.

note Remember that you can use ABS if you want to ignore the sign of a number.

Rounding a money sum requires a little more work. The intention is that any sum up to and including 0.005 should be rounded to the lower whole number, and any sum greater than 0.005 should be rounded up to the next whole number. For example, 48.167 would become 48.17 and 48.162 should become 48.16, rounding to the nearest penny, cent, pfennig, centime or whatever.

This is rather more than the action of INT or FIX alone, and the secret is to work with 100 times the money number. Suppose, for example, that we want to round amounts of 48.776 and 32.583. Using INT or FIX on these would chop them to an integer number of pounds, which would hardly be welcome. Now if we multiply each of these by 100 we will get 4877.6 and 3258.3 and rounding on these number will make them rounded to the nearest penny. Using INT directly, however, would chop them down to 4877 and 3258. both rounded down, and we would want to round the first number up rather than down. This is done by adding 0.5 before rounding:

```
CLS
A = 48.776
B = 32.583
newa = (INT((100 * A) + .5)) / 100
newb = (INT((100 * B) + .5)) / 100
PRINT " This rounds to £"; newa; " and £"; newb
```

Figure 6.8. Using INT in a routine that will round numbers to two decimal places.

The key to all this is in the expressions in the fourth and fifth lines. As always, when an expression contains a lot of brackets it needs some experience to make sense of it, so we'll use this one as an example. This applies as much to constructing these lines as to understanding them.

We start with (100 * A) + .5 which multiplies the number by 100 and adds 0.5. For the first number this converts to 4877.6 + 0.5 = 4878.1, and for the second number the conversion is to 3258.8. The next action outside this set of brackets is INT, which will chop these quantities to 4878 and 3258 respectively. Finally, the result of all this is divided by 100, giving 48.78 and 32.58, the rounded quantities that we need.

The general rules for rounding are:

1. Multiply by a power of ten (10, 100, 1000 etc) to make the number contain only one place of decimals.
2. Add 0.5.
3. Take the INT of this.
4. Divide by the same power of ten as was used in step 1.

Actions like this can be done by using a defined function, see Chapter 13, and also by using CSNG and CINT, see below. In general, this routine needs to be used only when you want to use a rounding factor other than 0.5 for your own purposes.

Number type conversions

There are several functions (actions) that will convert one type of number to another. These actions are not needed very often, and they have to be used with care because you need to understand exactly what it is they do. Nothing that you can do with a number will ever improve its precision, and the only reason for conversions is to make all numbers into a common format. You can, however, use CINT for rounding in place of the INT form used in Figure 6.8, and the main value of these actions is that they round automatically.

```
CLS
a% = 44
b = 44.5678
c# = 44.523458779#
PRINT CSNG(a%)
PRINT b
PRINT CSNG(c#)      PRINT
PRINT CINT(a%)
PRINT CINT(b)
PRINT CINT(c#)
```

Figure 6.9. Conversion actions: CSNG converts to a single-precision floating-point number, CINT to an integer number.

When this runs, you can see how the numbers have been treated. In each case, the appearance of the integer 44 is unchanged. No conversion affects an integer, because it is the lowest form of number as far as decimal places are concerned.

note

Note that using CSNG(a%) prints 44 and not 44.00000.

The CSNG action also has no effect on the number b which is a single-precision number in any case, but the double-precision number c# is 44.52346. This latter step is a true rounding, not just a chopping down. This also applies to the CINT set, because the two floating point numbers are rounded to 45, not chopped to 44.

Conversions down, to a smaller number of decimal places, are always rounded. Conversions up from variables, such as CDBL(a%), are very seldom needed. If you use, for example:

```
a = 1/3
b# = 1/3
```

then the first variable a will be .3333333 and the second, b# will be .3333333333333333 in accordance with single and double-precision respectively.

The list of conversion functions is shown below:

CINT	–	**convert to integer**
CLNG	–	**convert to long integer**
CSNG	–	**convert to single precision**
CDBL	–	**convert to double precision**

Testing and Branching

Testing a variable

An important action in any computing language is testing, and the small programs in this book contain many examples of tests being carried out. Tests are often associated with *looping*, and Chapter Eight takes this use further. In this Chapter we are concerned with what can be tested and what form of tests can be used.

A test is used in order to make some sort of decision, for example whether to print the value of a variable or ignore it, to take a new page, clear the screen, repeat a piece of program or whatever. Testing is the important step that is always followed by some sort of *Branch*, meaning that the program will do one action if the test succeeds and another action if the test fails.

note Any test will have only two possible results, FALSE or TRUE, there are no MAYBE or PERHAPS results. FALSE is represented in the memory of the computer by the number 0, TRUE by the number -1.

The tests that are used in loops are usually part of the loop statement (such as LOOP UNTIL or DO WHILE) and are noted in Chapter 8. The form of test that is independent of loops is the IF test and, once you know how this one works, you will find it easy to use all the rest.

The IF test starts with IF, tests the quantities, and uses the word THEN to separate the test from the branch action that will be done. For example:

```
IF a$ = "Smith" THEN PRINT "Pass"
```

consists of the keywords IF and THEN, with the test a$ = "Smith" and the branch action PRINT "Pass". The test is either TRUE or FALSE, the content of a$ is either "Smith" or it is not. When the test returns TRUE, the PRINT action is carried out; when the test returns FALSE, the PRINT action is omitted.

This very simple use of IF...THEN accounts for the majority of test steps in programs, but very much more can be achieved. In particular, there are several ways in which the IF...THEN statement can be used, and there are many other ways in which the test can be formulated. We'll take these one at a time, starting with the test methods.

The arithmetical operators can be used in tests, in various combinations. The main three signs in the group are = < and >, which compare the size of numbers and the ASCII codes of string characters. These signs can be combined, so that >= means equal to or greater than, <= means equal to or less than, and <> or >< means not equal to. Note that some older versions of BASIC do not allow the use of >< as an equivalent to <>. You would, of course, use these operators in connection with variable names for numbers or strings rather than with constants.

The = sign tests for exact equality, so that if your test is:

```
IF x = 2
```

then for x equal to 1.9999999 the test will fail. Similarly if you test:

```
IF A$ = "Smith"
```

the test will fail if A$ is "smith" or "Smith " (extra space) or anything that is not *precisely* equal. This is one of the failings of computing languages that they do not allow for human errors like this, and there is a whole field of study (fuzzy logic) which aims to put this right – some day. The inequality signs can be used singly or in combination. The meaning of:

```
IF a% > 4
```

is that the test will succeed if the value of a% is more than 4. Since a% is an integer, this means that the value of a% must be 5 or more for the test to succeed, If we used variable a in place of a%, then the test would succeed for value of a of 4.001 and so on. The < sign tests for the value on the lefthand side being less, so that:

```
IF x < 10
```

will be true for x being 9.999 or less, for example. By using <> or >< we can test for non-equality, as in:

```
IF A$<>"END"
```

which will be true for as long as A$ is not assigned with the string "END".

The use of => and =< can often make tests more stringent. For example, if the test in the form:

```
IF X = 5 THEN GOTO END
```

then we expect to end the program for a value of X equal to 5, but what happens if X takes the value 5.01? The answer is that the test will return FALSE, because this is not exact equality. By writing the test as:

```
IF X >= 5 THEN GOTO END
```

we avoid such problems, because a value of 5.01 for X will make this test return TRUE.

Make use of <= and >= if there is any reason to believe that the test might be comparing two items that would not necessarily be exactly equal.

When tests involve integers, there is less need to use this type of testing, because there is no danger of an integer variable taking a value that is not equal to an integer. You still need to beware of testing a quantity whose value might jump, in this example, from four to six without ever being exactly equal to five.

String tests

String testing is done on the basis of ASCII values of characters. Two letters are identical if they have identical ASCII codes, so it's not difficult to see what the identity sign, = , means when we apply it to strings. It's not so easy to see how we use the > and < signs until we think again about ASCII codes. The ASCII code for A is 65, and the code for B is 66. In this sense, A is 'less than' B, because it has a smaller ASCII code. If we want to place letters into alphabetical order, then, we simply arrange them in order of ascending ASCII codes.

The tests will recognise this, so that a test such as:

```
IF A$ > "M" PRINT "Second half"
```

will be true if A$ has been assigned with any letter from N to Z, and for all the lowercase letters a to z.

This is a point to watch. A lowercase letter in ASCII code uses a number which is 32 more than its uppercase counterpart, so that 'A' is coded as 65 and 'a' as 97. A test such as the one illustrated will be TRUE of any lowercase letter. QBASIC can use a string function, UCASE$, to make a temporary conversion to upper-case for the purposes of a test, see Chapter Nine.

String testing is not confined to a string of single letters, however. Suppose we test for string "WHAT" being less than string "WHEN". The first letters of the two words are tested and, because they are identical, no decision can be made. If the first word had been "HAT" the test would have been returned as TRUE simply by comparing the first letters. If no decision can be made on the first pair of letters, the second letter of each word is compared. Again, no decision can be made, so that the third letter of each word is taken. This time the TRUE decision can be returned and there is no need to look at the rest of the string.

- If two long strings are identical, then they must contain the same letters in the same order.

This letter-by-letter comparison can yield some unexpected results. In an index, we would place the lines:

```
Address, 27
Address use,29
```

in that order, but if these are compared using an IF test, the second phrase will be rated as coming earlier in ranking. The reason is that the whole of the first word is identical in both strings, so that the decision is made by comparing the comma in the first line with the space in the second. In ASCII terms, the space is code 32 and the comma is code 44, so that the space precedes the comma.

Logic tests

The tests using the arithmetical operators are useful, but there is another set of operators that can be used, the logic operators, consisting of the words AND, EQV, IMP, NOT, OR and XOR. The words AND, OR, XOR and NOT are sometimes called the Boolean operators in honour of the mathematician George Boole of Lincoln whose work laid the foundations of computing science. The operators EQV and IMP are not so commonly used. As with arithmetical operators, the action of a logic operator is to return TRUE or FALSE when it is used to test a relationship.

The NOT operator is unary, meaning that it needs only one argument, one item to work on, and it gives a TRUE result if what it precedes is NOT TRUE. If you are not accustomed to this, it can look very confusing, and a few examples will help. The secret is to work in terms of TRUE and FALSE only, and to start with any term that is enclosed in brackets. For example, what do you expect from the lines:

```
a% = 2
PRINT NOT (a% > 1)
```

when this runs? The answer is worked out by looking first at 2 > 1, which is what a% > 1 amounts to. This is TRUE and since NOT TRUE is FALSE, the answer must be the code for FALSE, which is 0 and this is what is printed.

If we programmed:

```
a% = 2
IF NOT (a% > 1) THEN PRINT "Not so"
```

then the message would be printed for this value of a%, but not if a% were 1, 0 , -1 or any other value less than +1.

Using PRINT with an arithmetic or a logic comparison will print the numbers 0 or -1, meaning FALSE or TRUE respectively. If you want to print any other message you need to use an IF..THEN test as indicated above.

- Numbers used in such tests must be integers – the Logic operators are meaningless as applied to single or double-precision numbers.

Try another one:

```
IF NOT("A" > "B") PRINT "Quite true"
```

When we compare strings, the ASCII codes count, and the ASCII code for "B" is 66, more than the code for "A" which is 65. "A" > "B" is therefore FALSE, and NOT FALSE gives TRUE, -1, so that the phrase is printed. By the same token, NOT ("B" > "A") gives 0, FALSE.

Using PRINT NOT(0) will give -1, since NOT FALSE must be TRUE, and equally obviously, NOT(-1) gives 0. If your nerves are up to it, try PRINT NOT(7) and see if you can explain the result. If it's baffling, please turn to the explanation at the end of this chapter.

The other logic operators, AND, EQV, IMP, OR and XOR need two quantities to work on. These quantities can be number comparisons or string comparisons, and the important point once again is that each side of the AND, OR or XOR word should be something that can be resolved to TRUE or FALSE. Each of these operators will give a result that depends on the state of the quantities that are being prepared, and in TRUE/FALSE terms these are shown in Figure 7.1. Note that if Binary numbers are being compared, 1 is used for TRUE and 0 for FALSE (since there is no -1). See the end of this Chapter for the uses of these operators on binary numbers.

Tables for A (OPERATOR) B

AND Table:	A	B	Result
	False	False	False
	False	True	False
	True	False	False
	True	True	True

TRUE only if A is TRUE and B is TRUE

EQV Table:	A	B	Result
	False	False	True
	False	True	False
	True	False	False
	True	True	True

TRUE only if A and B both TRUE or both FALSE

IMP Table:	A	B	Result
	False	False	True
	False	True	True
	True	False	False
	True	True	True

FALSE only for A TRUE and B FALSE

OR Table:	A	B	Result
	False	False	False
	False	True	True
	True	False	True
	True	True	True

FALSE only for both A and B FALSE

XOR Table:	A	B	Result
	False	False	False
	False	True	True
	True	False	True
	True	True	False

TRUE for A TRUE or B TRUE but not both TRUE

Figure 7.1. Truth tables for the logic operators. A and B are the items being compared, each of which can be TRUE or FALSE.

For example, if we have the test:

```
IF (7>3) AND (5>2) THEN PRINT "This is true"
```

then we can expect the phrase to be printed. Working out the items in the brackets we have 7>3 is TRUE and 5>2 is TRUE, so TRUE AND TRUE = TRUE. The Law of AND is that the result is TRUE only if the items that are connected are also both true. If one item is FALSE, the result is also FALSE. On that basis, then you would expect the result of:

```
PRINT (5>6)AND(7>4)
```

to be FALSE, as it is, because one term is FALSE.

As applied to strings, AND is used to check that a combination of conditions is true, as, for example.

```
IF A$="Smith" AND n%=45
```

which is TRUE only if both tests are separately TRUE. You can use AND more than once in such a line to make comparisons of more than two items.

The OR operator will give TRUE if one item is TRUE, no matter whether the other is TRUE or FALSE. Only if both items are FALSE will the result of OR be false. A typical use of OR is:

```
IF answer$ = "Y" OR answer$ = "y"
```

to test for the Y answer either as lowercase or uppercase. This is more appropriately dealt with by using UCASE$, see Chapter 8, but OR can be very useful for other comparisons such as:

```
IF name$="Sinclair" and age = 60
```

once again testing for either of two conditions to be TRUE. You can, of course, use several conditions separated by OR to test more than a pair of conditions.

The XOR action is closer to what we usually mean by OR in everyday life, meaning one or the other only, not both. One unique feature of XOR is that is can be used in a form of coding and decoding:

```
CLS
REM Code and decode
a% = 56
PRINT "Original is"; a%
x% = a% XOR 33
PRINT " Code is"; x%
y% = x% XOR 33
PRINT "Decoded figure is"; y%
```

Figure 7.2. Using XOR in a coding and decoding action.

When any number is XORed with another number, a key, the result will in general be a changed number. When this changed number is XORed again with the same key, the original number is restored. This feature of XOR is widely used for passwording, though usually in more elaborate forms.

note Remember that you would normally be using these operators with variable names.

Making the branch

The IF test can be used in the one-line form that has been demonstrated so far, with the action that follows THEN being a simple one-stage one like a PRINT or END. For anything more elaborate we need to use either a GOTO, a GOSUB, a CALL or an extended IF test. The subjects of GOSUB and CALL are dealt with in detail in Chapters 11 and 12 respectively, and this Chapter deals mainly with GOTO and the extended IF test.

A GOTO statement forces the program to jump to a new place, not taking the normal sequence of the next following line. The position for a GOTO can be identified by using a label name, a name followed by a colon. Such a label name must not be any of the reserved names of QBASIC.

note If you always type label names in lowercase you will see them turn to uppercase when you press ENTER if they are keywords. This will alert you to the incorrect use of a name.

```
CLS
a% = 5
b% = 6
IF a% < b% GOTO outhere
PRINT "It's not true"
END
outhere:
PRINT "a% is less than b%"
END
```

Figure 7.3. An IF test which uses a GOTO to jump over a line of a program.

Figure 7.3 uses the GOTO outhere following the test to jump over the first of the two PRINT lines – the first PRINT line can never be run while the variables have the values shown here. Try reversing the values, and see the first PRINT line run. Note that if you remove the END line just ahead of label outhere: then both PRINT lines will run when a% is greater than b%.

Using GOTO, you can jump ahead as many lines as you like, and it is also possible to jump back so as to repeat a piece of program. As Chapter 8 explains, however, using GOTO to repeat lines is very undesirable in a modern programming language, and in QBASIC there is never any need to use GOTO at all.

note You should regard GOTO as a statement that is intended to allow you to run programs written for older versions of BASIC, rather than something to use in your own programs.

The preferred way of dealing with the result of an IF test is either to use GOSUB or CALL (and of the two, CALL is preferred nowadays) or to form an extended IF test. The use of GOSUB and CALL will be covered in later Chapters.

An extended IF test uses the familiar form of IF up to the THEN part, and subsequently takes a new line. As many lines as you need can be taken for items that have to be carried out when the test succeeds, and the set is ended with the key words END IF. All of the lines will be ignored if the test fails.

```
CLS
a% = 10
INPUT "type a number, please, between 1 and 20
(ENTER)"; b%
IF a% > b% THEN
  PRINT " My number was larger than yours"
  PRINT " I shall reduce it to zero"
  b% = 0
  PRINT " My a% is"; a%; " and your b% is now"; b%
  END IF
END
```

Figure 7.4. An extended form of IF test, using END IF to mark out the end of the action lines.

In Figure 7.4 if the number you enter is less than 10, the messages are delivered and the reassignment of b% is made. If the number you enter is greater than 10, the program simply ends.

The important point about all this is that the use of an extended IF allows you to specify several lines of action without the need to jump to another part of the program, or call up any routine for carrying out these actions. More importantly, you can put other options into this test:

```
CLS
a% = 10
INPUT "type a number, please, between 1 and 20
(ENTER)"; b%
IF a% > b% THEN
  PRINT " My number was larger than yours"
  PRINT " I shall reduce it to zero"
  b% = 0

  ELSE
    PRINT "Your number was greater than mine"
    PRINT "I shall reduce a% to zero"
    a% = 0
  END IF
PRINT " My a% is now"; a%; " and your b% is now"; b%
END
```

Figure 7.5. Using the option ELSE in an IF...ENDIF test to provide a set of lines that deal with the opposite result of the test.

By using ELSE in this way, you can provide a set of lines that are run when the test result is FALSE as well as a set for the test being TRUE. This allows the IF test to be used for a large variety of purposes in a much simpler way than was possible on older varieties of BASIC.

You can elaborate this to use ELSE IF to carry out a second test if the first test returns a FALSE result, and you will see this form of the IF...END IF set of lines in programs. When you start to use ELSE IF, however, you need to plan very carefully to ensure that what you are doing is correct, and it can help considerably if you make a decision chart for what you want to do.

CONDITIONS	RULES			
	1	2	3	4
Is age >= 60?	Y	Y	N	N
Is home owned?	Y	N	Y	N
ACTIONS				
Grant short-term	Y		Y	
Grant long-term	N		Y	
Check with Head Office		Y	Y	

Figure 7.6. A typical decision chart that can be used to plan IF tests.

By checking against a chart like this you can program an extended IF test to carry out the correct actions, and Figure 7.7 shows the lines that would result from this Chart, using PRINT statements to show the ACTIONS columns – a real-life example would require considerably more than this.

```
CLS
INPUT "Age, whole years: ", age%
INPUT "Is home owned (Y/N): ", ans$
ans$ = UCASE$(LEFT$(ans$, 1))
IF age% >= 60 THEN
   IF ans$ = "Y" THEN PRINT "Grant short-term loan"
   IF ans$ = "N" THEN PRINT "Refer to Head Office"
   ELSE IF ans$ = "Y" THEN PRINT "Grant loan, short or
   long term"
   IF ans$ = "N" THEN PRINT "Refer to Head Office"
   END IF
END
```

Figure 7.7. Implementing the decision table with IF tests.

The first IF concerns age, and a TRUE result here allows the next two lines to be used. These deal with the state of ans$ (Y or N) and print the appropriate response. The ELSE then introduces the actions that have to be taken when the first IF test is FALSE, and this again consists of the two tests for ans$ with the appropriate responses.

When any IF test looks like needing too much in the way of ELSE and ELSE IF lines, it is wise to consider other methods, such as SELECT..CASE in Chapter 12 because it is just too easy to become tangled in a mass of ELSE and ELSE IF lines, with considerable uncertainty about what conditions will trigger each.

Binary numbers

The numbers that the computer deals with are all in binary form, using only the digits 0 and 1. Though the PC machine works with numbers that use at least 16 binary digits or bits, the effects of using binary numbers can be understood using only 8 bits, and this section will use these as illustrations – memory works in these 8-bit, single byte, units in any case.

The truth tables for logical operators as they extend to binary numbers use 1 for True and 0 for False, so that the AND truth table can be written as:

A	B	Result
0	0	0
0	1	0
1	0	0
1	1	1

to show the action on a single byte. This shows that the result of an AND action is 1 only when both inputs are also 1, and when one number is ANDed with another, each bit of one number is compared separately with the corresponding bit of the other number. If we take, for example the numbers which in ordinary (denary) scale as 7 and 14, these in binary are 0000111 and 0001110 respectively. The result of 7 AND 14 will be :

0 0 0 0 1 1 1
0 0 0 1 1 1 0

0 0 0 0 1 1 0

which translates to 6, so that the statement:

```
x% = 7 AND 14
```

will assign x% with 6. When the logic operators are used with integer numbers, then, the results will depend on the binary values of these numbers – there is no simple way of predicting the action without checking the binary number codes. This applies only to integers – the logical operators are meaningless on single and double-precision numbers and can be applied to characters only when ASC has been used to find the ASCII code for a character.

Tailpiece

The puzzle at the start of this chapter concerned PRINT NOT(7), which when you try it gives -8. If we imagine that numbers are represented as eight bits, then 7 is:

0 0 0 0 0 1 1 1

and NOT(7) must be the inverse, which is:

1 1 1 1 1 0 0 0

with the initial 1 meaning a negative number. To find the value, you have to add 11111111 and invert:

1 1 1 1 1 0 0 0 +
1 1 1 1 1 1 1 1

1 1 1 1 0 1 1 1 which inverts to:

0 0 0 0 1 0 0 0 which is 8.

Introducing Loops

Repetitive actions

One of the activities for which a computer is particularly well suited is of repeating a set of instructions over and over again and every computer language is equipped with commands that will cause repetition. QBASIC is no exception to this rule, and it is equipped with more of these repeat commands than is usual for any variety of BASIC. We'll start with one of the simplest though, nowadays, little used, of these repeater actions – GOTO.

GOTO, as you know from Chapter Seven, means exactly what you would expect it to mean – go to another point in the program, forward or backward. Normally a program is carried out by executing the instructions in the order in which the lines are placed in the memory. Using GOTO can break this arrangement, so that a line or a set of lines will be carried out in a different order, or carried out over and over again. The command word GOTO requires something following it to indicate where to go. In older forms of BASIC this was a line number, but in QBASIC you can use a label name, a marker for a line.

When a label is used, the point to which you want GOTO to take you is marked by a statement such as *loopit:*, the label name followed by a colon which can be placed on a preceding line of its own, or made part of a multi-statement line in which there are statements following the colon. Label names can be in lower or upper case.

Figure 8.1 shows examples of a very simple repetition, or *loop*, which has been written to illustrate this method. The program starts with a printed message, but the GOTO in the second line ensures that the third and fourth lines are never executed – the GOTO causes a jump over them. At the label 'loopit', the print line will be repeated endlessly, forcing you, when you run this one, to stop it by pressing the Ctrl-Break keys.

```
PRINT "This is the start"
GOTO loopit
PRINT "This is never seen"
END
loopit : PRINT "Looping fills your screen"
GOTO loopit
```

Figure 8.1. GOTO used for both forward and backward jumps.

In this example, the only action has been printing, and the label name was placed as the first item in a line that contained the PRINT statement.

Now an uncontrolled loop like this is not exactly good to have, and GOTO is a method of creating loops that we prefer not to use if anything else is available. GOTO allows you to get to any point that you care to mark with a label name or number. Because of this, it's all too easy to get a GOTO wrong by placing the name or number at the wrong position. This is more likely when you are working with a long program, and you can't see on the screen the line that you want to go to.

One of the acceptable uses of GOTO is as a way of testing a program. By inserting a GOTO and a label name, you can avoid using a section of program which you know is not yet ready for use. If you write programs in the correct way, in small sections, you should not need even this action.

A lot of varieties of BASIC offer little in the way of any other options, but QBASIC offers four, and one of them is the FOR...NEXT loop. As the name suggests, this makes use of two new instruction words, FOR and NEXT. The start of the loop is marked with the word FOR, and the end with the word NEXT. The instructions that are repeated are the instructions that are placed between FOR and NEXT, and the important point about this type of loop is that the number of repetitions is strictly fixed.

```
CLS
FOR n% = 1 TO 10
  PRINT "QBASIC is the champion!"
NEXT
```

Figure 8.2. Using the FOR...NEXT loop for a counted number of repetitions. Note the indentation to mark the repeated action.

The line which contains FOR must also include a number variable which is used for counting, and numbers which control the start of the count and its end. In the example, n% is the counter variable, and its limit numbers are 1 and 10. The NEXT is in the last line, and so anything between the FOR line and the NEXT line will be repeated. To make this more obvious, the lines that are included in the loop have been typed indented, making it much easier to see what is being repeated.

As it happens, what lies between these FOR and NEXT lines is simply the PRINT instruction, and the effect of the program will be to print 'QBASIC is the champion!' ten times. At the first pass through the loop, the value of n% is set to 1, and the phrase is printed. When the NEXT instruction is encountered, the computer increments the value of n%, from 1 to 2 in this case. It then checks to see if this value exceeds the limit of 10 that has been set. If it doesn't, then the PRINT line is repeated, and this will continue until the value of n exceeds 10 – we'll look at that point later. The effect in this example is to cause ten repetitions.

- Note the use of an integer variable, n%, since only small whole numbers are being used.

You don't have to confine this action to single loops either. Figure 8.3 shows an example of what we call *nested loops*, where one loop is contained completely inside another.

```
CLS
FOR n% = 1 TO 10
        PRINT "Count is"; n%
        FOR j = 1 TO 1200: NEXT
        CLS
NEXT
```

Figure 8.3. Using nested loops – one loop inside another. The inner loop here acts as a time delay, and a SLEEP statement could have been used in its place.

When loops are nested in this way, we can describe the loops as being *inner* and *outer*. The outer loop starts in the second line, using variable n% which goes from 1 to 10 in value. The next line is part of this outer loop, printing the value that the counter variable n% has reached. We then create another complete loop. This must make use of a different variable name, and it must start and finish again before the end of the outer loop. We have used variable j this time, and we have put nothing between the FOR part and the NEXT part to be carried out. All this loop does, then, is to waste time, making sure that there is some measurable time between the actions in the main loop.

The last action of the main loop is clearing the screen, and the NEXT is placed in the final line. The overall effect, then, is to show a count-up on the screen, slowly enough for you to see the changes, and wiping the screen clear each time. In this example we have used NEXT to indicate the end of each loop. We could use NEXT j and NEXT n% if we liked, but this is not essential. It also has the effect of slowing the computer down slightly, though the effect is not important in this program. When you do use NEXT j and NEXT n%, you must be absolutely sure that you have put the correct variable names following each NEXT. If you don't, the computer will stop with a 'NEXT without FOR' error message – meaning that the NEXTs don't match up with the FORs in this case. Just to rub it in, the listing in the Edit window will show the offending word in reversed colours. If you had omitted a NEXT, you would get a 'NEXT missing' message, but it would refer to the line in which the loop started, with the editing cursor placed in that line, at the FOR part. This example shows the value of indenting each loop, because the indentation shows very clearly where each loop starts and stops, and makes the program much easier to check.

note The outer loop uses n% for speed, but the inner loop uses j, a single-precision number – there's no point in trying to speed up processing in a part of the program that is intended to waste time!

In fact, there is no need ever to use a loop for a time delay, because QBASIC includes the command SLEEP in the form SLEEP 5 for a five minute delay. If you use SLEEP 0 the effect is like an INKEY$ loop waiting for any key to be pressed, but without using any dummy variable.

Even at this stage it's possible to see how useful this FOR...NEXT loop can be, but there's more to come. To start with, the loops that we have looked at so far count upwards, incrementing the number variable. We don't always want this, and we can add the instruction word STEP to the end of the FOR line to alter this change of variable value. We could, for example, use a line like:

```
FOR n% = 1 TO 9 STEP 2
```

which would cause the values of n to change in the sequence 1, 3, 5, 7, 9. When we don't type STEP, the loop will always use increments of 1.

Figure 8.4 illustrates an outer loop which has a step of -1, so that the count is downwards. Variable n starts with a value of 10, and is decremented on each pass through the loop. Once again an inner loop forms a time delay so that the countdown takes place at a civilised speed. This is a particularly useful way of slowing the count down, and it reveals that you need to use a count of 3000 to get about one second of delay. This is a good measure of how fast QBASIC runs.

```
CLS
FOR n% = 10 TO 1 STEP -1
  PRINT n%; " seconds and counting"
   FOR j - 1 TO 3000: NEXT
  CLS
NEXT
PRINT"Blastoff!"
```

Figure 8.4. A countdown program, making use of STEP to decrement the number in each loop.

- This is not the only way of causing a time delay, and Chapter 22 illustrates some others that make use of timing signals within the computer.

Every now and again, when we are using loops, we find that we need to use the value of the counter, such as n% or j, after the loop has finished. It's important to know what this will be, however, and Figure 8.5 brings it home. This contains two loops, one counting up, the other counting down. At the end of each loop, the value of the counter variable is printed. This reveals that the value of n% is 6 in after completing the FOR n% = 1 TO 5 loop, and is 0 after completing the FOR n% = 5 TO 1 STEP -1 loop. If you want to make use of the value of n%, or whatever variable name you have selected to use,,you will have to remember that it will have changed by one more step at the end of the loop. You can, of course, use negative values of n% in loops.

```
CLS
FOR n% = 1 TO 5
  PRINT n%
NEXT
PRINT "n% is now"; n%
FOR n% = 5 TO 1 STEP -1
  PRINT n%
NEXT
PRINT "n% is now"; n%
```

Figure 8.5. Finding the value of the loop variable after a loop action is completed. This is always one more step than the specified end of the loop.

A very revealing program snippet is illustrated in Figure 8.6. In this example the counter n is a single-precision number, so that the STEP amount can be a fraction, in this case 0.01. The values of n, however, do not reveal a simple count of 1, 1.01, 1.02 and so on, and the last quantity that is printed is 4.99002. This is a reminder of the approximate methods that are used in converting to binary numbers and what you see on screen is a result of adding up each approximation. This bears out an important point – that a counting variable should *not* be a floating-point number and, if it is, you should not rely on the final count being useful.

```
FOR n = 1 TO 5 STEP .01
  PRINT "Fractional"; n
NEXT
```

Figure 8.6. A count that uses a single-precision variable, revealing the cumulative effects of the lack of precision.

One of the most valuable features of the FOR...NEXT loop, however, is the way in which it can be used with number variables instead of just numbers. Figure 8.7 illustrates this in a simple way. The letters a%, b% and c% are assigned as numbers in the usual way, but they are then used in a FOR..NEXT loop. The limits are set by a% and c%, and the step is obtained from an expression, c% / b%. We shall see this technique being used in some loops in the following chapter. The rule is that if you have anything that represents a number or can be worked out to give a number, then you can use it in a loop like this. One point to watch is that the integer division can give rise to numbers that you might not expect because of the rounding up or down that is used when the result of a division is assigned to an integer variable (3 / 2 = 2 for example).

```
CLS
a% = 2 : b% = 5 : c% = 10
FOR n% = a% TO c% STEP c% / b%
        PRINT n%
NEXT
```

Figure 8.7. A loop instruction that is formed with number variables. Remember the effects of integer division.

Loops and decisions

It's time to see loops being used rather than just being demonstrated. A simple application is in totalling numbers. The action that we want is that we enter numbers and the computer keeps a running total, adding each number to the total of the numbers so far. From what we have done so far, it's easy to see how this could be done if we wanted to use numbers in fixed quantities, like ten numbers in a set. The program of Figure 8.8 does just this. The program starts by clearing the screen and setting a number variable 'total' to zero. This is the number variable that will be used to hold the total, and it has to start at zero. As it happens, QBASIC arranges this automatically at the start of a program, but it's a good habit to ensure that everything that has to start with some value actually does. We couldn't, incidentally, use the shorter name TO for this variable, because TO is a reserved word, part of the FOR...NEXT set of words.

```
CLS
total = 0
PRINT TAB(11)"TOTALLING NUMBERS PROGRAM"
PRINT:PRINT "Enter each number as requested"
PRINT "The program will keep a running total"
FOR n% = 1 TO 10
  PRINT "Number"; n% " please ";
  INPUT j: total = total + j
  PRINT "Total so far is"; total
NEXT
```

Figure 8.8. A number totalling program for a set of ten numbers, using a FOR..NEXT loop.

The next three lines print a title and issue instructions, and the action starts with the FOR...NEXT loop which will repeat the actions of the following three lines ten times. You are reminded of how many numbers you have entered by printing the value of n% each time, and the INPUT step allows you to enter a number which is then assigned to variable name j, a single-precision number. This is then added to the total in the second half of the line, and the loop then repeats. At the end of each pass through the loop, the variable total contains the value of the total, the sum of all the numbers that have been entered so far.

It's all good stuff, but how often would you want to enter exactly ten numbers? It would be a lot more convenient if we could just stop the action by signalling to the computer in some way, perhaps by entering a value like 0 or 999. A value like this is called a *terminator*, something that is obviously not one of the normal entries that we would use, but just a signal. For a number-totalling program, a terminator of 0 is very convenient, because if it gets added to the total it doesn't make any difference. The terminator is detected by an IF test.

IF, as you know, has to be followed by a condition. You might use conditions like IF n% = 20, or IF nm$ = "LASTONE" for this purpose. After the IF condition, use the word THEN, followed by what you want done, all within the same line. You might simply want the loop to stop when the condition is true. This can be programmed by placing a GOTO, with a line label name following THEN. If this is the label for the last line in the program, the program will end when the condition is true. The alternative is to test whether the program should keep running, and go back if this is so.

Now if all of that sounds rather complicated, take a look at the simple illustration in Figure 8.9. We can't use a FOR...NEXT loop here because we don't know how many times we will want to go through the loop, so we have used IF...THEN to control the loop. The instructions appear first, and we make the variable 'total' equal to zero before the loop starts. Each time you type a number in response to the request, the number that you have entered is added to the total, and following line prints the value of the total so far. The following line contains the loop controller. IF is used to make the test, and in this case, the test is to find if n is not zero. If it's not, then we go back to the labelled line that starts the loop. The sign that is made by combining the less than and greater than signs (< and >), is used to mean 'not equal'.

```
CLS
PRINT TAB(15)"Another Total Finder"
PRINT:PRINT"The program will total numbers for you"
PRINT"until you enter a zero"
total=0
backhere:
  INPUT"Number, please ";n
  total=total+n
  PRINT"Running total is ";total
  IF n<>0 THEN GOTO backhere
PRINT"End of totalling"
```

Figure 8.9 A running-total program which can't use FOR...NEXT. It uses an IF test which decides whether or not to loop.

Note that the indenting was done during typing and not by the Editor – it serves to show the extent of the loop. The effect is that if the number which you typed in was not a zero, the IF test will send the program back to the labelled line again for another number. This will continue until you enter a zero. When this happens, the IF test *fails* and the program goes to the last line. This announces the end of the program and, since there are no more lines, the program stops. If you press ENTER without having typed a number, then the program takes this as equivalent to entering a zero, and stops. Not all varieties of BASIC behave so sensibly.

This example uses just one test with its IF, but you aren't limited to just one. You could, for example, decide to terminate if either a 0 or 999 was entered. In this case, your IF line could read:

```
IF n<>0 AND n<>999 THEN backhere
```

making two conditions. You can also use the word OR when you make a test, such as:

```
IF n=0 OR n=999 THEN...
```

but you would have to be careful in a number totalling program that 999 did not get added to your total. You have to be careful about where you place some of these tests. Chapter Seven has already dealt with the type of IF tests that you can use.

Breakout

Sometimes you find that you need to leave a FOR...NEXT loop before the count has been completed. You might, for example, have a number of inputs in the course of a loop that allows 1000 inputs, and want to end after only 20. Another common option is to have a title followed by a time delay loop that waits for 25 seconds, but which allows you to break out by pressing any key if you don't want to wait. Now you can use an IF test to break out of any loop but, when the loop is a FOR...NEXT one, there's a possibility that the unfinished count can cause trouble later.

```
CLS
FOR n% = 1 TO 1000
  INPUT "name, please (type X to end) "; name$
  IF UCASE$(name$) = "X" THEN EXIT FOR
NEXT
PRINT"End of entries"
```

Figure 8.10. Breaking out of a name-entry loop, so that you don't have to enter 1000 names.

The name is input in the usual way, and the next line tests the name. If the name is "X", which could be x or X because of the use of UCASE$, then the loop is cancelled by using the EXIT command. The syntax of EXIT is that it must be followed by a word that indicates the type of loop and, in this case, that word is FOR. Now you could just as easily have programmed:

```
IF UCASE$(Name$) = "X" THEN END
```

with the same effect, but leaving the program not properly finished, with some value assigned to n%. Ending a loop in this way can be risky in some varieties of BASIC, though QBASIC cleans-up after you if you work in this way.

```
CLS
PRINT TAB(5)"The prologue..."
PRINT:PRINT"...wait, or press a key."
FOR j=1 TO 20000
  k$=INKEY$:IF k$<>"" THEN EXIT FOR
NEXT
PRINT"Next item..."
```

Figure 8.11. Breaking out of a time delay loop. As before, the breakout action makes use of a reassignment of the counter variable.

The time delay in this case must include a type of statement we have not met so far (but see Chapter Eight). When a string variable is assigned with INKEY$, the effect is to assign whatever key is pressed at that instant. If no key is pressed, then what is assigned is a blank string. By testing the value of k$ we can tell if a key has been pressed, and the use of the assignment and the test in a loop is a convenient way of waiting for a reply that uses just one key, with no need to press ENTER. The principle, however, is the same – the loop must be ended by using EXIT followed in this case by FOR to indicate the type of loop.

Very few versions of BASIC offer you any more than a simple FOR...NEXT loop, some don't even have the ELSE command. QBASIC, however, offers you a choice of several very different types of loop, one of which (WHILE...WEND) is intended to allow you to run programs written in other varieties of BASIC rather than for use in new programs.

All loops should contain some condition for ending, and this condition can be a positive one (END if TRUE) or a negative one (END if NOT FALSE). The condition can also be tested at either the start or the end of the loop. If the condition is tested at the start of the loop, the statements of the loop will not run if the test gives a FALSE result. If the test is made at the end of the loop, the loop will always run at least once, even if the test gives a false result. The FOR...NEXT loop tests at the start, but we sometimes need to use a test at the end, and we certainly need to be able to test for conditions other than number counts.

QBASIC provides a DO...LOOP form which can be used either way. The loop starts at DO and ends at LOOP, but it can be tested by using WHILE or UNTIL. If the loop starts with DO WHILE, with a test following, the loop will run if this test gives a TRUE result; the end of the loop is marked by the word LOOP. If the loop is formed by using DO at the start and LOOP UNTIL at the end, with a condition following UNTIL, the loop will always run at least once.

note The QBASIC form of this loop allows WHILE or UNTIL to be used at either end – one is a positive test, the other negative. For example, DO WHILE K = 5 is equivalent to DO UNTIL K <> 5; and LOOP WHILE K <> 10 is equivalent to LOOP UNTIL K = 10.

Yes, an example would certainly help, so cast an eye on Figure 8.12. This is another version of an old friend, the number-totalling program. This time, as well as making total=0, we have j=1 near the start. This is needed because of the way that a DO UNTIL loop works, testing at the start of the loop. What this means is that the loop will be repeated for as long as j is *not* zero. When the program starts, however, you will not have input any number j by this stage, and j would be zero if we did not assign a number to it.

```
CLS
PRINT TAB(5)"More Totals"
total = 0 : j = 1
PRINT:PRINT"Enter numbers for totalling; 0 to end"
DO UNTIL j = 0
   INPUT j
   total = total + j
   PRINT "Total so far is"; total
LOOP
PRINT"End of entry"
```

Figure 8.12. A number-totalling program that makes use of the DO UNTIL...LOOP form of loop. Note the dummy value of j (j=1) assigned to ensure that the loop starts correctly.

Without this j=1 step, the program would finish as soon as it got to the UNTIL test. This is something that you have to be careful about, particularly if you have used any of the older versions of BASIC that did not have this form of loop. If you find when you run a program that a DO UNTIL..LOOP type of loop appears not to run, then this is the first thing to suspect.

The steps in the loop are familiar, and we needn't go over them again. The important points to note are that the variable j is tested at the start of the loop, and that the end of the loop is marked by the word LOOP. There's no need for IFs and THENs here, and you can nest DO...LOOP loops inside each other. The only thing to watch is that you place the test at the correct end of the loop.

```
CLS
PRINT TAB(5); "More Totals"
total = 0
PRINT : PRINT "Enter numbers for totalling; 0 to end"
DO
   INPUT j
   total = total + j
   PRINT "Total so far is"; total
LOOP UNTIL j = 0
PRINT "End of entry"
```

Figure 8.13 The totalling program rewritten to use a test at the end of the loop.

This shows that the use of a test at the end of a loop is more satisfactory in this case, and for many others, because it avoids having to assign a dummy value to variable j before the loop starts.

tip If you find that a dummy value would be needed for a DO WHILE loop, rewrite it as a LOOP UNTIL type.

Take a look at another example, Figure 8.14, this time using READ...DATA inside the loop. This is a program which simply reads a number of data items from a list until it encounters an X. The loop is tested at the end with the condition that the loop continues until an X is found as the value of a$.

```
CLS
DO
READ a$
PRINT a$
LOOP UNTIL a$ = "X"
DATA Glenfiddich, Glenmorangie, Laphroaig
DATA Islay Mist, Glenduff, X
```

Figure 8.14. Using a DO...LOOP UNTIL form of loop to read data from a list.

The loop consists of reading and printing the value of a$ until the X is found, so that the program prints the list of tasty DATA items.

Now in this example, the testing is done at the end of the loop, so that when the X is found it is printed before the test is made. If the test were made in the form:

```
DO WHILE a$<>"X"
```

at the start of the loop, it would still print the X because the READ and PRINT actions follow the test. You can get round this by reversing the positions of the READ X$ and PRINT X$ lines, but this will start the list with a blank line.

The unadorned DO...LOOP is not quite perfect for this type of example – the test must be made either at the start or at the end of a loop, and the read and print actions are between these points, so that either the X is printed at the end of the list, or a blank line is printed at the start.

Ideally, in this loop, there would be a test just following the READ X$ item, and this would end the loop. The correct solution is not difficult to find – the word EXIT which in this example would need to be followed by DO to indicate the type of loop.

```
CLS
DO WHILE a$ <> "X"
   READ a$
   IF a$ = "X" THEN EXIT DO
   PRINT a$
LOOP
DATA Glenfiddich, Glenmorangie, Laphroaig
DATA Islay Mist, Talisker, X
```

Figure 8.15. Using EXIT to terminate a loop where a test is needed within the loop.

Figure 8.16 shows yet another use for the loop using DO WHILE. In this case, it acts as a *mugtrap*. A mugtrap (polite name – *data validator*) is a piece of program that tests whatever you have entered. If what you have entered is unacceptable, like a number in the wrong range, then the mugtrap refuses to accept the entry, shows by a message on the screen why the entry is unacceptable, and gives you another chance. Mugtraps are very important in programs where a piece of incorrect entry might stop a program with an error message.

```
CLS
INPUT " Type a number in range 1 to 5 "; n%
DO WHILE n% < 1 OR n% > 5
PRINT "Unacceptable answer - 1 to 5 only"
INPUT n%
LOOP
PRINT "You picked"; n%
```

Figure 8.16. Incorporating a DO WHILE loop into a mugtrap.

For an expert this is no problem, a crafty command will get back to the program. For the inexperienced user, the error message seems like the end, and it's likely that the whole lot will be lost, even if it took all day to enter the data.

In this example, then, you are invited to enter integer numbers in the range 1 to 5, perhaps as part of a menu. If the number that you enter is in this range, all is well, but if not (try it!), then the DO WHILE loop swings into action. This prints an error message of your own, and gives you another chance to get it right. That's the essence of a good mugtrap, and the DO WHILE loop is ideal for forming such traps. Note, despite the emphasis on numbers in some examples, that the DO form of loop is just as much at home with strings. You can have lines like:

```
DO WHILE Name$ <> "X"
```

to allow you to keep entering names into a list, or

```
DO WHILE UCASE$(AN$) <> "Y" AND UCASE$(AN$) <> "N"
```

to make a mugtrap for a Y or N answer. Don't forget the use of UCASE$ to avoid having to test for y and n as well as for Y and N.

While we're on the subject, the DO WHILE...LOOP action is a very useful one to use with INKEY$. Figure 8.17 shows such a loop used to produce a wait until ready effect. The DO WHILE loop will keep repeating for as long as INKEY$ is a blank, and there is no need in this case to assign a variable such as k$ to INKEY$ (see Chapter Eight).

```
CLS
PRINT "Press any key..."
DO WHILE INKEY$ = "": LOOP
PRINT "That's It"
```

Figure 8.17 Using DO WHILE...LOOP with INKEY$.

The WHILE...WEND loop

QBASIC can also use the WHILE..WEND loop, which is the exact equivalent of DO WHILE...LOOP. Because WHILE..WEND tests only at the beginning of the loop, it is not such a flexible type of loop as the DO..LOOP, and it is present in QBASIC only to allow programs written for other varieties of BASIC to be run without the need to alter each WHILE..WEND loop. There is no need to make use of it in your own programs.

Last pass

When you start writing programs for yourself, designing a loop often appears to be difficult. It's not, but you need to approach it with some method. The best way is to write down what the loop conditions are to start with. What conditions do you want at the start of the loop, for example? If the loop *must* run at least once, then a DO...LOOP UNTIL should be used. Do you need a counter in the loop which will have to be set to some starting value? In such a case, you might want to use a FOR...NEXT loop, and you then need to decide what to call the counter variable. If your loop has nothing to do with numbers, or if it has no preset count, then the DO WHILE...LOOP or DO...LOOP UNTIL type is likely to be more useful. Once again, though, you have to look for the starting conditions. Remember that the either the WHILE or the UNTIL form of test can be made either at the DO or at the LOOP end, making this type of loop by far the most convenient to use of the types devised to date.

Next, you have to think of what is to be done in each pass of the loop. This might be some string action, or some number action, or a bit of both. The really important bit, however, is to decide what will end the loop. You might want to end a counting FOR...NEXT loop before the true end of the count, in which case please take care to remember the use of EXIT, followed by the name of the loop.

Finally, it's possible to get yourself tied up in testing a loop. Suppose, for example, you have designed a loop that calls for the entry of 1000 names, and you want to check that it ends correctly when you enter an 'X', or after 5000 entries. Needless to say, you don't check it by going through all 5000 entries. You can either alter the count to 5 for testing, or you can alter the count after stopping – but for such items, see Chapter 16 on the subject of *Debugging*.

Strings and String Handling

Reminders

We have been using string variables for some time now, but Figure 9.1 is a reminder about this use of variable names for words and phrases. Once again, a name can be chosen, following the same rules as for a number variable name, but with the distinguishing feature that the last character of the name must be $, or a DEFSTR statement must be used, or a name defined as a string name.

```
CLS
a$ = "The Modern PC"
b$ = " rules "
c$ = "O.K.?"
PRINT a$ + b$ + c$
PRINT a$; b$; c$
```

Figure 9.1. Using string variables. These are distinguished here by the use of the dollar sign.

Names such as A$, ABC$, Nameofit$, Any_name_you_like$ are all valid string names, starting with a letter, containing not more than 40 characters and ending with the dollar sign (unless a range of letters has already been declared as string variable starting letters). Whatever you assign to such a name, using the ordinary form of assignment with the equality sign, must be surrounded by quotes. You can, for example, use assignments like a$="A string" and name$="Ian Sinclair" and so on.

You can also make use of READ and DATA lines to carry out string assignments. The READ line will consist of statements such as READ A$, Name$, Phone$ and so on, and the DATA line will carry data such as:

```
DATA Engineer, Harry Tibbs, 007-516-223
```

It's important to note that you don't normally have to surround the items in the DATA line with quotes, though it doesn't do any harm if you do. If you have any items that contain commas, however, then it's a different story. There's a big difference between the lines:

```
DATA Tibbs, Harry X.
```

and

```
DATA "Tibbs, Harry X."
```

The first DATA line will be read as having two items, each of which will have to be read into a different variable name. The second DATA line contains just one item, consisting of a name that includes a comma. Any comma that is not enclosed by quotes is taken as a marker dividing two data items, so if you want to have an item that contains commas, then that item *must* be surrounded by quotes.

In Figure 9.1 the three lines carry out the assignment operations, and the following two lines show how these variable names can be used. Notice that you can mix a variable name, which doesn't need quotes around it, with ordinary text, which must be surrounded by quotes. You can, for example, have a line such as:

```
PRINT "It's called "; name$"
```

to print a string that has been assigned to a variable name$ following the text that is within quotes. You have to be careful when you mix these two, because it's easy to run words together. Note how a space has been left on each side of the word 'rules' in Figure 9.1. If you omit this space, you will see this word run together with the words on each side. A space is printed in by typing a quote, then pressing the spacebar, then typing another quote.

You can use a string variable name for longer phrases if you like. The limit to the number of characters that you can assign to a string variable is 32767. There isn't much point in printing messages in the form of strings if you only want the message once but, when you continually use a phrase in a program, this is one method of programming it so that you don't have to keep typing it. Chapter Five demonstrated the use of INPUT with string variable names.

String operators and functions

So far we have looked briefly at how to input strings and how to print them. The important feature about the use of strings, however, is string functions, the really eye-catching and fascinating actions that the computer can carry out using strings. What's a string function, then? As far as we are concerned, it's *any* action that we can carry out with strings. That definition doesn't exactly help too much, I know, but let's look first at an example of the only string operator:

```
CLS
a$ = "ONE"
b$ = "TWO"
PRINT a$ + b$
a$ ="12": b$ = "34"
c$ =a$ + b$
PRINT c$
```

Figure 9.2. Concatenating or joining strings. This is not the same action as addition – see later for details of the VAL function.

This example shows two strings, a$ and b$, being assigned. a$ is assigned to ONE and b$ to TWO – remember that you must use quotes in an assignment like this. The next line then shows what you get for a$+b$. What is printed on the screen is ONETWO, the two strings run together. The + sign, then, is a kind of operator for strings, but the operation is not addition in the way that we add numbers. To distinguish it, this use is called *concatenation*. The rest of the program shows that concatenation works in the same way even if the strings are of number quantities. If you PRINT a$ or PRINT b$ after the program has been run, you will see 12 for a$ and 34 for b$, but c$ is 1234, not 46. The + is not an addition sign as far as strings are concerned, it is a joining sign.

Concatenation can be useful if you have carried out actions on two different strings and you then want to join them. Suppose, for example, that you have a mailing list program, and to save on memory space you allow names of up to ten characters only. When a name is entered, you just don't chop off all the characters after the tenth. This would result in JONATHAN MILKMAN being chopped to JONATHAN M because the space counts as a character. The more sensible method is to separate the surname from the forename, and then chop each to ten characters. Both parts of JONATHAN MILKMAN then can be joined again. If the surname is long, as with SILAS PREPONDERANCE, then the name appears as SILAS PREPONDERA, which is enough to recognise it. Concatenation is the only string operator, and we can turn now to the string functions.

The string function UCASE$ has already been demonstrated, and there is a corresponding LCASE$ function which will convert uppercase letters in any string to lowercase. As for numbers, a function acts on a string to produce some modified form of string, and we can now look at some other string functions. Figure 9.3 shows a program that prints THE PC COMPUTER as a title. What makes it more eye-catching is the fact that the word is printed with twelve asterisks (*) on each side. The asterisks are produced by a string function whose instruction word is STRING$.

```
CLS
a$ = STRING$(12, "*")
PRINT TAB(4); a$ +"THE PC COMPUTER" + a$
```

Figure 9.3 Using concatenation along with STRING$ to make a frame for a title.

STRING$ means 'make a string out of', and it has to be followed by two items placed within brackets and separated by a comma. The first of these items is the number of identical characters that you want to put into this string. The second item is the character itself. In this example, we've used the * character and it has had to be placed between quotes.

STRING$ is a useful way of creating strings of as long as you like, using just one character, and it's particularly useful when graphics characters are used. There are, however, some minor strings attached, as it were. The first is that you can't create a string of more than 32767 characters, so that the first number in a STRING$ expression has to be 32767 or less (in fact, it should be considerably less, and you will get a message 'Out of String Space' if you try to use such giant strings). This is hardly a deprivation, because it's very unusual to want strings of this length, which are longer than will fit on the screen.

The other point about STRING$ is that the second item in the brackets can be a number, with no quotes. Each character that is used in QBASIC is represented by a ASCII code number. In place of the asterisk that we have used between quotes, then, we could have used the number 42, making the instruction into STRING$(12, 42), which is shorter.

The number characters of normal ASCII code extend only from 32 to 127. The code numbers above 127 are used by the computer for other purposes, and we can choose how we make use of them. Figure 9.4 gives a flavour of this, allowing the use of all sorts of characters that don't appear on the keyboard.

```
CLS
a$ = STRING$(12, 169)
PRINT TAB(4); a$ + "QBASIC STRINGS" + a$
```

Figure 9.4. Using ASCII numbers above 128 in a STRING$ statement.

By using the number 169 in the STRING$ command in the second line, we select the bent-bar shaped character rather than an English letter character. This same character can be typed by pressing the ALT key down and typing the digits 1 6 9 on the number keypad at the righthand side. The full list of character shapes will be listed in the manual for your computer or for your printer.

Long and short of It

String variables allow us to carry out a lot of operations that can't be done with number variables. One of these operations is finding out how many characters are contained in a string. Since a string can contain up to 32767 characters, an automatic method of counting them is rather useful, and LEN is that method. LEN has to be followed by the name of the string variable, within brackets, and the result of using LEN is always an integer number so that we can print it or assign it to a number variable.

Figure 9.5 shows a useful example of LEN in use. This program uses LEN as a way of printing a string called title$ centred on a line. This is an extremely useful routine to use in your own programs, because its use can save you a lot of tedious counting when you write your programs.

```
CLS
title$ = "PC QBASIC Computing"
tb% =(80 - LEN(title$)) / 2
PRINT TAB(tb%); title$
REM Now print your other text.
```

Figure 9.5. Using string function LEN to measure string length so that a phrase can be centred automatically.

The principle is to use LEN to find out how many characters are present in the string 'title$'. This number is subtracted from 80 in this example, and the result is then divided by two. If the number of characters in the string is an even number, then the number tb% is rounded up, but even if we had used a single-precision number which could accept a .5, it would be ignored by TAB when the string is printed. Note how brackets have been used in the second line. The easiest way of writing a line like this is to start at the innermost brackets. For example, you know that you need to find the length of the string, title$, so you write LEN(title$) first. You have to subtract this from 80, so you then put this in, to get 80 - LEN(title$). The whole of this, not just LEN(title$), must be divided by two, so you must place brackets around it all, to get:

```
(80 - LEN(title$))/2
```

which is then assigned to tb%.

You will find that this inside to outside approach pays off when you have to work with lots of brackets. If you are uncertain about using brackets, be thankful that you are programming in BASIC, and not in the language called LISP (the name is said to mean Lots of Irritating Silly Parentheses). The whole process of centring could be done in one line, but I have shown it in three lines so that you can see what the steps are. In Chapters 11 and 12, we'll look at ways of rewriting actions like this so that they can be called up when we want them, just like another instruction word.

Slicing to the left of them

The next group of string operations that we're going to look at are called slicing operations. The result of slicing a string is another string, a piece copied from the longer string. Note that this is a copying process, nothing is removed from the longer string when the copy is made. The piece that is copied can be printed or assigned as you please. String slicing is a useful way of finding what letters or other characters are present at different places in a string.

All of this might not sound terribly interesting, so take a look at Figure 9.6. The strings a$, b$, c$ and d$ are assigned in the first few lines. The STRING$ function is used to make a string that consists of one space. This is not the simplest method (which would be s$=" ") for a single space, but is very useful if you want a number of spaces (say 10 or 20).

```
CLS
a$ = "Personal"
b$ = "Computer"
c$ = "Macintosh"
d$ = "hinder"
s$ = STRING$(1, " ")
PRINT "QBASIC on a " + LEFT$(a$, 1) + s$ + LEFT$(b$,
1) + s$ + LEFT$(c$, 3) + LEFT$(d$, 3) + "e"
```

Figure 9.6. Extracting letters from strings by slicing using LEFT$. Note that the last line is typed into the Editor as one single line – it has been split up here so that it can be reproduced on a page.

In this example, there is just one space assigned to the variable s$, so that we can use it to space words. The next step is to print some slices from a$, b$, c$ and d$ on the screen. Now how did the phrase 'PC Machine' appear? The obvious answer is by slicing chunks out of the strings. The instruction LEFT$ means 'copy part of a string starting at the left hand side'. LEFT$ has to be followed by two quantities, within brackets and separated by a comma. The first of these quantities is the variable name for the string that we want to slice, a$ in the first example. The second is the number of characters that you want to slice (copy, in fact) from the left hand side. The effect of LEFT$(a$,1) is therefore to copy the first letter from 'Personal', giving 'P'.

Long lines are a problem if you want to print out a program from the Editor, because characters beyond the end of the line do not print. There is no problem on screen because you can scroll sideways to see the end of a long line. The best solution for printing is to load the program file into a wordprocessor and print from there.

Eyes right

String slicing isn't confined to copying a selected piece of the left hand side of a string. We can also take a copy of characters from the right hand side of a string. This particular facility isn't used quite so much as the LEFT$ one, but it's useful none the less. Figure 9.7 illustrates a simple use of this instruction to avoid having to use the whole of a complicated code number.

```
CLS
READ D$
PRINT "Part No. is "; RIGHT$(D$, 6)
DATA PD1Q-747-164027
```

Figure 9.7. Using the righthand slicing action to extract a number (in string form) from the righthand side of a string.

Take a look, for example, at the code number on your telephone bill. There are other serious uses like this. You can, for example, extract the last four figures from a string of numbers like 010-242-7016. I said a string of numbers deliberately, because something like this has to be stored as a string variable rather than as a number. If you try to assign this to a number variable, you'll get a silly answer. Why? Because when you type:

```
N = 01-242-7016
```

the computer assumes that you want to subtract 242 from 10 and 7016 from that result.The value for N is -7248, which is not exactly what you had in mind! If you use N$="010-242-7016" then all is well.

Middle cut

There's another string slicing instruction which is capable of much more than either LEFT$ or RIGHT$ and can, in fact, be used to replace both of them if you want. The instruction word is MID$, and it has to be followed by three items, within brackets, and using commas to separate the items. Item 1 is the name of the string that you want to slice, as you might expect by now. The second item is a number which specifies where you start slicing. This number is the number of the characters counted from the left hand side of the string, and counting the first character as 1. The third item is another number, the number of characters that you want to slice, going from left to right and starting at the position that was specified by the first number.

```
CLS
A$ = "Using Common putty."
B$ = MID$(A$, 7, 3) + MID$(A$, 14, 3) + MID$(A$, 3, 3)
PRINT B$
```

Figure 9.8. Making use of the MID$ statement to extract any part of a string.

It's a lot easier to see in action than to describe, so try the program in Figure 9.8. A$ is assigned with the phrase "Using Common putty." and the following line then assigns a new string, B$, which is made out of slices from A$. The first slice uses MID$(A$,7,3). If you count the characters in A$, including spaces, you'll find that the seventh character is the C of Common. Remember that the counting for MID$ starts at 1, not at 0 like so many other computer counting actions. The slice starts with the C, and is of three characters, 'Com' from this part of the phrase. The other two slices also take three characters each, to make up the word 'Computing', which is what appears on the screen.

One of the features of all of these string slicing instructions is that we can use variable names or expressions in place of numbers. Figure 9.9 shows a more elaborate piece of slicing which uses an expression, along with a random number:

```
CLS
INPUT "Your surname, please ", NAM$
L% = LEN(NAM$)
R% = RND * L% + 1
COD$ = UCASE$(MID$(NAM$, R%, 1))
PRINT "Todays code letter is "; COD$
```

Figure 9.9. Slicing a variable input from the keyboard, using a position determined by a random number, and converting the sliced letter to uppercase.

The action all starts innocently enough in the second line with a request for your name. Whatever you type is assigned to variable NAM$, and in the following line the length of this string is found and assigned to integer variable L%. The next line then generates a number, at random, which lies between 1 and L%. We have seen this done earlier, and there are more details in Chapter 12. This random number, assigned to R%, will be a whole number because an integer variable can hold only a whole number. It is then used in to select one of the letters from your name, and this selected letter is converted to uppercase. Finally, you are informed that this letter is your code letter for today.

It's a simple example, but the point is important – that whatever appears in the number part of MID$ (or LEFT$ or RIGHT$) can be a number variable. Could you now take this piece of program, and alter it so that you got a group of letters of random length? The number of letters should not be more than half the number of letters of your name, so that for Taylor, I might get AY or YLO for example.

Now we can get quite a lot of interesting effects from these slicing methods, particularly when we start to use them in loops. Take a look at Figure 9.10 for an example, which does odd things with the letters of your name:

```
CLS
INPUT "Your name please"; nam$
L% = LEN(nam$): C% = L% / 2 + 1
FOR N% = 1 TO C%
PRINT TAB(45 - N%); MID$(nam$, C% - N% + 1, N% * 2 - 1)
NEXT
```

Figure 9.10. A program that creates a letter pyramid from your name.

The program prompts you to enter your name in the second line, and the name is assigned to nam$. In the next line, we use LEN so that the number variable L% contains the total number of characters in your name. This will include spaces and hyphens – nobody's likely to use asterisks and hashmarks! There follows then a loop which uses the half of the total number of characters, plus one, as its end limit. In the action lines, number variable N% starts at 1, and this number, along with the variable C% determines both the position and the string that is extracted.

Suppose you type as your name DONALD. This has six letters, so variable L% is assigned to 6, and C% is the whole number part of L/2+1 (equal to 4). There then starts a loop of 4 passes. In the first pass you print at position TAB 44, because N%=1, and 45, N% = 44. What you print is the name MID$(nam$,4,1). With N%=1 and C%=4, then C%–N%+1 is 4–1+1, which is 4, and N%*2–1 is 2–1, which is 1. What you print, then, is the fourth letter of the name. On the next run through the loop, N% is 2, C%–N%+1 is 3, and N%*2–1 is 3. What is printed is MID$(nam$,3,3), which is NAL. The loop goes on in this way, and the result is that you see on the screen a pyramid of letters formed from your name. It's quite impressive if you have a long name! If your name is short, try making up a longer one. You may end up with an incomplete name depending if you have typed an even or odd number of letters.

Ways with spaces

There are three string functions that deal with spaces. SPACE$ will create a number of spaces specified by an integer number in brackets:

```
CLS
s$ = SPACE$(5)
b$ = "NAME" + s$ + "OF" + s$ + "THE" + s$ + "GAME"
PRINT b$
```

Figure 9.11. Using SPACE$ to place a set of spaces into a string, used in this example for spacing words.

In addition, there are two functions that remove spaces, though not spaces between words. One of the annoying features of using a computer is that only absolutely identical items are regarded as equivalent. Suppose, for example, that you have a program that asks for a name and will produce a set of notes about that person (check with the Data Protection Act!). Most programs of that type will create a new file if the name is not recognised, but the snag is recognition, because if the name in the file is Sinclair, then typing the name with a space either in front or following will result in a failure to recognise the name.

Figure 9.12 shows a way around this using LTRIM$ and RTRIM$. LTRIM$, as the name suggests, will trim spaces from the left hand side of a string, and RTRIM$ will chop the spaces from the righthand side:

```
CLS
nam$ = " Sinclair "
end$ = " Books"
PRINT nam$ + end$
PRINT LTRIM$(nam$) + end$
PRINT RTRIM$(nam$) + end$
a$ = LTRIM$(nam$)
a$ = RTRIM$(a$)
PRINT a$ + end$
```

Figure 9.12. Using LTRIM$ and RTRIM$ to chop off spaces, and showing how to trim both sides.

The example also shows how to trim both sides, since this is not obvious. Using LTRIM$ and RTRIM$ allows the recognition of names that have been entered with spaces or read from a disk with unwanted spaces.

Tying up more strings

It's time now to look at some other types of string functions, starting with two that are important when your program handles numbers. The first of these is VAL, and it's used to convert a number that is in string form back into ordinary number form so that we can carry out arithmetic. Suppose, for example, that we have NR$="3.4". NR$ is a string, and if we carry out PRINT NR$+"2", then the result is 3.42, not 5.4. This is because numbers which are in string form cannot be added, and no other form of arithmetic is possible either. If you have a number in this form, then you can convert by using VAL. You can, for example, use A=VAL(NR$) to convert the number from its string form in NR$ to the number variable form as A. As usual, QBASIC will choose whether to store this as an integer or as a float.

There's an instruction that does the opposite conversion, STR$. When we follow STR$ by a number, number variable, or expression within brackets, we carry out a conversion to a string variable. We can then print this as a string, or assign it to a string variable name, or use string functions like LEN, TO and all the others. Figure 9.13 illustrates these processes – with a warning!

```
n$="22.5":v=2
CLS:PRINT
PRINT n$;" times ";v;" is ";v*VAL(n$)
PRINT
v$=STR$(v)
PRINT" There are ";LEN(v$);" characters in ";v$;"!"
PRINT
PRINT n$;" added to ";v$;" is not ";n$+v$
```

Figure 9.13. Using VAL and STR$ – with a warning about the space preceding a number.

The first three lines show that we can do arithmetic on N$ if we use VAL with it. The fifth line converts the number variable V into string form, using the string name of V$. Now V has been assigned to the number 2, and we would expect just one character to be present in the string. Using LEN reveals that there are two! The reason is that when we use STR$ to convert a floating-point number into string form, a space is left at the left-hand side of the string in case we want to put in a sign, + or –. This space is, of course, an invisible extra character, which explains why 2 appears to consist of two characters, and 42 of three characters. The last line shows the strings being concatenated, just to emphasise the difference between string variables and number variables.

The reason why

You may by now be wondering why on earth we might want to use numbers in string form, when we have all this carry-on about converting between string form and number form. One reason is that string form is often very convenient. Just to give an example, you can enter anything in string form, using something like INPUT X$ or LINE INPUT X$. If you have INPUT X, then what you enter must be a number, and only a number. You can't, for example, enter 27A. If you do, then you'll just get the usual Alert Box message to remind you that only a number is acceptable, and 27A isn't an ordinary number.

Now if you and only you are to use the program, this might be acceptable, but if a non-programmer is to use it, then this error message might cause a lot of confusion. If you use an input which is to a string variable, then items like 27A will be accepted. You can then use VAL to extract the number part. This use of VAL, however, works only if the string starts with a number. You can extract the number 27 from 27A, but not from A27. If you type A27 as your answer, then VAL will give the number 0. When a reply consists of mixed numbers and letters, you will have to make use of string slicing, like X$= RIGHT$(X$,2) to get rid of the letters before you use VAL.

There's another reason for needing VAL. Up until now, we've used INPUT as our only way of getting a value into a program when it is running. INPUT, if you remember, causes the program to hang up until you press the RETURN key. There's another way of getting a character from the keyboard, though, which uses a different instruction word, INKEY$, a function that we have already met. The important point about this one is that it has to be assigned to a string variable. You can use K$=INKEY$, but not K=INKEY$. The other point about INKEY$ is that it scans the keyboard. This means that at the instant when the line that contains K$=INKEY$ is executed, the computer checks to find if any key is being pressed. If no key is pressed, the computer makes K$ equal to a blank string and goes on its merry way.

If you want to make use of K$=INKEY$ to get something from the keyboard, then, you have to arrange for the instruction to be repeated in a loop until a key is pressed. Figure 9.14 shows this in action. In the REPEAT loop, K$ is assigned to INKEY$, so that the computer will test the keyboard at this point. If K$ is a blank string, we want this action to repeat, and this is done by the UNTIL test, which reads:

```
LOOP UNTIL K$ <> ""
```

This means that if K$ is a blank string because no key was pressed, the loop will repeat, and will break out only when K$ is no longer a blank.

```
CLS
PRINT "press any KEY...."
DO: k$ = INKEY$
LOOP UNTIL k$ <> ""
PRINT "Your key was "; k$
PRINT "Number value "; VAL(k$)
```

Figure 9.14. The use of INKEY$ to get one character from the keyboard, without the use of the ENTER key. Using INPUT$ is easier.

Note how a blank string is typed as a pair of quotes with nothing between them – you just tap the quotes key twice to get this. The program will therefore hang up, repeating the INKEY$ loop, until you press a key. You only need to press one key and, unlike INPUT, you don't have to follow it with pressing the ENTER key. The following lines show the effect of what you have done. This is where VAL is really essential, because K$ is a string. If you want to use a number value here, then you can assign something like V%=VAL(K$). V% will always be an integer, because INKEY$ allows you one key only, and one digit key can't give you a fraction!

Why should we need STR$? Let me give you just one example. Suppose you have a program which accepts numbers. These might be catalogue numbers of gifts, for example. Now when the computer lists are printed, we might want numbers like 1, 12, 123 to be printed out as 0001, 0012 and 0123 respectively, using four characters. It's quite difficult to arrange this if the program prints number variables, but it's simple if you use strings.

```
CLS
INPUT "number, please "; V
V$ = STR$(V)
L% = LEN(V$) - 1
V$ = "0000" + RIGHT$(V$, L%)
V$ = RIGHT$(V$, 4)
PRINT V$
```

Figure 9.15. Using numbers in string form to print in four-digit format with zeros ahead of the number.

The program gets a number from you, and you should try the effect of numbers like 3, 45, 624, 1234 and so on, keeping to positive numbers of four digits or less. The number is converted to string form as V$ and then the length L% of this string is found, and 1 subtracted. This, remember, is because STR$ always places a blank space before the first digit of the number.

We don't want to have this when we print the number, so we subtract 1 from L%. The string is then concatenated with the string '0000' and only the number part of V$ is added. This is done by using RIGHT$(V$,L%). For example, if N=23, then LEN(V$) will be 3, and L=2. The program will then take the last two characters of V$, '23' and add them to '0000', to get '000023', then take the last four digits of this, which are '0023', to be printed.

Note how a variable name like V$ can be reassigned several times in the course of a program like this. You could, of course, use different variable names at each stage of the process, but it's more economical to reassign the same name, and it makes things easier to follow. This is because you know that V$ is always being used to hold the quantity that you are working with. There are lots of other manipulations like this that become easy when STR$ is used. Another example would be adding letters to a number. Could you design a piece of a program that asked for your name and your age, and then took the first three letters of your name and joined them to your age to give a code like SIN60? Having done that, could you make the program of Figure 9.15 cope with negative numbers by testing for a negative sign and keeping it as a separate variable?

ASC and CHR$

If you hark back to Chapter Two and earlier parts of this one, you'll remember that we introduced the idea of ASCII code. This is the number code that is used to represent each of the characters that we can print on the screen. We can find out the code for any letter by using the function ASC, which is followed, within brackets, by a string character or a string variable. The result of ASC is a number, the ASCII code number for that character. If you use ASC("PC"), then you'll get the code for the 'P' only, because the action of ASC includes rejecting more than one character.

```
CLS
DO
  PRINT " Press a key, please (Esc to stop)";
  DO: k$ = INKEY$
    LOOP UNTIL k$ <> ""
  PRINT " ASCII code is "; ASC(k$)
LOOP UNTIL k$ = CHR$(27)
```

Figure 9.16. Using ASC to find the ASCII code for letters. This example uses the inner loop for the INKEY$ action, and the outer loop to repeat the ASC finding. Note that the Esc key gives ASCII 27.

You are asked to press any key, and an outer loop starts which will repeat all the actions of the program until the Esc key (ASCII 27) is pressed. The INKEY$ loop is used to get the character from the keyboard. The ASCII code for whatever key has been pressed is then obtained by using ASC(K$), and printed. When you run this, you will find that keys which don't produce anything on the screen will still give an ASCII code. Keys such as the spacebar, the DEL-left and Esc keys, for example, all give their own codes, but the F-keys do not, nor does the Delete key, though the Del key on the number keypad gives code 46 (the full stop code). You have to get out of this one by pressing Esc which in QBASIC uses the code 27.

ASC has an opposite function, CHR$. What follows CHR$, within brackets, has to be a code number, and the result is the character whose code number is given. The instruction PRINT CHR$(65), for example, will cause the letter A to appear on the screen, because 65 is the ASCII code for the letter A.

Figure 9.17 is a short program that allows you to enter numbers, and see what their effect is on the screen. The numbers that can be used for this CHR$ action extend from 0 to 255. The numbers from 0 to 31 produce a variety of graphics character on the screen. The more usual functions of these are as *action* code numbers, which produce effects like backspacing the cursor, clearing the screen and so on. In fact, for this range of numbers, you will find that using ASC to find a key ASCII code does not necessarily produce the same result as using CHR$ to find the character for that code. The reason is that the machine uses the codes in the range 0 to 31 that it gets from keys to perform actions, but substitutes a set of characters for the actions when required to do so by CHR$. The number 32 is the ASCII code for the spacebar, and the numbers from 33 to 255 will all produce various characters, including the Greek letters.

```
DO
 CLS
 INPUT " Number, please "; n%
 PRINT : PRINT " Character is "; CHR$(n%)
 PRINT : PRINT " Press any key to proceed"
  DO WHILE INKEY$ = "": LOOP
LOOP UNTIL n% = 27
```

Figure 9.17. Using CHR$ to convert an ASCII code number into a printed character.

One of the main uses of CHR$ is in producing these alternative alphabets, the other is for coding messages. Every now and again, it's useful to be able to hide a message in a program so that it's not too obvious to anyone who reads the listing. Using ASCII codes is not a particularly good way of hiding a message from a skilled programmer, but for non-skilled users it's good enough. The codes can be kept in a DATA line, read in one by one, converted in characters by using CHR$, and printed. Figure 9.18 shows an example – it wouldn't keep a skilled programmer in the dark, but it could still be useful.

```
CLS
PRINT " What does PC mean?": PRINT
PRINT " Press any key for the answer"
  DO WHILE INKEY$ = "": LOOP
FOR J% = 1 TO 27: READ N%
  PRINT CHR$(N%);
NEXT
END
DATA 32,72,111,119,32,97,98,111,117,116
DATA 32,80,114,111,98,108,101,109,32
DATA 67,114,117,110,99,104,101,114
```

Figure 9.18. Using ASCII codes to carry a coded message, and then using CHR$ to obtain the character that corresponds to a code number.

The Law about order

We can compare one number variable with another, using the >, < and = signs. We can also compare strings, using the ASCII codes as the basis for comparison, as was noted in Chapter 6. This process can be taken one stage further, though, to comparing complete words, character by character. Figure 9.19 illustrates this use of comparison using the = and > symbols:

```
CLS
A$ = "qwerty"
PRINT : INPUT " Type a word "; B$
IF A$ = B$ THEN PRINT " Same as mine!": END
IF A$ > B$ THEN SWAP A$, B$
PRINT " Correct order is "; A$; " then "; B$
END
```

Figure 9.19. Comparing complete words for alphabetical order.

A nonsense word is assigned – it's just the first six letters on the top row of letter keys. You are then asked to type a word, and you should use lowercase letters. The comparisons are then carried out. If the word that you have typed, which is assigned to B$ is identical to qwerty, then the appropriate message is printed, and the program ends. If qwerty would come later in an index than your word, then the next line is carried out. If, for example, you typed 'peripheral', then since q comes after p in the alphabet and has an ASCII code that is greater than the code for p, your word B$ scores lower than A$, and the strings are swapped round. QBASIC does this by using the useful command SWAP. When SWAP is followed by two variable names, separated by a comma, it will do what the name suggests – swap the values. This is the command that has been used following the IF test.

The next line will then print the words in the order A$ and then B$, which will be the correct alphabetical order. If the word that you typed comes later than qwerty – for example 'tape' – then A$ is not greater than B$, and the test fails. No swap is made, and the order A$, then B$, is still correct. Note the important point though, that words like 'qwertz' and 'qwertx' will be put correctly into order – it's not just the first letter that counts. If you are thinking of using this for indexing, however, remember that upper-case (capital) letters always come well before lower case letters in ASCII code, so that XYZ would always come ahead of abc. For indexing, you should compare the UCASE$(A$) with UCASE$(B$) to get this right. The SWAP command applies to number variables as well as to string variables.

String ends

Another useful command is FRE. If you type PRINT FRE(1), then the machine will print the number of bytes of memory that you can use for string data. By having a line such as:

```
IF FRE(1)<1000 THEN PRINT "No room - please record
data" : GOSUB makespace
```

you can detect when memory is running short, and then record your data – the GOSUB statement and the recording of data will be dealt with later.

Finally, QBASIC provides an excellent command, INSTR. This is used to find if one string is contained in another. Its simplest form is:

```
X%= INSTR (A$, B$)
```

to find if B$ is contained in A$. If it is, then X% is the position number of the first letter of B$ that is found in A$. If B$ is not contained in A$, then X% is zero. X% will always be zero if B$ is longer than A$. You can, of course, use the form:

```
PRINT INSTR(a$,b$)
```

if you just want to see the number.

Figure 9.20 shows a simple example of this function in action. Names are assigned to strings, and the following lines make the tests, so that you can see how they work out. Notice that the strings have to be exact for the function to work – it's no good looking for 'Bert' if what is contained in the string is 'bert' or 'BERT', for example.

```
CLS
A$ = "Albert Hall"
B$ = "Richardson, Bertram"
C$ = "Sinclair, I"
PRINT " In "; A$; " ; bert is located at "; INSTR(A$,
"bert")
PRINT " In "; B$; " ; Bert is located at "; INSTR(B$,
"Bert")
PRINT " In "; C$; " ; BERT is located at "; INSTR(C$,
"BERT")
```

Figure 9.20. Illustrating the action of INSTR to find if one string is contained within another.

To leave you with a thought, suppose you had a string:

```
A$="YESyesYUPyupSUREsureOKok"
```

and you asked for a yes/no answer. You could get INSTR to look through this. If the result of X=INSTR(Answer$,A$) is zero, then the answer wasn't any form of YES! The other point about INSTR is that you can specify at which character in the string you start the search. This is done by putting in a number as the first item within the brackets. The other items are used as before, with commas between them. For example, if you had:

```
X%=INSTR(5,A$,B$)
```

the computer would start at character number 5 of A$, and look from that position to find if B$ was present. This can be useful if you are, for example, looking for a space between a forename and a surname. The program might be misled if there was a space just before the name, so using INSTR(2,A$,B$) would skip over this first space and concentrate on looking for the second one. The number X% that you can get from this can then be used in a string slicing instruction to separate out the words. Magic!

Finally, there are two less-used string functions, HEX$ and OCT$ which are of interest mainly to programmers in machine code who need to convert numbers into the Octal (scale of eight) or hexadecimal (scale of sixteen) format. This short example shows how these functions are used:

```
CLS
a% = 25
b& = 7314088
c = 456.78
PRINT a%; " is "; HEX$(a%); " in hex."
PRINT b&; " is "; HEX$(b&); " in hex."
PRINT c; " is "; HEX$(c); " in hex."
PRINT
PRINT a%; " is "; OCT$(a%); " in octal"
PRINT b&; " is "; OCT$(b&); " in octal"
PRINT c; "is "; OCT$(c); " in octal"
```

Figure 9.21. Using OCT$ and HEX$, rather specialised actions.

The number that is used should be an integer or a long integer and any other number will be rounded to an integer or long integer, as is illustrated.

Complex Data

Put it on the list

The variable names that we have used so far are called *scalar variables;* each one can hold one value. Scalar variables are useful but they have their limits. Suppose that you had a program which allowed you to type in a large set of numbers. These might be examination marks, goals scored, league points, money saved or any other such list of numbers. How would you go about assigning a different variable name to each item? It would be very unsatisfactory if you had to assign a new variable name to each item, and if you had to put in an INPUT line for each input. It would be far better if you could have just one INPUT routine that could be used in a loop, but to do this we need a different type of variable:

```
CLS
FOR N% = 1 TO 10
  A%(N%) = RND * 100 + 1
NEXT
PRINT : PRINT
PRINT TAB(18); "MARKS LIST" + STRING$(19, 32)
PRINT : PRINT
FOR N% = 1 TO 10
  PRINT TAB(10); "Item "; N%; TAB(19); "received ";
  A%(N%); TAB(34); " marks."
NEXT
END
```

Figure 10.1. An array of subscripted number variables. It's simpler than the name suggests. The long line should be typed without splitting it.

The first four lines of this program generate an (imaginary) set of examination marks. This is done simply to avoid the hard work of entering the real thing (even for assessed work). The variable A%(N%) in the third line is something new, though. It's called a *subscripted variable,* or *array variable,* and the subscript is the number that is represented by N%. The name 'subscripted' that we use has nothing to do with computing, it's a name that was used long before computers were around. How often do you make a list with the items numbered as 1, 2, 3.. and so on? These numbers 1, 2, 3 are a form of subscript number, put there simply so that you can identify different items. Similarly, by using variable names A%(1), A%(2), A%(3) and so on, we can identify different items that have the common variable name (and variable type) of A%. A member of this group like A%(2) has its name pronounced as 'A%-of-two'. We have also used TAB to good advantage to make the listing look neat – without the TABs it looks very ragged as you'll see if you remove them.

The usefulness of an array is that it allows us to use one single variable name for the complete list, picking out items simply by their identity (subscript) numbers. Since the number can be a number-variable or an expression which yields a number (such as LEN(A$)), this allows us to work with any item of the list. The main restriction is that the list can normally be of only one variable type, either number or string and, as usual, it's often better to convert numbers into string form so that we can use strings. The example shows the list being constructed from the FOR...NEXT loop with each item being obtained by finding a random number between 1 and 100, and then assigned to A%(N%). Since A% is a variable name for an integer number, this is an integer number array, and the N% is the subscript number. You can use any number variable as the subscript, but it will always be chopped to an integer, and you can't expect to be able to refer to item A%(2.5). In the example, ten of these marks are assigned in this way, and then the list is printed. It makes for much neater programming than you would have to use if you needed a separate variable name for each number.

So far so good, but one point has been omitted. Try altering the loop, so that it reads FOR N% = 1 TO 11, and then run the program. You'll get an error message that says 'Subscript out of range', and the line that creates the array number, the third line, will be highlighted. QBASIC provides automatically for the use of subscript numbers of 0 up to 10, but no higher. The computer has to be prepared by an additional statement for the use of numbers greater than 10 – the preparation consists of getting some more memory ready to receive the data. When you use DIM (meaning dimension), the memory is allocated for the array, and cannot be used for anything else until the program is ended or until some other allocation of memory is made. A line such as DIM A%(11) allows you up to twelve items in an array, in fact, because we can use A%(0) if we like, but you must not attempt to use A%(12) or any higher number. You will get the error message again if you do so.

If you want to use array numbers starting at 1 you can do so by starting your program with OPTION BASE 1. An alternative is to use DIM in the form:

```
DIM A% (1 TO 100)
```

which allows numbers 1 to 100 to be used.

The important DIM instruction consists, in its simplest form, of naming each variable that you will use for arrays – and following the name with the maximum number, within brackets, that you expect to use. You aren't forced to use this number, but you must not exceed it. If you do, and your program stops with an error message, you will have to change the DIM instruction and start again – which will be tough luck if you were typing in a list of 100 names! Note that you can dimension more than one variable in a DIM line, as Figure 10.2 shows. Even though you don't have to use DIM when you use numbers of 10 or less, it's a good habit to do so. The reason being that it avoids wasting memory space, by making the most efficient use of the memory.

```
CLS
DIM A%(12), N$(12)
PRINT TAB(10); "Please enter names and marks"
FOR N% = 1 TO 12
  INPUT " Name "; N$(N%)
  INPUT " Mark "; A%(N%)
NEXT
CLS : total% = 0
PRINT TAB(16); "Marks List"
PRINT : FOR N% = 1 TO 12
  PRINT TAB(10); N$(N%); TAB(40); A%(N%)
  total% = total% + A%(N%)
NEXT
PRINT : PRINT
PRINT " Average was "; total% / 12
```

Figure 10.2. Using strings in one array, and numbers in another. The arrays have been dimensioned, using DIM, because numbers greater than 10 are to be used.

This example extends the use of array variables another step further. This time you are invited to type a name and a mark for each of twelve items. When the list is complete, the screen is cleared and a variable called 'total%' is set to zero. The list is then printed neatly, and on each pass through the loop the total is counted up so that the average value can be printed at the end. The important point here is that it's not just numbers that we can keep in this list form. The correct name for the list is an array of one dimension, and this example uses both a string array (N$) and a number array (A%). The dimension in this case is the single subscript number that is used to identify each item, and later on we'll be looking at arrays that have more than one dimension.

The DIM statement has another use, which applies to ordinary (scalar) variables as well; it can declare the *type* of an array or scalar variable. So far, we have been using the old style distinguishing marks like $, &, ! and # to determine the variable type, but these are peculiar to older versions of BASIC and are not used in any other language. Other languages *declare* that a name will be used and say what type of variable it is.

In QBASIC, this is done by using DIM...AS. For example:

```
DIM NAM AS STRING
DIM NAMLIST(100) AS STRING
```

declares NAM as a single scalar string variable, and NAMLIST as a string array. The array is distinguished by the use of the brackets in the DIM statement, and the key word AS must separate the name of the variable from the type.

note The types are INTEGER, LONG, SINGLE, DOUBLE, STRING or any other data type that you have defined – see Chapters 12 and 19.

note We should not dismiss the use of old style nam$ and num& too lightly. It is often very difficult when you are programming in other languages to remember what data type is allocated to a name, and the use of the BASIC distinguishing marks can be very useful in this respect – you don't need to keep looking back at the place where the names were declared.

QBASIC also provides ways of testing the dimensioning of an array by using UBOUND and LBOUND functions. This is not something that you need to use very often, if at all, and the syntax is of the form:

```
x% = LBOUND(array%)
```

for a simple (one-dimensional) array – in the example the number that is returned in x% is the lower limit of the array (usually 0, but sometimes 1 or higher). Similarly UBOUND will return the upper limit , which is likely to be more useful to know. For an array of more than one dimension you have to specify which dimension you want the boundary for, so that:

```
x% = UBOUND(matrix%,2)
```

will return the upper limit for the second dimension of matrix% – see later for multi-dimensional arrays.

While we are on the topic of arrays and their uses, there's a small side road to explore. If we fill arrays by using a READ...DATA set of instructions, it is sometimes useful to be able to select a set of DATA to read. This can be done by using RESTORE. The normal use of RESTORE is to set the DATA *pointer* to the start of a data line, so that the data line can be read again from the start. If RESTORE is followed by a label name (or a line number) however, that data line will be used for reading, along with any data lines that follow it if the read requires more than one data line.

This action is demonstrated in Figure 10.3. You are asked which of three lists you want to use, and the REPEAT...UNTIL loop keeps an INKEY$ instruction running until you enter a number that is within the acceptable range. Once you have done so, this number is used to select a data line by using a label name following RESTORE in three test lines. In fact, only two lines need to be tested, because if the number a is not 1 or 2 it must be 3. Once the correct DATA line has been selected by its label, then the array can be read. In this example, the array is used only to read one item, but you can see that this could be used to select much more information when the data comes in sets of this type.

```
CLS
PRINT " Which list do you want (1 to 3)?"
PRINT
DO
  INPUT a%
LOOP UNTIL a% > 0 AND a% < 4
IF a% = 1 THEN RESTORE british
IF a% = 2 THEN RESTORE german
IF a% = 3 THEN RESTORE italian
FOR n% = 1 TO 4: READ a$(n%): NEXT
PRINT " Now pick a number, 1 to 4"
DO
  INPUT x%
LOOP UNTIL x% > 0 AND x% < 5
PRINT a$(x%)
british:
DATA Rover, Aston-Martin, Jaguar, Vauxhall
german:
DATA BMW, Mercedes, Porsche, Opel
italian:
DATA Alfa Romeo, Fiat, Lancia, Ferrari
```

Figure 10.3. Selecting a DATA line with RESTORE and using a label name. Reading into an array allows an item to be picked out.

With the added facility of arrays, we can now begin to think of much more powerful programs, because we can now deal with lists of items without having to program any more than we would for one single item. We can, for example, enter items into a list with the type of routine that is illustrated in Figure 10.4. In this example, a DO WHILE loop has been used, but there has to be a test for number, because the dimensioning of the loop must not be exceeded. This is always a problem, because if you use a very large dimension number, you will be reserving a lot of memory that you might in fact not use; and if you dimension too little, you may run out of room for your data.

```
CLS
PRINT TAB(18); "NUMBERS": PRINT
n% = 1: DIM a%(100): nr% = 1
DO WHILE (n% <= 100 AND nr% <> 0)
  PRINT " Please enter number, zero to end ";
  INPUT nr%: a%(n%) = nr%
  n% = n% + 1
LOOP
CLS
PRINT TAB(16); "NUMBER LIST"
PRINT : PRINT
FOR j% = 1 TO n% - 2
PRINT TAB(20); a%(j%)
NEXT
END
```

Figure 10.4. Entering items in a list in such a way that dimensioning is not exceeded.

In this example, the main entry loop uses DO WHILE...LOOP, with the condition for continuing written as:

```
(n% <= 100 AND nr% <> 0)
```

meaning that the loop will continue for as long as both conditions, n% not exceeding 100 and number nr% not zero, are true. The important points, however, are that a number is input and allocated to an array place. In this example, the number has been allocated indirectly, using INPUT nr%, followed by a%(n%)=nr%. This is not essential, because you could use INPUT a%(n%) just as easily. When you want to do a lot of checking on an entry, however, it's easier to use an intermediate, and it's also useful to have a record of the entry to use in the DO WHILE condition. Since n% is incremented in the loop, you couldn't test a%(n%)<>0 in the WHILE part of the loop and you would have to use a%(n%-1) instead, and assign some dummy value to a%(0). Using an intermediate variable name can make for a lot less typing, and a neater-looking program.

Incidentally, did you test that the DO WHILE loop would terminate correctly? It's easy enough to test for the ending when zero is entered, but to test the alternative ending for 100 entries, you need to break the loop by pressing the Ctrl-Break keys. Press F6 until you get to the Immediate screen and then type n%=98 (ENTER), and use F6 to get you back to the Edit screen.

Pressing F5 will then get you back to the loop, and you can enter the remaining numbers, and watch as all 100 entries, most of them zeros, are listed.

Another aspect of working with arrays is display. As you will have seen from the previous example, the display can be far from satisfactory if the numbers just scroll up the Results screen, leaving you with no time to look at them. What is needed is some method of paging the listing so that the numbers can be inspected, and Figure 10.5 shows what can be achieved.

```
CLS
DIM a%(100)
FOR n% = 1 TO 100
  a%(n%) = 2 * n%: NEXT
PRINT TAB(18); "NUMBERS": PRINT : PRINT
FOR n% = 1 TO 100
  IF n% / 20 <> INT(n% / 20) THEN
     PRINT a%(n%)
       ELSE
          PRINT " Press any key..."
          DO WHILE INKEY$ = "": LOOP: CLS
  END IF
NEXT
```

Figure 10.5. Displaying a list, with paging to ensure that you have time to read the list.

The array is created for you this time to save the labour of typing it, and the important point is the display. I'm assuming that the display has to be in the form of one item per line, because if you can accept more than one item per line then large amounts of data can be displayed by using a PRINT a%(n%);" "; action in the printing loop. In this example, the list is paged by testing the value of the control number, n%, in the FOR...NEXT loop. The test is for n%/20<>INT(n%/20), which is true except for n% values of 20, 40, 60, and so on, all multiples of 20. When the test is true, some lines are skipped, and the numbers are printed normally. When the test is not true, at a multiple of twenty, the intermediate lines swing into action. The first of these prints the message to press any key, and then the next line contains an INKEY$ loop, using DO WHILE...LOOP, and a CLS to clear the screen for the next lot of numbers. The next page, then, will be printed whenever you press any key.

String arrays

A string array is formed in much the same way as a number array, but with the usual dollar sign or any of the alternative methods of declaration. As before, you can make use of arrays with subscripts up to 10 without dimensioning but, if you want to use higher numbers, then you must have a DIM line. As with number arrays, declaring a string array will cause the computer to allocate some memory for that array whether you need all of the memory or not. However, the machine may not be able to prepare as much memory as you need, a complication that does not arise with numbers.

The problem is that strings are not of fixed length. When you specify an array of numbers, then the amount of storage is fixed – five bytes for each float number, for example. This cannot be done for string arrays, because a string can consist of anything up to 32767 characters, each character needing a byte of storage. The allocation of memory for string arrays, therefore, needs to be flexible, so that strings can be stored wherever there happens to be memory available. QBASIC has to keep track of this use of memory, so that working with string arrays is considerably more complicated than working with number arrays. All this complication, however, is concealed from you – it's dealt with by QBASIC – and all you ever know about it is that the machine seems to deal with some string array actions more slowly than it deals with number array actions.

Figure 10.6 illustrates a simple string array in use. You are asked to type in twelve names to be used in the array with each name assigned to an array item. Having the names in the array allows printing in any arrangement of columns you like, as the example shows, using two commas to separate the names, but you have to be careful with the size of columns, because a long name may overlap from one column to another.

```
CLS
DIM name$(12)
FOR n% = 1 TO 12
  INPUT "Name, please "; name$(n%)
NEXT
CLS : PRINT TAB(19); "NAMES": PRINT
FOR n% = 1 TO 12 STEP 2
  PRINT name$(n%), , name$(n% + 1)
NEXT
END
```

Figure 10.6. Filling and displaying a string array of names which can be of any reasonable size. The spacing has to be altered for long names.

Figure 10.7 shows how the use of fixed length string array items can make printouts easier. In this example, the items are imaginary code names, and you can try the effect of deliberately typing names that are too large. As you enter the name, there is no indication that the name is too long, because the chopping action only comes when the names are stored in the array. It would be better if the program did not just chop the names to size, but test each and report to you that a long name had been chopped, and show what was being entered. This looks like a good exercise in program modification for you.

```
CLS
DIM code(12) AS STRING * 5
FOR n% = 1 TO 12
  PRINT " Code for item"; n%; " is "; : INPUT code(n%)
NEXT
CLS : PRINT TAB(19); "CODES": PRINT
FOR j% = 1 TO 12 STEP 3
  PRINT code(j%), code(j% + 1), code(j% + 2)
NEXT
END
```

Figure 10.7. Using a string array with fixed length strings which do not require the use of the dollar sign.

The distinguishing feature here is that a string that has been declared in the way illustrated in the second line does *not* need to use a dollar sign or the DEFSTR statement to identify it as a string (or string array as in this case). By using the modified form of the DIM statement that includes AS STRING we ensure that this is recognised as a string, and by also using the modifier *5 we ensure that each string is of five characters length. The great advantage of such strings is that the machine can work with them at very high speed.

Using arrays

Arrays are very useful for storing sets of related items, whether number or string, and for arranging items for display on screen or on paper. Their main purpose, however, is to allow searching and sorting. The programming of these actions can become very complicated, so much so that most of us are grateful to use standard subroutines that are freely available, and much of this type of work belongs in the Advanced category.

For the moment, however, we can give some thought to how we might find items in a list of names. Suppose, for example, that you had an array that consisted of names, and you wanted to pick out all the names that started with the letter J. This is comparatively easy to program, because the use of an array allows you to use a FOR...NEXT loop to select each item in turn and test it. Figure 10.8 shows a simple example, in which names have been put in by using a READ...DATA statement, and you are asked to specify the initial letter that you are looking for:

```
CLS
FOR n% = 1 TO 10
  READ name$(n%)
NEXT
DO
  CLS : PRINT "Please type first letter"
  PRINT "type 0 to end searching"
  INPUT n$: n$ = LEFT$(n$, 1)
  j% = 0: IF n$ = "0" THEN EXIT DO
  FOR n% = 1 TO 10
  IF UCASE$(n$) = UCASE$(LEFT$(name$(n%), 1)) THEN
    PRINT name$(n%): j% = 1
    END IF
  NEXT
  IF j% = 0 THEN PRINT "No matching name found"
  PRINT "Press any key to proceed"
    DO WHILE INKEY$ = "": LOOP
LOOP UNTIL n$ = "0": PRINT "End."
DATA George, Helen, Mary, Bert, Jim
DATA Alan, Mike, Patsy, Jill, Pete
```

Figure 10.8. Searching a list for names with a given starting letter.

Some safeguards are needed, however. To start with, you need to check that more than one letter has not been typed, and this is done by selecting the first character of the reply string. The next point is that the list might not contain any names with the letter that you have chosen. The testing must allow for this, and print a suitable message in this event. It's very unsatisfactory to have any program that gives you no answer. Even if the answer is that no name has been found, this should be announced on the screen, rather than leaving the user wondering if something has gone wrong.

Finally, if the list contains more than one name with the selected initial letter, then all the matching names must be printed, not just the first one. All this is provided for in the example.

The placing of the names into the array is straightforward enough, but in the eighth line, you have the statement n$ = LEFT$(n$,1). This reassigns n$ to be the first letter of the original value of n$, the letter you typed. This is the way of ensuring that if you type more than one letter, only one is used for selection. Following this is j%=0. The number variable j% is being used here as a *flag*, a method of signalling something. In this case it is used to signal whether or not any matching names have been found. If a matching name is found in the list, the value of j% is set to 1, otherwise it is left at 0. At the end of the search, we can test the value of j% to find if we have to print a message about not having found any matching names.

The search is then done, using a FOR...NEXT loop. In this loop, the important line is:

```
IF UCASE$(n$) = UCASE$(LEFT$(name$(n%), 1)) THEN
```

This compares n$, converted to upper case, with the first letter of name$(n%), also converted to upper case. The first letter is picked out in the usual way, using LEFT$. If the comparison is true – meaning that a match has been found – the name is printed and the flag variable j% is set to 1. With j%=1, the test following the NEXT will not print the message, and there is a pause so that you can read whatever name or message is produced. The DO...LOOP UNTIL loop continues until a 0 is typed. Note that the zero is tested for and forces the program to skip to statement following the UNTIL statement. This avoids having to press another key to get out after you have pressed 0.

Sorting array items into order is something that could take up a complete book by itself. The simplest sort methods such as the *bubble-sort* are reasonably easy to understand, but dismally inefficient in action, so that we'll look at them only very briefly as an introduction to the subject. In the rest of this Chapter we'll look at number and string sorting and some of the more advanced actions involving arrays.

Number sorting

One very common requirement in number lists is to sort the lists into some kind of order, either ascending or descending. Many textbooks list a bubble-sort for this purpose, and a routine of this class is illustrated in Figure 10.9.

The bubble-sort works by looking through the items in pairs, swapping positions if the numbers (in this example) are in the wrong order. Each time a swap is done a flag is set making the loop repeat and the whole array is checked over and over again until no swaps have taken place in a run.

The bubble-sort is easy to understand, but requires a lot of time if you are working with long lists, though it is quite efficient when the number of items in a list is small, below 50 for example. A much better method for long lists of numbers is the *quicksort*. It's certainly not an easy sort to understand, and

```
CLS
DIM j%(100)
FOR n% = 1 TO 100
  j%(n%) = RND * 100
NEXT
PRINT "Sorting now"
DO
  p% = 0
  FOR x% = 1 TO 99
    IF j%(x%) > j%(x% + 1) THEN SWAP j%(x%), j%(x% +
    1): p% = 1
  NEXT
LOOP UNTIL p% = 0    FOR n% = 1 TO 100
  PRINT j%(n%); " ";
NEXT
```

Figure 10.9. A simple bubble-sort routine used on numbers. It's slow but, on a fast machine and with only 50 numbers, it can look fast enough.

it's even more difficult to explain without going through the action step by step. That's something you can do for yourself by putting suitable PRINT and K$=INKEY$ lines into your program so, in this book, I'll leave out the explanations except to say that in all fast sort routines, the array is divided into two parts, and comparisons and swaps are done between corresponding items on the two parts.

The quicksort is shown in Figure 10.10. It sorts a list of random numbers using a version of the display routine illustrated earlier. Even this sort isn't breathlessly fast for three hundred integers, and it can be noticeably slower than the bubble-sort for small numbers of items.

The numbers have been created in this example by using RND*1000, so that they range from 1 to 1000. In the printing routine, the display is a simple type which packs the numbers as close together as the format string allows – this makes it possible to see all of the numbers on one screen page.

The sorting routine starts at the reminder line and occupies the following 24 lines. The dimensioning of the minor arrays q% and r% is rather haphazard – they don't need to be dimensioned to the full 300 of the main array, and the dimensioning shown here is on the generous side. The dimensions can be calculated, but the method is decidedly complicated, and a cut-and-try approach is easier.

```
CLS : m% = 300: DIM a%(m% + 1)
PRINT "Please wait - creating file"
FOR n% = 1 TO m%
a%(n%) = RND * 1000: NEXT
REM sort
PRINT "Please wait- sorting numbers"
DIM q%(50), r%(50)
p% = 1: q%(1) = 1: r%(1) = m%
DO
  u% = q%(p%): d% = r%(p%): p% = p% - 1
  DO
  j% = u%: L% = d%: x% = a%(INT(u% + d%) / 2)
    DO
      DO WHILE a%(j%) < x%
          j% = j% + 1
      LOOP
      DO WHILE x% < a%(L%)
          L% = L% - 1
      LOOP
      IF j% > L% THEN EXIT DO
      SWAP a%(j%), a%(L%)
      j% = j% + 1: L% = L% - 1
    LOOP UNTIL j% > L%
    IF j% < d% THEN
      p% = p% + 1: q%(p%) = j%: r%(p%) = d%
      END IF
    d% = L%
  LOOP UNTIL u% >= d%
LOOP UNTIL p% = 0
REM display
CLS
FOR j% = 1 TO m%
  PRINT a%(j%);
NEXT
END
```

Figure 10.10. A quicksort used on numbers, providing a very fast action for this size of array.

The important line to look for is SWAP, in which the array values are exchanged if they are not in ascending order. This is the line which needs to be altered if you are sorting any other type of variables. If, for example, you want to sort strings rather than numbers then each a%(j%) would be replaced by a$(j%), or by whatever variable name that you wanted to use. If you want to sort into descending order, then you need to change the routine around considerably so it's much easier to print the sorted array in reverse order (FOR N=M to 1 STEP -1) or to shift the numbers into another array using statements such as:

```
FOR j% = 1 TO m%
g%(j%) = a%(m% - j% + 1)
NEXT
```

and then use the printing routine to print the array g% instead of array a%.

Remember that if you have files of numbers or strings on disk, then there is little point in creating BASIC subroutines to sort them, because MS-DOS has its own routines for sorting files into order – this applies to number or to word files. For example, if you have the SORT program in a directory called MS-DOS, and an unsorted file in a directory called PFOLIO you can use a direct MS-DOS command:

```
C:\MSDOS\SORT < C:\PFOLIO\oldfile > C:\PFOLIO\newfile
```

The unsorted numbers in oldfile will then be used to create a sorted list in newfile – all without using QBASIC.

Finding an item

The next topic as far as numbers are concerned, is locating a number in a list that has been put into ascending order. For a list that is not in order, you need to check each item in turn as was demonstrated for strings earlier, but for sorted lists a very much faster subroutine exists in the form of a *binary chop*. The principle is to break the list in two, and find which half contains the number that is being looked for. This part is then halved in turn, and the process is repeated until the number is found or the search is abandoned. The usefulness of the routine lies in the fact that it needs very few loops, because even a very large list can be reduced to one item with a surprisingly small number of repeated halvings. The technique is even more useful for string items, as shown in Figure 10.11.

The list is a simple one – each number in the list is double its position number so the 44th number, for example, is 88. This makes it easy to check that the results of the subroutine are correct. If you create and use a set of random numbers, the test will be useless because the numbers need to be in order first and, once they are in order, it can still be tedious checking that they are correct. Go for an easy life every time where preliminary testing is concerned – the most advanced stuff can wait.

```
CLS : m% = 300: DIM a%(m%)
PRINT "Please wait - creating list"
FOR n% = 1 TO m%: a%(n%) = 2 * n%: NEXT
PRINT "List ready"
REM Find routine
DO
  PRINT "Please type number required": INPUT a%
  lo% = 1: hi% = m%: flag% = 0: mi% = 0
  DO
    mid% = INT((hi% + lo%) / 2)
    IF a% = a%(mid%) THEN flag% = 1: EXIT DO
    IF a% < a%(mid%) THEN
      IF mid% = lo% THEN mi% = 1
      hi% = mid% - 1
    END IF
    IF a% > a%(mid%) THEN
    IF mid% = hi% THEN mi% = 1
    lo% = mid% + 1
    END IF
  LOOP UNTIL (flag% = 1 OR mi% = 1)
  REM Printout
  IF (flag% = 1) THEN
    PRINT "Item is No."; mid%
    ELSE PRINT "No such item"
  END IF
  PRINT "Press Y to repeat search": k$ = INPUT$(1)
  LOOP UNTIL UCASE$(k$) <> "Y"
END
```

Figure 10.11. A binary chop routine being used to find a number in a list.

The main loop starts by asking for the required item. This is INPUT in the usual way and is then assigned to variable a%. The next line then initialises the variables that will be used. The variable lo% (*not* 10) is used to carry the lowest subscript number which in this array is 1. If you intend to use a%(0) in your array, then this assignment has to be altered, or the a%(0) item will never be found. The highest subscript number, passed as variable m% from the main program, is assigned to hi%. The quantities flag% and mi% are both flags, used respectively to report an item found or missing. For most purposes, one or both of these can be used to detect success.

The main loop of the finding portion starts with the DO that follows the initialisation, and consists of a loop which will continue until the item is found or reported missing. The search actions then lie in the remaining lines. These actions consist of tests and alterations to the variables. The first action is the calculation of mid%, a subscript number that lies about mid-way between lo% and hi%. The first of the three tests that follow then checks to see if the wanted item is exactly equal to the array member a%(mid%). If it is, then flag%, which was initially set to 0 is set to 1 (meaning item found) and the EXIT DO directs to the end of the loop, so that the LOOP UNTIL action can be used to terminate the loop correctly. If, as is likely on the first pass, the items are not equal, then the test for a% < a%(mid%) is made. If this is true, then the value of a% lies in the first half of the set of subscripts, and the high end of the number range can be taken now as the old middle range. We need to test in this subroutine at this point to find if mid% has been reduced to the value of lo%, because if this has happened, the whole range has been tested and the item is missing.

This is the first part of the action, and it is used to alter the mi% flag so that this flag can be detected at the LOOP UNTIL stage. The next action applies if mid% has not been reduced to lo% – the value of hi% is made equal to mid%-1. This will restrict searching from now on to the lower half of the group of subscripts. If a% has not been less than a%(mid%) and is not equal, then the test for a%>a%(mid%) must succeed. Here again there is another test, for mid%=hi%, which means once again that the whole group has been searched with no success. The alternative is to alter the value of lo% so that the upper part of the group will be searched next time. The program then loops back until either the item is found or the variable mid% reaches either lo% or hi% without matching the item.

The thing to note in testing this routine is how little difference in time there is between finding an item in the middle and one at either end. An item in the middle of the array will be found on the first pass through the loop, whereas an item at either end will require several passes. The maximum number of passes, however, is small even for very long lists. As the name 'binary search' indicates, the number of passes is n, where 2^n >= number of items. For example, 128 items would take at most 7 loops, since 2^7=128. This is a very efficient search, but you must remember that the items need to be in order before the search can be used. If you want to use this routine with disk files, it is a good idea to use a batch file to sort the files into order before loading in your BASIC program that makes use of the files.

Sorting string lists

Sorting string lists can be done in much the same way as we sort number lists, except that a string array has to be declared and filled first. The most popular sorting algorithm is the *Shell-Metzner* which is illustrated in Figure 10.12 alongside a brief routine that puts in some names to sort. The Shell-Metzner (named after its two inventors) is rather simpler than the quicksort, and performs very well with large string arrays. The basis is like that of any of the faster sorting methods – to compare items which have subscripts that are about half the list number apart, and then to alter the gap until items next to each other are sorted. In the listing of Figure 10.12, the sort is shown as a subroutine, adapted for QBASIC and running as fast as you can expect of a string sort.

Static and dynamic arrays

For most users of QBASIC, how an array is stored in the memory is not of great important as long as it *is* stored but, for anyone wanting to create or use the stored bytes in the memory, it can be rather important. As is noted in several parts of this book, the microprocessor of the PC uses a piece of memory called the *Stack* for temporary storage. Anything stored on the Stack is retained only for as long as it is needed. By contrast, most variables are stored in a more permanent way, using memory positions in a portion of memory called the *Data Sector.*

Items stored on the stack are called *dynamic*, because they are created and destroyed; those in the data sector are *static* because they are normally retained even when a program is ended (until another program is started or the machine is switched off). When you use static arrays, the space is allocated before the program runs – if you try to reserve too much space, the program won't start. When you use dynamic arrays the space is not allocated until the program is running, so that an overflow will stop the program. Note that only a dynamic array can be redimensioned, see later.

There are two main ways in which you can determine how array variables are stored. The more important one is how you use the DIM statement. If you use it with a number, such as DIM A$(100) then the array will be static, and if for any reason the array cannot be created you will be informed before the program runs. If you use DIM with a number variable, such as DIM A$(b%), then the array will be a dynamic one and any error messages will be delivered only when the program runs.

This is rather a subtle difference, and the use of a variable for DIM is quite often for an entirely different reason – to allow a variable to carry a maximum value throughout a program.

```
CLS
m% = 10:
FOR n% = 1 TO m%: READ a$(n%): NEXT
PRINT "Sorting now...": PRINT
REM Sort routine
y% = 1
DO WHILE y% < m%
  y% = 2 * y%
LOOP
DO
  y% = INT((y% - 1) / 2): IF y% = 0 THEN EXIT DO
  jt% = m% - y%
  FOR j% = 1 TO jt%: k% = j%
     DO
        z% = k% + y%
        IF a$(z%) <= a$(k%) THEN
          SWAP a$(z%), a$(k%)
        END IF
          k% = k% - y%
        IF k% <= 0 THEN EXIT DO
     LOOP
  NEXT j%
LOOP
REM Printout
FOR n = 1 TO 10: PRINT a$(n): NEXT
PRINT : PRINT
PRINT "Press any key..."
DO WHILE INKEY$ = "": LOOP
END
DATA "Hepzibah, Perry G.", Anemone, Produlus
Gigantica, Zoetrope
DATA Blow the wind southerly, X-ray techniques,
Collected thoughts, Young's Ts
DATA Linkers for assembly, Disaster fund progress
```

Figure 10.12. A Shell-Metzner sort routine being used on a small number of strings.

The other way that the difference can be enforced is by what are known as *metacommands*. A metacommand is a command to the QBASIC interpreter rather than a program instruction, and all such commands start with a dollar sign, such as $STATIC, $DYNAMIC and *must* be preceded by REM (these are the only remarks the interpreter will pay any attention to). These commands are made before any DIM statement for an array, and will override the use of a number or variable in the DIM statement. For example:

```
REM $STATIC
DIM NAM$(x%)
```

causes NAM$ and all arrays from this point onwards to be created as static arrays. Note that using REDIM, see below, always dimensions a dynamic array. In addition, an array variable that has been declared as COMMON, see Chapter 24, will be a dynamic array unless it has been specifically declared as STATIC.

Redimensioning an array

In older forms of BASIC, an array was static and its dimensions were fixed. For example if you use DIM A$(100) early in a program, then you would get an error message if you later wanted to reduce the amount of memory being used and put in the statement DIM A$(50).

This still applies if you use static arrays, but if you use dynamic arrays such as by the lines:

```
a%=100
DIM A$(a%)
```

then you can later redimension, for example by using REDIM A$(50). If you dimension an array for the first time using REDIM it will be a dynamic array.

ERASE and CLEAR

The ERASE statement frees the memory used by a dynamic array, allowing it to be re-assigned. For a static array, it sets each element of the array to a zero or blank. The syntax is of the form ERASE X$, where X$ would have been declared as an array.

The CLEAR statement is more drastic – it zeros all variables, array or otherwise, resets everything, and can also change the stack size if used in the form:

```
CLEAR ,,1024
```

in which the stack is set to a size of 1024 bytes, or 1K.

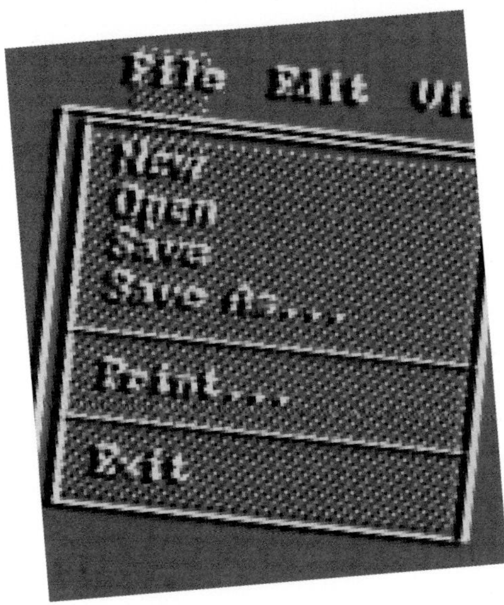

Menus, Subroutines and Functions

Parts of this Chapter show only sections of programs, or programs that have been shortened to emphasise the use of the keywords.

Menus

We saw in Chapter 10 how RESTORE, followed by a label name, can be used to make a choice of items that are to be read from a READ...DATA list. Very often, though, we want to present the user with a menu on screen. A menu is a list of choices, usually of program actions. By picking one of these choices, we can cause a section of the program to be run. One way of making the choice is by numbering the menu items, and typing the number of the one that you want to use. We could use a set of lines such as:

```
IF K =1 THEN GOTO First
IF K =2 THEN GOTO Second
```

and so on. There is a much simpler method, however, which uses a new instruction ON N GOTO, where N is a number variable, an integer in this example. You can use any number variable, of course, not just N, and a very common name here is choice because this reminds you of what the number is to be used for.

Figure 11.1 shows a typical menu that uses this instruction. The screen is cleared, and then the menu items are presented on the screen, followed by the invitation to you to pick one item by typing its number. At this point, the label *choose* is used so that the whole procedure can be repeated if an incorrect choice is made.

```
CLS
PRINT TAB(18); "MENU": PRINT
PRINT "1. Enter name."
PRINT "2. Enter phone number."
PRINT "3. List all names."
PRINT "4. List local numbers."
PRINT "5. End program.": PRINT
REM choose
PRINT " Please select by number (1 to 5)"
DO:
  DO: k$ = INKEY$: LOOP UNTIL k$ <> ""
  k% = VAL(k$):
  IF k% >= 1 AND k% <= 5 THEN EXIT DO
  PRINT "Incorrect choice - please try again"
LOOP
ON k% GOTO namin, phone, namlist, numlist, endit
outplace:
END
namin: PRINT "Names entered here.": GOTO outplace
phone: PRINT "Phone numbers here.": GOTO outplace
namlist: PRINT "Name list here.": GOTO outplace
numlist: PRINT "Local numbers here.": GOTO outplace
endit: PRINT "End of program": GOTO outplace
```

Figure 11.1 A very simple form of menu program, using GOTO and label names.

The INKEY$ loop keeps the program looking for a key until you make your choice, which is tested with a mugtrap. VAL has to be used, remember, because INKEY$ produces a string variable, and you can't compare a string with a number (even if a red rose sometimes looks like a carrot). By using k%=VAL(K$) you get a integer number variable K% which holds a number that is in the correct form to be compared. If you had pressed a letter key, the effect is the same as that of pressing a number key in the correct range.

The choice is then made by using the ON k% GOTO instruction. Now what happens here? If k% equals 1, then the first label name (or line number) that follows GOTO is used. If k equals 2, then the second label name or line number following GOTO is used, and so on. All that you have to do is to arrange the label names or line numbers in the same order as your choices. You don't have to use long label names, but it helps greatly in following the program if you make the names *mean* something. In this example, the line numbers simply lead to PRINT instructions to keep the example reasonably short. Note that the last item in a menu like this should always be a QUIT option, which lets you leave the program. There is nothing quite so frustrating as a program that won't let you get away. Note also that the label name 'outplace' is used because EXIT is a reserved word.

GOSUB subroutines

This type of menu selection is useful, but an even more useful method makes use of *subroutines*. A subroutine is a section of program which can be inserted anywhere that you like in a longer program. It's inserted by typing the instruction word GOSUB, followed by the label name or line number in which the subroutine starts. When your program comes to this instruction, it jumps to the line that is indicated by the name or number that follows GOSUB, just as if you had used GOTO. Unlike GOTO, however, GOSUB offers an automatic return. The word RETURN is used at the end of the subroutine lines, and it will cause the program to return to the point immediately following the GOSUB statement.

```
CLS
t$ = "Practical PC"
GOSUB centre
t$ = STRING$(LEN(t$), "-")
GOSUB centre
LOCATE 4, 2
PRINT " Neat, isn't it?"
END
centre:
nr% = LEN(t$)
PRINT TAB((80 - nr%) / 2); t$
RETURN
```

Figure 11.2 Using GOSUB for the simplest type of subroutine, compatible with earlier versions of BASIC.

When the program runs, a phrase is assigned to the string variable t$. The next line is GOSUB centre, which means that the program must jump to the routine which starts at the label word 'centre'. In this line, nr%, the number of characters in t$, is found. The following line then prints t$ centred on the screen. The last line of the subroutine consists only of the word RETURN. As the name suggests, this returns the program to the position immediately following the GOSUB that started the subroutine.

In the first instance, that RETURN means to the fourth line which carries out another assignment of T$, this time to a string of underlining dashes. Once again, calling GOSUB centre in the next line causes this new value of t$ to be printed centred, and the RETURN this time makes the program return to the following line. With a GOTO, you are stuck with just one destination line number, but the RETURN at the end of a GOSUB makes sure you return to the command which follows the GOSUB. Even if you have a multi-statement line like:

```
T$ = "MENU": GOSUB centre: PRINT "NOTES"
```

then the subroutine will return correctly, in this case to perform the PRINT action.

One important point in this simple example is the use of END at the end of the main program. A subroutine should be used only by *calling* it, which means the use of GOSUB. If the subroutine can be run in any other way, then when the RETURN is found, there is nowhere to return to, and you get an error message. Subroutines must be placed so that they can never run by normal program action. The best way to ensure this is to place the subroutines following the END statement at the end of the main program. An alternative, not used very much, is to make the first line of a program a GOTO main that leads to the main program, and have all the subroutines placed between this line and the main label. See for yourself the effect on Figure 11.2 of removing the END statement.

Now for the application to menus, Figure 11.3 shows subroutines in use as part of a (totally imaginary) games program. The PRINT lines offer a choice of items, and then you are invited to choose by pressing a number key. The point at which you are invited to select by number is labelled, so that this instruction can be repeated if an incorrect choice is made.

The familiar INKEY$ action is put into the subroutine labelled 'choice' and a mugtrap action follows. This time, the number is selected by using choose%=ASC(k$)-48. The reasoning here is that any key will give an ASCII code, and by subtracting 48 from the ASCII code for a number, you get the number itself. This is easier to mugtrap, because a letter key will simply produce a number that is out of the correct range. This is an alternative to the use of VAL.

The choice is then carried out by the ON choose% GOSUB statement. This time, however, the program will return to whatever follows the choice. For example, if you pressed key 1, then the subroutine that starts at label 'blood' is carried out, and the program returns to the ON choose% GOSUB line to check if you might also want subroutines 'fang', 'doze' or 'pyramid'. Note that you can use a label more than once if you want to summon the same subroutine for different choices.

```
CLS : PRINT
PRINT TAB(8); "Choose your monster."
PRINT
PRINT TAB(2); "1. Vampire."
PRINT TAB(2); "2. Werewolf."
PRINT TAB(2); "3. Zombie."
PRINT TAB(2); "4. Mummy."
PRINT TAB(2); "5. Flying Picket."
PRINT
DO
  PRINT " Select by number 1-5 please."

  DO
    GOSUB choice
    choose% = ASC(k$) - 48
    IF choose% >= 1 AND choose% <= 5 THEN EXIT DO
    PRINT "Incorrect choice"
  LOOP

  ON choose% GOSUB blood, fang, doze, pyramid, doze
  PRINT : PRINT " Want another choice? Type y or n"
  GOSUB choice
LOOP UNTIL UCASE$(k$) <> "Y"
END
choice:
DO: k$ = INKEY$: LOOP UNTIL k$ <> "": RETURN
blood: PRINT "Blood, blood, bootiful blood!": RETURN
fang: PRINT "Howl, snarl, gnash!": RETURN
doze: PRINT "I obey, master, I obey": RETURN
pyramid: PRINT "Come to mummy, do": RETURN
```

Figure 11.3 Using the ON k% GOSUB form of subroutine call in an imaginary game.

Since the value of choose% is still 1 at this point, the program then skips over these other choices and ends. If the first subroutine had altered the value of choose%, however, you could find that a second subroutine was selected following the first one. Never make any other use of the variable name that you have selected for ON choose% GOSUB. Using the name choose% for this variable is a good way of reminding yourself of this.

A subroutine is extremely useful in menu choices, but it's even more useful for pieces of program that will be used several times in a program. Take a look at Figure 11.4 by way of an example. The subroutine is an elaboration on the INKEY$ routine. The trouble with INKEY$ is that it doesn't remind you that it's in use, there's no question mark printed as there is when you use INPUT. The subroutine in this example remedies that by causing an asterisk to flash while you are thinking about which key to press. The asterisk is flashed by alternately printing the asterisk and a backspace and delete step. To make the rate of flashing reasonably slow, I've added another subroutine, a delay that uses a simple FOR...NEXT loop.

```
CLS : PRINT "Press any key "
GOSUB flash
PRINT "You pressed "; K$
END
flash:
K$ = "":
DO WHILE K$ = ""
  K$ = INKEY$
  PRINT "*"; : GOSUB pause
  PRINT CHR$(29); CHR$(32); CHR$(29); : GOSUB pause
LOOP: RETURN
pause:
FOR N = 1 TO 500: NEXT: RETURN
```

Figure 11.4. An INKEY$ subroutine that flashes an asterisk while waiting for a key to be pressed.

The asterisk is flashed by alternately printing the asterisk and the delete steps, PRINT CHR$(29);CHR$(32);CHR$(29);, with a time delay between them. The PRINT CHR$(29) causes the cursor to move one step back, but this does not wipe out the character in this position. To do this, you print a blank using CHR$(32), and then since the cursor will have moved one step right you need to use CHR$(29) again. Do not forget to use the semicolons to keep printing in the same line, otherwise you will see the asterisk moving down the screen. To make the rate of flashing reasonably slow, I've put in a delay using a FOR...NEXT loop.

Note that the subroutine uses INKEY$, which does not stop and wait for a key to be pressed, so making the loop in the subroutine run until a key is pressed. At the time when a keypress is detected, the asterisk will have been erased, so that the routine does not stop with an asterisk still showing. It's a small point, but one that can save a lot of bother. There is also a delay between pressing the key and getting the subroutine to return because the pause routine has to run first. You can get rid of the delay by adding the line, following k$=INKEY$, of:

```
IF k$ <> "" THEN EXIT DO
```

which allows you to jump out of the loop, avoiding the pause subroutine.

While we're on the subject of menus, there's another subroutine, in Figure 11.5, which can make a menu look more interesting. This is a visual menu choice, and its use brings several advantages to your menus. One is that you don't have to have the items of the menu numbered, because you don't choose by number. Instead, a little arrow flashes next to the first item of the menu. This arrow can be shifted by using the cursor keys, the ones which are marked with the vertical up or down arrows. Since the program makes it impossible to shift the arrow beyond the menu items, no sort of testing or mugtrapping of the answer is needed.

The choice is passed back to the main routine as a number CH%, which you can then use in a line such as:

```
ON CH% GOSUB.
```

Try it for yourself, and see how much better it looks compared to the traditional menu. It would be preferable to be able to use the mouse, but QBASIC makes no provision for that.

The subroutine needs to have some values passed to it. The title is passed as T$, and two integer numbers are also needed also. One of these is ST%, which is the line where the first item of the menu appears. The other is NR%, the number of items on the menu. The actual menu items are placed in a DATA line which can be anywhere in the program. If you have more than one menu, you can use RESTORE to get the correct set of data items. Once these quantities have been assigned, the subroutine can be called. In the example, the numbers have been set up to start on line 2 and use four items only.

The subroutine starts at label 'startit' by printing the title, centred, and then activating the cursor up and down keys. You will find that the cursor keys do not give ASCII codes, so that special methods of reading them are needed. The method that is used is that of generating an interrupt, and more details of this process are contained in Chapter 22. What it means is that, if a designated key is pressed, the action of the computer, whatever it happens to be at the time, is interrupted and a subroutine run. It's up to you to say what subroutine this should be, and we designate that key(11) should run the subroutine *upwards*, and key(14) should run the key *downwards*. The key

```
REM Use cursor keys on numeric keypad only.
CLS
T$ = "Your Choice"
ST% = 2: NR% = 4
GOSUB startit

LOCATE 12, 2: PRINT "You chose option "; CH%
END
upwards: PS% = PS% - 1: RETURN
downwards: PS% = PS% + 1: RETURN
startit:
PRINT TAB((80 - LEN(T$)) / 2); T$
ON KEY(11) GOSUB upwards
ON KEY(14) GOSUB downwards
FOR J% = 1 TO NR%
LOCATE ST% + J% - 1, 5
READ MENU$: PRINT MENU$
NEXT: PS% = ST%
DO
  LOCATE PS%, 1: PRINT CHR$(175)
  FOR J = 1 TO 1000: NEXT
  LOCATE PS%, 1: PRINT CHR$(32)
  KEY(11) ON: KEY(14) ON
  FOR J = 1 TO 1000: NEXT
  KEY(11) OFF: KEY(14) OFF
  K$ = INKEY$
  IF K$ = CHR$(13) THEN CH% = PS% - ST% + 1: RETURN
  IF PS% > ST% + NR% - 1 THEN PS% = ST%
  IF PS% < ST% THEN PS% = ST% + NR% - 1
LOOP
DATA Input data,Output Data,Check Data,Alter Data
```

Figure 11.5. A menu routine that allows you to pick with the cursor and the ENTER key.

whose code number is 11 is the cursor up key, and the key with code 14 is the cursor down key. These are the cursor up and down keys on the *numeric keypad* – the main cursor up and down keys on a modern keyboard are reached in a different way, and can be used only if the Num Lock key is disabled, or its state tested.

note The key action is sluggish because of the delays.

Key Numbers 12 and 13 are used for cursor left and right, again on the numeric keypad only, and numbers 1 to 10 are the function keys, so that you can cause a subroutine to run by pressing one of these keys. Simply stating the subroutines for specified keys, however, does not in itself make the keys respond – for that you need on and off statements so that you can control the parts of the program in which these keys are active. Having specified these keys and their subroutines, we then start reading the menu items and printing them.

Variable ST% is used to make sure that the items are placed on the correct lines. The LOCATE command makes sure that the items are all tabbed to column number 5. At the end of setting-up, using PS%=ST% passes the value of ST% (4 in this example) to another variable PS% which is used to control the position of the arrowhead. The main DO loop prints the arrowhead, waits, deletes the arrowhead and then looks for a key being pressed while it waits. During this time, the detection of keys 11 and 14 is switched on so that if either cursor key is pressed in this interval, one of the subroutines 'upwards' or 'downwards' will be run. The INKEY$ statement then looks for the ENTER key being pressed and, if it is, the program assigns CH% and returns. The movement of the cursor, expressed as PS%, is then checked to make sure that it cannot be above or below the menu items.

The idea in the CH% calculation is that ST% is the number of the first screen line which contains a menu item, and PS% is the one that the arrow points to. If the arrow is still on the first line, PS%-ST%+1 is 1-1+1=1, if the arrow is on the second line, then PS%-ST%+1 is 2-1+1=2 and so on. If you only use the menu subroutine once, then you can substitute numbers in place of ST% and NR%. The key detection for keys 11 and 14 is on only in the interval during which the arrow is deleted. This avoids leaving an arrowhead behind when a key is pressed, but if you want greater key sensitivity, you could use the key on statements at the start of the subroutine and cancel at the end. The problem of deleting an unwanted arrow would then have to be tackled by using a LOCATE and PRINT CHR$(32) statement in each of the arrow subroutines before the value of PS% was changed.

The value of PS% is then tested. If this has gone out of limits, then it is returned to the opposite limit. If PS% would place the arrow above the top menu item, it's placed at the bottom item. If the value of PS% would put the arrow below the bottom item, then it is returned to the top. This sort of action is called *wraparound*. The loop is broken only when the ENTER is pressed. You could, of course, alter this so that the ESC or TAB or any other key operated this action. Now try it out in your own programs!

Defined functions

A subroutine of the simple type, using GOSUB and RETURN, is a hangover from older forms of BASIC, and one that is not entirely satisfactory because of its use of global variables and the way it can be run accidentally if it is not placed following the END line of a program.

A global variable, as Chapter Two noted, is one that can be used in all parts of a program, including subroutines. The advantage is that such a variable can be used by all subroutines without any special actions to make it available, but the drawback is that it might be altered unintentionally by such routines. For example, a program that contained the lines:

```
N%=15
PRINT N%
GOSUB delay
PRINT N%
.....
END
delay:
FOR N%=1 to 1000
NEXT
RETURN
```

would print out two values for N%, one before the subroutine runs and another one after because the subroutine has also used N%. When all variables are local, a program has to be written carefully, preferably by one person, to avoid this sort of thing. This goes against the grain of modern programming in which programs are written by teams, each tackling a piece, and making use of subroutines which can be used on more than one program.

Even the simplest subroutines that you write and use cannot usually be copied from one program and used unchanged on another because of the likelihood of conflicts of variables, particularly if the subroutine needs to make use of variables from the main program, alter them, and pass on their altered values.

The other problem of subroutines, the need to ensure that a subroutine is not entered by accident, is answered by placing all subroutines following the END line of a program. It would nevertheless be useful if a subroutine could be placed anywhere and was *transparent* to the main program, meaning that the program would pass over it unless it had been called using a GOSUB.

The modern form of a subroutine, called a *Procedure,* is dealt with in Chapter 12 along with other modern additions to QBASIC, but even in older versions of BASIC there was one form of routine which answered both of these criticisms of subroutines. This is the *defined function* and, although most defined functions are used for number examples their range of actions can extend to strings, making them a very useful addition to the QBASIC toolkit.

A defined function is one that you write for yourself, and the definition must be placed early in a program, before the function needs to be used. It is transparent to the main program, so that there is no need to place it at the end. QBASIC contains two such defined functions, one called FUNCTION which is not found in earlier versions of BASIC, and the other DEF FN which is extensively used in other versions. In this Chapter we shall look at the older DEF FN type.

The definition starts with DEF FN, following which you need a name, one that must not be the name of an existing function. If you pick an existing name, you will see the name appear in upper-case letters – assuming that you have sensibly used lowercase for all your typing. Following DEF FNname, there is an equality sign and, on the righthand side of this is placed the formula that will define the function. For example, this could be SQRT(a^2+b^2) which finds the square root of the sum of the squares of two numbers.

The important point about the use of a defined function like this is that it always uses *parameters* enclosed in brackets. For example, the function that is defined by:

```
DEF FNsumofsq(a , b) = SQR(a ^ 2 + b ^ 2)
```

has the letters a and b within brackets. These letters are *stand-in* variables, used because two variables are needed in the function. When the function is used, it can be called with FNsumofsq(3,4) or with FNsumofsq(x%,y%) or whatever two quantities you like; as long as there are two of them and they are numbers. This ability to specify any two variables is very valuable, and in other languages it is extended to a procedure in order to allow much more freedom in programming than BASIC normally possesses.

The variables that are used inside the defined function, a and b in this example, are local variables. Inside the function, they have the values that are passed to them when FNsumofsq is called, but if you attempt to print values outside the function you will find none. For example:

```
DEF FNsumofsq(a,b) = SQR(a ^ 2 + b ^ 2)
x%=4: y%=5
print FNsumofsq(x%,y%)
print a,b
```

will print nothing for a and b.

note One oddity is that if you type, for example, def fnsumofsq as above, the 'def' part will be converted to uppercase, but the 'fn' part will not. The operation of the function is not affected.

The quantities that are passed into a defined function are its *input parameters*, and these are represented in the example by a and b. The correct name for these is *formal parameters*, the stand-in variables, with x% and y% being the real or working parameters, the ones that the calculation is applied to. You can, however, use the same variable names of a and b for the quantities that you pass to the function – because the a and b that are used in their function are local, there is no confusion.

The quantity that is passed out from the defined function is obtained from the function itself, by using k = FNsumofsq(x%,y%) or, as in the example, a PRINT statement. There is no provision in this simple form for passing more than one quantity out from the defined function.

With all that out of the way, it's time to look at some more examples. When a defined function is used with numbers, it is defined with a number form of name like DEF FNsumofall(a,b,c,d) or DEF FNaverage(a,b,c,d) and so on. When a defined function has to return a string (not necessarily using strings as its input) its name must include the dollar sign, such as DEF FNstringbits$(a$,b%). An example will make this more clear:

```
DEF FNbitofstring$ (A$, n%) = UCASE$(LEFT$(A$, n%))
CLS
A$ = "this is a test string"
FOR n% = 1 TO LEN(A$)
  PRINT FNbitofstring$(A$, n%)
NEXT
```

Figure 11.6. A defined function whose input is a string and an integer, and whose output is a string.

note The important point here is that a function whose output is a string must be a string function, with the $ sign at the end of the name, and one which provides a number output is a plain number defined function. It is not the inputs that determine whether the defined function is a string one or a number one, only the output.

More advanced DEF FN

The original type of defined function was a considerable improvement on older methods when it started to appear in BASIC around 1979, but it suffers from the handicap of requiring the whole action to be described in one statement on one line. QBASIC allows an extended form of DEF FN to be used, which follows the same scheme as many other functions by marking a start and an end, and containing as many lines as you like between these two. This allows very much more to be accomplished in a defined function.

note: This should not be confused with the more advanced FUNCTION which is also available, see Chapter 12.

As an example, one function that is very useful in engineering is the *cartesian to polar* function, which is used in the process of converting a position in x,y cartesian form into polar form which consists of a distance and an angle. Figure 11.7 shows the relationships between the two systems of specifying the position of a point P. The angle is the angle of the direction of the point P from the origin, measured to the x-axis. The distance from the origin to P is given by the root of the squares of the x and y coordinates, and the angle is found from using ATN.

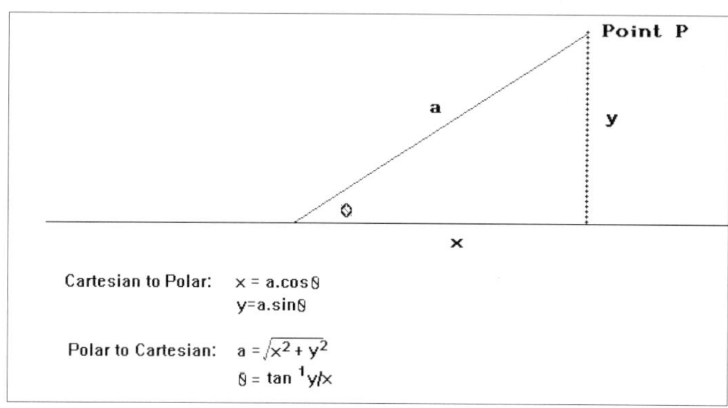

Figure 11.7. The connection between cartesian and polar coordinates.

Electrical AC theory makes considerable use of polar notation for amplitude and phase, and some geometric and navigational formulae require positions to be specified in polar coordinates, using a distance and an angle found in this way. The example of Figure 11.8 shows the calculation done in a straightforward piece of program and also by using the extended form of defined function.

The more interesting part of this example is the extended defined function, taking up the lines between the DEF part and the END DEF. The contents are much as they would be for a Procedure (see Chapter 12) and all variables other than those contained in brackets are local, so that, in this example, printing quantities 'lg' and 'theta' outside the defined function would return zero values. Note also that the defined function is called by assignment to a dummy variable 'a' which is not used and which has zero value.

```
CLS
CONST rad = 180 / 3.1416
INPUT "X and Y values"; a, b
PRINT "R is "; SQR(a ^ 2 + b ^ 2)
PRINT "Angle is "; ATN(b / a); " radians"
DEF fncarpol (x, y)
    lg = SQR(x ^ 2 + y ^ 2)
    theta = ATN(y / x) * rad
    PRINT "Size is "; lg
    PRINT "Angle is "; theta; " degrees"
END DEF
a = FNcarpol(a, b)
```

Figure 11.8. An extended form of define function.

Since the function prints the values of lg and theta as they exist inside the function you can add a line:

```
PRINT lg, theta
```

following the last line to establish the important point that lg and theta have no values outside the function. The principle of local variables is very important, because it allows a function like this to be copied from one program to another without the need to alter any of the internal lines. The variables that are used inside the function cannot be in conflict with variables used outside, because they are local to the function. When the function is called, the values in the variables a and b are transferred to the local variables x and y. The values of a and b cannot be changed by the function, not even if the function used local variables called a and b.

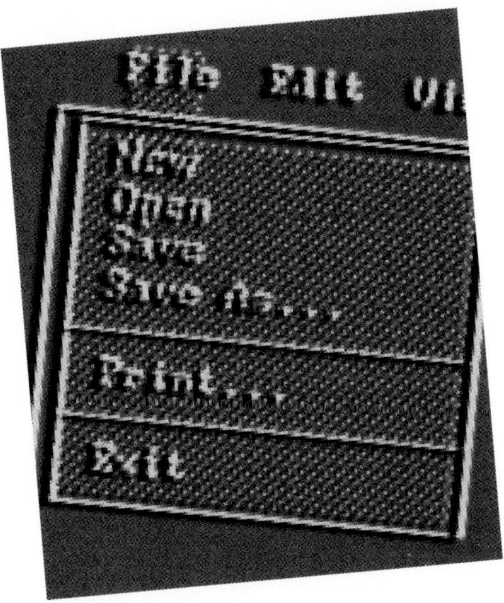

Procedures, Advanced Functions and Select Case

The QBASIC statements that are the subject of this Chapter are all modern enhancements of BASIC, intended to bring the language into line with the many other modern programming languages. In particular, they allow you to write in BASIC programs which are tightly organised as they would be in a good version of PASCAL – if that is what you want. You can, of course, opt to use QBASIC as you might once have used GW-BASIC but, if you do so, you are missing a lot. The use of the more advanced features isn't easy but, once you have mastered the methods, you'll be reluctant to go back to the older methods.

Old style BASIC forces you to use only the types that are provided, which are sometimes only integer, single and string, along with arrays of each. Other languages are often not too generous with data types, often omitting the string type, but most of them allow you to define a data type of your own. This is also possible in QBASIC, and having declared a type of your own, you can declare variables of that type, either scalar (single) or array. Figure 12.1 shows a type being created and used.

```
CLS
TYPE oneday
  daynr AS INTEGER
  monr AS INTEGER
  notes AS STRING * 80
  END TYPE

REM watch size of array - must not exceed 64K
REM Put some values in

DIM page(1 TO 365) AS oneday
page(1).daynr = 1
page(1).monr = 1
page(1).notes = "Happy New Year"
page(32).daynr = 1
page(32).monr = 2
page(32).notes = "First of February celebrations"

REM Show values printed

n% = 1
PRINT page(n%).daynr; "/"; page(n%).monr; "/1993 - ";
page(n%).notes
```

Figure 12.1. A type being defined and used as an array variable.

The TYPE must be defined in terms of existing types. This does not restrict you to just INTEGER, LONG, SINGLE, DOUBLE and STRING because, if you defined one type, it could be used as a type in a second TYPE definition. The definition starts with the keyword TYPE followed by the name of the type. The next few lines then define what elements make up this type; in this example they are two integers and a string. Unusually, the maximum length of the string must be stated following the asterisk sign. The definition of the new type ends with the keywords END TYPE.

note If you are going to use an array variable of this type, you must check that it will fit inside 64K. In this example, the string will be of 80 bytes and the integers of 2 bytes each, so that the array size for a 365-page array will be around 365 x 84, which is 30660 – well within the limit of 65536. You will get an error message if you try to run when the array is too large.

The next point concerns the declaration and use of an array of this type – a single variable follows much the same pattern. The DIM line makes the array consist of elements from 1 to 365, because page(0) would be meaningless in this context. For any single element of the array, such as page(1), the component parts are referred to by using a dot followed by the component name as defined for the type, so that page(1).daynr refers to the day number for page(1), an integer, and page(32).notes refers to the string for the 1st of February.

The use of a type that you have defined for yourself allows you to create variables that contain more than one piece of information, and these variables can be scalar or array. This is particularly useful for filing purposes, see Chapters 18 and 19, and can replace the older methods that are used for filing purposes.

The user-defined type is called a RECORD in some programming languages.

Procedures

The simple GOSUB...RETURN type of subroutine has the drawbacks of using global variables and of not being transparent to the program, see Chapter 10. This has made older forms of BASIC look very primitive compared to other programming languages which have used better forms of subroutine right from the beginning, and QBASIC allows you to make use of a much improved form, a procedure whose keywords are CALL, SUB and END SUB. There are several ways in which these can be used, so it's important to approach the use of these by way of simple examples at first – an entire program written in this form will be illustrated later. In this book we will call the QBASIC procedures *Subs* to distinguish them from the older type of subroutines.

Each Sub is programmed separately from the Main program. The Editor maintains them in alphabetical order allowing you to edit and even delete them as required. All this is done to emphasise that a Sub is a isolated piece of program that can be called up when required, but which does not depend heavily on the main program.

An important point to remember about QBASIC procedures or Subs is that their variables are local unless you decide otherwise. What you may need to determine is just how local they are, and this is a point that can often cause confusion.

The syntax is straightforward enough. A Sub is defined by the word SUB followed by a name (following the usual conventions for naming anything within QBASIC) and the definition is ended by END SUB. These lines are transparent – they are ignored when the program runs – so there is no need to place them following the end of the main program. The Sub is called by using the word CALL followed by using the name that has been typed in the definition. You can call another Sub from within a Sub, but you cannot define another Sub inside a Sub. Figure 12.2 shows an example that illustrates the local and global variables aspect of a Sub and a main program.

```
DECLARE SUB demo ()CLS
DIM SHARED n%
n% = 10
CALL demo
PRINT "a% outside is"; a%
PRINT "b% outside is"; b%
END

SUB demo
  a% = 2 * n%
  b% = 3 * n%
  PRINT "a% inside is"; a%
    PRINT "b% inside is"; b%
END SUB
```

Figure 12.2. A demonstration of a SUB using one global variable and two local variables.

Note that when you type the definition SUB demo, you are taken to a new screen of the Editor – return to the main program by using the View – Subs menu (press the F2 key). The SUB is placed following the main program by the Editor no matter where you type it.

A SUB must *not* start with a blank line. If you try to put in a blank line the Editor will convert it into a comment line.

In this example, the variable n% is made global, something that is not necessary when you are using GOSUB...RETURN subroutines. The line that makes n% global is:

```
DIM SHARED n%
```

which ensures that any Sub can use variable n% and alter its value.

By contrast, the variables a% and b% in the Sub are local variables. They are assigned values in the Sub, which are printed, but once the Sub has ended these values no longer exist. This is the same sort of use of local variables as we saw illustrated for DEF FN in Chapter 10.

Once the program has been saved, the line:

```
DECLARE SUB demo ()
```

will have been put in by the Editor though you may prefer to type it in yourself. When this line appears, you can alter the CALL demo line to:

```
demo
```

omitting the CALL. This is optional, and you may feel more at home using CALL to mark the place where the Sub is called.

Now take a look at Figure 12.3 (overleaf). This uses another Sub, demo2, that is called from the first one, demo, to emphasise the points about local and global variables. The variable n% is truly global – it is printed from within demo2 to prove it. The variables a% and b% which exist in demo however, do not exist in demo2. They are local to demo and are not passed on or made available to demo2 in any way.

The point about how local is local is an important one, and we need to look deeper into it. Figure 12.4 shows a small change made in the way that these routines are arranged.

In Figure 12.4 (overleaf), the printout that you see when the program runs reflects the effect of declaring variables a% and b% as being SHARED in the Sub demo. You might expect that SHARED would have the effect of making a% and b% available to the demo2 Sub which is called from demo, just as declaring n% as SHARED in the main routine causes n% to be available in both demo and demo2. The opposite is true. By using SHARED a%, b% as the first line in Sub demo, we make it possible for a% and b% to pass values *back* to the main program. These variables are now shared with the program that called demo, not the one that demo calls.

The important difference between these two is that n% has been declared in a DIM SHARED statement. You are not allowed to use a DIM SHARED statement in a Sub, so that this cannot be used to allow variables to be passed on the Sub demo2. You can use DIM in a Sub, but not with SHARED.

```
DECLARE SUB demo2 ()
DECLARE SUB demo ()
CLS
DIM SHARED n%
n% = 10
CALL demo
PRINT "a% outside is"; a%
PRINT "b% outside is"; b%
END

SUB demo
  a% = 2 * n%
  b% = 3 * n%
  PRINT "a% inside demo is"; a%
  PRINT "b% inside demo is"; b%
  CALL demo2
END SUB
SUB demo2
  PRINT "n% in demo2 is "; n%
  PRINT "a% in demo2 is "; a%
  PRINT "b% in demo2 is "; b%
END SUB
```

Figure 12.3. The variable n% is global to the new subroutine, but variables a% and b% are not passed on.

The summary so far is:

1. Any variable used in a Sub is purely local to that Sub unless it has been declared as SHARED.
2. A SHARED variable is only shared with the main program, not with any other called program.
3. A global variable created using DIM SHARED in the main program is available to *all* Sub procedures.
4. You cannot use a DIM SHARED statement in a Sub.

```
DECLARE SUB demo2 ()
DECLARE SUB demo ()
CLS
DIM SHARED n%
n% = 10
CALL demo
PRINT "a% outside is"; a%
PRINT "b% outside is"; b%
END

SUB demo
  SHARED a%, b%
  a% = 2 * n%
  b% = 3 * n%
  PRINT "a% inside demo is"; a%
  PRINT "b% inside demo is"; b%
  CALL demo2
END SUB

SUB demo2
PRINT "n% in demo2 is "; n%
PRINT "a% in demo2 is "; a%
PRINT "b% in demo2 is "; b%

END SUB
```

Figure 12.4. Using SHARED for declaring variables a% and b% has an effect you might not expect.

The next step to look at is how to pass quantities to and from Subs without using global declarations in the main program. Figure 12.5 (overleaf) shows how this is done. Each Sub is called and defined with a dummy variable (a formal variable) name or names in brackets. The DECLARE, CALL and SUB lines must all match. Use the Editor's Search-Change action for doing this if you are working on elaborate programs.

```
DECLARE SUB demo2 (p%, q%)
DECLARE SUB demo (x%)
CLS
n% = 10
CALL demo(n%)
PRINT "a% outside is"; a%
PRINT "b% outside is"; b%
END

SUB demo (x%)
  a% = 2 * x%
  b% = 3 * x%
  PRINT "a% inside demo is"; a%
  PRINT "b% inside demo is"; b%
  CALL demo2(a%, b%)
END SUB

SUB demo2 (p%, q%)
  PRINT "n% in demo2 is "; n%
  PRINT "p% in demo2 is "; p%
  PRINT "q% in demo2 is "; q%
END SUB
```

Figure 12.5. Passing variables between Subs without using global variables.

In this example, the printout appears as:

```
a% inside demo is 20
b% inside demo is 30
n% in demo2 is 0
p% in demo2 is 20
q% in demo2 is 30
a% outside is 0
b% outside is 0
```

and the logic of it all is as follows.By calling demo(n%), the value of n% is transferred to the local internal variable of x%, which is not shared in any way. In Sub demo, values of a% and b% are calculated, and by using CALL demo2(a%,b%) these values are transferred to the local variables p% and q% in Sub demo2. In this Sub, a% and b% have no meaning, but p% and q% hold the values that have been passed on.

When a SUB is declared, the type of each parameter can also be declared if you are not using the distinguishing characters (such as $,!,%,&,#). The form of declaration is:

```
DECLARE SUB trial (name AS STRING, month AS INTEGER)
```

The types can be INTEGER, LONG, SINGLE, DOUBLE, STRING, a user-defined type or ANY. Specifying ANY allows a variable to be used for any declared type.

This deals with passing values on, but what of passing them back? Figure 12.6 shows one method, in which the variable r% in Sub demo2 is made available to Sub demo by including it as one of the parameter list in CALL demo(p%,q%,r%):

```
DECLARE SUB demo2 (p%, q%, r%)
DECLARE SUB demo (x%)
CLS
n% = 10
CALL demo(n%)
PRINT "a% outside is"; a%
PRINT "b% outside is"; b%
END

SUB demo (x%)

  a% = 2 * x%
  b% = 3 * x%
  PRINT "a% inside demo is"; a%
  PRINT "b% inside demo is"; b%
  CALL demo2(a%, b%, c%)
  PRINT "c% in demo (after demo2) is "; c%
END SUB

SUB demo2 (p%, q%, r%)
PRINT "n% in demo2 is "; n%
PRINT "a% in demo2 is "; p%
PRINT "b% in demo2 is "; q%
r% = p% + q%
PRINT "r% in demo2 is "; r%
END SUB
```

Figure 12.6. Returning a value by using a variable in the parameter list.

In this program, printing the value of c% in Sub demo gives the value of 50 that has been passed back as formal parameter r% in the parameter list. We can therefore place items in this list for passing back as well as for passing on, provided that the assignments are made in the Sub.

Another method of passing a values back is shown here using SHARED in the Sub in which a variable is created:

```
DECLARE SUB demo2 (p%, q%)
DECLARE SUB demo (x%)
CLS
n% = 10
CALL demo(n%)
PRINT "a% outside is"; a%
PRINT "b% outside is"; b%
END

SUB demo (x%)
  a% = 2 * x%
  b% = 3 * x%
  PRINT "a% inside demo is"; a%
  PRINT "b% inside demo is"; b%
  CALL demo2(a%, b%)
  PRINT "c% in demo (after demo2) is "; c%
END SUB

SUB demo2 (p%, q%)
SHARED c%
PRINT "n% in demo2 is "; n%
PRINT "a% in demo2 is "; p%
PRINT "b% in demo2 is "; q%
r% = p% + q%
PRINT "r% in demo2 is "; r%
c% = r%
END SUB
```

Figure 12.7. Passing a value back by way of a SHARED variable declared in the Sub where is it assigned.

In this example, the SHARED c% statement is in the Sub demo2 which is called by Sub demo, called in turn by the main routine. When the print out appears, however, it is evident that c% has no value in Sub demo, it is still a local variable. It does, however, have a value back in the main routine. Using SHARED in a Sub does not necessarily make a variable available to the routine that called the Sub, only to the Main program (it might, of course, be the main program which called the Sub). Local variables stay determinedly local unless you are generous with your SHARED declarations – try adding SHARED c% into the Sub demo lines.

Can we pass a variable value down to a Sub called from a Sub by using SHARED? The answer is 'No' – we can only use SHARED to pass a value back to the Main program not forward to a new subroutine. If you want values passed forward you must either use global variables in the Main program, or parameters in the Sub.

There is another twist to passing a value back. When we call up a Sub in the form CALL routine (variable list), the list of variables is enclosed in brackets, such as:

```
CALL sumitall (a%,b%,c%,d,e,f)
```

and if any of these variables is changed within the Sub, this changed value will be available to the part of the program that called the Sub. In the example above, if a% is 5 when the Sub is called and 10 when it ends, the value of a% will be 10 in the program after the Sub has been run.

There is another way of calling a Sub, however, by using the name only. This is not possible until DECLARE SUB lines have been placed at the start of the main program. Once these lines have been created, you can use either 'CALL subname' or just 'subname' as you please. There is an important syntax difference, however. When you use 'CALL subname' each variable name *must* be enclosed in brackets. When you use 'subname' you should normally not enclose variable names in brackets. If you put brackets round a variable name for a subroutine called in this way, that variable will not have a changed value passed back. This is illustrated in Figure 12.8 (overleaf).

```
a% = 5
Sub1 a%
PRINT "After Sub1, a% is"; a%
SUB2 (a%)
PRINT "After Sub2, a% is"; a%

SUB Sub1 (a%)
a% = a% * 2
PRINT "Sub1 has changed a% to"; a%
END SUB

SUB SUB2 (a%)
a% = 2 * a%
PRINT "Sub2 has changed a% to"; a%
END SUB
```

Figure 12.8. Preventing a variable from being exported from a Sub by enclosing its name in brackets.

The DECLARE SUB lines in this program have been created when the program was first saved, and the calls to the Subs are being made by using the Sub names only. The difference is that Sub1 is followed by the variable name without brackets, and Sub2 is followed by the variable name within brackets. When this runs, you can see that both subroutines alter the value of a%, but Sub1 returns the altered value and Sub2 does not.

If you do not want to make use of this facility, it is better to stick with the CALL Sub1 type of call.

Passing arrays

An array variable can be passed to a Sub as easily as any other variable, but the syntax needs to be noted. When a Sub is defined, any array variable that it will use should have its name declared and followed by empty brackets. The Editor will remove any number you place between the brackets. In addition, when a call is made using an array, the brackets should be empty, so that you use lines such as:

```
CALL (a$()) or just a$()
CALL NAMEADDR$() or just NAMEADDR$()
```

depending on which way you want to call the Subs:

```
DECLARE SUB Sub1 (a$(), b$())
REM Passing arrays   CLS
DIM a$(5)
DIM b$(2, 2)
FOR j% = 0 TO 5
  READ a$(j%)
NEXT
FOR j% = 0 TO 2
  FOR k% = 0 TO 2
    READ b$(j%, k%)
  NEXT
NEXT
CALL Sub1(a$(), b$())
PRINT a$(5)
PRINT b$(1, 1)
END
DATA arc, base,chapter,delta,effort,find
DATA abacus,basic,carol,destined,element,force,
ginger,hotel,ink

SUB Sub1 (a$(), b$())
a$(5) = "CHANGED"
b$(1, 1) = "ALSO CHANGED"
END SUB
```

Figure 12.9. Passing array values to a Sub, using empty brackets in the CALL statement and also in the definition.

On occasions, you may want to pass a single array value, and this is done by specifying a value within the array brackets, so that:

```
CALL Alterit(a$(4))
```

will use a Sub called Alterit to work on A$(4), one item in an array.

Note: An array can be static or dynamic, and one way of determining the difference is to use the DIM statement. Using DIM a$(25), for example, makes A$() a static array. Using something like DIM a$(b%), where b% has been assigned with a number, makes the array dynamic. An array that has been declared using COMMON is also dynamic unless it has been dimensioned as STATIC. For the differences between static and dynamic arrays, see Chapters Two and 10.

With that lot out of the way, we can now look at other variants on Sub use, in particular at STATIC variables. The usual subroutine variables are local unless declared otherwise, and they have no value outside the Sub. In normal use, this means that these variables are created afresh each time the Sub is called.

This is not always desirable, sometimes we need to have a variable in a Sub which will keep its value from one call to another, even though this value is not available outside the Sub. This is possible by declaring the variable as STATIC. Static storage of a variable means that it is stored in the main memory of the computer throughout a program. The more usual storage of local variables is in temporary memory, the *Stack memory,* which is used during the Sub and cleared out at the end of the Sub.

Figure 12.10 shows the essential difference. In Sub1, the variable j% is printed and incremented. The value at the time of printing will be 0 because no other values has been assigned, and after printing the incrementing action changes this to 1. This values, however, is lost along with j% itself when the Sub ends, so that each time Sub1 is called, the value of j% is printed as 0.

```
DECLARE SUB sub1 ()
DECLARE SUB sub2 ()
CLS
REM Static and dynamic
PRINT "Start here"
FOR n% = 1 TO 10
CALL sub1
CALL sub2
SLEEP 1
REM time delay
NEXT

SUB sub1
PRINT "Value of counter j% is"; j%; "in Sub1"
j% = j% + 1
END SUB

SUB sub2
STATIC j%
PRINT "value of j% in Sub2 is"; j%
j% = j% + 1
END SUB
```

Figure 12.10. Demonstrating the difference between a dynamic and a static variable.

By contrast, in Sub2, j% is declared as STATIC. At the end of the Sub, the value that has been assigned to j% is saved even though the variable itself no longer exists, and when Sub2 is called again, this value is restored, as the printout shows.

A variable that has been declared as STATIC in a Sub is nevertheless still a local variable, with no value in any other part of the program – try adding a PRINT j% to the main routine.

You can also declare a whole Sub as being STATIC, in which case all of its variable values will be preserved for the next time it is called.

The QBASIC FUNCTION

In Chapter 10 we said that the simple BASIC DEF FN could be extended in QBASIC to a more useful form which allowed the definition to extend over several lines. This stretches the use of DEF FN considerably, but QBASIC also allows the use of a FUNCTION which extends the idea rather further and corresponds to the FUNCTION type used in other programming languages.

A FUNCTION is defined and used in a way that is very similar to a Sub, so that this description does not need to be extensive. The name of the Function can carry a marker such as $, !, # and so on to indicate the type of data that the Function will return. You can declare a Function as STATIC, so that its variable values are preserved from one call to the next, though all are local to the Function. The inputs to the function are contained in the parameter list that follows the name, and the output is decided by a line of the form:

```
variable name = expression
```

within the Function. The end of the Function definition is marked by END FUNCTION, and such a Function is transparent to the program.

Figure 12.11 illustrates a Function of this type being created and used. When you want to type in the statements of the Function, use the Edit menu of the QBASIC Editor and select New FUNCTION.

```
DECLARE FUNCTION geteqn! (a!, b!, c!)
REM Using a FUNCTION
CLS
a = 2.5
b = 5.4
c = 2.2
y = geteqn(a, b, c)
PRINT "Y is"; y
END

FUNCTION geteqn (a, b, c)
  REM Solve equation
  geteqn = a ^ 2 + 6 * b + c
END FUNCTION
```

Figure 12.11. Declaring and using a Function. Note that the value is passed back by using an assignment to the name of the Function, and that a line in the Function must also make this assignment.

As for a Sub, the DECLARE statement is put in by the Editor when the program is saved for the first time. The use of the ! marker is not essential, because the single-precision number variable is the default. You must use suitable names for string and other types, however.

note The function is called by assigning its name to a variable, or by using a 'PRINT function_name' type of statement.

Using SELECT...CASE

The third of these advanced statements is SELECT...CASE, which is used for menus in place of the ON K% GOSUB type of action. The reason is that SELECT CASE is considerably easier to use for most menu actions, and it allows a better range of traps for unsuitable entries to be built in, reducing the amount of checking that you would need to do otherwise.

Figure 12.12 shows this method being used for a conventional type of menu in which an item is referred to by number – this has been cut to the bare minimum to concentrate on the use of SELECT CASE. The variable that is used for selection is N%, so that the menu lines start with SELECT CASE N%, the syntax for starting this type of action.

```
CLS
PRINT "Please pick by number, range 1 to 3, 0 to end"
DO
  INPUT N%
  SELECT CASE N%

    CASE IS < 1
      EXIT DO

    CASE IS = 1
      PRINT "First choice"

    CASE IS = 2
      PRINT "Second choice"

    CASE IS = 3
      PRINT "Third choice"

    CASE IS > 3
      PRINT "Out of range - please try again."
  END SELECT
LOOP
```

Figure 12.12. A SELECT...CASE menu incorporated in a loop. Note that testing for variable range is part of the SELECT...CASE action.

There is a difference between SELECT...CASE and ON n% GOSUB. SELECT...CASE allows much more flexible checking of the value of the variable; in lines that start with CASE IS and then perform a test using any of the usual operators such as <, > and = in any combination. This has been emphasised in this example by using SELECT...CASE within a DO loop, so that each action can be carried out and then the menu re-used by way of the DO...LOOP statement. The first test in the example is CASE IS < 1, which allows you to leave the loop for any input that is less than unity, zero or a negative integer. We can use CASE IS > 3 to continue the loop for any input that is outside the range. SELECT...CASE can be used without the DO...LOOP construction, but by using the loop the menu can be made a central part of a program, with every subroutine or procedure that is called returning to it.

If SELECT...CASE is not enclosed in a loop, making a choice will end the SELECT...CASE when any subroutine that has been called returns.

You can use CASE ELSE much as you use ELSE in an IF statement to account for choices that are not included in the list. One benefit of using SELECT..CASE is that the choice is not necessarily determined by numbers. You can use letters or words to make your choices, as shown in Figure 12.13 below:

```
DECLARE SUB savit ()
DECLARE SUB usit ()
DECLARE SUB setitup ()
CLS
PRINT "please select by name -"
PRINT "setup, use, record, leave"
INPUT reply$
SELECT CASE reply$
  CASE IS = "setup"
    CALL setitup
  CASE IS = "use"
    CALL usit
  CASE IS = "record"
    CALL savit
  CASE ELSE
    PRINT "No choice made"
END SELECT

SUB savit
PRINT "Saving file"
END SUB

SUB setitup
PRINT "Set up being done"
END SUB

SUB usit
PRINT "Using routine"
END SUB
```

Figure 12.13. Illustrating the use of SELECT..CASE using names rather than numbers, and using CASE ELSE to cater for any other entries.

In this example, the reply is a string, and the SELECT...CASE construction also uses the strings for selection. Any replay that is not recognised comes into the CASE ELSE category, and in a real-life program this would be used to make the choice repeat in a loop.

You could make your reply string each of the same length and use INPUT$(number) in place of INPUT.

Working with Numbers

Translating formulae

The earliest computer programming languages were for scientific and engineering use. Translating formulae so that the computer could deal with them was a very important feature. It was so important, in fact, that one of the main languages in the early days was called FORTRAN, which was an abbreviation of FORmula TRANslation. FORTRAN is still used, and the BASIC language which is used by all microcomputers is considerably based on the ideas and methods of FORTRAN. For this reason, BASIC is a language not to be despised if your needs or interests are in programming of this type.

A lot of languages that are more highly regarded either by academics or for business use are grossly inferior to BASIC at working with formulae, and even worse at handling strings. If you haven't had some practice, however, it's not always straightforward to convert a formula written in a reference book into the form of a BASIC expression. The order in which the terms of the formulae are written will not usually be the order in which you want them evaluated, so you must either change the order or make use of brackets to obtain the correct expression.

Examples are very helpful here, but one person's example is another's confusion, so please bear with me if the formulae that you want to use are not shown here. Remember that you don't have to derive the formulae for yourself for most purposes, you simply take them from a reference book. You need to know, of course, what variable values have to be supplied, and what the formula does, and you also need to know any limitations, but in general this is all. You get into a different league when you start to generate your own formulae.

We'll take as our first example the formula for calculating the volume of a sector of a sphere, shown in Figure 13.1(a). Like many formulae, this uses no sign for multiplication. Quantities that are printed together are intended to be multiplied, so that the formula requires you to multiply 2 by Π by the value of r(squared) by h, and then divide the answer by 3. Note that this uses the constant pi, which can be assigned with a value of 3.14159265. Now in the expression, there is one power taken, and this action will have precedence no matter where we put it. It makes sense, in any case, to start with this item, getting the value of r squared. Suppose that we use variable names R and H, then the expression that is shown in Figure 13.1(b) is the BASIC expression for evaluating the formula.

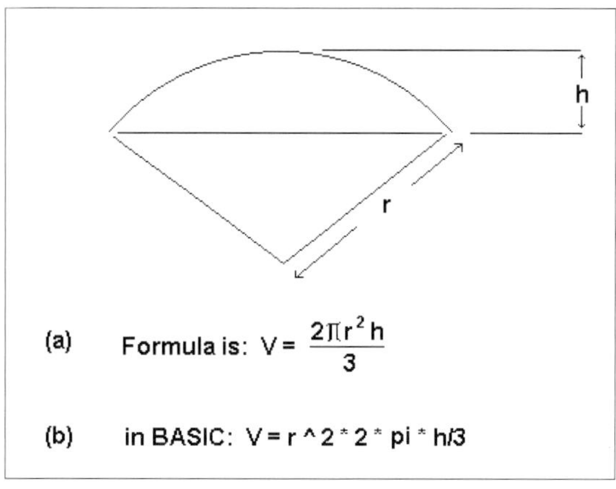

h
r
(a) Formula is: $V = \frac{2\Pi r^2 h}{3}$
(b) in BASIC: V = r ^ 2 * 2 * pi * h/3

Figure 13.1 A formula (a) and its BASIC equivalent (b).

The variable V is used for volume, and the main point to note is that we have to insert the multiplication * and division / signs that BASIC demands. Because all the operations apart from finding the square are of equal precedence, we can write the rest of the expression from left to right and be reasonably confident that it will work as planned. However, if you are in any doubt, try a few examples with simple numbers and check that you get what you expect. In this example, the answers will always have more places of decimals that you would expect, and we'll look at how to round them off later. This business of testing with numbers whose result you already know is important, because unless you do this, the results of your programs can be totally misleading – and you won't know!

The real problems come when the formula is not in the form that you want. If you have a smattering of algebra then you may be able to rearrange the formula to suit. We can't in this book, cover all the mathematical actions of formula rearrangement except to give one example of where it is needed, and how it is done. Suppose that you want to draw out the shape of an ellipse on the screen. If you make use of x and y coordinate numbers, then you can choose a set of x numbers, and find the y numbers that will give positions on the ellipse. The formula for the ellipse, however, will be shown in books in the form of Figure 13.2(a)0. To be useful, we need this in the form y = ... and the steps for changing into this form are shown in Figure 13.2(b).

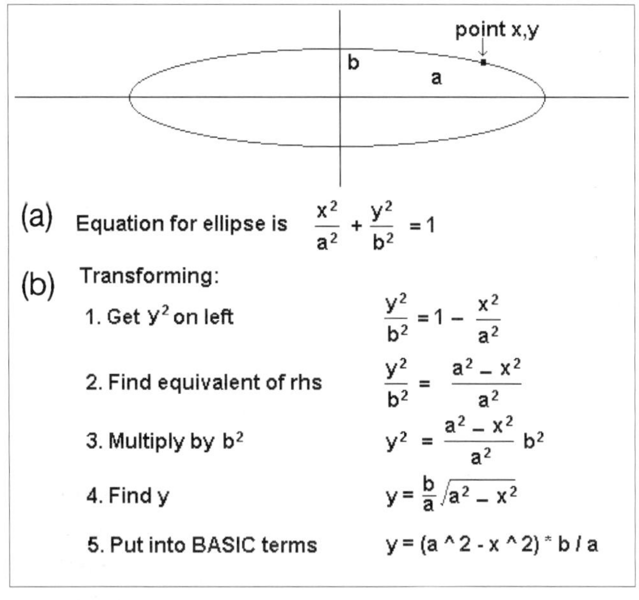

Figure 13.2 A textbook formula (a) and the process of changing the variable (b).

Once we get to the final form, however, we can write the expression that we need, which is:

```
Y=(A^2-X^2)^0.5*B/A
```

and this is the expression that we shall use to find each value of Y for a given value of X. Remember that a set of X values ranging from 0 to A will give only one quarter of the ellipse corresponding to both A and B positive. For the other parts, you need to consider the results of +A and -B, -A and +B and -A and -B. If you want to draw an ellipse or any other geometrical figure, Chapters 20 and 21 contain the instructions.

A very common requirement if you are working with probability in statistics is the factorial of a number. This is obtained from a formula in which the number is multiplied by the number one less, and then by the next number down, and so on down to 1. For example factorial 5, written as 5! is 5*4*3*2*1. Another way of writing this is that 5!=5*4!, and this leads to a method of finding factorial by what is called *recursion*, repeating a formula. If we keep to simple BASIC, then the factorial of a number X can be found from a routine such as is shown in the example of Figure 13.3.

```
  CLS
INPUT "Number"; x%
IF x% <= 0 THEN PRINT "Unsuitable number": END
GOSUB fact
PRINT j%
END

fact:
j% = x%: IF j% = 1 THEN RETURN
FOR n% = x% TO 2 STEP -1
  j% = j% * (x% - 1): x% = x% - 1
NEXT
RETURN
```

Figure 13.3. A routine which calculates a factorial using straightforward methods.

The important point here is to ensure that if the number X% is 1, then the factorial value is also 1, and this is done by the test in the first line of the subroutine. The method that is shown must test for the number being zero, negative, or fractional, because the factorial function is meaningless for such quantities.

The recursive version of this is shown in Figure 13.4. Recursion is the action of a subroutine calling itself. An old joke is that the Computing Dictionary's entry for recursion is:

Recursion – See Recursion

Such an action was not possible in older versions of BASIC, one of its features that was greatly criticised by academics. The plain fact, however, is that recursion is never (well, hardly ever) really needed and most programmers would not notice if they were no longer allowed to use it.

```
  CLS
INPUT "Number"; x%
j% = 1
IF x% <= 0 THEN PRINT "Unsuitable number": END
GOSUB fact
PRINT j%
END
fact:
j% = j% * x%
x% = x% - 1
  IF x% > 1 THEN GOSUB fact
RETURN
```

Figure 13.4. A recursive solution, which will bomb out if you pick too large a number, anything more than seven.

One of the problems of using recursion is that it piles up a set of GOSUBs all waiting for their RETURN statements. This is done using a piece of memory set aside for the purpose and called the Stack. In this example, any more than seven nested GOSUBs will make the stack overflow, stopping the program.

note As far as factorials are concerned, a lot of time and trouble in calculating factorials of numbers greater than 10 can be saved by using Stirling's formula:

$$x! = x^x e^{-x} \sqrt{2\pi x}$$

Figure 13.5 shows this in use with the expression evaluated using natural logarithms as QBASIC does not provide for ordinary base ten logs. This avoids having to evaluate large powers.

```
CLS
CONST pi = 3.1416
REM Can use more decimal places for pi
INPUT "integer number (10 or more)"; n%
IF n% < 10 THEN PRINT "Formula inexact for this
number": END
GOSUB stirling
PRINT "Value is"; fact
END

stirling:
logfact = n% * LOG(n%) - n% + .5 * LOG(2 * pi * n%)
fact = EXP(logfact)
RETURN
```

Figure 13.5. A routine that uses Stirling's formula for a large factorial – this is accurate to better than 1% for numbers of 10 or greater.

Finally in this section, we need to look at what has to be done if the formula is in the shape of a series. A series means that the result is found by using a loop, adding up a set of terms that are obtained from an expression. A series of this type is used to evaluate many quantities that are not usually provided as functions in small computers. For example, the series for evaluating the inverse hyperbolic tangent is:

$$\text{arctanh}(x) = x + \frac{x^3}{3} + \frac{x^5}{5} + \frac{x^7}{7} + \frac{x^9}{9} + \ldots$$

If you don't know what this means you'll feel better for not asking. The point is that the quantity can be found by substituting a value for the variable x and finding a value for the series.

The trouble with any kind of series like this is knowing where to stop, because most series like this are infinite. A practical, though arbitrary, solution is to continue until the term that you are evaluating adds less then 1% to the total value. This requires a loop which cannot be of the FOR...NEXT type, since the number of repetitions cannot be fixed in advance. Figure 13.6 shows a suitable subroutine for this particular series, but note that this series converges only when the value of X is 1 or less.

```
CLS
CONST pi = 3.1416
INPUT "Number (less than 1)"; x
IF x >= 1 THEN PRINT "Impossible to evaluate": END
GOSUB series
PRINT "Angle is "; w; " radians"
PRINT "which is "; 180 * w / pi; " degrees"
END
series:
w = x: n% = 3
DO WHILE (x ^ n% > w / 100)
  w = w + (x ^ n%) / n%
  n% = n% + 2
LOOP: RETURN
```

Figure 13.6 A series for calculating an inverse hyperbolic tangent, put into the form of a QBASIC subroutine.

If X>1, then each term is larger than the one before it, and the total keeps growing until it becomes too large for the computer to store. This is a common thing to look out for in series, particular series for trigonometric functions, and it's always a good idea to put a trap for an illegal number in the subroutine, as has been done here – it prevents a long wait from being ended by an OVERFLOW error notice. Even if you avoid 1, however, the series can take impossibly long times to evaluate, as you will find out if you try it with 0.9, 0.99, 0.999 and 0.9999 . It's likely that your patience will run out on the last of these, so you might like to alter the trapping to include numbers of this size also.

Functions

Quantities such as trigonometrical ratios, square roots, hexadecimal equivalents and so on are dealt with in QBASIC by the use of functions. To remind you, a function of a number is a quantity that is obtained by the use of various actions on the number. The number (or a variable that takes number values) is called the *argument* of the function, and for many functions has to be enclosed in brackets. These functions can include operations in sequence and the summing of one or more series. In the computing sense, functions can also include actions on strings, and the main thing that they have in common is that the function uses a statement word (not a symbol) and that it needs an operand or argument, which can be a number or a string depending on the type of function.

The main number functions are listed in Figure 13.8 (opposite), along with their effects. The trigonometric functions on this list merit particular attention, because they cause a lot of trouble to programmers who are working with trigonometrical formulae. These formulae are often the simplest way of obtaining certain graphics effects including drawing graphs. The functions that are most used are SIN, COS and TAN, all of which are provided in QBASIC. What you need to watch, however, is that each of these functions needs an argument which is an angle in radians. If you are working with angles in degrees you need to convert from degrees to radians which requires the use of Pi defined as a constant. The relationship is that Pi radians are 180°.

The reverse problem occurs when you need to use the inverse trigonometric functions, ASIN, ACOS or ATN. These find the angle (in radians) whose sine, cosine or tangent, respectively, has the value which is used as the argument. These are called inverse functions because they find the angle rather than the function of an angle. A lot of work with trigonometry calls for the inverse SIN (ARCSIN) and inverse COS (ARCCOS) rather than the ARCTAN, but only the ARCTAN (ATN function) is provided in QBASIC. These actions can be provided by using simple defined functions with Pi defined as a constant.

```
CONST pi = 3.1416
DEF FNasin(X) = ATN(x / SQR(-x * x + 1))
DEF FNacos(X)= -ATN(x / SQR(-X * X + 1)) + Pi/2
```

so that using FNasin or FNacos either by assignment to another variable or by a PRINT statement will provide these functions.

The other conversion that is often needed is that between natural and common logarithms. QBASIC supplies only natural logarithms and, confusingly, uses LOG rather than the conventional LN for the purpose. Figure 13.7 shows how the common logarithm can be obtained, using the defined constant for the natural log of ten.

```
CLS
CONST loge = 2.3026
DEF FNlog10 (x) = log(x) / loge
DEF FNalog10 (x) = exp(x * loge)
PRINT "Log10 of 50 is"; FNlog10(50)
PRINT "Antilog of 1.9031 is"; FNalog10(1.9031)
```

Figure 13.7. Using common (base 10) logarithms derived from QBASIC's LOG function and EXP (antilog) function.

The use of common logarithms is important in all branches of Electronics because of the use of logarithmic decibel ratios for comparing wave amplitudes.

ABS()	Absolute value, stripped of - sign.
ASC()	ASCII code for first character of string.
ATN()	Angle in radians whose tangent is supplied.
CDBL()	Convert number to double-precision format.
CINT()	Convert number into integer form (if possible).
CLNG()	Convert number into long integer (if possible).
COS()	Give cosine of argument (angle in radians).
CSNG()	Convert number into single-precision form.
CVD()	Convert number in random access file form into double precision form.
CVDMBF()	Convert number in random access file form to IEEE format, double precision
CVI()	Convert number in random access file form into integer form.
CVL()	Convert number in random access file into long integer form.
CVS()	Convert number in random access file form into single-precision form.
CVSMBF()	Convert number in random access file form into IEEE format, single precision
DEFDBL	Declare letters for double precision variables.
DEFINT	Declare letters for integer variables.
DEFLNG	Declare letters for long integer variables.
DEFSNG	Declare letters for single precision variables.
EXP()	Exponential (e) raised to power of argument.
FIX()	Strip fractions to give integer.
INT()	Convert to integer by rounding to next lower-value integer.
LOG()	Give logarithm to base e of argument.
RANDOMIZE	Provide starting number (seed) for random number generation.
RND()	Provide random fraction.
SGN()	Sign of number.
SIN()	Sine of argument (angle in radians).
SQR()	Square root of argument.
TAN()	Tangent of argument (angle in radians)

Figure 13.8. The main number functions of QBASIC.

Using a small list of defined functions to supplement the existing functions of QBASIC, there are few actions in trigonometry that cannot be handled easily and competently. Figure 13.9 shows a list of defined functions for other quantities such as hyperbolic functions that are used in engineering work and which are sometimes called for in formulae.

```
Trigonometry

  SECANT             DEF FNsec(X) = 1 / COS(X)
  COSEC              DEF RNcx(X) = 1 . SIN(X)
  COTAN              DEF FNct(X) = 1 / TAN(X)
  ARCSIN             DEF FNasn(X) = ATN(X /SQR(-X * X + 1))
  ARCCOS             DEF FNacs(X) = -ATN(X / SQR(-X * X +1)) + PI/2

Area and Volume

  Arean of circle    DEF FNAcir(R) = PI * R ^ 2
  Area of sphere     DEF FNAsph(R) = 4 * PI * R ^ 2
  Volume of sphere   DEF FNVsph(R) = (4 * PI * R ^ 3) / 3

Quadratic wquations of the form:

  A * X ^ 2 + B * X + C + 0

have the two solutions given by:

  DEF FNH(A, B, C) = (-B + SQR(B ^ 2 - 4 * A * C)) / (2 * A)
  DEF FNJ(A, B, C) = (-B - SQR(B ^ 2 - 4 * A * C)) / (2 * A)
```

Figure 13.9 Some defined functions for actions that are not already in function form.

Other functions

Of the other functions that do not fit into the arithmetic, trigonometry and logarithm set, the one that is most used is the random number function, RND. A random number should be one that is picked in a way that is completely random, like the spinning of a roulette wheel or the picking of a card. A random number produced by QBASIC, or any other version of BASIC, is not truly random in this sense. Computers work to rules, and any number that is produced by a set of rules cannot ever be truly random, as we shall show. The method that is used by the RND routine is to start with a number called a *seed*, and from there to produce a sequence of numbers that is nearly random. Because the numbers are produced by rules, however, you always get the same sequence of numbers from using the same seed.

QBASIC has two commands that relate to random numbers, RND and RANDOMIZE. RND used by itself in the form PRINT RND or X=RND gives a fraction that extends to nine places of decimals and which is reasonably random. This allows you to generate whole numbers which are fairly random, as if picked from a hat, by using a defined functions such as:

```
DEF FNrand%(d%)=rnd*d%
```

Other versions of BASIC require this to be written as INT(RND*d%+1). In QBASIC, the use of the integer defined function rounds up or down, avoiding the need for adding one to the random number before taking the integer part.

By using RND in the form RND(-1), you can get a random fraction which is the same each time the function is called. This can be useful for testing, as can RND(0) which repeats the last random fraction that was used.

Numbers obtained by using RND are random enough for simple purposes (like picking the lucky number at a fete) but because they are calculated numbers the sequence must eventually repeat. They are certainly not random enough for statistical purposes.

The other keyword concerned with random numbers is RANDOMIZE. By using RANDOMIZE 10, for example, you force the RND function to take the number 10 as its seed, and though the numbers are still reasonably random, the same sequence is always produced. By using RANDOMIZE with a number that is always changing, like TIMER (see Chapter 22), you can avoid such sequences.

MAX and MIN

Some versions of BASIC contain the functions MAX and MIN which will find the maximum or minimum value, respectively, of a list of numbers. These functions are not as useful as you might imagine, because each item on the list has to be typed, as in MAX(V1,V2,V3,V4,V5...), and there is no provision for looking through all the items in an array just by using the name of the array. Since this is normally what you want to do when you are looking for a maximum or minimum, we can write a routine that does just that and so fill in the absence of any MAX or MIN actions in QBASIC. Such a routine is shown in Figure 13.10 (overleaf).

```
CLS
DIM n%(100)
FOR j% = 1 TO 100
  n%(j%) = RND * 1000
NEXT
GOSUB maxit
PRINT "Largest is"; mx%
END
maxit:
mx% = n%(1)
FOR j% = 2 TO 100
  IF n%(j%) > mx% THEN mx% = n%(j%)
NEXT: RETURN
```

Figure 13.10. Finding the maximum value in a list (array) of numbers.

The principle is to make MX% equal to the first item in the array, and then to search all the other items so as to compare their values. If any item has a value greater than that of MX%, then MX% is assigned that value so, by the time the list has been searched, MX% carries the maximum value. You can write a similar subroutine for MN%, the minimum, by altering the main line to read:

```
IF n%(j%) > mn% THEN mn% = n%(j%)
```

Integer arithmetic

QBASIC allows you to work with integer division using quotient and remainder. If you use 5\3, using the backslash as the division sign, you get the answer 1, and using 5 MOD 3 gives 2, the remainder. You can therefore do quotient and remainder division with integers. For some purposes, this is very much more useful. If, for example, you are working with time, it's much better to get a time of 40 minutes 35 seconds than 40.5833333 minutes , and this type of arithmetic applies also to any work with the old imperial units of feet, pounds, rods, perches, poles, roods, furlongs and all the rest of them.

The listing of Figure 13.11 demonstrates how a time that is given as a fractional number of hours can be converted to a string in hours, minutes and seconds form, using an extended DEF FN format. The fractional form is input to the function as variable t, and FIX(t) finds the number of whole hours in this time. By using FIX, no rounding is performed; the fraction is simply chopped off, so that the fractional part can be found by subtracting the FIX part from the original variable. The variable r is then the fraction of an hour, and by multiplying by 60 this is converted into minutes and a fractional part. Repeating the action gives seconds, and the use of an assignment to an integer s% ensures that rounding is upward for 0.5 seconds or more.

```
CLS

DEF FNtimeconvert$ (t)
  STATIC h%, r, m%, s%
  h% = FIX(t): r = (t - h%) * 60
  m% = FIX(r): s% = (r - m%) * 60
  FNtimeconvert$ = STR$(h%) + ":" + STR$(m%) + ":" +
  STR$(s%)
END DEF

INPUT "Type time as a fractional number of house,
like 1.54"; tm
PRINT "Time is"; FNtimeconvert$(tm)
```

Figure 13.11. Using a function for a conversion from fractional hours form to a string containing hours minutes and seconds.

note STATIC is used for the variables in the function. This is done to keep these variables local rather than to preserve their values.

Manipulating number arrays

A multi-dimensional array is called a *matrix*, and can have a variety of uses. In Adventure games, for example, a multidimensional string matrix can be used to store location information, and two-dimensional number matrices can store screen image data. Arrays of this type are filled and used in very much the same ways as we have looked at for a single dimensional list, so that there is not much point in going over the more elementary uses. The use of number matrices can get us into highly mathematical topics, and of these, only one is likely to be useful to more than a few readers. This is the use of a number matrix for solving simultaneous equations. If you don't know simultaneous equations from a Waldorf salad then you should skip this section, but if you find that you need to solve equations of the form:

```
3.5x + 2.7y = 99.27
17.4x + 9.8y = 465.98
```

then this could be a very useful subroutine for you. Figure 13.12 shows the subroutine with only a very brief calling program. It is not confined to just two simultaneous equations, but the time that is needed will be greatly lengthened if a large number of equations are to be solved.

```
CLS : f$ = "###.###"
k(1, 1) = 3.5: k(1, 2) = 2.7
k(2, 1) = 17.4: k(2, 2) = 9.8
g(1) = 99.27: g(2) = 465.98: n% = 2
GOSUB solve
PRINT : PRINT "x=";
PRINT USING f$; ans(1)
PRINT "y%=";
PRINT USING f$; ans(2)
END
solve:
flag% = 0:
FOR j% = 1 TO n% - 1            y% = j%: x = k(j%, j%)
  FOR h% = j% + 1 TO n%
    IF k(h%, j%) > x THEN y% = h%: x = k(j%, h%)
  NEXT h%
  IF x = 0 THEN PRINT "No possible solution": flag% = -1: END
  IF y% = j% THEN GOTO skip
  FOR f% = 1 TO n%: z = k(j%, f%)
    k(j%, f%) = k(y%, f%): k(y%, f%) = z
  NEXT
    SWAP g(j%), g(y%)
skip:
  FOR h% = j% + 1 TO n%
    x = k(h%, j%) / k(j%, j%
    FOR f% = j% TO n%
      k(h%, f%) = k(h%, f%) - x * k(j%, f%)
    NEXT f%: g(h%) = g(h%) - x * g(j%)
  NEXT h%
NEXT j%: ans(n%) = g(n%) / k(n%, n%)
FOR j% = n% - 1 TO 1 STEP -1: z = 0
  FOR h% = j% + 1 TO n%
    z = z + ans(h%) * k(j%, h%)
  NEXT
  ans(j%) = (g(j%) - z) / k(j%, j%)
NEXT
RETURN
```

Figure 13.11 An equation-solving subroutine and small calling program to illustrate its use.

If you want to use this as a general subroutine for solving equations that might use several more unknown quantities, then the calling program will have to be more elaborate. On the other hand, if you always need to solve equations for the same form, then you could have a calling routine which contained a loop, and filled the matrix by using lines such as:

```
INPUT"NUMBER OF EQUATIONS"; N%
FOR B% = 1 TO N%
PRINT "EQUATION"; B%;" COEFFICIENT OF X ";
INPUT K(B%,1)
```

and so on. The way that the numbers in the equations correspond to the matrix and the list values are shown in Figure 13.13, and the results are taken from another list 'ans'

```
Equations:

3.5x + 2.7y = 99.27
17.4x + 9.8y = 465.98

Matrix form:
    3.5   2.7    99.27
   17.4   9.8   465.98

K(1,1) = 3.5 K(1,2) = 2.7 G(1) = 99.27
K(2,1) = 17.4 K(2,2) = 9.8 G(2) = 465.98

Solutions:

L(1) = 22.5 ...this is value of x
L(2) = 7.6 ...this is value of y
```

Figure 13.13. How values in the equations correspond to the matrix values.

The subroutine uses a variable flag% to determine whether the results are valid or not, and this can be used to suppress the printing of results if the equations cannot be solved. In this example, flag% has not been used because the equation that is supplied is guaranteed to have solutions. Note the use of PRINT USING, see Chapter 14, to avoid rounding errors from being printed. It would be unusual in equations of this type to need to work to more than three places of decimals.

For anyone who needs to work with number matrices, the next six listings are of some useful manipulations in straightforward subroutine form, providing you are already familiar with matrix methods. Figure 13.14 (overleaf) shows a subroutine for the scalar multiplication of a three-element matrix.

```
scalmult:
FOR h% = 1 TO n1%'
  FOR j% = 1 TO n2%
    FOR k% = 1 TO n3%
      b(k%, j%, h%) = a(k%, j%, h%) * z
    NEXT
  NEXT
NEXT
RETURN
```

Figure 13.14. A subroutine for scalar multiplication of a matrix.

Scalar multiplication means multiplying each element of the matrix by the same value, so that for a three-dimensional matrix, three loops must be used. The dimension values are the numbers n1%, n2% and n3%, and each element in the matrix is multiplied by the number z, to give the new matrix b(i,j,k). If you want to adapt the routine to a two-dimensional matrix, then one loop and its variable can be omitted.

Figure 13.15 illustrates matrix addition of two-dimensional matrices A and B, in which the action consists of adding similar elements of each matrix to form a corresponding element of the result.

```
matadd:
FOR j% = 1 TO n2%
  FOR h% = 1 TO n1%
    c(h%, j%) = a(h%, j%) + b(h%, j%)
  NEXT
NEXT
RETURN
```

Figure 13.15. A subroutine for the matrix addition of two-dimensional matrices.

The dimensions of the matrix have to be assigned to the numbers n1% and n2% in the calling routine.

Element multiplication is illustrated in Figure 13.16, and it follows much the same scheme as the element addition of the previous example, with each element of the answer obtained by multiplying corresponding elements of the original two-dimensional matrices.

```
elmult:
FOR j% = 1 TO n2%
  FOR h% = 1 TO n1%
    c(h%, j%) = a(h%, j%) * b(h%, j%)
  NEXT
NEXT
RETURN
```

Figure 13.16. A subroutine for element multiplication of two matrices.

This action is *not* the same as matrix multiplication, illustrated in Figure 13.17 in which each term of the new matrix is the sum of multiplied terms from the original matrices.

```
matmult:
FOR h% = 1 TO n1%
  FOR j% = 1 TO n2%
    c(h%, j%) = 0
    FOR k% = 1 TO n3%
      c(h%, j%) = c(h%, j%) + a(h%, k%) * b(k%, h%)
    NEXT
  NEXT
NEXT
RETURN
```

Figure 13.17. A subroutine for matrix multiplication .

Note that for this type of multiplication, three dimension numbers have to be provided to the subroutine, and there is no provision for checking that these are correct in this simple subroutine.

Another operation is matrix transposition, meaning the exchange of rows and columns, for which the subroutine of Figure 13.18 (overleaf) can be used when the matrix has two dimensions.

```
transpose:
FOR h% = 1 TO n1%
  FOR j% = 1 TO n2%
    b(j%, h%) = a(h%, j%)
  NEXT
NEXT
RETURN
```

Figure 13.18. Transposition of a square matrix.

Finally, Figure 13.19 shows a subroutine for inverting a two-dimensional matrix – assuming that this is possible. Inversion is a lengthy process, comparable to string sorting in its use of memory, so it's advisable to precede this subroutine with a screen warning that the action can take some time to complete. In this example, the message has been incorporated into the subroutine itself, and there is provision for using a flag as well as for printing a warning if the matrix cannot be inverted. The routine applies to a square matrix – one which has the same number (n) of rows as it has columns. The matrix to be inverted is v, and the inverted matrix is k.

IEEE number format

The IEEE (Institution of Electrical and Electronic Engineers, USA) form of number is a way of coding numbers in binary with high precision, and is standard in many modern programming languages. To cater for older versions of BASIC which do not use this format, the functions MKSMBF$, MKDMBF$, CVSMBF and CVDMBF have been included in QBASIC. The two string functions convert a single or double-precision number (respectively) to Microsoft string format as used in files (see Chapter 19), and the two number functions convert back into IEEE format. These functions are required only for a few program conversions, and are not likely to be much used.

```
CLS
DEFINT A-J, L-U, W-Z
REM Create a test matrix to solve
v(1, 1) = 1: v(1, 2) = 3: v(2, 1) = 4: v(2, 2) = 2
n = 2: REM Two dimensional matrix
GOSUB invert
PRINT "Results are:"
PRINT " k(1,1)="; k(1, 1)
PRINT " k(1,2)="; k(1, 2)
PRINT " k(2,1)="; k(2, 1)
PRINT " k(2,2)="; k(2, 2)
END
invert:
PRINT "Please wait..."
flag% = 0
FOR j = 1 TO n
  FOR h = 1 TO n
    k(j, h) = 1 - ABS(SGN(j - h))
  NEXT
NEXT
FOR j = 1 TO n - 1
  IF v(j, j) = 0 THEN GOSUB errit: GOTO outpoint
  FOR h = j + 1 TO n
    m = v(h, j) / v(j, j)
    FOR p = 1 TO n
      v(h, p) = v(h, p) - m * v(j, p)
      k(h, p) = k(h, p) - m * k(j, p)
    NEXT
  NEXT
NEXT
FOR j = n TO 1 STEP -1
  FOR p = 1 TO n
    FOR h = j + 1 TO n
      k(j, p) = k(j, p) - v(j, h) * k(h, p)
    NEXT
  k(j, p) = k(j, p) / v(j, j)
NEXT
NEXT
outpoint: RETURN
errit:
PRINT "No solution possible..."
flag% = 0
RETURN
```

Figure 13.19. The inversion of a matrix – this can be a lengthy routine for a large matrix. A calling routine is shown.

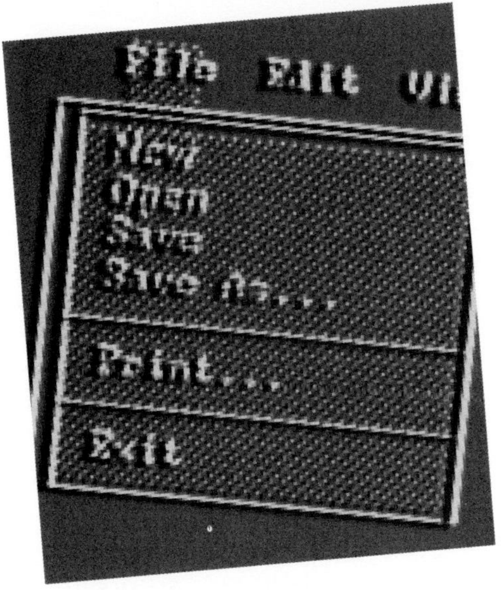

Print Control

Printers and PRINT statements

The reasons for needing a printer are obvious if you use your PC for business purposes. You can hardly expect your accountants or the income tax inspector to look at accounts that can only be shown on screen. It would be a total waste of time if you kept your stock records with a computer, and then had to write down each change on a piece of paper, copying from the display on the screen. For all of these purposes, and particularly for wordprocessing, the printer is an essential part of the computer system. Output on paper is referred to as hard copy, and this *hard copy* is essential if the computer is be of any use in business applications. For wordprocessing uses, it's not enough just to have a printer, you need one with a high quality output whose characters are as clear as those of a first class electric typewriter.

Even if your computer is never used for any kind of business purpose, however, you can still run up against the need for a printer. If you use, modify or write programs in QBASIC, the printer can pay for itself in terms of your time. Trying to trace what a program does from a listing that you can see only a few lines at a time on the screen is very frustrating. Even a very modest program may need a hundred lines of BASIC. Trying to check a program of a hundred lines when you can only see a dozen or so at a time is like bailing out a leaky boat with a teaspoon.

With a printer attached to your PC you can print out the whole listing, and then examine it at your leisure. If you design your programs the way you ought to, using a *core* and subroutines (see Chapters 15 and 16), then you can print each subroutine on a separate piece of paper. In this way, you can keep a note of each different subroutine, with variable names noted. On each sheet you can write what the subroutine does, what quantities are represented by the variable names, and how it is used. If you have a wordprocessor that allows you to add one piece of text to another, you can keep your subroutines filed separately and merge them into a main program whenever you want, allowing you to construct programs painlessly using your library of tested subroutines.

Granted, then, that the use of a printer is a high priority for the really serious QBASIC user, what sort of printers are available? The PC type of machine in its natural state allows virtually any printer to be attached, thanks to the provision of both a parallel Centronics port and a serial port. This opens up the way for the use of any of the printers which are offered at such attractive prices in the magazines. It also allows you to use an existing printer, providing that it is one of the universal type, and not a 'special', intended to work with just one make of computer.

The normal hard copy print statements of QBASIC are Print from the Edit menu (selected with the mouse from the File menu) to list to the printer and LPRINT which prints text from a QBASIC program. In addition, statements that include file numbers can be used provided that the file number has been allocated to the printer by using the OPEN command (see Chapters 18 and 19). For example, using:

```
OPEN "prn" FOR OUTPUT AS #1
```

allows hard copy printing to be done by using the PRINT #1 statement. The advantage of this is that by using PRINT #n%, the print can be switched between screen and printer according to the value of the variable n%.

If the printer is not connected or is switched off, statements such as LPRINT or PRINT #n%, or the use of the Print option from the File menu of the Editor, all cause the computer to hang up until the printer is connected and switched on. Any fault that prevents printing, whether a printer not switched on, turned offline, or out of paper, causes a *Device Fault* message, and clicking on <OK> will allow you to regain control and sort out the problem.

Print Fielding

The topic of *print fielding* will be completely new to you if your computing has been learned on older types of machines, and it's a topic that rightly belongs in the category of more advanced programming. Print fielding is concerned with how a quantity, string or number, is presented in a given space on the screen or on paper. Fielding is not so much concerned with the position of print on the screen or paper page, which is dealt with by TAB, LOCATE, and AT, but with the actual quantity itself. The field that is referred to is the space in which something is printed, and fielding means how the printed text or numbers will be arranged within this space. For example, you might want a number printed with only two places of decimals, with decimal points lining up, with dollar or pound signs and so on. Figure 14.1 illustrates what is meant by a field in this sense (the word is also used in other senses, see Chapters 18 onwards).

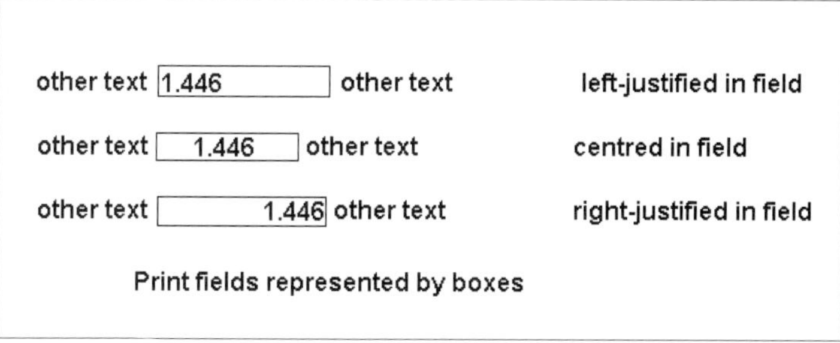

Figure 14.1. The meaning of field as applied to printing on screen or on paper.

In this diagram, the field is represented by a rectangle which can be placed anywhere on the screen. Some data is printed in this space, and other text is printed outside the boundary of the field. Within the field, however, data can be printed to the left, to the right or in the centre. The width of the field is the number of columns that are reserved for data, and if the data does not fill the field then we can control how the data is arranged in it. Figure 14.2 shows an example of fielding carried out with text.

```
CLS
name$ = "Fielding, Henry"
PRINT USING "\   \"; name$
f$ = "\   \"
PRINT USING f$; name$
PRINT USING "!"; name$
PRINT USING "&"; name$
END
```

Figure 14.2. Fielding carried out on text with PRINT USING.

In this example, the screen is cleared, the name is then printed USING the field string "\   \", with three spaces between the backslash signs. The number of characters between the quotes means that the field will be of this width, five characters in all. When the name is printed then, only five characters will appear, and it's the first five as you'll see when you run this. If the name is of fewer characters than is needed to fill the specified space, then it is left-justified, with the first letter of the name at the lefthand side of the field of five characters width.

The field string can be assigned to a variable, using a line such as F$="\ \", and there are two other possible characters that can be used in place of the backslashes and spaces. One is !, which causes just the first character of a string to be printed, and the other is & which causes the whole string to be printed in the normal way. The reason for needing the & character is that you might be using a PRINT USING statement within a loop, and need to print the first character of one string followed by the whole of another. This would be done by a command of the form:

```
PRINT USING A$;B$
```

where A$ specifies a single character on one pass through the loop and the whole string on another pass. The separator can be a comma instead of a semicolon, which has no effect on the form of the printing, unlike the effect of the comma used to separate printed items normally into zones.

Qnote If you use a semicolon or a comma in a list of items to print, they have the usual spacing effects.

The corresponding expression for the printer is LPRINT USING but, since the action is identical, there is no point in repeating all of the examples with LPRINT in place of PRINT unless you want to check out a new printer. Throughout this Chapter, then, you can assume that what applies to PRINT also applies to LPRINT.

PRINT USING, as applied to strings, does not easily perform the task that we most often need, that of centring a string in a line, and we have already looked at routines for that purpose. Where PRINT USING comes into its own with strings is when you are working with several columns and want to ensure that no name overruns the width of its column. Take a look at the result of running Figure 14.3, for example.

In this listing, the fielding string has been much more elaborate so as to set up three fields well within the width of the screen, each with different numbers of characters and therefore separated by different numbers of spaces. The effect of using this fielding to create a column of names is then illustrated. The great advantage of using fielding for this type of display, as distinct from TAB, is that it's so much easier to ensure that names do not overlap, and that the spaces between the columns are rigidly maintained. Fielding like this, however, takes more planning than the simple use of TAB, and may require the data being chopped to fit.

```
CLS
x$ = "\            \"
y$ = "\                    \"
z$ = "\            \"
FOR j% = 1 TO 5
  READ a$, b$, c$
  PRINT USING x$; a$;
  PRINT USING y$; b$;
  PRINT USING z$; c$
NEXT
DATA "C. Rook",Charlie Fahnsbahns,"L. Ranley"
DATA "P.Plod","Frank N. Stein","Dr. Acula"
DATA "D.S. Pair",No Kim Bin Hir,"P.Lum"
DATA "S.Bond",Percy Flage,"O.B. Livion"
DATA "K. Kong",Paul Roger XIV,M. Hat
```

Figure 14.3. Using a more elaborate fielding so that text can be put into three fields.

Formatting numbers

Formatting control strings have some useful applications in printing text, but they really come into their own when you want to print numbers, particularly money amounts and items in columns. As before, the string quantity that follows the word USING determines how the number is arranged in its field, and this string can be assigned to a variable, or simply placed in quotes following USING.

For the formatting of a number, the string can consist of a number of hashmarks, to specify digit positions in the field, and other characters . , + * $ ^ which specify the way the number is to be displayed. What this amounts to is that you can insert various characters into the fielding string. The characters you are most likely to use for most purposes are the decimal point and the comma. By using these you can make your numbers appear the way you want to see them.

You can use as many commas as you want although there must always be a hashmark preceding a comma but you are limited to one decimal point per field. The arrangement of hashmarks, decimal point and commas should then appear as you would want to see your numbers arranged. QBASIC makes no concessions to the continental use of commas and points (comma for decimals, point for thousands). This is odd at a time when virtually every program is available in an international form, and the same neglect is exemplified later for the floating dollar sign. The program in Figure 14.4 prints a set of numbers, each set using a different field specification.

```
CLS
FOR n% = 1 TO 5
  RESTORE forms
  FOR x% = 1 TO n%
    READ f$
  NEXT
  RESTORE nums
  FOR j% = 1 TO 5
    READ d
    PRINT USING f$; d
  NEXT
    x = TIMER: DO: LOOP UNTIL TIMER >= x + 1
    PRINT
NEXT
END
forms:
DATA"##,###.##","##.#","#,###.#","#.#","#####"
nums:
DATA 1.57,11.236,10143.2,1071623,237.145
```

Figure 14.4. A program to demonstrate number fielding.

The loop that starts in the second line prints five sets of numbers, and the correct field specification is obtained in the following three lines. The RESTORE forms statement ensures that the data for the field specification is taken from the line following the 'nums' label, and by using the loop FOR x%=1 TO n%, you end up with f$ assigned to the nth item in the DATA line. The RESTORE nums line then picks the number data, and the loop that uses variable j% reads various numbers so that they can be printed with the required format. When each loop of number printing is completed, the DO loop using TIMER makes the program wait so that you can take a look at the group of figures before the next fielding string is assigned.

```
     1.57
    11.24
10,143.2                First set
%1,071,623.00
   237.15

     1.6
    11.2
    %10143.2            Second set
    % 1.1E+06
    %237.1

     1.6
    11.2
%10,143.2               Third set
%1,071,623.0
   237.1

     1.6
    %11.2
    %10143.2            Fourth set
    %0.1E+07
    %237.1

     2
    11
 10143                  Fifth set
 %1071623
   237
```

Figure 14.5. How the numbers appear as printed from the program.

Figure 14.5 shows the results of all this as printed on paper. The first fielding string uses a total of nine characters, so all fields are nine characters long. The numbers are justified to the right of the field and, since two hashmarks have been shown following the decimal point, numbers with more than two places of decimals are rounded to two decimal figures. The numbers are placed with the decimal points lining up, which is ideal for displaying tabular data. One of the supplied numbers cannot be displayed in this field, because it has 7 figures and no decimal point. It would therefore consist of ten characters if we added a decimal point and two figures following the point. Since this amount of space is not available, the number is printed with incorrect fielding rather than chopping the number to size or not displaying it at all.

Note the effect of rounding on 11.236, which is printed as 11.24, 11.2 or even 11. This automatic rounding can save you a lot of program effort, but you need to be careful that it is doing what you expect it to. If, for example, you are working with such things as compound interest, you may be calculating to four decimal places, but displaying a rounded amount only. You have to ensure that the rounding does not work against you!

The other sets of figures follow this pattern, with rounding when the decimal places are not displayed, and incorrect fielding if the total number of places is insufficient. Note in the last set that the effect of the formatting string "#####" on 1.57 is to print this number as 2, rounding up to the nearest whole number, which is what the format calls for. The figure of 1.49 would be rounded to 1 in this position. In general, when you are working with numbers, it's better to allow for more places than you need preceding the decimal point, and for as many as you want following. If you need to display with three decimal places, and you are expecting numbers up to 502614 for example, use #,###,###.### as your formatter so that if a larger number comes along unexpectedly, you are not treated to the sight of a number incorrectly placed in its field.

Standard form

For a lot of purposes, particularly in science and engineering applications, you might need to print numbers in standard form. If you have never met standard form before, this is no place to start making its acquaintance, and Appendix A is a brief introduction. A number is fielded into standard form by using four *carats,* the little inverted V symbols on the 6 key at the top of the keyboard. The number of these symbols is important – fewer than four and you just get an error message, more than four and your figures will include these marks.

In the Standard form of QBASIC, however, the output is not in the European standard of using a digit between 0 and 9 before the decimal point. Instead, figures are printed with a zero preceding the point, no matter what you happen to specify with hashmarks in the template. The template, in fact, affects only the number of places following the decimal point. If no decimal places are specified, as by using "#^^^^" as the formatting string, then there will be a digit or digits preceding the decimal point.

```
DATA"#^^^^","#.#^^^^","#.###^^^^","#.##^^^^","#.####^^^^"
nums:
DATA 1.57,11.236,10143.2,1071623,237.145
```

Figure 14.6. The DATA lines for using Standard form for printing numbers.

Figure 14.6 shows a change to the DATA line of the previous listing, so that you can see the effect of printing the same numbers in standard form with various field specifiers.

```
2E+00
1E+01
1E+04                       First set
1E+06
2E+02

0.2E+01
0.1E+02
0.1E+05                     Second set
0.1E+07
0.2E+03

0.157E+01
0.112E+02
0.101E+05                   Third set
0.107E+07
0.237E+03

0.16E+01
0.11E+02
0.10E+05                    Fourth set
0.11E+07
0.24E+03

0.1570E+01
0.1124E+02
0.1014E+05                  Fifth set
0.1072E+07
0.2371E+03
```

Figure 14.7. The number output from the previous program.

The results are shown in Figure 14.7. Note how the single digit preceding the decimal point is shown only when there is no place following the point.

In standard form, a number that is only fractional is shown as having a negative *exponent* (the figure following the E). If the number is a negative number, then there will be a negative sign preceding the figure before the decimal point and, if you are not using standard form, this negative sign will take up one of the places allocated for a digit. This can lead to your line-up of decimal points being disturbed if the remaining number of places preceding the point is insufficient. You can test this for yourself by using the program of Figure 14.6 and making all the numbers in the 'nums' line negative. If, however, you place a negative sign before each first hashmark in the format strings, then the sign will be correctly printed only where it is needed, and will *not* affect the positioning of the figures.

Money amounts

Printing money amounts is likely to be a requirement for a lot of applications. You can place into a field any money sign that is provided for on your keyboard, and since keyboard symbols are provided for most European languages, that makes QBASIC useful for accounts programs in most languages that are likely to be needed. The simplest way of placing a money unit sign is to have it at the head of a formatting string, as for example:

```
f$="£##,###.##"
```

which puts the British Pound symbol at the head of a ten character field. You can place whatever symbol you need in this position, or in a similar string. Using the money symbol at the head of the field is not always satisfactory in visual terms, however, as Figure 14.8 shows.

```
CLS
f$ = "£###,###.##"
FOR n% = 1 TO 5: READ d
  PRINT USING f$; d
NEXT
DATA .25,1.76,23.4,2176,31261.22
```

Figure 14.8. Printing money amounts with a pound sterling sign. You must make sure that your printer is using the PC-8 character set.

Printing the pound sign has in the past been a problem, particularly for owners of the older Epson and similar dot-matrix printers. The problem originated in there being no agreed ASCII code number for the pound and the PC machines use ASCII code 156 which is not used by the normal US character set of the Epson printer. If the English character set is printed, then each hashmark is printed as a pound. This problem is an endemic one, and will haunt everything you do until you replace the printer with a more modern one.

All modern dot-matrix and laser printers allow selection from a number of character sets, of which the PC-8 set matches that used in the PC machines, so that whatever you can obtain on the screen you can also print. This has eliminated the problem of printing the pound sign provided that the printer user has read the manual and realises the importance of using the correct character set.

When the program runs on the screen, you can see that the pound sign has been placed at the start of the field, but it looks much too remote for most of the figures. What is needed is what is called a *floating* pound symbol, one which will just precede the first figure of a money sum.

This ability to float the symbol is provided in PRINT USING – but only for the dollar sign. Programs like QBASIC seem to lag many years behind Windows and Lotus 1-2-3 in providing for currencies other than the dollar. To float the dollar (which sounds like an economist's prescription) requires putting two dollar signs at the start of a fielding string, though following any + or - sign, if used. This is followed by the usual set of hashmarks that mark out the field size for your money amounts. Figure 14.9 shows the change that is needed to the listing in Figure 14.8, and the results of running the program.

```
f$ = "$$###,###.##"

        $0.25
        $1.76
       $23.40
    $2,176.00
   $31,261.22
```

Figure 14.9. Altering one line of the previous listing so as to make the dollar sign float, and the resulting printout.

Cursor positioning

On the screen the cursor can be placed by using the LOCATE statement as noted earlier, but this does not always make it easy to place the cursor if you do not know the current position. For example, if you want to place the cursor two rows down and five columns across from its current position you need first of all to know the row and column number of the current position. These are provided by the functions CSRLN and POS. Figure 14.10 illustrates these functions in use printing positions on the screen.

```
CLS
LOCATE 5, 5
PRINT "Demonstration of cursor control"
PRINT
FOR n% = 1 TO 5
  Row% = CSRLIN
  Col% = POS(0)
  PRINT "Position "; n%; "(Press any key)"
    DO
    LOOP WHILE INKEY$ = ""
  LOCATE (Row% + 2), (Col% + 5)
NEXT
```

Figure 14.10. Using CSRLIN and POS to find the position of the screen cursor.

note POS needs a *dummy argument*, in the form POS(0), so that it can return a number to the variable (Col% in this example).

The function LPOS performs much the same action for a printer, but for column number only. The argument of LPOS is the printer port number, of which 0 and 1 signify LPT1, the usual printer port, and 2 can be used for LPT2 or 3 for LPT3. LPOS can be used when characters are sent one by one to a printer, allowing LPOS to count them in and perform some action such as a new line, printing a vertical bar symbol, or whatever is needed after a set number of characters. You seldom need this action.

The SCREEN statement

SCREEN can be used in a variety of ways, of which the most straightforward is SCREEN n%, with n% used to determine the screen mode. The uses of the various mode numbers depend on the type of graphics adaptor fitted, and for the almost universal VGA type, the modes are shown in Figure 14.11.

```
SCREEN 0: Text only. Video pages 0 to 7 (depending on video memory)
    text modes of:      40 x 25     40 x 43     40 x 50
                        80 x 25     80 x 43     80 x 50
with up to 64 colours.

SCREEN 1: 320 x 200 graphics. Video page 0 only
        text:           40 x 25     16 colours

SCREEN 2: 640 x 200 graphics. Video page 0 only
        text:           80 x 25                 16 colours

SCREEN 7: 320 x 200 graphics. Video pages 0 to 7 (depending on video
memory)
        text:           40 x 25                 16 colours

SCREEN 8: 640 x 200 graphics. Video pages 0 to 3
        text:           80 x 25                 16 colours

SCREEN 9: 640 x 350 graphics. Video pages 0 to 1
        text:           80 x 25 or 80 x 43      16 colours

SCREEN 10: 640 x 350 graphics. Video pages 0 to 1
        text:           80 x 25 or 80 x 43      Monochrome only

SCREEN 11: 640 x 480 graphics Video page 0 only
        text:           80 x 30 or 80 x 60      256K colours

SCREEN 12: 640 x 480 graphics. Video page 0 only
        text:           80 x 30 or 80 x 60      256K colours

SCREEN 13: 320 x 200 graphics. Video page 0 only
        text:           40 x 25                 256K colours
```

Figure 14.11. SCREEN modes usually available with the VGA graphics adaptor fitted.

Altering the SCREEN automatically clears any existing display. In general, you will not use SCREEN to any great extent until you start to work with graphics, Chapter 20.

The WIDTH statement can be used to determine a screen layout (but only for some fixed layouts), a line width for a disk file (see also Chapters 18 and 19), or a printer width. For use with screens, WIDTH 40,25 forces the screen to be of 40 columns and 25 rows, and only the numbers 40 or 80 can be used for the number of columns, with 25, 30, 43, 50 or 60 being used for rows if you are using VGA (older screen display cards will not support the larger number of rows).

The use of WIDTH LPRINT 90 allows the printer to use 90-character rows. You can use whatever printer width your printer can support, depending on the size of type (font size) that has been selected.

note Many of the statements that concern screen display are subject to limits that depend on the type of adaptor used, and many of the examples in the QBASIC Help pages contain the words – 'This example requires a colour adaptor'. This is a hangover from the past. Early PC machines were fitted with a monochrome display with little of no graphics capability, and later machines used the CGA (colour graphics adaptor) which allowed low-resolution graphics. Of these two, the CGA adaptor was needed to demonstrate many of the QBASIC examples. Virtually all PC compatible machines now being manufactured and sold use the much later VGA type of screen adaptor which, whether colour or monochrome, possess better resolution than the older types, so that all examples can be used on VGA.

Sectioned screens

The VIEW PRINT statement allows you to use parts of the screen independently for text purposes – see Chapter 21 for the VIEW statement that performs a similar type of action for graphics outputs. Figure 14.12 gives a flavour of what can be achieved.

```
CLS
PRINT " This is a title line which will not scroll"
VIEW PRINT 12 TO 24
PRINT "This is where scrolling takes place"
FOR n% = 1 TO 2000
  PRINT "A";
  FOR j = 1 TO 10: NEXT
NEXT
PRINT "End of scrolling"
SLEEP 2
CLS
END
```

Figure 14.12 Using VIEW PRINT to establish an independent text window.

The first PRINT statement prints on the top line of the normal screen but, subsequently, the VIEW PRINT line establishes that the new screen area is from line 12 to line 24. All print actions now take place in this set of rows, and this includes scrolling and screen clearing, so that these actions have no effect on the upper part of the screen.

The use of VIEW PRINT is quite simple, but you have to remember to use the statement before each PRINT or CLS that is intended to set up the section of screen. The most useful action in a program is often to keep a title and a reminder strip in view while other actions are concentrated in lines 2 to 23, and this is easily done by using LOCATE on the full screen to put in the title and reminders, and then using VIEW PRINT 2 TO 23 to establish the *window* for the rest of the print actions.

Program Design

Newcomers to programming always assume that learning the language (BASIC, PASCAL, C or whatever) is the main hurdle that they have to face. This is probably a hangover from trying to learn French at school and some programming languages are almost as rich in irregular verbs. The main obstacle to fast learning, however, is the design of the program, the work that needs to be done before a line of the program can be written. In the past, this has been easier for BASIC than for other languages and since academics never take a language seriously unless it is difficult to learn (and almost impossible to use for any non-academic purpose) BASIC is now catching up. QBASIC gives you the choice – you can, if you like, use it as easily and as casually as classic versions like GW BASIC, or you can treat it as a modern *structured* language and learn as much about computing from it as you would from any other favoured language.

A program is written to solve a problem and to start with you need to know if the problem can be solved using a computer. Computers are machines which obey instructions and which work in a way that has been decided by their designer. Just to illustrate this, think of a pocket calculator. A pocket calculator is useful, but you cannot ask it to name the best-looking car in the world. There are two reasons for this. One is that the calculator is designed to carry out a limited range of actions with numbers. It can't *name* anything, nor has it been programmed with any names of cars. The other reason is that items like 'good looking' are human value judgements that only a human can make. If you want to use a computer to solve a problem, then, the problem must be one that can somehow be reduced to numbers or logical actions, and you need a program that will carry out the actions. It's programs that solve problems, not computers. Having said that, you do need a computer that is capable of running your program.

Every problem looks different, but the steps that you need to use in writing a program to solve a problem are similar for all problems. First of all you have to decide whether the problem can be solved with a program. A computer cannot decide which is the best applicant for a job, for example. If, on the other hand, you could draw up a checklist of skills and a set of points that could be awarded for answers to questions, you could reduce the choice to a number of points, and this the computer could cope with. 'Best' it doesn't understand; 'most points' it can be made to work with. It's important to remember that when you find a computer used in any form of selection that the value judgements have been made by humans at some stage, and the computer is doing little else than acting as a scoreboard. This applies particularly to programs for decision making of any kind, ranging from the strictly business type (shall we invest £50K in Consolidated Wotsits?) to the possible pleasure (like computer dating).

note It is also possible to use the computer to provide plausible-looking nonsense based on ancient superstitions, but this does not make the output any more logical or sensible. Stars have as little effect on computers as on anything else.

If the problem is one that can be solved by using the computer then the next item is to decide what sequence of steps will lead to a solution. The important point here is sequence. A computer does one thing at a time, and the program sets out what this sequence of steps will be. Once you have decided what sequence is needed, you are well on the way to creating a program. Typical steps would be putting data into the computer, making calculations or rearrangements, and printing data out (using the screen or the printer). For a longer program, you might have steps of typing data in, saving data on a disk, replaying data, rearranging or selecting data, and printing data. No matter how simple or how complicated the program is, the sequence has to be correct, or you can't design the program correctly.

Take a simple example. Suppose you had to produce sets of prices which showed item names, price before VAT, VAT amount and price including VAT. This is certainly a problem that can be solved using the computer, because it deals with words and numbers, and all it has to do is make calculations. At its simplest, the program might require you to enter the name of the item and its pre-VAT price. The screen would show these items. The calculation part of the program would then swing into action, producing the amount of VAT, and the total price. The next step would be to print this extra data on the screen. This is a simple three-step program outline, and from it a program could be written. You could summarise the steps in a diagram, as in Figure 15.1, with the steps arranged in order from top to bottom.

1. Ask for name of item

2. Ask for pre-VAT price

3. Print item name, total price, VAT amount.

Figure 15.1. An outline of a very simple program.

Too simple? Perhaps, but the value of something like this is that you can build upon it. Suppose, for example, that you wanted to keep entering items and prices and getting the information until you entered X as the name of an item. This means using a loop, as you know, and it makes the plan look as in Figure 15.2.

1. Repeat

2. Ask for name of item

3. Ask for pre-VAT price

4. Print item name, total price, VAT amount.

5. Until X entered

Figure 15.2. The plan extended to allow for a loop.

This time, the loop has been marked out with the words REPEAT at the start and UNTIL at the finish. For any loop, we need an ending condition, and this has been stated at the UNTIL position. The main outline of the program has stayed very much the same, however. This type of program design is much easier than the use of flowcharts, because it's easier to go from a simple plan to a more complicated one. Always start your program design with a simple plan and add the complications later. In this way, you can design the program better, test it in stages and, if necessary, make changes that will not affect too much of your program. Design like this is called *top-down,* because you start with the most important items, at the top of your list, and work down to the detail later. The method of using words to describe the action steps is called *structured English* though it can, of course, be done in any language.

Now suppose you wanted to complicate things even further. The task now is to enter the list of items and prices, end it with item X, record the whole list on a disk and, when the disk is played back, produce a printout of item, price, VAT and total all on paper. This only means modifications to the plan, not a new plan, as Figure 15.3 shows.

1. Repeat
2. Ask for name of item
3. Ask for pre-VAT price
4. Save on disk
5. Until X entered

NEXT

1. Repeat
2. Read from disk
3. Print item name, total price, VAT amount.
4. Until X read

Figure 15.3. The plan extended further, with a subroutine indicated.

The plan keeps to its order of actions, but this time it consists of two sections. The first section is a loop that accepts entries and saves data on a disk. The ending condition is the usual X, but this time it leads to a second loop, marked in this example by the NEXT in the plan. In this loop, the data is taken from the disk, tested, the calculations made and the results printed on paper. The sequence in each loop is just as it was in the simple plan, but this is now a primitive database program. Any program that consists of entry of data, storage (particularly on disk) and then calculation, selection or rearrangement of data, is a database program. The database of the title is the collection of data that has been stored on the disk.

As we go through this and following chapters, then, we shall be working to simple plans and looking at pieces of program that carry out the actions that are needed in the plans. When you design your own programs, you can draw up plans for yourself, and make use of the program sections in this book to carry out the actions that you want. You can also make use of routines from other programs that you see in print. Even if you do not fully understand how these routines work (and if they are machine code routines that's not unusual) you can always use them provided you know what they do. Knowing what they do means knowing what has to be put in, what happens to it, and what comes out, and it's on that basis that we'll be working with program sections in this book.

Two points are important here. One is that experience counts in this design business. If you make your first efforts at design as simple as possible, you'll learn much more from them. That's because you're more likely to succeed with a simple program first time round. You'll learn more from designing a simple program that works than from an elaborate program that never seems to do what it should. We have already dabbled with the design of simple programs, and I want to show you that this is all you ever need! The second point is that program design has to start with the computer switched off – preferably in another room! The reason is that program design needs planning, and you can't plan properly when you have temptation in the shape of a keyboard in front of you. Get away from it!

Put it on paper

Program design always starts with a pad of paper. For myself, I use a 'student's pad' of A4 which is punched so that I can put sheets into a file. This way I can keep the sheets tidy and add to them as I need. I can also throw away any sheets I don't need, which is just as important. Even a very simple program is probably going to need more than one sheet of paper for its design. If you then go in for more elaborate programs, you may easily find yourself with a couple of dozen sheets of planning and listing before you get to the keyboard. These sheets are important because not only do they form the basis of your listing, and help to trace where a fault may have occurred, they also act as the basis of your documentation.

Never assume that your program will not need some sort of manual. Even if only you ever use it, there will come a day when you can't quite remember what you had to enter at some stage, or in what order some quantities were printed out. A lot of commercial programs use HELP pages, but paper documentation is much more satisfactory. It doesn't need any memory or disk space, and you can look at it before you even start using the program. If you keep your design notes in an orderly state they will form the basis of such a guide, even if it amounts only to a sheet or two.

Another point about preparing such documentation is that it may assist you to see what features might usefully be added to the program. I must stress the word usefully. Too many commercial (and some non-commercial) programs are grossly overloaded with features of questionable utility, all of which combine to make the programs run slower, take up more disk and memory space, and make the manual twice as large as it need be. Worse still, on such programs it's often very difficult to find how to do the comparatively simple things you want to do because there is so much to wade through. QBASIC itself shows what happens when a program grows, but has to retain features from earlier versions. Start with a simple program, and add only what you find to be necessary and useful.

Start, then, by writing down what you expect the program to do. You might think that you don't need to do this, because you know what you want, but you'd be surprised. There's an old saying about not being able to see the wood for the trees, and it applies very forcefully to designing programs. If you don't write down what you expect a program to do, it's odds on that the program will never do it. The reason is that you get so involved in details when you starting writing the lines of BASIC that it's astonishingly easy to forget what it's all for.

If you write it down, you'll have a goal to aim for, and that's as important in program design as it is in life. Don't just dash down a few words. Take some time about it, and consider what you want the program to be able to do. If you don't know, you can't program it! What is even more important is that this action of writing down what you expect a program to do gives you a chance to design a properly structured program. Structured in this sense means that the program is put together in a way that is a logical sequence, so that it is easy to add to, change, or redesign.

If you learn to program in this way from the start, your programs will be easy to understand, take less time to get working and will be easy to extend so that they do more than you first intended. In particular, your structure should make use of the building bricks of computing: input, computation and display. This means that your outline plan should consist of these elements – what you need to add is just what you want input, worked with and displayed, and what order of actions will do what you require. QBASIC makes this type of work particularly easy, but since QBASIC is so different from older forms of BASIC you may have to unlearn some bad habits (like line numbers) or be reminded that better ways exist.

All of this is made easier if you design using a core and subroutines. If you get the program working using the simplest and most direct methods, you can easily elaborate it later. Tired of a slow running sort routine? Replace the subroutine with a different one, and you can concentrate on your mouse programming, knowing that what you are doing should not interfere with the running of the rest of the program. At one time other programming languages were greatly superior to BASIC in this respect, but the introduction of the SUB procedure and the FUNCTION to QBASIC allow for local variables to be used, insulating the subroutines from the main program and allowing you to swap one subroutine for another much more easily.

To highlight the differences more clearly, we can take a look at the development of two programs, one in this chapter using the traditional GOSUB...RETURN system, the other, in Chapter 16, using the more modern CALL...SUB type of statements. The first is cheap and cheerful (an amusement rather than a utility) and the second is a slightly more serious effort. Both, however, have deliberately been kept simple and in a raw state anything longer than these examples demands far too much typing and is likely to inhibit you from trying them for yourself. It's important for you to practice the development of a program, so that short examples are of paramount importance.

A simple word game

Figure 15.4 shows the program outline plan for a simple word game. The aim of the game is to become familiar with the names of countries and their units of currency. The program plan shows what I expect of this game.

Aims.

1. **Present the name of an country on the screen, picked at random.**
2. **Ask what its currency unit is called.**
3. **Reply must be correctly spelled.**
4. **User must not be able to read correct answer from the listing.**
5. **Give one point for each correct answer.**
6. **Allow two chances at each question.**
7. **Keep a track of the number of attempts.**
8. **Present a score as number of correct answers out of number of attempts.**

Figure 15.4. An outline plan for a simple game.

It must present the name of a country, picked at random, on the screen, and then ask what the name of its currency is. A little bit more thought produces some additional points. The name of the currency will have to be correctly spelled. A little bit of trickery will be needed to prevent the user (son, daughter, brother or sister) from finding the answers by typing LIST and looking for the DATA lines. Every game must have some sort of scoring system, so we allow one point for each correct answer. Since spelling is important, perhaps we should allow more than one try at each question. Finally, we should keep track of the number of attempts and the number of correct answers, and present this as the score at the end of each game. Now this is about as much detail as we need, unless we want to make the game more elaborate. For a first effort, this is quite enough, because if we design it correctly, we can add as much elaboration as we like later. How do we start the design from this point on?

The answer is to design the program in the way that an artist paints a picture or an architect designs a house. That means designing the outlines first, and the details later. The outlines of this program are the steps that make up the sequence of actions. We shall, for example, want to have a title displayed. Give the user time to read this, and then show instructions. There's little doubt that we shall want to do things like assign variable names, dimension arrays, and other such preparation. We then need to play the game. The next thing is to find the score, and then ask the user if another game is wanted. It all has to be put it down on paper and Figure 15.5 shows what this might look like at this stage.

1. Display title, then instructions.
2. Display name of country.
3. Ask for name of currency unit.
4. Use INPUT for reply.
5. Compare reply with correct answer.
6. If correct, add 1 to score, and ask if another one is wanted.
7. If incorrect first reply, allow another try without incrementing number of tries.
8. If second reply incorrect, select another question.
9. Game ends when user types n or N in reply to 'Do you want another one' message (or does not type y or Y)

Figure 15.5. Extending the plan.

Foundation stones

Now, at last, we can start writing a chunk of program. This will just be a foundation, though. What you must avoid at all costs is filling pages with BASIC lines at this stage. As any builder will tell you, the foundation counts for a lot. Get it right, and you have decided how good the rest of the structure will be. The main thing you have to avoid now is building a wall before the foundation is complete!

Figure 15.6 shows what you should aim for at this stage. There are only fifteen lines of program here, and that's as much as you want. This is a foundation, remember, not the Empire State Building. It's also a program that is being developed, so use some REM lines to point to where there might be changes.

```
REM Prepare variables
CLS : GOSUB ttlname
REM title line
GOSUB tellem
REM instructions
GOSUB setup
DO
GOSUB playit
REM play the game, chaps
GOSUB score
REM Present score
GOSUB ask
REM Another game?
LOOP UNTIL INSTR("Yy", k$) = 0  END
```

Figure 15.6. A core or foundation program for the example.

The REM lines allow you to put notes in with the program. These notes will not be printed on the screen when you are using the program, and you will see them only when you edit. In Figure 15.6, I put the REM notes on lines which immediately follow the main lines. This way, I can edit out all the REM lines later when the program is complete, tested, and working perfectly. REMs are very useful, but they make a program take up more space in memory, and run slightly slower.

Keep one copy of a program with the REMs in place, and a working copy without them. That way you have a fast and efficient program for everyday use, and a fully detailed version that you can use if you want to make changes. After a little practice, you may feel that you can dispense with a lot of REM lines in any case, because if you use meaningful label names for your GOSUBs, you need hardly use them.

Let's get back to the program itself. As you can see, it consists of a set of GOSUB instructions, with references to subroutines that we haven't written yet. That's intentional. What we want at this point, remember, is foundations. The program follows the plan of Figure 15.5 exactly, and the only part that is not committed to a GOSUB is the main DO loop that is terminated by the use of INSTR("Yy",K$). When INSTR("Yy",K$) runs, we get 1 if Y is pressed and 2 if y is pressed. If K$ is neither y nor Y, then INSTR gives 0, meaning that the string we are seeking is not contained in 'Yy'. It is simple, but very useful.

Take a good long look at this fifteen-line piece of program, because it's important. The use of all the subroutines means that we can check this program easily – there isn't much to go wrong with it. We can now decide in what order we are going to write the subroutines. The wrong order, in practically every example, is the order in which they appear. Always write the title and instructions last, because they are the least important to you at this stage. In any case, if you write them too early, it's odds on that you will have some bright ideas about improving the game soon enough, and you will have to write the instructions all over again.

A good idea at this stage is to type a REM at the start of each GOSUB line that is not yet written, or which you don't yet need to use. This saves a lot of time when you are testing the program, because you don't have the delay of printing the title and instructions each time you run it, or problems trying to run subroutines that are not written.

First developments

The next step is to get to the keyboard and enter this core program. You might want to place REMs before each GOSUB in order to make sure that the main loop works before you go any further. The next step is to record this core program and then keep adding to the core. If you have the core recorded, then you can load this into QBASIC, add one of the subroutines, take out its REM and then test. When you are satisfied that it works, you can record the whole lot again, using the same filename (unless you want to keep the early versions). Next time you want to add a subroutine, you start with this version, and so on.

This way, you keep on the disk a steadily growing program, with each stage tested and known to work. Again, this is important. Virtually always, testing takes very much longer than you expect and it can be a very tedious job when you have a long program to work with. By testing each subroutine as you go, you know that you can have confidence in the earlier parts of the program, and you can concentrate on errors in the new sections. This is even more important when you use the CALL..SUB type of routines, see later.

The next thing we have to do is to design the subroutines. Some of these, such as title and instructions, may not need much designing as far as their programming is concerned. This does not mean that you should start with them, because such details can wait. A simple routine to start with is the one that asks if you want another game, and waits for a Y or N reply. This is a straightforward INKEY$ routine, Figure 15.7. You could use INPUT$ in your own version.

```
ask:
PRINT " Would you like another game?"
PRINT "Please answer Y or N"
DO: k$ = INKEY$: LOOP UNTIL k$ <> ""
RETURN
```

Figure 15.7. The ask subroutine, all ready to use.

The next task is what you might think is the hardest part of the job – the subroutine which carries out the playit action. In fact, you don't have to learn anything new to do this. The Play subroutine is designed in exactly the same way as we designed the core program. That means we have to write down what we expect it to do, and then arrange the steps that will carry out the action. If there's anything that seems to need more thought, we can relegate it to a subroutine to be dealt with later.

As an example, take a look at Figure 15.8. This is a plan for the Playit subroutine, which also includes information that we shall need for the setting-up steps.

1. **Keep the answers as DATA lines containing ASCII codes. Read into an array.**
2. **Keep list of countries in another DATA line, to be placed in another array.**
3. **The number that selects the country also selects the codes for the answer.**
4. **Use variable tr% for number of attempts.**
5. **Use variable sc% for score.**
6. **Use variable go% to record number of attempts at one question.**

Figure 15.8. The plan for the playit subroutine.

The first item is the result of a bit of thought. We wanted, you remember, to be sure that some smart user would not cheat by looking up the answers in the DATA lines. The simplest deterrent is to make the answers in the form of ASCII codes. It won't deter the more skilled, but it will do for starters. I've decided to put all of the answers in order in DATA lines in the form of a string of ASCII codes for each answer, with each code written as a three-figure number. The capital letters of ASCII will use two figures only, the small letters three, so making them all into three figures simplifies things. You'll see why later – what we do is to write a number like 86 as 086, and so on. That's the first item for this subroutine.

The next one is that we shall keep the names of the countries in an array. This has several advantages. One of them is that it's beautifully easy to select one at random if we do this. The other is that it also makes it easy to match the answers to the questions. If the questions are items of an array whose subscript numbers are 1 to 10, then we can place the answers in DATA lines and read these also as a string array. Even neater would be to make both questions and answers part of the same array, a two-dimensional array. Another possibility would be to keep the names and the answers in DATA lines, and use RESTORE. This is not quite so neat, however.

The next thing that the plan settles is the names that we shall use for variables. It always helps if we can use names that remind us of what the variables are supposed to represent. In this case, using sc% for the score and tr% for the number of tries looks self-explanatory. The third one, go% is one that we shall use to count how many times one question is attempted. Finally, we decide on a name for the array that will hold the country names and the ASCII codes, q$.

At this point, watch for reserved names. It is only too easy to use names for variables or labels that are reserved (PLAY and EXIT are examples). The Editor will catch these, but it saves time if you avoid them in the first place.

Play time

Figure 15.9 shows what I've ended up with as a result of the plan in Figure 15.8. The steps are to pick a random number, use it to print the name of a country, and then find the answer. That's all, because the checking of the answer and the scoring is dealt with by another subroutine.

```
playit:
RANDOMIZE TIMER
go% = 0: pick% = RND * 10 + 1
retry:
CLS : PRINT " The country is - "; q$(pick%)
PRINT : PRINT " The currency is the - ";
INPUT x$: tr% = tr% + 1
GOSUB checkit
REM Find correct answer
RETURN
```

Figure 15.9 .The playit subroutine that generates the random number and picks a name.

Always try to split up the program as much as possible, so that you don't have to write huge chunks at a time. As it is, I've had to put another subroutine called checkit into this one to keep things short.

We start the playit subroutine by using RANDOMIZE TIMER to ensure that RND does not produce predictable sequences. The next step is to clear the variable go% to make sure that it does not contain a value from a previous run. This is not important when playit runs first, but in the course of the program it will be called many times, and go% must not be allowed to keep increasing.

The second part of this line then picks a number, at random, lying between 1 and 10 and this random number is assigned to variable pick%. The following lines are straightforward stuff. We print the name of the country, selected from the array by using pick%, that corresponds to the random number, and ask for an answer, the currency of that country. The section following the INPUT then counts the number of attempts, using tr%. This is the logical place to put this step, because we want to make the count increment by one each time there is an answer. Now it's chicken-out time. I don't want to get involved in the reading of ASCII codes right now, so I'll leave it to a subroutine which I'll write later. The REM reminds me what this new subroutine will have to do, and the Playit subroutine ends with the usual RETURN.

Dealing with the details

With the playit subroutine added and the program saved on disk, we can think now about the details. The first one to look at should be one that precedes or follows the playit step, and I've chosen the score routine. As usual, it has to be planned, and Figure 15.10 shows the plan. The correct answer will be contained in a variable called a$ – note that we can use a simple string variable a$ and a string array like a$(1) as separate variables – the value of one has nothing to do with the value of the other.

1. **For a correct answer, increment sc%, go to the next question.**
2. **For a first incorrect answer, with go%=0, allow another try. Decrement tr%, and increment go%.**
3. **For a second incorrect answer, with go%=1, pass to the next question, and make go%=0 again.**

Figure 15.10. Planning the score routine.

The correct answer a$, obtained from a separate subroutine, is compared with the input answer x$. Each time there is a correct answer, the number variable sc% will be incremented, and we can go back to the main program.

More is needed if the answer does not match exactly. We need to print a message, and allow another go. If the result of this next go is not correct, that's an end to the attempts. At this point, you might later want to include some sound. We could have a short beep to announce a mistake, and a long one for a correct answer. Write it down.

Figure 15.11 shows the program subroutine that has been developed from this plan – which is rather more complicated than you might think. This is an illustration of the extended I...ENDIF statement of QBASIC, and it allows these choices to be made in a more straightforward way than older versions. It's best understood in sections – which is how it was written and how it was typed.

```
score:
PRINT
IF x$ = a$ THEN
  sc% = sc% + 1
  PRINT " Correct - your score is now "; sc%
  PRINT " in "; tr%; " attempts."
  GOSUB dely
  RETURN

  ELSEIF go% = 0 THEN
    PRINT " Not correct - but it might be your spelling!"
    PRINT " You get another go free. "
    tr% = tr% - 1
    GOSUB dely
    go% = 1
    GOSUB retry
    GOSUB score
    RETURN

      ELSE
      go% = 0
      PRINT "No luck - try the next one"
      GOSUB dely
      RETURN
END IF
```

Figure 15.11. The score subroutine written. This allows for the three possibilities of the plan.

The PRINT statement is used to add a blank line, and this is done no matter what else follows. The next line deals with a correct answer. If the answer was correct, the good news can be printed and the subroutine can RETURN.

If the answer at this stage is not correct, though, the ELSE IF section swings into action. This tests the value of go% and, if it is zero, causes a message to be printed with further instructions. The answer subroutine is then called again so that the user can try another answer entry, and this answer is tested again. Note that this is an example of a form of recursion.

Now there's a piece of cunning here. The number variable go% starts with a value of 0. When there is an incorrect answer, however, and go% is still 0, the program prints the message about being allowed another chance, and goes to the answer subroutine. One of the actions of this path, however, is to set go% to 1. When you answer again, with go%=1, another path will be used, and if your second answer is wrong, the last section that starts with ELSE will run. This puts go% back to zero for the next round, prints a sympathetic message, pauses, and then lets the subroutine return.

Now that we've got the bit between our teeth, we can polish off the rest of the subroutines. Figure 15.12 shows the subroutine that deals with filling the arrays. It also shows the dimensioning and initialising steps that occur right at the start of the program.

```
REM At start of program
DIM q$(10), a%(10
tr% = 0: sc% = 0: go% = 0

REM read in questions and answers
setup:
FOR j% = 1 TO 10: READ q$(j%): NEXT
FOR j% = 1 TO 10: READ a$(j%): NEXT
RETURN
```

Figure 15.12. The setup subroutine for dimensioning and array filling.

At the start, the arrays are dimensioned and all the variables for the scoring system are reset to zero. You might think it more logical to dimension the arrays in the setup subroutine, but QBASIC objects to this, and such a step really does need to go right at the start.

The array q$ that will be used for the names of the countries, and the array a$ of numbers in string form that give the answers, is filled in the routine, using a data list, and that's it. We can write the DATA lines later, as usual.

Next comes the business of finding the answer, at the label name of checkit. We have planned this, so it shouldn't need too much hassle. Figure 15.13 shows the program lines.

```
checkit:
a$ = ""
FOR j% = 1 TO LEN(a$(pick%)) STEP 3
  a$ = a$ + CHR$(VAL(MID$(a$(pick%), j%, 3)))
NEXT:
RETURN
```

Figure 15.13. The lines that extract the ASCII codes and get the answer from them.

The variable pick% is the one that we have selected at random, and it's used to select one of the strings of ASCII numbers, a$(pick%). Since each number consists of three digits, we want to slice this string three digits at a time, and that's why we use STEP 3 in the FOR...NEXT loop. The answer string, which we call a$, is then built up. The value of a$ is set to a blank in the first part of the first line to ensure that we always start with a blank string, not with the previous answer, which would also be a$.

The string a$ is then built up by selecting three digits using MID$, converting to the form of a number by using VAL, then to a character by using CHR$. Remember that when you have a lot of brackets like this, you read from the innermost set to the outermost. This character is then added to a$, and this continues until all the numbers in the string have been dealt with. That's the hard work over. This result a$ is then used in the score subroutine to determine whether the input answer is correct or not.

Figure 15.14 is the subroutine for the instructions, a set of straightforward PRINT lines. These have been arranged to fit into a narrow screen, but you can rewrite them if need be. The instructions subroutine ends with an INKEY$ loop so that you need to press the spacebar to get to the game. Following that, Figure 15.15 is the title subroutine.

```
tellem:
CLS : PRINT TAB(15); "INSTRUCTIONS": PRINT
PRINT TAB(2); "The computer will supply you with the name"
PRINT " of a country. You should type the name of its"
PRINT " Currency - make sure that your spelling is"
PRINT " correct, and that you start your reply with a"
PRINT " capital letter. Press RETURN to enter your "
PRINT " reply. The computer will keep the score for "
PRINT " you. You get two shots at each name."
PRINT TAB(2); "Now press the spacebar to start."
DO: k$ = INKEY$: LOOP UNTIL k$ = " "
RETURN
```

Figure 15.14. The instructions – always leave these until you have almost finished.

```
ttlname:
CLS : PRINT TAB(33); "CURRENCY GAME"; : PRINT
GOSUB dely: RETURN
```

Figure 15.15. The title program lines.

The title portion includes a delay to give you time to read the title. Finally, Figure 15.16 shows the DATA lines and the time delay subroutine. The names of the countries occupy two DATA lines, and the ASCII codes for the answers are put into strings in four lines. The delay routine is a simple one that uses the TIMER variable.

```
DATA Albania,Holland,Greece,Norway,Colombia
DATA Turkey,Malaysia,Indonesia,Pakistan,China
DATA "076101107","071117105108100101114","068114097099104109097"
DATA "075114111110101","080101115111","076105114097"
DATA "082105110103103105116","082117112105097104","082117112101101"
DATA "082101110109105110098105"

dely:
k = TIMER: DO
    LOOP UNTIL TIMER >= k + 1
RETURN
```

Figure 15.16. The DATA lines with the name of the countries and the coded answers.

Now we can put it all together, and try it out. Because it's been designed in sections like this, it's easy for you to modify it. I have deliberately chosen a very simple theme just for this purpose. You can use different DATA, for example. You can use a lot more data – but remember to change the DIM in the initialisation step. You can make it a question-and-answer game on something entirely different, just by changing the data and the instructions. You can add some sound beeps, for example, or add more interesting display effects.

One major fault of the program is that once an item has been used, it can be picked again, because that's the sort of thing that RND can cause – the same country can even be picked twice in succession. You can get round this by swapping the item that has been picked with the last item (unless it was the last item), and then cutting down the number that you can pick from. For example, if you picked number 5, then swap numbers 5 and 10, then pick from a total of 9. This means that the RND(10) step will become RND(D%), where D% starts at 10 (or whatever number you use), and is reduced by 1 (using D%=D%-1) each time a question has been answered correctly. In this way, the game ends when all of the possible questions have been answered correctly.

There's a lot, in fact, that you can do to make this program into something a lot more interesting. The reason that I have used it as an example is to show what you can design for yourself at this stage using only the simpler statements of QBASIC. Take this as a sort of construction set to rebuild any way you like. It will give you some idea of the sense of achievement that you can get from working with QBASIC. As your experience grows, you will then be able to design programs that are very much longer and more elaborate than this one.

Designing with Extended QBASIC

The index program

The second example makes use of aspects of QBASIC that are not available in earlier versions of interpreted BASIC (though they are present in several compiled BASICs). Figure 16.1 shows a program outline plan for a simple indexing program. The aim is to be able to type in words and page numbers, edit out any mistakes and then display or print the list sorted into alphabetical order. I know that this can be done in about five lines using an MS-DOS batch file, but that's not relevant here. The outline program plan shows what I expect of the first attempt at this program. It must allow me to enter words, with suitable prompting, and page numbers. It should keep a tally of the number of words, and prevent the array from becoming overfilled. It must then allow me to edit each word or number in case of mistakes. The lists should then be sorted into alphabetical order, and finally presented either on the screen or to the printer.

1. Repeat
2. Enter phrase and page number
3. Until finished
4. Sort list
5. Ask – screen or printer
6. Output list on screen or printer.
7. END

Figure 16.1. The simple outline plan for an indexing program.

All of this hinges on a plan to use arrays to hold name and number. At this point, we might think hard about whether we want to use one array to hold both, or separate arrays. We often want to print an index in a form like byte, 38 using a comma to separate the two. If we want to do this, then we have to remember that we certainly can't type the comma if we choose to keep both name and number in one array. This is because the comma is taken to mean that more than one item is being entered. By using separate arrays, we can type the input using a comma, which seems more natural. The other point is that we might eventually want to merge items in which the same name appears with different page numbers. For example, if we have the items:

```
memory,22
memory,58
```

then it's likely we'll want to combine these in the form:

```
memory,22,58
```

This is not so easy if the name and the number are contained in one array item. On balance, then, two arrays seem to be indicated, as we can use name$ and number$ for them. Why use a string array to hold a number? Simply because we can do more with strings, and since we aren't going to perform any arithmetic with the number there doesn't seem to be much point in keeping it as a number array.

From this, the core program can be written, and when we start to use the QBASIC Editor with the modern type of subroutine, only the core part of the programs (plus the testing routine) will remain on screen when we are listing and testing – you can switch to any other subroutine by using the View menu. The core appears as in Figure 16.2.

```
'Start of main program
'input of words and numbers - REM out until ready
REM getit
GOSUB testin    ' temp entry
' editing of list
REM editit
' sorting of list
sortit
' display of list
dispit
' restore and clear
END
```

Figure 16.2. The core program for the index. Note that this program doesn't do anything yet.

To make use of the modern aspects of QBASIC, we need to work with the more advanced type of subroutine, and these can be declared in advance. We shall also declare variables in advance, so that there is no need to use markers such as $, !, % and so on. This type of usage brings QBASIC into line with other modern languages.

note This is all optional. If you call a subroutine using CALL, there is no need to declare it. If you call it by simply using its name, you need to use DECLARE. You can also opt to continue using variable names such as past%, incr$ or precise! should you prefer to.

Figure 16.3 shows what you should aim for at this stage. This lists the variables and the subroutines that will be used, with comment lines as reminders. This type of start needs much more planning than the simpler use of QBASIC illustrated in the first part of the Chapter, but since the planning has to be done anyway, why not do it thoroughly from the start – one of the criticisms of older BASICs is that you could go ahead in an unplanned way and get out of difficulties by dirty methods, like a crafty GOTO. This sounds like an advantage, but for more elaborate programs it could result in immense complication, especially for anyone trying to unravel what was happening.

```
REM initialising actions
DEFINT A - Z
CONST max = 26
' change this later
DECLARE SUB getit ()
DECLARE SUB editit ()
DECLARE SUB dispit ()
DECLARE SUB pagit ()
DECLARE SUB sortit ()

DIM SHARED nam(max) AS STRING, number(max) AS STRING

testin:
RESTORE
FOR j = 1 TO max
READ nam(j), number(j): NEXT
RETURN
DATA Memory,22,catalogue,35,zero,47
DATA abacus,62,ROM,64,RAM,67
DATA port,67,bus,68,digit,69,data,70
DATA RISC,71,random,72,read,73,write,74
DATA set,75,instructions,75,codes,76,clear,77
DATA cable,78,buffer,79,guide,80,inject,82
DATA serial,83,parallel,83,start,85,stop,85
```

Figure 16.3. The definition lines for subs, and the testin routine for testing.

note An extra subroutine has been included. Testin is purely for testing – it avoids the need to have to type in data each time the program is to be tested, and it can be removed, along with its calling line, when the program is running satisfactorily. Writing a test routine like this can help considerably in debugging a new program, see Chapter 17.

Declaring the items such as integers, constants and subroutines (and, in other programs, functions as well) is no extra burden because you should have provided for these in your plan. One considerable benefit is that you can see at a glance what subroutines will be called and which ones make use of an array. The test routine need not be written at this stage, but it is an advantage to do so because it creates some data in the form that you want it and will test if the program can handle it correctly. The subroutines must then be designed on paper. As an example, take a look at Figure 16.4

1. Set item number to zero
2. Repeat
3. increment item number
4. Input words and number
5. Check for limit – out if exceeded
6. Until comma entered.

Figure 16.4 An outline plan for the entry procedure.

This is a plan for the word/number input procedure, which also includes information that we shall need for the setting-up steps. The plan starts by setting an item number at 0, then follows a loop in which the item number is incremented, the name and number are input, with the item number is printed so that you can keep a check on what has been done. The program then checks for the limit – the loop will have to be left if this has been reached. If the subroutine does not end in this way, then it is terminated by entering a comma and pressing the ENTER key.

When you are working on the core, each procedure is entered by using the Edit menu, selecting New SUB. This prompts for the name of the new SUB, and switches you to a screen which shows the SUB name and END SUB lines so that you can type whatever you want between these two.

If you are altering an older program to QBASIC SUB format, each time you edit out the GOSUB and remove the colon (such as changing GOSUB testin: to just testin), you will see this Subroutine editing screen, and you can cut the subroutine lines from the old version and paste into the new SUB space, then edit the lines.

Entry subroutine

Figure 16.5 shows a first attempt at a suitable entry subroutine which carries the name of 'getit'.

```
SUB getit
STATIC n AS INTEGER
CLS
PRINT "Enter name, number, ENTER (comma, ENTER to end)"
n = 0: DO
  n = n + 1: PRINT TAB(2); "Item"; n; ": ";
  INPUT nam(n), number(n)
  IF n = max THEN PRINT "Last item": EXIT DO
LOOP UNTIL nam(n) = ""
END SUB
```

Figure 16.5. A listing for an entry subroutine. Note that n is defined as an integer, so the % sign is not used.

The first line is a title line, and the second line deals with variable n. This is to be a STATIC variable, mainly because in an expanded version of this program we might need its value to remain unchanged between calls to this routine. As always, n is a local variable.

note A procedure should use local variables as far as possible. The only variables that have been declared as shared by all subroutines are the name and number arrays. The constant 'max' is also shared.

The screen is cleared, a reminder is printed (this could be put in later), variable n is set to 0 (important, since this is a static variable) and the entry loop then starts in the next line with the item number being incremented. This is the best place to increment the number, because it means that all the input and testing will be carried out with this same item number. The item number is printed, and the INPUT statement gets the inputs to the array. The next line then tests for the last entry number having been reached, and prints a suitable message if it has, then leaves the loop. Finally comes the looping condition, which is that the name is not a blank. These few lines can be typed into place, and tried out by running this routine from the core, using REMs to prevent anything else from running.

The routine appears to do just about what we need when we test it, and that's another important point. The testing must check for three things in particular. One is that the entries are as you would expect, another is that the program ends as you expect (a blank entry or reaching maximum entry number). The other thing is that no silly entry causes problems. In this case, ending the routine before the maximum number has been input is not straightforward, because you have to press ENTER, then a comma and then ENTER again. This is because of the use of INPUT name$, number$. We can live with this for the moment, and tidy it up later, because the essential thing is to get a working overall scheme.

Later, we can substitute a routine that uses a DO WHILE loop terminated by maximum value, and which takes an entry for name$, tests it, exits if it is the ENTER key, and only if it is a genuine name prompts you for a page number. Later, remember, not now. The only other likely problem is entering a name, then pressing ENTER. What happens, though, if another name is entered here? The answer is nothing – it can't be detected. A small rethink will be required later, along the lines of testing the ASC code for the first character of the entry and rejecting it if it is not a digit.

One final point to note is that the true number of genuine entries is n-1 if the entry is terminated by pressing ENTER with no data, because the last entry is always a blank one, but the number is max if the entry is terminated by coming against this limit. There will be some work to do on all this later, but at this stage it just goes into the documentation. When the program is running, these fine points can be sorted out with the knowledge that it should still work after the amendments have been carried out. That, after all, is the whole point of working with subroutines in this way.

For testing what happens when a maximum number of entries is used, alter the value of constant max temporarily to 5 or some other convenient number.

The Edit subroutine

We can leave sorting and display for the moment, because we already know how to tackle these points, and we'll turn now to the editing routine. The essentials here are to display items, amend them as needed and ensure that they are corrected in the list. In a later version we might be able to reproduce something like the excellent screen editing of QBASIC to do this, because that part of QBASIC is designed to work on ASCII files of the type that we are entering. Perhaps in a V3.0 of this program, we might make our lists by using the QBASIC editor, and then recording the results on disk, but that's beyond our scope just at the moment (but see Chapter 18 onwards). What we need must be reasonably simple, but capable of letting us see what we want and correcting the mistakes.

The new lines of code are shown in Figure 16.6 and are the minimum that will serve. We have not used any fancy system of visual selection to display and pick out entries, because at this stage such a routine would take up a disproportionate amount of time to develop and would hinder the completion of the outline program.

```
SUB editit
STATIC n AS INTEGER
CLS
PRINT "Do you want to edit the list (Y/N)?"
DO
  k$ = INKEY$
LOOP UNTIL k$ <> ""
IF INSTR("Nn", k$) <> 0 THEN EXIT SUB

DO
  PRINT "Type item number range 1 to"; max; " only"
  INPUT n
  LOOP UNTIL n >= 1 AND n <= max
PRINT "Item"; n; ": is "; nam(n); ","; number(n)
  INPUT "Your changes:"; nam(n), number(n)

END SUB
```

Figure 16.6. A simple one-off edit subroutine which relies on typing a new entry to replace a faulty one.

The correction is of a very simple type – just displaying the existing item and then making another input. If your typing is precise, you might have so few corrections to make that this system is perfectly adequate – remember that there is no point in adding embellishments for their own sake or, worse still, to show how good your grasp of QBASIC is.

Once again, variable n is static so that it will keep its value if needed in a later version. The routine has been written so that it appears once after entry and, when a correction has been made, it is not recalled. Would this really be sufficient, or would we want to be able to recall this routine later? In a later version it might be preferable to use a menu structure with SELECT..CASE so that items such as entry, editing, sorting and printing could be carried out in whatever order we wanted. A menu structure would also allow the addition of other options such as read 'file from disk' when we get round to these points.

The next step is display and printing. Display on the screen is straightforward, because it has been done already in the course of editing. You have to decide at this point whether to use a subroutine to serve both purposes, or to write a new one for final display. Since we want to allow the possibility of printed output as well as screen, we might as well make this a new routine. The choice of printer or screen destination will have to be made before the data is printed and Figure 16.7 shows this part of the program.

```
SUB dispit
OPEN "lpt1" FOR OUTPUT AS #1
OPEN "con" FOR OUTPUT AS #2
CLS : PRINT "Type (P)rinter or (S)creen"
DO: k$ = INPUT$(1)
  ctrl = INSTR("PS", UCASE$(k$))
LOOP UNTIL ctrl <> 0
CLS
FOR n = 1 TO max
' need to use ctrl to specify screen or printer here
  PRINT #ctrl, nam(n); ","; number(n)
  IF UCASE$(k$) = "S" THEN
  IF n / 20 = n \ 20 THEN pagit

  END IF
NEXT
END SUB
```

Figure 16.7. A display subroutine that offers the choice of screen or printer.

A novelty in this routine is that the choice of screen or printer is done by allocating the device number as variable ctrl, using the numbers of 2 for the screen and 1 for a printer. This form of action is dealt with in more details later (Chapter 19), but the essence of it is that when a number is assigned by using the OPEN statement, a PRINT #1 will print to the device with that number. This makes it easy to write a single routine rather than one for printer and one for screen.

When the message about using screen or printer appears, it is tested in a DO..LOOP UNTIL set of lines until a satisfactory answer is obtained. The test uses the assignment to ctrl of the results of INSTR and, because the answers are in the order "PS", INSTR will return 1 for P and 2 for S, but 0 for any other answer. Using UCASE$ ensures that there are no silly errors caused by using the wrong case of letter. This value of ctrl can then be used to terminate the loop, and for determining whether the printout goes to screen or to printer. Do not use the P option unless you have a printer connected and on line.

If the screen option is chosen, you want to avoid having the data scrolling past you with no time to watch. The screen output is therefore paged. This is done using the test:

```
if n / 20 = n \ 20 then pagit
```

This uses the two different division operators in a way that has been illustrated earlier. It pages the screen output into 20 line units. You might, of course, want to page your printer output as well and, since the only difference between screen and printer is the reference number (1 or 2) it should be easy to alter pagit to cope with either by testing the value of variable ctrl. The pagit routine in its simple form is shown in Figure 16.8.

```
SUB pagit
STATIC g AS STRING
PRINT "Press any key for next page"
g = INPUT$(1): CLS

END SUB
```

Figure 16.8. The routine for paging text on screen.
This could be adapted to page for the printer as well.

This as it exists at present is very straightforward and could have been incorporated into the test for 20 lines. All that is left is to put in the sort routine and, once again, that's something that we have covered before. On the basis that you keep it simple until you are sure of what you are doing, we'll use the straightforward string sort. Figure 16.9 shows the final listing for this part of the routine, using the Shell-Metzner sort (see Chapter 10).

The only changes from the earlier examples of sorts are the addition of another SWAP for sorting the number array along with the nam array and the use of Ucase$ in the test so that names are sorted into the correct order no matter whether they are in upper or lower case. This is important, because if ASCII code order is taken, any word in capitals is placed ahead of a word in lower case. For example, if you had the words Zebra and abacus, then the order of an ASCII sort would be Zebra followed by abacus, placing the uppercase always before the lowercase. By using UCASE$ in the test, we avoid all such troubles. Once again, a quick test reveals that the routine works.

note A marker variable xc is used as one of the tests for ending a loop. If this is not used a GOTO will be needed to make the loop work, and older versions of BASIC used to program the Shell–Metzner sort with a tangle of GOTO lines.

```
SUB sortit
STATIC y AS INTEGER, jt AS INTEGER, k AS INTEGER
STATIC z AS INTEGER, xc AS INTEGER

PRINT "Sorting...please wait": y = 1
DO WHILE y < max: y = 2 * y: LOOP
DO
  y = INT((y - 1) / 2): IF y = 0 THEN EXIT DO
  jt = max - y
  FOR j = 1 TO jt: k = j
   DO
     xc = 0
     z = k + y
     IF UCASE$(nam(z)) <= UCASE$(nam(k)) THEN
       SWAP nam(z), nam(k)
       SWAP number(z), number(k)
       k = k - y
       xc = 1
     END IF
   LOOP UNTIL (xc = 0 OR k < 1)

  NEXT
LOOP
END SUB
```

Figure 16.9. The sorting subroutine, using a conventional Shell-Metzner sort.

All the testing so far will have been done with the aid of READ...DATA lines, and these will be kept until we can be absolutely sure that the program works perfectly. Once that has been accomplished, we can delete these lines and put in the initialisation that we need in order to make this a useful program. We shall also have to alter the entry routine to make sure that constant max is assigned with the actual maximum number of entries once entry is complete. Using an array of 300 entries would be enough for the indexing of a small book. Obviously, if your needs require more than this, you can extend the dimensioning to suit yourself, but for large numbers of entries, there are other methods open to you and, in particular, you would probably want to keep the entries, both before and after sorting, on a disk file. Now you have a working program, you can start to embellish it as you please. In all of this work, you may, if you have read school texts of computing (many written in the 60s), be surprised to see no elaborate flowcharts or other planning aids. The reason is that when you plan to make use of standard subroutines, the use of flowcharts is unnecessary. Providing that you draw up a plan of what the program will do and in what sequence, you can build the program in stages as I have demonstrated, knowing that you can rely on each stage which has been used in other programs, and testing each stage, old or new, as you go. This is one very great benefit of programming in this core and subroutine form, and another is the ease with which you can alter the program to suit yourself.

Debugging

Digging out the bugs

In computing language, a fault in a program is called a *bug*, removing faults is called *debugging* and someone who puts the faults there is, of course, called a *programmer*. Your programs can exhibit many kinds of bugs, and these are indicated by the error messages that you get when you try to run them. Some of these messages are pretty obvious. 'Label does not exist', for example, means that you have used a command like GOTO cornbelt or GOSUB cornbelt and forgotten to write label cornbelt.

There are two types of bugs, and the differences between them mean that they have to be tackled in different ways. If, for example, you have spelled the name of a statement incorrectly, like 'pribt', this mistake can be picked up early on by the Editor. If you type, as has been recommended, using lowercase lettering, you will not see this word appear in uppercase when you press the ENTER key, indicating that it is incorrect. When you try to run, the Editor will check the lines and draw your attention to this one before allowing the program to start. This allows you to make changes before the program is run – the Editor will not even allow you to run the program until the changes are made.

This type of bug, a *pre-run bug,* will almost always be caught by the way that the Editor of QBASIC checks all the lines of a program when you try to run it. The other type of bug, a *run-time bug,* cannot be caught in this way, however. Suppose you have in a program the lines:

```
DIM a%(20)
FOR n% = 1 TO 30
a%(n%) = rnd * 50
NEXT
```

then the check that the Editor makes will not reveal this fault, because each line has the correct syntax. It is only when the value of n% reaches 21 that this will be caught as a *Subscript out of range* error. The loop will have run through 20 passes by this time, and data will have been generated. All you can do is abandon the run, correct the mistake and start again.

As it is, the most common fault message is *Syntax error,* picked up by the pre-run checking of the Editor. This message invariably means that you have wrongly used some of the reserved words of BASIC. You might have spelled a word incorrectly, like NXT instead of NEXT. You might have used a reserved word as a variable or subroutine name (other error messages can be caused by this). You might have missed out a bracket, a comma, a semicolon, or put a semicolon in place of a colon or a comma.

The most common mistake, missing out a space before or after a command word, is caught by the Editor when you press the ENTER key for that line. Any spelling errors of command words, or missing spaces which allow command words to be joined to other words, can be easily found if you always enter your programs using lower-case. Since the computer always converts all reserved words to upper-case, you will find that mistakes are highlighted by being still in lower-case. Machines can't tell what you meant to do, they can only slavishly do exactly what you tell them. If you haven't used BASIC in exactly the way the machine expects, you'll find a syntax error being reported.

A common run-time error is *Illegal Function call*. This usually means that something silly has happened involving a number. You might, for example, have used LOG(-5), which is an obvious mistake, but it's not so obvious if the command happens to be LOG(N%), and N% has been changed to a value of -5. Anything that makes use of numbers, like MID$, LEFT$, RIGHT$, STRING$, and others can have an incorrect number used – and this will cause this type of error which can be caught only when the program runs. You will also find that using a negative number in SQR(N), a negative or zero value in LOG(N), and other mathematical impossibilities will cause this error message. The cause shouldn't be hard to trace, because the machine tells you which line caused the trouble by switching back to the Editor with the offending line highlighted.

note Each error message gives you the options of going back to the Editor by clicking on <OK>, or of obtaining Help by clicking on the <Help> option. In many cases you may find that the <Help> is not particularly helpful unless you already know what is going on.

Even when you have eliminated all of the syntax errors and improper arguments, you may still find that your program does not do what it should. The most difficult faults to find are those that have arisen from errors in planning, because it is much more difficult to find such errors when there are no error messages to find them for you. You may find, for example, that a loop is never completed, or an input is never asked for, or a subroutine runs even when you don't want it. These things can occur in programs that are totally free of syntax errors or run-time errors. Of all these types of errors, the never-ending loop is one of the most awkward.

QBASIC does what any BASIC of the '90s should do – it gives you a lot of ways of finding out exactly what has gone wrong. One of the most powerful of these is the Ctrl-Break key combination. This stops the action of the machine which can be continued when you press F5. This can be very useful for bug-hunting in screen display routines as well as in loops. What you possibly don't know, however, is that you can print out the values of variables, and even alter values while the program is stopped, making use of the Immediate window, and then make the program resume by using the F5 key.

You cannot, however, make use of f5 to continue if you have called up an edit, or changed the program statements in any way. This will give a message such as 'Cannot continue'. Suppose, for example, you are running a program which uses a slow count, and you press Ctrl-Break at some early stage. The program stops. Suppose that the counter variable is N% and the count is to 1000. Try typing ?N% in the Immediate window, and press ENTER. This will give you the value of N%. Now type N=998 (say) in the Immediate window and press ENTER. Press f5 to resume, and you will then see the count start again – but at 998!. This is an excellent way of testing what will happen at the end of a long loop. Testing would be a rather time-consuming business if you had to wait until the count got there by itself. The use of the Ctrl-Break key method of tracing a fault can be very handy, because it allows you to print out the state of the variables at any stage in the program, and then carry on.

Trace and single-step

One valuable way of checking what is going on in a program makes use of the Trace and Single-step features of the Editor. Single-stepping means that each statement of the program is run and the Editor then waits for another command for you, such as another single-step. The F8 key can be used to make each step happen. When a program runs one statement at a time like this you can use the Immediate screen to check the value of variables (if there is any doubt). If a line such as K% = 5 has just been run, there is not much point in checking K% because it will be 5, but for a line such as K% = RND * 5 you would want to know what number had been assigned to K%.

When you use single-step, it can often be helpful to know which step is being run, and switching Trace On will do just this. When you take this option of the Debug menu, it is shown with a dot against it, and this will remain to show that Trace is switched on until you select again to turn tracing off. The effect of Trace on is to highlight the statement at which the single-step has stopped. For example, if you single-step and Trace the program lines of:

```
FOR n% = 1 TO 100
PRINT n%
  FOR j% = 1 TO 2: NEXT
NEXT
```

the steps in tracing will look as follows. The first use of the F8 key starts the outer loop, so that the Editing screen shows the program with the PRINT n% statement highlighted:

```
FOR n% = 1 TO 100
PRINT n%
  FOR j% = 1 TO 2: NEXT
NEXT
```

showing where the step action has ended. Use F4 to switch to the Results screen to see the number that has been printed. The next press of the F8 key returns you to the Editing screen with the program looking as:

```
FOR n% = 1 TO 100
PRINT n%
  FOR j% = 1 TO 2: NEXT
NEXT
```

indicating that the inner loop is about to be run for one pass. When F8 is pressed again, the highlighting shifts:

```
FOR n% = 1 TO 100
PRINT n%
  FOR j% = 1 TO 2: NEXT
NEXT
```

and this is highlighted again with the next press of F8 because this inner loop runs twice. Another press takes you to the second NEXT.

```
FOR n% = 1 TO 100
PRINT n%
  FOR j% = 1 TO 2: NEXT
NEXT
```

so that the outer loop has now been completed. When you remember that you can print out variable values by using the Immediate screen, switch between Edit and Immediate by using F6 and switch between Results and Edit using F4, this is obviously a very powerful way of checking what happens in a loop.

The obvious disadvantage is that a loop of 1000 passes could take a long time. However, you should not need to go through a loop like this. What you are usually interested in is what makes a loop keep running or what makes it end prematurely, so you need to study the variables that are tested in the loop, at the start (DO...WHILE), the end (LOOP...UNTIL), or in the middle (such as IF x%=>5 THEN EXIT DO). You do not need to go through every pass of a loop to check these because you can either:

a) Make the loop a shorter one, for example by using FOR n% = 1 TO 5 in place of 1 TO 1000.

b) Alter the value of a variable in the loop using the immediate screen so that the loop finishes after one more pass.

note The Trace feature can also be placed into the program by using the TRON and TROFF statements. The keyword TRON in a program turns the tracing on and TROFF turns it off. Using trace on is not particularly rewarding if you do not single-step the program, however.

Using single-step and a trace is an excellent way of finding why a program sticks in a loop or why an assignment seems to be incorrect, but in some cases it can be rather too long-winded. This is particularly true when a program contains a lot of calls to SUB procedures, each of which is known to run well, so that there is no point in single-stepping through each SUB. For such eventualities, the Procedure Step (using F10) is very useful, because it treats a call to a SUB as a single step, so that the actions of the procedure are carried out, but the only steps are call and exit, allowing you to see what has been changed by the procedure without going through every step.

Quite often you know exactly at what point a program fails without needing to single-step at all. For such cases, the ability to set breakpoints is very valuable. A breakpoint is, as the name suggests, a point at which program action will be held suspended, allowing you to print (using the Immediate screen) and alter variables. The F9 key is used to toggle breakpoints, ie pressing F9 turns a breakpoint on and pressing it again at the same place turns it off.

In use, the cursor is placed where you want the program to stop, and the F9 key pressed. There is no indication, unfortunately, at this point of the breakpoint being placed in that line. When the program is run, however, it will stop at the breakpoint, and the statement will be highlighted. You can then read and/or change variable values as you wish and use the F5 key to continue the program.

note You can set a break point for a single statement in a line, but not for each statement in a line that contains several statements separated by colons. Pressing the F9 key for a second time in a line will cancel the effect of the first action.

You can set as many breakpoints as you like, but for most cases only one or two will be needed to make the program yield its secrets. Since the breakpoint leaves no visible trace, you need to use the Clear all breakpoints command to remove all of the breakpoints before you resume testing on the program.

Unavoidable errors

There are occasions when an error in a program may be totally unavoidable. This is particularly true of mathematical functions like SQR and LOG which cannot accept a negative number, or of string actions which depend on using the length of a string. Feeding in a negative number to these mathematical functions, or a string of zero length to some string actions can therefore cause an error message at run time.

By far the best way of dealing with such errors is to trap them, testing numbers for being negative, and strings for length, but in a very few cases there is no way at all of avoiding a run-time error in some line. The method of dealing with this is the use of an ON ERROR line, and this is dealt with in Chapter 22 along with other actions that are triggered by some event.

Testing

Testing a program is, as often as not, as important and as difficult as designing it in the first place. A whole volume could be written about the topic, but in the confines of this Chapter, only a few hints will be noted for the type of testing that you need to do when the program is known the be running:

1. For preliminary testing use a subroutine which contains data in READ...DATA lines to avoid the need to enter data on every test.
2. Always test with limit values. If, for example, you have a limit of 20 characters in a string entry, try a 21-character string and a blank string. Check the effect of entering numbers that are too large or too small.
3. Where any sorting or selection is used, test with values that can be checked – an example is illustrated in Chapter 19.
4. Test every procedure and function – some may never run with normal data.

QBASIC Serial Filing Techniques

What is a file?

I have used the word 'file' in the course of this book to mean a collection of information of any type which can be recorded on disk. Programs in BASIC are one type of file, the only type, incidentally, which permits the use of the LOAD and SAVE commands from the Editor. The SAVE and SAVE AS commands save the program as a set of ASCII codes, which is a more versatile type of file for BASIC programs because it can be used by QBASIC, by some DOS routines like TYPE, and by most standard wordprocessors and editors (including WordStar, WordPerfect and many others). This, of course, also allows you to prepare your QBASIC program files with the aid of these and similar text programs.

note You can prepare a QBASIC program with a wordprocessor only if it is set to produce ASCII files. In general, the Editor of QBASIC is so good that it would be pointless to use anything else, and the only reason for mentioning this is because you might want to prepare files on a machine that did not have QBASIC, such as a portable.

In this chapter, however, I shall use the word 'file' in a narrower sense, to mean a collection of data that is separate from a program. For example, if you have a program that deals with your household accounts, you would need a file of items and money amounts. This file is the result of the data gathering action of the program, and it preserves these amounts for the next time you use the program. It would be pointless to write such a program if all the data needed to be typed in afresh each time you wanted to use it.

Taking another example, suppose that you devised a program which was intended to keep a note of your collection of vintage 78 rpm recordings. The program would require you to enter lots of information about these recordings, such as title, artists, catalogue number, recording company, date of recording, date of issue and so on. This information is a file, and at some stage in the program, you would have to record this file. When you load a BASIC program and RUN it, it starts from scratch. All the information that you fed into it the last time you used it has gone – unless you recorded that information separately. This is the topic that we're dealing with in this chapter, recording the information that a program uses or *filing* the information. In this Chapter, we look at the roots of the subject and at one type of filing that QBASIC can carry out.

Knowing the names

You can't discuss filing without coming across some words which are always used in connection with filing. The most important of these words are record and field, illustrated in Figure 18.1.

A record is a set of facts about one item in the file. For example, if you have a file about vintage steam locomotives, one of your records might be used for each locomotive type. Within that record, you might have wheel formation, designers name, firebox area, working steam pressure, tractive force and anything else that's relevant. Each of these items is a field, an item of the group that makes up a record. Your record might, for example, be the SCOTT class 4-4-0 locomotives. Every different bit of information about the SCOTT class is a field, the whole set of fields is a record, and the SCOTT class is just one record in a file that will include the Gresley Pacifics, the 4-6-0 general purpose locos, and so on. Take another example, the file called 'British Motorbikes'. In this file, BSA is one record, AJS another and Norton is another. In each record, you will have fields. These might be capacity, number of cylinders, bore and stroke, gear ratios, suspension system, top speed, acceleration and whatever else you want to take note of. Filing is fun – if you like arranging things in the right order.

The importance of filing is that all of the information can be recovered very quickly, and that it can be arranged in any order, or picked out as you choose. If you have a file on British Motorbikes, for example, it's easy to get a list of machines in order of cylinder capacity, or in order of power output, or any other order you like. You can also ask for a list of all machines under 250 cc, which ones used four-speed gearboxes, which were vertical twins and which were two-strokes. Rearranging lists and picking out items is something which is a lot less easy when the information exists only on paper.

```
                FILE
Record 1
              Field 1 Index number 1
              Field 2 Type 1
              Field 3 Wheel formation 1
              Field 4 Tractive force 1
              Field 5 Working pressure 1
              Field 6 Firebox area 1
Record 2
              Field 1 Index number 2
              Field 2 Type 2
              Field 3 Wheel formation 2
              Field 4 Tractive force 2
              Field 5 Working pressure 2
              Field 6 Firebox area 2
Record 3
              Field 1 Index number 3
              Field 2 Type 3
              Field 3 Wheel formation 3
              Field 4 Tractive force 3
              Field 5 Working pressure 3
              Field 6 Firebox area 3
```

Figure 18.1. Records and Fields in a File.

Disk filing

In this book, because we are dealing with QBASIC and its very advanced filing systems, we'll ignore filing methods that are based on DATA lines in a BASIC program. Though you may be experienced with the use of filing with disk, I'll explain filing from scratch in this Chapter. If it's all familiar to you, please bear with me until I come to something that you haven't met before. To start with, there are two main types of files that we can use with a disk system, *serial files*, and *random access files*. The differences are simple, but very important.

A serial (or sequential) file places all the information on a disk in the order in which the information is received, just as it would be placed on a cassette. If you want to get at one item, you have to read all of the items from the beginning of the file into the computer, and then select. There is no way in which you can command the system to read just one record or one field. More important, with such files you can't easily change any part of a record, or add more records in the middle of such a file. Any such action has to be done by reading the whole file and making alterations while the file is in memory, then rerecording the whole file.

A random access file does what its name suggests – it allows you to get from the disk one selected record or field without reading every other one from the start of the file. You might imagine that, faced with this choice, no-one would want to use anything but random access files. It's not so simple as that, though, because the convenience of random access filing has to be paid for by a lot more complication. For one thing, because random access filing allows you to write data at any part of the disk, it can be very easy to wipe out valuable data with a badly designed program. There is also a problem of choosing which record to read. We'll start in this Chapter, by looking at serial files, which are easier to design and use and which are suitable for a large variety of purposes. Random access files are dealt with in Chapter 19.

Serial filing on disk

We'll start by supposing that we have a file to record, called CAMERAS. On this file we have records (such as Nikon, Pentax, Canon, Yashica and so on). For each record we have fields like Model, Film Size, Shutter speed range, Aperture range (standard lens), Manual or Automatic, and so on. How do we write these records? First of all, we need to arrange the program that has created the records so that it can output them in some order. Figure 18.2 for example, shows how we might arrange this part of a QBASIC program (using the older type of statements) so as to input a number of records, with five fields to each record.

The number of fields is five, so the fields are input from the keyboard using a FOR n% = 1 TO 5 loop. The number of records isn't fixed, so we use a DO..LOOP UNTIL loop, which keeps putting out records until it finds one called "X" or "x", which is the terminator. If we need to make a test for the terminator at the start of a loop, then it's better to use a DO WHILE..LOOP form. Note that we haven't used an array for holding these items, because an array has to be dimensioned, and we don't know in advance how many items we will have. Instead of storing the items in an array for future use, they will be recorded on disk. The points where the disk recording routine would be fitted are shown in the REM lines. Each item, field or record, is treated as a string. This is because strings are easier to work with and produce an ASCII file on disk that is compatible with the files of other forms of text.

Organising the fields in this way allows you to have the fields as long or as short as you like, and they will eventually be recorded on the disk in the same form. QBASIC also allows you to gather fields into units called records, but for this purpose fixed length strings must be used (see Chapter 12). The main point of serial filing is that you can use fields widely varying lengths without the waste of space that you get when you need to declare a fixed length, and all shorter strings are padded out with blanks. The use of these

```
CLS : rc$ = "": x% = 0: DIM field$(5)
REM would need to open file here
PRINT TAB(27); "DATA ENTRY": PRINT
PRINT TAB(2); "Type x% for record name to end entries"

DO
  PRINT TAB(4); "Name of this record ";
  INPUT rc$
  IF UCASE$(rc$) = "x%" THEN EXIT DO
  REM need to record this name on disk
  x% = x% + 1
  FOR n% = 1 TO 5
    PRINT TAB(5); "Field item "; n%; " is ";
    INPUT field$(n)
    REM each item will be recorded
  NEXT
LOOP UNTIL UCASE$(rc$) = "x"

REM end of entries
REM would need to close file
PRINT TAB(2); "There are"; x%; " records in this file"
```

Figure 18.2. The form of a filing program, showing how data has to be arranged for a serial file.

fixed length strings is, however, essential when random access filing is needed, and we'll deal with it under that heading. Remember, however, when you reach that point that the use of records is just as valid when you want to use serial filing.

The illustration above uses ordinary strings as the type of variables being filed, but remember that you can declare a type of your own. You might, for example, create a type that consisted of a string, two integers and a single-precision number. A variable of this type could be assigned and filed using the same sort of lines as in the example.

That deals with the organisation of the data for putting on to disk, but how do we actually put it on the disk? There are several stages, and the first one is to open up the file. This means assigning a reference number, otherwise known as a *stream* or *channel number*, and a filename which will be recorded on the disk, and there are two varieties of this statement, one for writing and one for reading. The stream number is a purely temporary thing which is used from the time that a file is opened until it is closed, and you might use a variable name for this purpose. Having assigned a stream number, you must not OPEN again with the same number until the first file that used the number has been closed. Apart from that, though, you are free to assign stream numbers as you please. The OPEN statement will cause the disk to spin and the filename to be recorded.

Once the file has been opened for writing, with the filename on the disk, you can place data on to the disk using a statement of the form PRINT #5 or WRITE #5. The '5' in this example must be the same as the reference number or stream number that was used in the OPEN statement, because this is how the machine recognises files. Each time you want to make use of a file that has been opened, you must use this file stream number which has been established by the earlier OPEN statement.

The purpose of using the filename and the stream number is to organise data. The disk stores all data in units of 512 bytes. It wouldn't make sense to spin the disk and find a place on the disk just to record one byte at a time, so when you record or read a disk, it's always one complete sector, or as much of a sector as possible, at a time. Some of the memory of the computer has to be used to hold data which is being gathered up for recording, or which is being replayed. The stream number is an identifying number for the piece of memory, called a *buffer*, that is being used, so that the machine finds the correct data in the correct part of the memory. Using this stream number avoids the need for you to have to allocate parts of the memory to use in this way as buffers. The memory which is used for this purpose is reserved by a command in a file that runs when the Master disk is used to load in QBASIC.

- The CONFIG.SYS file of your PC will probably contain a line such as:

```
BUFFERS 30
```

which decides how many buffers can be used (all open) at any particular time. If you write a program that needs to keep a large number of buffers open you might have to change this number.

Opening the file

After that short diversion, back to our filing program. Before we start to gather the data together for filing, we need to 'open the file' for the data. This is done using the OPEN "aircraft.dat" FOR OUTPUT AS #1 command. OPEN has to be followed by a filename, which can specify a drive and/or directory path. If you do not specify any drive or path, as in this example, the file will be recorded on the same directory as contains the QBASIC files.

note Using OUTPUT has disadvantages, as we shall see later, so that using APPEND is almost always preferable. For the sake of illustration, however, we shall use OUTPUT here and explain the differences later.

The filename OPEN must be followed by one of the keywords INPUT, OUTPUT or APPEND (or for other purposes RANDOM or BINARY). For networked files, the keywords ACCESS and LOCK (also followed by qualifying words) can be used, but we'll ignore this. The next keyword is AS and it has to be followed by file number (the # is optional) in the range 1 to 255. You can also specify a buffer size, such as LEN=256 if you want to use a different buffer size (the default is 512 bytes).

When a large program can generate and file a large amount of data, then you really need to keep the program and the data directories separate. The standard filename extension for data is .DAT, so it makes sense to use this unless you have some pressing reason to use something else. When you are developing a program that will go through a large number of stages, it's a good idea to put the stage number into the main title as, for example, CAMERA01.DAT. When this first line is executed, the disk spins for a short time, preparing for the file, and the filename appears on the directory/catalogue if you interrupt the program and type DIR. The buffer space will also be prepared in the memory and allocated to the stream number which, in the examples, has been 5.

In some program examples, files may be opened and closed by various subroutines or procedures so that when an OPEN line occurs, you may not be able to tell in advance what number to allocate. This can be solved by using the FREEFILE function, in the form:

```
filenum% = FREEFILE
```

which returns the next available channel number as the integer filenum% (or whatever variable you want to use) so that this variable can be used in an OPEN statement.

Printing to the file

It's at this stage that we need to make use of the loops in the writing program. Within these loops, we need to have a line something like:

```
PRINT #5, field$
```

in which PRINT #5 means 'put the information out to the buffer whose stream number is 5' (the stream number that was selected for the OPEN statement) so that PRINT #5 will eventually put out to the disk system the data that follows. The PRINT #5 statement can be used exactly as you would use the PRINT statement, and so can be followed by strings, numbers, commas and so on. There's an alternative, WRITE #5, which is used particularly where strings are concerned and, for most general purposes, WRITE #5 is more useful if you are recording more than one item in each statement. In this Chapter, we will use PRINT #5 because WRITE #5 has no advantages for the type of examples used here. In this example, what is being printed to the file is field$. There is no need to use an array, such as Field$(N%) here, because the items are recorded to the disk/buffer in order and no array is needed. We also need to write the record name, and this is done within the loop, by using a line such as:

```
PRINT#1,rc$
```

Figure 18.3 shows the complete example of a very short and simple program of this type which has been adapted from the first example.

```
DECLARE SUB fields (rc$)
CLS : OPEN "aircraft.dat" FOR OUTPUT AS #5
REM APPEND better, see text
rc$ = ""
DIM SHARED x AS INTEGER
PRINT TAB(27); "DATA ENTRY": PRINT
DO WHILE UCASE$(rc$) <> "X"
PRINT
  INPUT "Name of this record "; rc$
  IF UCASE$(rc$) <> "X" THEN CALL fields(rc$)
LOOP: REM end of file
PRINT x; " records on file ."
CLOSE
END

DATA Country of origin,Type,Engines,Empty weight
(kg),Accommodation

SUB fields (recordname$)
PRINT #5, recordname$: x = x + 1
RESTORE
FOR n% = 1 TO 5
  READ head$
  PRINT head$; " "; : INPUT field$
  PRINT #5, field$
  NEXT
END SUB
```

Figure 18.3. A simple serial file writing program which writes a record with five fields. The field titles are stored as a DATA line in this example, making the routine easy to adapt to your own uses.

The programming makes use of a DO WHILE form of loop, with a subroutine used for the field inputs and the disk filing statement. You can enter anything you like into this, but it makes more sense to enter something that you can easily check. Since the file is called 'aircraft.dat' a set of items has been put into a DATA line to act as headings. You can, of course, easily change this program so that it has another title that suits the information that you might want to use, and a completely different set of headings.

Before we move on, consider what this program has done. It has created a file called aircraft.dat on the QBASIC directory, and allocated a channel number of 5 to it. It has stored the data as it came along, in the sequence of RECORD, then FIELD. Finally, the file has been recorded and closed by using CLOSE.

This last step is very important. For one thing, you don't actually record on the disk any of the information in this short program until the CLOSE statement is executed. That's because it would be a very time-consuming business to record each item of a file at a time. What the filing system does, remember, is to gather the data together in memory. This is the buffer piece of memory and its contents will be written to the disk only under one of two possible circumstances. One is that the buffer is full, so that there is a complete buffer-load to write. The other is that there is a CLOSE type of statement in the program. For a large amount of data, the disk will spin and write data each time the buffer is full. The CLOSE statement then writes the last piece of data, the one which doesn't fill the buffer. It also writes a special code number, called the *end-of-file* code (EOF). This can be used when the file is read, as we'll see later.

If you forget the CLOSE statement, you'll leave the buffer unwritten, with no EOF – and cause a lot of problems both in your programs and possibly with that disk. Forgetting the CLOSE is called *leaving your files open,* and you wouldn't like to be seen like that, would you? It's possible to use something like CLOSE #5 but since CLOSE deals with any and all open files, this is easier and more certain. The biggest danger is when you are testing a program. If there is an error, such as a syntax error, which stops the program from running, there will be no CLOSE carried out, and the files will be open. If you had typed a lot of data, you would lose it if you then went on to correct the program and run it again. The correct procedure is to close all of the open files. In this example, it's easy – you only have to type CLOSE and press RETURN. For a large program, you would probably find it better to write an ON ERROR GOTO line which, when an error occurred, closed files and ended, see Chapter 22. This would automatically ensure that files are never left open. The CLOSE ensures that your data on all file stream numbers are recorded.

When you use an INPUT statement, as in this example, to gather up the data, you can find that with a lot of data you will hear the disk start and stop at intervals. That's an indication of the buffer transferring data to the disk. You won't see on the screen what you type on the keyboard while the transfer is taking place, but the time that's needed to write a sector is fairly short, and no characters will be lost. In this example, there is nothing like enough data to fill a buffer. You will hear the disk spin when the OPEN command is executed, and again when the CLOSE command is executed, but not at any time between these two unless you enter a huge amount of data.

note: You can use the INPUT$(5,#1) type of statement in place of INPUT if you know that each file consists, in this example, of five characters. In general, actions such as INPUT$ or PRINT that are available for screen control are also available, when used with a channel number, as file control.

You can use a diagnostic function FILEATTR to determine what type of file you have opened. The form of the function is:

```
PRINT FILEATTR (5,1)
```

in which the first number of integer variable in the brackets is the channel number and the second is a code for the type of information. If this second code is 2, then the file channel number is returned (not particularly useful when you had to specify it anyway). If the code 1 is used, the number that is printed (or assigned to a variable) describes the type of file OPEN statement as:

1 ....Input

2 ....Output

4 ....Random

8 ....Append

32 ....Binary

One disadvantage of using the program of Figure 18.3 is that each time you use it a new file of the same name is created, wiping out the old file. This is a considerable disadvantage which can be avoided by altering the OPEN statement to:

```
OPEN "aircraft.dat" FOR APPEND AS #5
```

When APPEND is used, specifying a new file name simply creates a new file just as using OUTPUT would; but if a file already exists it is added to, not substituted. For almost all applications, then, it is preferable to use APPEND.

note: There is another form of OPEN statement in QBASIC that is more compatible with the system used for older versions. You should not use it on new programs, only as a way of running older programs with the minimum of changes. This follows the OPEN keyword with a MODE2$, a string that determines how the OPEN statement will work. For details, see the HELP page under the heading of OPEN statement Alternate Syntax.

Getting your own back

Having created a file on disk, we need to prove that it has actually happened by reading the file back. You can read this file in quite a surprising number of ways, because it is an ASCII file. If you don't have QBASIC running, you can use the DOS TYPE command or, if BASIC is running but you don't have the filing program to hand, you can use the QBASIC Editor to show the files in the directory and open the data file. You can even edit the data file with the QBASIC Editor. To delete a file you can use the DOS commands ERA filename, DEL filename, or, in BASIC, the KILL "filename" direct command. Once again, KILL is a BASIC command and, as such, can be used within a program or from the Immediate window.

We need to look now at a QBASIC program to read and make use of this file. A program which reads a file must contain, early on, a command which opens the file for reading. This is OPEN "aircraft.dat" FOR INPUT AS #6 and it must use the same filename as was used to write the file. If we recorded a file using the name 'aircraft.dat',then we can't expect to be able to read it if we use 'cameras' or any other name. Misspelling can haunt you here, because if you specify a filename such as aircraft or AIRCRAFT.DAY you get only the response 'file not found' appearing in an error message window.

Remember that if a program crashes in this way you should close the open file by typing in the Immediate window the word CLOSE (press ENTER). Once the file has been opened, we can read data with INPUT #6 (or LINE INPUT #6), just to establish that we don't have to use the same number as we had when we recorded the file. This is then followed by the variable name that we want to assign to each item. This statement reads an item from the disk, and allocates it to a variable name, for printing the item or other use, according to what we have programmed. The number of reads can be controlled by a FOR...NEXT loop, if the number is known, or it can make use of the EOF marker, if it isn't known.

By testing for NOT EOF(#6), meaning 'not the end of file for file number 6', we can make the program stop reading the file at the correct place. The example of Figure 18.4 shows both methods in use.

The number of fields has been five, so that a FOR...NEXT loop can be used to control the input of the fields. The number of records, however, has not been fixed by a FOR...NEXT loop, so we have to keep reading the file until the EOF byte is found. This is done by testing EOF in a DO..LOOP UNTIL type of loop. If EOF is found, then the file is closed and the program ends. As you can see, the EOF(6) test has been put at the END of the loop, because EOF occurs after the last file has been read.

Qnote This is an important point if you are converting programs from the older BASICA or GW BASIC. In these versions, the test for EOF could be made at the start of a WHILE..WEND loop, but this cannot be done in QBASIC.

```
DEFINT A-Z
CLS : OPEN "aircraft.dat" FOR INPUT AS #6
PRINT TAB(27); "DATA DISPLAY": PRINT
DO
  INPUT #6, name$
  PRINT "Name of this record- "; name$
  RESTORE
  PRINT : FOR n = 1 TO 5
    READ head$: INPUT #6, gen$
    PRINT head$; " - "; gen$
  NEXT: PRINT
  RINT "Press any key for next record"
  k$ = INPUT$(1)
LOOP UNTIL EOF(6)
CLOSE : PRINT "End of file"
END
DATA country of origin,type,power,empty
weight,accommodation
```

Figure 18.4. Reading back a serial file(a), in this case the file that was created by the program of Figure 18.3.

If you attempt to read again from a file like this, you get the 'Input past end of file' error message, and the program stops. Unless you have arranged for an ON ERROR GOTO line to close files for you, the files will still be open. Leaving a reading file open is not quite such a disaster as leaving a writing file open, but it's still very undesirable. Note that the disk does not spin each time you press a key to get another record. This is because a complete chunk of data is read each time and, if the information that you want is all in one buffer load, the disk need not be used. Sorry if I seem to be labouring this point, but a newcomer to disk filing sometimes finds it difficult to remember. If you now try out the reading program you can see that we have the essence of a useful filing system here. It's quite common to have the data gathering and writing part of a program separate from the reading and analysing portion like this, but you can have the two parts combined into one single program with a menu choice if you like.

If you need to know the length of the file, you can use the LOF function, but this is not particularly useful for files of this type. The form of the function is:

```
x% = LOF (1)
```

where x% contains the file length in bytes. This type of action is more suited to binary files in which each byte is counted.

Now this simple example shows a lot about serial filing that you need to know. We have used PRINT #5 mainly because there was only ever one item at a time to put on to the file. If you have a whole set of items to put at one time, it's better to use WRITE #5, because you don't get any problems with formatting, such as you get with PRINT #5. For example, if you use PRINT #5, A$, B$ you set 18 spaces for each string because of the use of the commas, which is exactly as it would be when you use PRINT A$,B$. The choice of INPUT or OUTPUT so far, however, allows us to create a new file, to overwrite a file of the same name or to read a file. What we have not encountered so far is how to update a file. One method of file updating is that of adding more items to the end of the file and, as it happens, there is a particularly simple way of carrying this out by using the APPEND word following OPEN.

Appending data

A simple serial file has a number of advantages, prominent among which is the ability to use variable length strings. In the past, however, serial filing systems have allowed only one way of altering the serial file – that of reading the file in, altering it and writing it out again. The QBASIC serial files have a huge advantage in this respect as items can be added (appended) to the end of the file by altering the file OPEN statement. If you want to edit an item in an existing part of the file or delete a record or field, then the old-fashioned method must still be used, and we'll look at them later. For the moment, we'll take a look at how APPEND is used.

There is just one line of the data entry program of Figure 7.3 that needs to be altered. In place of the existing OPEN line, type in the replacement:

```
OPEN "aircraft.dat" FOR APPEND as #5
```

in which the words INPUT or OUTPUT have been replaced by APPEND. When this runs, new data will be added to the end of the existing file, and you can use the data reading program to check out that the new items have indeed been added. This is so beautifully simple that it invites the writing of a general entry subroutine in which you can pick (N)ew or (A)dd at an early stage. The reply to this can then be used to run either an OUTPUT or an APPEND line for OPEN, since this is the only difference between the routines, and the entry of data will take the same pattern as illustrated earlier. Things are not nearly so simple when you need to make alterations to records that are in the middle of a serial file.

Updating the file

There are two answers to the problem of updating a serial file, other than by appending new records. One possibility, which is the simplest one for short files, is to load the whole file into the memory of the computer, stored as an array or arrays, make the alterations (your BASIC program will have to be written so as to provide for this) and then write the file again, wiping out the earlier version. The other, much better, possibility is to open two files, one for reading and the other for writing. Working with two files open means that the computer maintains two buffers. You read one record from the reading file and you can, if you want, display it. If it's all right, it's then written – initially to the buffer. If the record has to be modified, you can do so. If extra records have to be added, this is equally simple, and no great amount of computer memory need be taken up with large arrays, no matter how much data is involved. Each time a buffer empties, the disk spins and a read or write takes place. This *simultaneous* operation is possible because of the use of different OPEN commands, which control different buffers. One complication is that the open files must have different filenames. In practice, it's a matter of writing your program to suit and Figure 18.5 (continued overleaf) illustrates the programming methods that are needed.

```
DECLARE SUB editit ()
DECLARE SUB change (j)
DEFINT A-Z
CLS
ON ERROR GOTO trap

DIM SHARED gen$(5)
x = 1
OPEN "aircraft.dat" FOR INPUT AS 6
OPEN "aircraft.new" FOR OUTPUT AS 5
REM note that 5 and 6 can be used instead of #5, #6
PRINT "Please specify record to be changed (number, RETURN)"
INPUT "Record Number "; reply
q = 0

DO
  FOR n = 0 TO 5
    INPUT #6, gen$(n)
  NEXT
  IF x = reply THEN CALL editit: q = 1
  FOR n = 0 TO 5
    PRINT #5, gen$(n)
  NEXT
  x = x + 1:
LOOP UNTIL EOF(6)
CLOSE
KILL "aircraft.bak"
```

```
NAME "aircraft.dat" AS "aircraft.bak"
NAME "aircraft.new" AS "aircraft.dat"
IF q = 0 THEN PRINT "No such record found"
PRINT "End of program"
END
trap:
IF ERR = 53 THEN RESUME NEXT ELSE GOTO 0

DEFSNG A-Z
SUB change (j)
PRINT "New value for item"; j;
INPUT gen$(j)

END SUB

SUB editit
DO
  CLS
  FOR n = 0 TO 5
    PRINT TAB(2); n; " "; gen$(n)
  NEXT: PRINT
  PRINT TAB(2); "pick item to alter (0 - 5), 6 to end"
  PRINT TAB(2); "(RETURN key not needed)"
  a$ = INPUT$(1): j = ASC(a$) - 48
  IF j >= 6 THEN EXIT DO
  IF j < 0 OR j > 5 THEN PRINT "Incorrect choice - 0 to 5 only"
  CALL change(j)
  LOOP
END SUB
```

Figure 18.5. Changing items in a serial file. This involves reading the file, changing items and then rewriting the file. In this example, the rewriting is under a different filename and the files are renamed after the changes have been made.

The principle is to read the items of a specified record, print them and then change an item or items before rerecording the file. The main problem is to find a neat way of doing this. In the example, the file AIRCRAFT.DAT is opened, the changes made and the file saved as AIRCRAFT.NEW. Once the files are closed, any file called AIRCRAFT.BAK is deleted, the old AIRCRAFT.DAT file is renamed to AIRCRAFT.BAK and the new file is renamed to AIRCRAFT.DAT. The actions of deletion and renaming are covered in Chapter 22 and will be only briefly described. A further complication is that if no file called AIRCRAFT.BAK exists the program will stop with an error message. Once again, the programming methods for avoiding this problem are detailed in Chapter 22.

The program of Figure 18.5 shows one approach which edits by the simplest possible method, asking you what you want to change specified by record number and item number. Note that the file names have been chosen so as to make the revised file be saved as a temporary file under the filename AIRCRAFT.NEW. At the end of the program, the original file is renamed as a BAK file, and the temporary file is renamed as the main aircraft.DAT file.

One point we have to be very careful about, however, is closing files. The CLOSE statement is used whenever the program has finished, and it could also be used in the ON ERROR GOTO line so as to ensure that if an error is encountered in the program or its files, then all open files are closed. During the course of experimenting with serial files, you may corrupt files and wipe out end of file marks. This will cause trouble at the UNTIL EOF(6) stage, and the program will normally stop with an error message and all files open. The use of an error trap, see Chapter 20, can ensure that all files are closed if an error occurs, but because such a trap is not straightforward in this program it has been omitted in the example.

The first five lines are concerned with initialisation and the last in this set is the ON ERROR GOTO trap statement, which switches the program to label 'trap' if any error occurs. This avoids any error message and the usual ending of the program when an error is found. Since the main reason for having this line is to ensure that the program does not stop if there is no file called AIRCRAFT.BAK, label trap is followed by a test for the File not Found type of error and, if this is what caused the stop, the program resumes. If any other type of error has caused the trouble, the GOTO 0 ensures that the program stops and the normal error message is printed.

The main array, GEN$ is dimensioned as SHARED so that it can be used by all procedures, and what follows is the filing part of the program. The input file is aircraft.dat and the output file is aircraft.new. You are asked which record you want to change, and the assumption here is that you know the records by number. If you don't, then you could alter this section of the program so that you either looked at each record, or searched for some feature, such as GEN$(0) (the record title) having a value like 'Beechcraft'. Given that the number is the method used here, though, the main loop starts with the DO line as usual. The principle is to read in the records, and increment the counter number x for each record until x is the number that you requested. If you have requested an impossible number, then the end-of-file will be met first, and the loop will stop.

When the correct record has been read, CALL editit transfers control to the section that allows you to alter the record. This is a straightforward editing routine which displays the whole record with item numbers, and asks you to press keys 0 to 5 to alter some aspect of the record, or key 6 to end the editing. After any change, the record is displayed again, so that you can check the change and possibly make another.

With the amendment made, the subroutine returns, and all records beyond the one you have edited will be read and rewritten until the end of the file. The main loop ends at the LOOP UNTIL EOF(6) line. The files are then closed, and the renaming starts. When you first use this program, there will be no aircraft.BAK file on the disk, so the command to kill the old aircraft.BAK file will cause an error if this file does not exist. This is dealt with by using the ON ERROR GOTO command, which will resume with no error message if the error is a 'File not Found' type. With this filename no longer on the disk, the original aircraft.dat file can be renamed as AIRCRAFT.BAK, and then the new AIRCRAFT.NEW file can be renamed as AIRCRAFT.DAT. This leaves you with a copy of the amended file, and also a copy of the previous version, a very useful feature to build into any program that uses files. This is followed by a test which will print an explanatory message if you happened to ask for a record number higher than the number of records in the file. The variable q is changed only if a record is found.

Serial filing is often dismissed as primitive, but it is relatively free of complications, and has the enormous advantage of allowing you to use unrestricted string sizes. The read-then-write action that is necessary to alter a file can be tedious when large files are being used, but the machine is doing the work, and the time required is not so very great. For any type of data that requires only appending rather than amending, and can be kept in the order in which it was entered, serial files are preferable to other types. Remember, incidentally, that editors and wordprocessors create serial files, so that the QBASIC editor can read (or alter) the files of the programs illustrated in this chapter.

Q note A statement such as PRINT #4, data$ is not specifically a serial file command, simply one that sends the data out along a specified channel. If the channels that you use are assigned to the printer or the screen then the effect of the command will be to print to either of these outlets. By using a statement of the form:

```
PRINT #ctrl%, data$
```

you can send data to a file, to the screen or to the printer depending on the number assigned to the integer variable ctrl%. This type of use has already been illustrated in Chapter 15.

To assign a channel number to screen or printer requires an OPEN statement in the usual form, but with filenames that are taken by the system as screen or printer. For example:

```
OPEN "LPT1" FOR OUTPUT AS #1
OPEN "CON" FOR OUTPUT AS #2
```

opens channels for printer and screen respectively, so that data can be sent along either path. You can also use the "COM1" filename to allow a file to be sent over the serial port. Using the OPEN "COM1:" type of statement requires considerable experience with serial communications and details have been omitted here – for an example, see the Help page for OPEN COM.

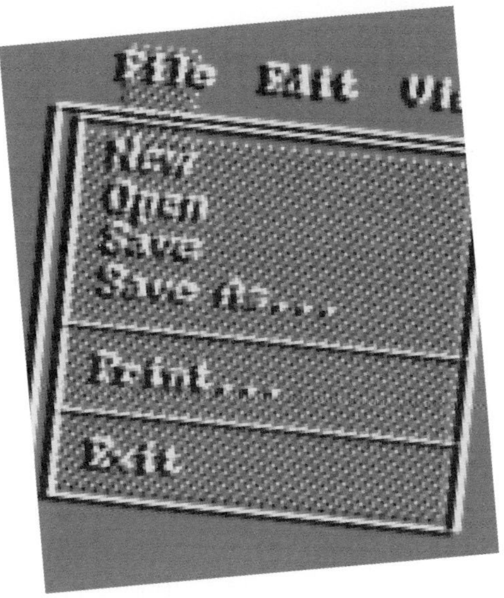

Random Access Filing

Fundamentals

Random access filing, as the name suggests, means that we should be able to get at any record (or set of records) on the disk without having to read all of the earlier records as well. This doesn't mean that we have to create a random access file by scattering bytes all over the disk (though we could), simply that it should be possible to locate and read any byte on the disk. As you might by now expect, this is not done by reading one selected byte but by reading one complete sector into buffer memory and working on it there.

In general, we can create and record a file using much the same general techniques as we have used for serial filing. We can then add to the file, replace items, change items and select items at random using random access techniques. The important point about such random access filing is that it's possible to extend a file so that the file length is much greater than could be held in the memory of the computer. As an alternative, of course, we can use the random access filing methods that we need for extending a file in order to create the file in the first place. With a random access file, we can extract single items or groups as we please and amend, delete or replace items, without the need to read the whole file into the memory and then back to disk as we did with the serial files. For most purposes, all that ever has to be read or written is one sector of the disk. This freedom, however, is bought at a price, the details of which are not easy to dig out from the Help pages.

Random access commands

The main random access commands of QBASIC are OPEN, PUT and GET. These open a file and save or load data but, in addition, there are a number of commands that deal with the way that the data is organised. QBASIC allows you to use two quite different methods. One is compatible with older versions of BASIC, and uses commands that set the size of each record and how the fields are packed into the record. The more modern system relies on creating a new data type, a RECORD, which is then filed just like any other variable, but which can consist of a mixture of other data types such as strings, integers and floating-point numbers.

Random access filing is possible only if each record in the file consists of the same number of fields, and each field in the record is of a specified size. There's nothing magical about random access filing. The name of the file is stored on the disk directory and the directory also contains the starting position of the file. From then on, it's easy. If you know that each record is 100 characters (bytes) long, for example, then it's easy to find the 4th record (numbering from 1) because it will start at the 300th byte in the file and the 17th record will start at byte 1600. Similarly if the 100 byte record consists of four names each of 25 characters, then it's easy to find the third name in a record by getting to byte 75 within that record.

Without these fixed lengths, random access filing is not possible in this comparatively simple form. Whatever method is used to prepare data, it must specify at some point how long each record will be, allowing you to specify each field, its name in the file and its length in number of characters/bytes. No matter what type of data you may specify, everything must be recorded and replayed in the form of a string of fixed length. The older system uses a FIELD statement, the more modern one uses a defined data TYPE.

The older system

The form of a FIELD statement is simple. It starts with FIELD #1 or FIELD #file%, for example, using the file channel (or reference) number. As usual, unless you have some rooted objection to the number, you might as well use 1. Using a variable such as file%, which can be assigned with the number 1 at some earlier stage, allows you some freedom when you are designing a program, in case you want to change the channel number (to avoid conflict with another file, perhaps) without having to change all the statements that use it.

Remember that using a variable as the channel number allows you to use the same PRINT #stream% form of command to screen or printer.

Having used the FIELD statement and the channel number, you then put in each variable name that you want to use in the file and its maximum size.

The syntax here is 'size AS name' and each name must be a string name. You can, for example have such items as 25 AS A$, 32 AS Add$ and so on. There must be one of these number AS string statements for each field that you use, and they are separated from each other and from the start of the FIELD statement by commas. The FIELD statement cannot be run until the file has been opened.

The OPEN statement is more straightforward, because much of it is as you would use it for a serial file. The keyword OPEN is followed by the filename as for a serial file, with RANDOM in place of INPUT, OUTPUT or APPEND this time, because a random access file permits two-way traffic. Following the name comes AS and then the file channel number. A space separates this from the record size, in the form LEN=50, so that a complete OPEN statement would be like:

```
OPEN "daybook.rnd" FOR RANDOM AS #1 LEN=50
```

- The LEN=50 part is optional – the length will be taken as 128 if this is not specified.

Any existing file of this name is opened for random access by this statement and if no such file exists, one will be created. No BAK files are created when you use random access filing, so there's nothing to stop you writing new data all over a valuable file if your program is badly designed. The length of the record, LEN=50 in this example, must match with the total of the lengths of the fields that are to be used. As you might expect, chaos results if you use a LEN figure which is too small. There is no problem with a larger length than is needed, because the data will be padded out to fit.

The record length is fixed at 128 characters, the standard buffer size for a random access file, unless you specify something different in the LEN part of the OPEN statement. For quite a surprising number of applications, 128 characters is a convenient record size but, if you are filing something much smaller, it would be a ridiculous waste of disk space.

Padding

Since each field in a random-access file must be of a fixed length, what do we do if the information does not fit? To start with, we ensure that any number information fits, by methods that we can look at later. The awkward items are strings like names and addresses. These are chopped if they are too long and padded out with blanks if they are too short. Unlike some versions of BASIC, QBASIC does not require you to write a lot of tedious loops in order to pad out short names. Instead, you can use two functions that will have a very familiar ring to anyone (like me) who used the good old TRS-80 disk system, or who have more recent acquaintance with MALLARD BASIC on the Amstrad PCW machines. These functions are LSET and RSET.

These keywords are compatible with GW-BASIC and BASICA statements for random access filing.

The names indicate the action, but the syntax will be unfamiliar unless you have used a similar filing system. LSET, for example, sets a string to the left of its field, fills out the right-hand side with blanks and assigns the field to the record. For example, using LSET A$=nam$ assigns A$ so that it contains nam$ followed by enough blanks to make up the correct field size, and puts this field into place in its record. You cannot assign correctly to field names other than by the use of these three commands, of which LSET is by far the most common. If the FIELD statement has used A$ AS 25, then the name in nam$ will be padded out to 25 characters, with the name at the start. As you might expect, if nam$ consists of more than 25 characters, it will be chopped to 25 characters by omitting characters at the right-hand side.

The word RSET works in a similar way, but it sets the string over to the right, putting the padding blanks on the left. This is most likely to be used when you have converted numbers to strings and want the numbers placed to the right-hand side of a field.

Numbers are treated in a rather special way. Since each item that is stored in a random-access file must be a string, the obvious thing to do is to convert each number into a string by using STR$. However, this is a slow action and, if you have to work with large files and a lot of numbers, it can noticeably increase the time that you spend just waiting. In addition, the conversions that are made by STR$ are to quite long strings, particularly for double precision numbers, and you have to make your fields long enough to hold all the characters.

QBASIC provides three sets of reserved words to cope with this conversion in a different and more useful way, once again familiar to former TRS-80 (and present PCW) programmers. The principle is to convert into string form not the number itself, but the code that is used to store the number. The result of this is strings that are often of very weird characters. If you try to print the result they are certainly not recognisable as numbers. The advantage is that an integer always codes as a 2-character string, a single-precision number as a 4-character string, and a double-precision number as an 8-character string. Figure 19.1 illustrates this with a short program that uses the codings, prints the characters and the lengths of the strings, and shows how we can convert them back into printable numbers.

```
A% = 65: B% = 16706
X = 22.45
D# = 216.45169#
A$ = MKI$(A%): PRINT A$; " ("; LEN(A$); ")"
B$ = MKI$(B%): PRINT B$; " ("; LEN(B$); ")"
X$ = MKS$(X): PRINT X$; " ("; LEN(X$); ")"
D$ = MKD$(D#): PRINT D$; " ("; LEN(D$); ")"
PRINT CVI(A$); "    "; CVI(B$)
PRINT CVS(X$); "    "; CVD(D$)
```

Figure 19.1. The effects of the MK and CV type of statements to convert between number form and string form. However, the string form is not the same as used by STR$, as this shows.

The number-to-string conversions are done by MKI$ (short integers), MKL$ (long integers) MKS$ (single precision) and MKD$ (double precision), using fixed string lengths of 2, 4, 4 and 8 bytes respectively. For a short integer, you can see reasonably easily how the scheme works. The number 65 is character A in ASCII code, so when the string version of 65 is printed, you get an A printed. The number 16706 is more of a surprise, because it gives BA. The ASCII code for B is 66, with A being 65, and 16706 is 66+256*65. This corresponds with the way that larger integers are stored as two bytes. The strings that correspond to single and double precision numbers are considerably more complicated unless you have a taste for mathematics. The program shows that the length allocated to each string has no connection with the number of digits in the number and is fixed only by the type of number, integer, single-precision or double-precision. Finally, the conversion back to number form is carried out by using CVI (integer), CVS (single-precision) and CVD (double-precision) respectively. The use of these words allows us to work with numbers in random-access files using smaller fields than would be possible if we had to convert with STR$ and VAL, and also with faster conversions.

An integer file

It's time to illustrate a random access file in action, first of all using the older form of statements. The fact that this is a simple illustration should not put you off – the techniques are exactly the same as you will need if you choose to use random access filing for more serious purposes. The example is in Figure 19.2 and, as before, the first line is an automatic way of ensuring that files will be closed if an error is found. If an error is found as the program runs then instead of the program stopping with the usual error message, it goes to the line labelled as getout which closes files and ends. The snag here is that you get no error message in this simple application, and it's a good idea to omit this line or put a REM at the start while you are testing the program.

```
ON ERROR GOTO getout
REM close file on error
FILE% = 1: LIMIT% = 100
OPEN "integer.rnd" FOR RANDOM AS #FILE% LEN = 2
FIELD FILE%, 2 AS A$
FOR N% = 1 TO LIMIT%
  A% = 1000 - N%: REM recognisable number!
  LSET A$ = MKI$(A%)
  PUT FILE%
NEXT
CLOSE

PRINT "Press any key to read"
K$ = INPUT$(1)
OPEN "integer.rnd" FOR RANDOM AS #FILE% LEN = 2
FIELD FILE%, 2 AS N$
DO WHILE N% <> 0
  INPUT "Item number, please (0 to end) "; N%
  GET FILE%, N%
  X% = CVI(N$)
  PRINT "Number is "; X%
  FOR J = 1 TO 2000: NEXT
  CLS
  LOOP
getout:
CLOSE : END
```

Figure 19.2. A simple random access file program that contains both the recording and the read-back sections.

Two variables are defined, FILE% assigned with 1 to act as a channel number, and LIMIT% to set a limit in a FOR...NEXT loop of items. The point of using variables for these quantities is to illustrate how easy it can be to adapt a program to other numbers when variables are used in this way. In this short example, of course, you could just as easily have used numbers 1 and 100 in the appropriate places.

The creation of the file uses the OPEN statement. The channel is as fixed by FILE%, equal to 1, and the name chosen for the file is 'integer.rnd'. This suggests that the integers are random, but in this example they quite certainly are *not* for reasons that we'll look at in a moment. The last part of the OPEN statement fixes the record size at 2, since only 2 bytes are needed to store an integer. Following the opening of the file, which starts the disk action, the FIELD statement uses the channel number again, and states that the variable to be filed is called A$ and consists of 2 bytes only.Having declared the sizes of record and of field, identical in this case since there is just one field per record, we can now put numbers into the file. The loop that does this uses the ending number set by LIMIT%. In the loop, the numbers that are to be filed are assigned to A% by using 1000-N%. The reason for doing this in a test is to provide easy recognition. If you use truly random numbers, you can't be sure when you replay the file if a given number is really the one that was originally filed in that position. By using a scheme like this, you can be sure that number 1 is 999, number 2 is 998 and so on, all easily recognised later.

tip This is useful for testing any filing system, because otherwise it's easy to miss a fault that makes the replayed item incorrect.

The LSET line places the string version of the number A% into a string A$, and sets it to the left. Since the string consists of only two characters, this may look rather unnecessary but it is essential. If you omit the LSET, you will find that A$=MKI$(A%) runs, but that you cannot find any numbers in the file when you replay it. The reason is that LSET and RSET are not just field padding statements, they are the statements that actually place the value of a variable into the file. You can't omit them!

In normal circumstances, there would be several lines of LSET or RSET statements to place the fields into the record in correct form, and following these you need to put the record on to the file. This is done using the PUT FILE% statement. If the record is of the default size of 128 bytes, this statement places the data on to the disk, but if the records are small, as they are in this example, the records are stored in a buffer piece of memory until the total length is around 128 bytes, upon which the assembled records are filed. Figure 19.3 shows a summary of these processes. At the end of the loop, the file is closed by using the CLOSE statement. Once again, CLOSE FILE% could be used, but CLOSE by itself closes all files.

1. **OPEN file, using filename and channel number. Add record length is not 128 characters.**
2. **FIELD to show size of each field in a record.**
3. **Convert any numbers, using MKI$, MKL$, MKS$ or MKD$.**
4. **Place items in fields using LSET (or RSET).**
5. **Use PUT to place record in file, GET to retrieve record.**

Figure 19.3. A summary of the processes involved in random access filing programs using the older commands.

The second part of the example shows how such a file can be read back. One golden rule here is that, unless you are trying to do something very clever (or risky), you should try to use statements in the same form when replaying as you did when recording. Accordingly, the replay program starts with the same form of OPEN as the recording program used. Note that the OPEN statement is identical, no matter whether we are writing, reading or extending the file. We can use FIELD once again to declare the form of the fields, and this time we have used 2 AS N$, with a different variable name.

The variable name of A$ need not be used this time – all that is going to be done is to take two characters from the file and assign them to a string variable and, provided that you declare some variable, it doesn't matter what the name is so long as it does not conflict with anything else that you use. With the file open and the FIELD statement executed, you can then use the file. In this case, we are going to read the file, to do so we have to specify which record we want to read. This is done by record number, and this is the weakness of random access files of this form. Unless you know the record numbers, you can't read the records. If the records that you are using have some natural number, like an employee record number, all is well. If not, then you have to find some way of associating each record with its *accession number*, as this is called.

In this example, of course, you simply type a number between 1 and 100, and the number appears. Since you know that the number that appears should be 1000-record number, you can check that the numbers are the correct ones. Asking for a number greater than 100 is not an error, you merely get the result of zero, assuming that the disk contains no other files. This is important, because it means that a random-access file can make use of more disk space that you might have intended. If this could be a problem, then your programs should include steps that limit the number of records that can be used.

Before we leave this example, it's important to point out that random access allows much more than is illustrated here. Once the file is opened and the FIELD statement executed, we can amend or extend the file as we like. This is done by specifying a record number with PUT in the same way as we have used GET in line 190. In other words, if you assign something to N$ in this second part of the program, you can use a statement like PUT FILE%,45 to change record number 45 to some other number. You can also use a statement like PUT FILE%,120 to create a record that did not exist in the original. Neither the OPEN nor the FIELD statement puts any limit on the number of files that you can create, and there's no restriction on the order in which you create them. If PUT is used with no record number, then the records are put into the file in order starting with 1, or with any specified number that is used in a preceding PUT statement. This freedom can cause difficulties, however, because it's quite possible to specify a record number that cannot be filed due to a lack of room on the disk. Because of this, random access files have to be planned carefully, usually by setting a limit to the number of entries and by making a dummy file with this number in order to clear space on the disk.

Using record types

The older system of random-access filing, using LSET, MKI$ and all the rest, is useful if you are converting programs written in GW-BASIC or BASICA. The system is cumbersome, however, and looks antique compared with the methods that are used by other modern programming languages. QBASIC provides the method of a user-defined data type as an alternative and, since this is much closer to modern methods, we shall illustrate this and use it in other examples. Figure 19.4 shows the same integer filing program adapted to this system, avoiding all the elaborate preparation that was required in the earlier example.

```
CLS
ON ERROR GOTO getout
REM close file on error such as request for record
zero
FILE% = 1: LIMIT% = 100
DIM A AS INTEGER
OPEN "integer.rnd" FOR RANDOM AS #FILE% LEN = 2
FOR n% = 1 TO LIMIT%
  A = 1000 - n%: REM recognisable number!
  PUT FILE%, n%, A
NEXT
CLOSE

PRINT "Press any key to read"
K$ = INPUT$(1)
OPEN "integer.rnd" FOR RANDOM AS #FILE% LEN = 2

n% = 1
DO WHILE n% <> 0
  INPUT "Item number, please (0 to end) "; n%
  GET FILE%, n%, A
  PRINT "Number is "; A
  FOR J = 1 TO 2000: NEXT
  CLS
LOOP
getout:CLOSE : END
```

Figure 19.4. The much simpler modern method of random access filing using a data type with the extended PUT and GET statements.

In this case, the integer that is to be filed is declared in a DIM statement as being of type integer, and the PUT and GET statements refer to the channel number, the record number and the integer variable name. If you compare this with the earlier example you will see how much simpler this method is for such an example where only one type of variable is involved. What we need to look at now is the use of this system with mixed data such as string, integer and float constituting one record. This requires the use of the TYPE statement to declare a variable of the specified type, following which the ordinary random-access methods can be used, but with some extensions when it comes to extracting parts from the record.

If you want to use information that consists of a string, an integer, two single-precision numbers and a long integer, then the modern method is much simpler. Just declare a user-defined type and assign variables of that type, then file these variables. This avoids all of the number conversion and other contortions of the older methods. You need to remember that you have to assess the individual fields of such a record by using the dot separator, such as in:

```
PRINT myrecord.name
```

but otherwise the method is much simpler.

A longer example

Our experiences with random access filing so far have been confined to simple programs, and these simple illustrations do not really bring out the peculiar advantages and disadvantages of random access methods. The main disadvantage for many purposes is the need to refer to each item by number, the accession number as it is called. For some purposes, the use of an accession number can be a positive advantage if the item is to be numbered anyhow. If, for example, your program keeps track of works personnel by using works number or of references in a book indexed by page number, then you have the number principle built-in, and all's well. For a lot of other files, however, including the very common name and address file, you do not want to have to remember a number in order to read a file. For such a case, there are established methods which are noted briefly (a full description would fill another two chapters) at the end of this Chapter.

The example developed here is a natural for accession number - a day memo book. Since each day of the year is numbered starting at 1 for January 1st, we can make the day number equal to the record number. For a daybook, you might not need anything apart from a note, but this program will allow for a cash input and cash output entries, a birthday name, and also for a 'Meeting at...' section that can be used when reading to indicate that this is an important event. Each record therefore consists of a note string, a string for a name (birthday name), the 'meeting at' string, cash in and cash out. Since the file is a random one, it follows that you can make an entry for any day in the year, and also read any entry that has been made. A further step would be to allow addition to a string or amendment of any string, or the summing of cash for a given month – but for the moment we'll concentrate on the essentials. As a sideline, we need to be able to convert from the more familiar 26/4/93 type of date format into a day number – and that needs some planning.

Like all programs, this starts as a core routine which is illustrated in Figure 19.5. This allows for screen setup, initialisation (particularly of records), menu display and then choice, the chance to repeat a menu item, and closedown

In order to use the more modern random file actions, a data type of DAYRECORD has been created, and the variable 'thisday' is declared of type DAYRECORD. This variable has been declared as shared, as are several others. This is done to avoid the need to pass them from one procedure to another, a pointless exercise in a comparatively short program like this.

Variables file% and note% are used as channel numbers, with file% used for the main random access file, and note% for a small serial file that holds the year and whether or not it is a leap year. The constant in this section is LENYR%, assigned with 365, the normal length of a year. Leap years are dealt with by using a quantity LEAP%, which will be false (0) or true(-1), by subtracting LEAP% from LENYR% – since subtracting a negative quantity is the same as adding a positive quantity, then LENYR% - LEAP% gives 366 on leap years and 365 on other years.

The next step is the filling of an array to be used in calculating day numbers. The principle here is that if the month is January, month 1, then the day number is just the number of the day in January. If the month is February, then the day number is 31 + date, because the number of days in January has to be added to the number of days in February, and so on. The array MON%(J%) therefore consists of the cumulative number of days, using 0 for January, 31 for February, and so on. Leap years are catered for by adding 1 for months following February, as we shall see later. The last item is the assignment to TRUE% and FALSE%, since these are not preassigned in this version of BASIC.

```
REM instructions
CALL instruct
  REM initialise records
CONST lenyr% = 365
DIM SHARED mon%(12), file%, note%, dno%, mno%, YEAR%, LEAP%
file% = 1: note% = 2
FOR j% = 1 TO 12: READ mon%(j%): NEXT
CONST TRUE = -1: CONST FALSE = 0
TYPE dayrecord
  comment AS STRING * 160
  meet AS STRING * 20
  bday AS STRING * 20
  cashin AS SINGLE
  cashout AS SINGLE
END TYPE
DIM SHARED thisday AS dayrecord
REM Actual program lines

DO
  REM menu
  CALL menu
  REM choose
  CALL choose
  REM Another?
  choice$ = "menu item"
  CALL another(choice$)
LOOP UNTIL choice$ = "N" OR choice$ = "n"
REM close and end
CALL getout
END
DATA 0,31,59,90,120,151,181,212,243,273,304,334
```

Figure 19.5. The core of the daybook program, showing the main portions as called procedures.

From this simple core, quite a considerable program has grown. It allows the creation of a file for one year, with one year per disk-file as presently constituted. Once a file for a year has been created, items can be entered for each day in the year. These items can also be read, with one item displayed per screen. No provision has been made for hard-copy, or for more elaborate displays or editing, and the menus are straightforward pick-number types. In short, this is just a starter to which you can add as much as you like to make it more useful or more appealing to you. The record size is 210 (a safe number for the size of a record). A blank file is created for each year when the program is first run for that year, so as to ensure that each space in the file is correctly allocated. This avoids the problem of reading rubbish from a file that has been placed on a disk that was previously used for other files.

The complete listing of the subroutines shows that it has grown considerably from the core outline. Much of this is because of mugtraps and other routines, notably the routine for converting a date in DD/MM format into a day number, allowing for leap years. The daybook is configured up to 1999, but could be used beyond this date with no adjustment needed for the foreseeable future (until the year%/400 test for an additional leap year becomes applicable).

To make the task of examining this program easier, we'll look at it in the order of the listing of the routines, though this is not the order in which they were written. This starts with Figure 19.6, the 'another' routine, which deals with the another question.

```
SUB another (k$)
CLS
PRINT TAB(2); "Do you want another "; k$; " (Y/N)?"
k$ = INPUT$(1)
END SUB
```

Figure 19.6. The 'another' procedure for answering 'Do you want another?' questions – the name of the item is passed as k$.

In this simple routine, the calling procedure assigns a string to use as k$ which will be Menu or Write or whatever is needed, and this routine prints the question and takes the answer, passing it back as a changed string variable.

Procedure 'badday', Figure 19.7, simply prints a message when a request for a date is impossible because you have typed something like 31-02.

```
SUB badday
PRINT " Bad day number - please try again "
CALL waithere
END SUB
```

Figure 19.7. The badday procedure, which simply prints an error message.

Procedure 'choose' in Figure 19.8 is rather more meaty, and it deals with the menu number selection – remember that you can select by letters or names if you like.

```
SUB choose

    k$ = INPUT$(1)
    k% = VAL(k$)

  SELECT CASE k%
    CASE IS = 1
      CALL newyear
    CASE IS = 2
      CALL writeday(daynr%)
    CASE IS = 3
      CALL readday(daynr%)
    CASE IS = 4
      CALL getout
    CASE ELSE
      END
    END SELECT
END SUB
```

Figure 19.8. The choose routine which selects the main procedures.

This identifies the main procedures as newyear, writeday and readday and deals with mugtrapping for numbers that are not in the correct range. Note that the routine is not used in a loop because this would have caused 'Press a key' actions to require two key presses. We now get to one of the important routines, Figure 19.9, getday which gets a day number from the date and returns the integer daynr%.

```
SUB getday (daynr%)
CLS : PRINT : PRINT TAB(5); "Please enter date now
-"
PRINT TAB(5); "Use format DD/MM or DD-MM"
BAD% = TRUE
DO WHILE BAD% = TRUE
  MYDATE$ = ""
  LOCATE 7, 5: FOR j% = 1 TO 5
  k$ = INPUT$(1)
```

```
  PRINT k$;
  MYDATE$ = MYDATE$ + k$: NEXT
  FOR j% = 1 TO 5: k% = ASC(MID$(MYDATE$, j%, 1))
    IF (k% > 47 AND k% < 58) OR j% = 3 THEN BAD% =
FALSE
  NEXT
  IF BAD% = TRUE THEN LOCATE 7, 5: PRINT SPACE$(79);
  LOOP
dno% = VAL(MID$(MYDATE$, 1, 2)): mno% =
VAL(MID$(MYDATE$, 4, 2))
  REM Check month and day to find daynumber
IF mno% < 1 OR mno% > 12 THEN
  PRINT " Bad month number"
  CALL waithere
  CALL getday(daynr%)
END IF
IF (dno% > 28) AND (mno% = 2) AND NOT LEAP% THEN
  CALL badday
  CALL getday(daynr%)
END IF
IF (dno% > 29) AND (mno% = 2) THEN
  CALL badday
  CALL getday(daynr%)
END IF
IF (dno% > 30) AND ((mno% = 4) OR (mno% = 6) OR
(mno% = 9) OR (mno% = 11)) THEN
  CALL badday
  CALL getday(daynr%)
END IF
IF (dno% > 31) THEN
  CALL badday
  CALL getday(daynr%)
END IF
daynr% = mon%(mno%) + dno%
IF LEAP% AND (mno% > 2) THEN daynr% = daynr% + 1

END SUB
```

Figure 19.9. The getday procedure which generates the important daynr% variable value.

The day number routine starts with a request to enter the date in DD/MM form. In fact, any form of divider can be used, so that DD.MM, DD,MM, DD-MM and so on are all equally acceptable. The important point is that this reply must consist of five characters, so that the first of September is entered as 01/09 and not as 1/9. This date entry is carried out within a loop so that it can be tested for incorrect entries like 1/12 or 234/5. The input uses an INPUT$ and if the date is of the wrong format, the use of PRINT SPACE$(79) wipes out the line so that another attempt can be made. So far though nothing prevents the acceptance of a date such as 32/13, and this has to be tested for separately.

The next section of the routine tests month and day numbers. Since the previous section has ensured that the date is in the correct format, we can use string slicing and VAL to get the day and the month numbers as variables DNO% and MNO%. These are then tested in a set of IF lines which are arranged so that if the test fails a message is printed and the date entry is restarted. The first test will reject month numbers less than 1 or more than 13, and the remaining tests are to establish the correct day number.

This is complicated by the use of unequal numbers of days per month, and is done on the basis of the old rule of '30 days hath September; April, June and November'. The first line, however, deals with Month 2, February. If the month number is 2 and the number of days exceeds 28 and the year is not leap, then we have an error, and the usual routines are invoked. The next line tests for a February with more than 29 days, with the same result if the test is true. The following line rejects months with more than 30 days if they happen to be months numbered 4, 6, 9, or 11 (April, June, September, November), and then a final line rejects any month with more than 31 days.

Since the array MON% has already been created in the initialisation section, the number of days from January 1st can now be calculated by adding the variable DNO% to MON%(MNO%). This is adjusted for leap years and month number greater than 2 in the following line to allow for the 366 day years. The end result is the number DAYNR% because this will be used as the accession number for the record whether for reading or writing.

The writeday procedure deals with the writing of a complete entry for a day, Figure 19.10.

```
SUB writeday (daynr%)
OPEN "daybook.rnd" FOR RANDOM AS #file% LEN = 210
CLS : PRINT
PRINT TAB(32); "Write to Daybook."
DO
  CALL getyear: REM find year
  CALL getday(daynr%): REM get day number
  CALL putit(daynr%): REM write to record
  CALL waithere: CLS
  choice$ = "write action"
  CALL another(choice$)
LOOP UNTIL choice$ = "N" OR choice$ = "n"
CLOSE #file%

END SUB
```

Figure 19.10. The writeday routine which opens the file and calls the procedures that will write to the file.

This opens the file, gets the day number, and calls procedure putit to place the data in the form of variable thisday to the file. This action can be repeated, using the DO loop, until you have written as many day notes as you want.

The next important procedure is putit, Figure 19.11, which takes the information for a day and places it into the variable thisday for putting into the file at the correct position.

This starts with an editing subroutine of a very simple type which asks for inputs and tests for length of input. This rejects any input that is too long (you have to type it all again, which is far from ideal), if the input is simply the return key no assignment is made. The string or number replay is then assigned using thisday, comment and so on for the individual fields. Following the entry of all of the data, the record is placed in the file using PUT #FILE%, DAYNR%, thisday in the usual way for a user-defined type. Note how much simpler this is compared to the older LSET and REST commands.

```
SUB putit (daynr%)
DO
  CLS : PRINT : PRINT TAB(3); "Please enter as prompted."
    PRINT TAB(5); "Pressing ENTER by itself makes no entry.": PRINT
    limit% = 160: strlen% = 161:
    DO WHILE strlen% > limit%
    PRINT TAB(5); "Comments for today (2 lines max.) "
    PRINT TAB(5); : LINE INPUT rep$
    CALL testrep(rep$, limit%, strlen%)
    LOOP
    thisday.comment = rep$
    limit% = 20: strlen% = 21
    DO WHILE strlen% > limit%
    PRINT TAB(5); "Meeting at (20 characters max.) ";
    LINE INPUT rep$: CALL testrep(rep$, limit%, strlen%)
    LOOP
    thisday.meet = rep$
    limit% = 20: strlen% = 21
    DO WHILE strlen% > limit%
    PRINT TAB(5); "Birthday today for (20 characters max.) ";
    LINE INPUT rep$: CALL testrep(rep$, limit%, strlen%)
    LOOP
    thisday.bday = rep$
    PRINT : PRINT TAB(5);
    INPUT "Cash in today.."; rep
    thisday.cashin = rep
    PRINT : PRINT TAB(5);
    INPUT "Cash out today..."; rep
    thisday.cashout = rep
    PRINT
    PRINT TAB(3); "Please check this entry for"; dno%; "/"; mno%; "/";
    YEAR%; "."
    PRINT TAB(5); "Press Y key to proceed, any other to repeat input."
    k$ = INPUT$(1)
    LOOP UNTIL k$ = "Y" OR k$ = "y"

   PUT #file%, daynr%, thisday
```

Figure 19.11. The putit procedure which gets the data and puts it on the file at the correct day number position.

The opposite action is performed by procedure readday in Figure 19.12.

```
SUB readday (daynr%)

OPEN "daybook.rnd" FOR RANDOM AS #file% LEN = 210
CLS : PRINT
PRINT TAB(35); "READ DIARY": PRINT
PRINT TAB(3); "You can now read your entry for any
day."
DO
  CALL getday(daynr%): REM get day number
  CALL readentry(daynr%): REM read entry
  choice$ = "read"
  CALL another(choice$)
LOOP UNTIL choice$ = "N" OR choice$ = "n"
CLOSE #file%

END SUB
```

Figure 19.12. The readday procedure which makes use of procedure getday again and calls readentry.

The steps for reading a record follow so closely the steps for writing a record that most of the procedures can be reused, which is the whole point of having them. The record reading routine starts by opening the random access file. The reading routine then uses the day finding procedure which accepts the input of a date and converts it into a day number for use as a record number. The main part of the reading routine is then carried out by procedure readentry in Figure 19.13.

```
SUB readentry (daynr%)

CALL getyear
GET #file%, daynr%, thisday   CLS : PRINT
PRINT TAB(29); "Date: "; dno%; "/"; mno%; "/"; YEAR%: PRINT
PRINT TAB(3); "Comments: "; thisday.comment
PRINT
PRINT TAB(3); "Meeting at: "; thisday.meet
PRINT
PRINT TAB(3); "Birthday of: "; thisday.bday
PRINT
PRINT TAB(3); "Cash in: "; thisday.cashin
PRINT
PRINT TAB(3); "Cash out: "; thisday.cashout
PRINT : PRINT "Press any key to proceed."
k$ = INPUT$(1)

END SUB
```

Figure 19.13. The procedure that gets the variable thisday and prints out the individual fields.

The routine is also straightforward, the reverse of the actions used to collect the fields into variable thisday and put it on the file. We now need to look at the first of the menu choices, the procedure that creates a new daybook random file for a year – Figure 19.14.

```
SUB newyear

CLS : PRINT TAB(34); "NEW YEARBOOK": PRINT TAB(34);
"============"
PRINT : PRINT TAB(5); "What year, please (1987 to 1997)"
YEAR% = 0:
DO WHILE YEAR% < 1992 OR YEAR% > 1999
  INPUT YEAR%
LOOP
IF YEAR% / 4 = YEAR% \ 4 THEN LEAP% = TRUE ELSE LEAP% =
FALSE
OPEN "notes.dat" FOR OUTPUT AS #note%
PRINT #note%, YEAR%, LEAP%
CLOSE #note%
PRINT TAB(5); "Year noted in file - please wait"
OPEN "daybook.rnd" FOR RANDOM AS #file% LEN = 210
thisday.comment = STRING$(160, 32)
thisday.meet = STRING$(20, 32)
thisday.bday = STRING$(20, 32)
thisday.cashin = 0!
thisday.cashout = 0!
FOR j% = 1 TO (lenyr% - LEAP%)
  PUT #file%, j%, thisday
NEXT
CLOSE #file%
PRINT "File created"
END SUB
```

Figure 19.14. The year creation routine, which fills the random file with blanks to avoid reading rubbish for an unwritten day. Note that FALS is part of the IF YEAR% etc line when entering the program.

This creation subroutine will be used only once on each data disk-file, since it sets up the serial file noting year and LEAP%, and then a dummy random-access file, filled with blanks, for a daybook for one year. This ensures that a read from the file at a point which has not been written to does not produce rubbish left over from an old deleted file in the disk. The year is requested at the start of the subroutine, and is tested to find if it divides evenly by 4, because this would make it a leap year. The variable LEAP% is used in a TRUE or FALSE way as an indicator from that point on.

To ensure that this data is available each time the daybook for that year is used, the year and the variable leap are recorded in a serial file called NOTES.DAT. Once this serial file has been closed, the main random dummy file is opened. This wipes out any other file of that name on the disk, so that you are not allowed to create another file for the same year on one disk. The length is specified as 210, allowing for the planned sizes of comment (160 characters), meeting place and birthday (20 each), cash in and cash out (both real numbers using 4 bytes each), and 2 bytes to spare. A FOR...NEXT loop then records the values assigned as fields of thisday into each record of this file, using FOR J%=1 TO LENYR%- (LEAP%) in order to make the file extend to 365 for normal years and to 366 for leap years, remembering that LEAP% = -1 for a leap year and 0 for others.

This action can take some time if you are using a floppy or other slow drive, so a 'Please wait' notice has been placed on screen while this is being done – there will be only a very short wait for hard disk users, particularly if a cache is being used. The file needs about 78K, so that it would be perfectly feasible to have more than one year on a disk, but the complications of altering filenames make it hardly worthwhile. The file is closed, then a message informs you when the file has been created, and the subroutine then returns you to the menu if you answer Y to the question. The disk now contains blocks of 210 bytes (356 of them, or 366 in a leap year) and you can place data into any of these blocks using the writing routine. A collection of procedures of a more minor nature is illustrated in Figure 19.15.

```
SUB getout

CLS
CLOSE
PRINT "END."

END SUB

SUB getyear

OPEN "notes.dat" FOR INPUT AS #note%
INPUT #note%, YEAR%, LEAP%
CLOSE #note%

END SUB

SUB menu

CLS : PRINT TAB(38); "MENU": PRINT TAB(38); "====": PRINT
PRINT TAB(5); "1. Create a file for a NEW YEAR.": PRINT
PRINT TAB(5); "2. Write to this years diary.": PRINT
PRINT TAB(5); "3. Read a days notes.": PRINT
PRINT TAB(5); "4. End.": PRINT
PRINT "Please choose by number (1 to 4):"

END SUB

SUB testrep (rep$, limit%, strlen%)

strlen% = LEN(rep$)
IF strlen% > limit% THEN
  PRINT "Too long- please try again"
  CALL waithere
END IF

END SUB

SUB waithere

SLEEP 1

END SUB
```

Figure 19.15. Some of the minor procedures.

Finally, the instruction lines are written in another procedure which is called each time the program starts, Figure 19.16. This procedure deals with the printing of the title and the brief instructions. These actions are straightforward, and need no further explanation.

```
SUB instruct

CLS
PRINT TAB(36); "YEARBOOK": PRINT TAB(36); "========"
PRINT : PRINT TAB(3); "This program allows you to set up a
notebook for an entire year."
PRINT TAB(2); "You use Option 1 only once each year, and
from then on use the other options"
PRINT "to enter items or read items. These are classed as
general notes, meetings,"
PRINT "birthdays, cash in and cash out. You specify dates
in the normal way and they"
PRINT "are converted to day numbers. The information you
supply will be stored in each"
PRINT "record.": PRINT : PRINT "Press any key to proceed."
k$ = INPUT$(1)

END SUB
```

Figure 19.16. The instruction procedure, called once on each run.

Indexed sequential action

Serial files are very useful for a lot of purposes, but not if you want to be able to obtain one record out of a very large number. The obvious alternative is random access filing, and we have just dealt with that topic. Random access filing in BASIC, however, suffers from one considerable snag. Unless you know the number of a record, you cannot get random access to that record. You can't, for example, get the record for TAYLORJ just by typing this name and, unless you happen to know that this is record number 273, that's it – you will have to search through the records one by one just as you would with a serial file. Programming with random-access filing so that you can recover items by name, or so that you can quickly list in alphabetical order of name, is by no means easy – but these are often precisely the actions for which we most need random access!

The solution to the problem was developed a long time ago, however, and is called by various names like *indexed random access, relative filing, ISAM* (Indexed Sequential Access to Memory) and so on. In the space that we have here we can only look briefly at the principles – but they are quite simple. In an ISAM filing system, each time a random access record is written, a serial file is also written. Into the serial file is put some key item, which is often the first six letters of the main field of the random access record. For example, if your random access record dealt with names and addresses, you could extract the first six letters of the surname, and this would be filed on a serial file along with the record number.

Now, when you want to search for a name, you don't have to search each record in the random access file, only the much shorter serial file. As an improvement on this, you could arrange a subroutine that read the serial file into an array each time the program was being closed down, and sorted the items into alphabetical order. Since each item is recorded along with its record number, the rearrangement of the items in the serial file does not jumble the record numbers. You could then use a very fast binary search routine to find the name you wanted in the serial file, and the program would read the record number and use it to get the record from the random access file. When you feel confident in using both types of file, have a go at this for yourself.

Binary files

The OPEN statement also allows the descriptive word BINARY to be used for a random access file. When a BINARY type of file is created, the information is held as a file of bytes, and access to the file is obtained by using GET and PUT, in the form:

```
PUT #1, 115, name$
```

or

```
GET #2, 7144, code%
```

in which the variable names represent the source of file data for PUT and the destination of file data for GET. Binary files can use SEEK as a function which returns the current position in the file that can be used by a PUT or GET which does not specify a position.

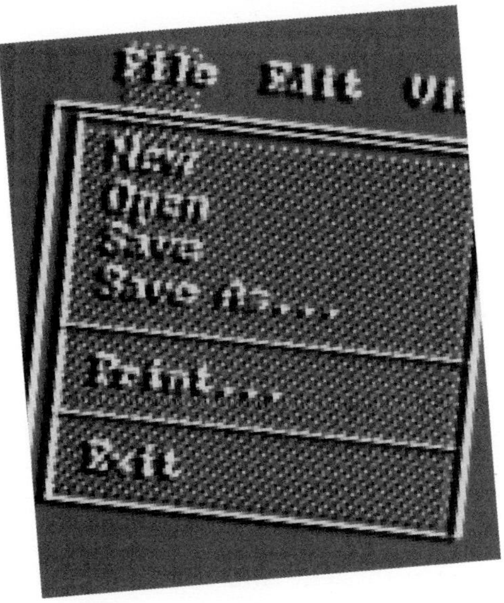

Graphics 1

Special effects and geometric shapes

Any modern computer is expected to be able to produce dazzling displays of colour and other special effects. The PC is no exception, but precisely what you can achieve depends on the version of BASIC you are using so, in this chapter, we'll start to look at some of the effects that are possible using QBASIC. To start with, we have to know some of the terms that are used, and the first of these is *Graphics*.

Graphics means pictures that can be drawn on the screen, and all modern versions of BASIC have instructions that allow you to draw such patterns. Some shapes can be produced on the screen along with text by using PRINT CHR$() statements, such as PRINT CHR$(185). These ready-made shapes are illustrated in your PC manual or in the manual for your printer and are the shapes that are built into the machine itself. You can make up strings that consist of these characters and then print each string as shown in Figure 20.1. These are simple enough to print at the left-hand side, but need to be printed line by line if you want to TAB them to a different position.

```
CLS
X$ = CHR$(204) + CHR$(185) + CHR$(10) + CHR$(200) + CHR$(188)
PRINT X$
```

Figure 20.1. Printing graphics strings.

This string consists of four characters with two printed on each line, and it can be printed as shown here on the left hand edge of the screen. You cannot, however, use TAB or LOCATE to print this shape anywhere else in a line. If you do, you will find that only the top half is correctly tabbed. You might think that you could replace CHR$(10) by SPACE$(78) so as to ensure shifting the lower part of the symbol but, for some curious reason, when SPACE$(78) is included in the string, the TAB and LOCATE functions no longer work and the symbol always appears at the left-hand edge! Since this rather limits the utility of graphics strings of this type, we'll leave it at that.

When it is switched on, your computer defaults to a *text screen* as its output screen as well as for its editing screen. In other words, it automatically sets up the screen so as to print words and numbers, plus the limited range of graphics symbols. You cannot use any of the large number of graphics drawing commands on such a screen. You can get round this by switching to a different screen layout which displays the graphics characters fully. This is done by typing SCREEN 1 for low-resolution (coarse textured) images, or SCREEN 12 for high-resolution (fine textured) images. There is a set of numbers that you can use with the SCREEN statement, but many of these are of little interest unless you have a machine with a CGA or Hercules graphics card. These are rather thin on the ground and now, for most purposes, using SCREEN 12 with the usual VGA graphics card permits a good standard of text and graphics display. The other screen layouts are noted in Chapter 14.

What you can do depends critically on the graphics card that you are using, so that the combinations of some commands with all the possible screen types can look very complicated. In this chapter, the only screen modes that will be considered are SCREEN 0, the text screen, and SCREEN 12, the high-resolution VGA graphics screen. If you use the Hercules, CGA or EGA graphics adaptor, see Chapter 14.

Vivid impressions

If you are using a colour monitor, you can, of course, display both text and graphics in colour. If you are using a monochrome monitor, then the colours will appear only as shades of black or white. The colour statement uses the word COLOR (US spelling, remember) which can be followed by up to three numbers, each one specifying a colour. For a text screen, SCREEN 0, the order of numbers is foreground, background, border and the meaning of the numbers is shown in Figure 20.2. As an illustration, try:

```
SCREEN 1
COLOR 13,5,1
CLS
```

which makes the foreground colour light magenta, the background dark magenta, and the border dark blue. This really is useful only on a colour monitor, because the contrasts are not so useful on a monochrome one. Note that if you omit the CLS then you will not see the background colour appear except where a character appears. You can use a COLOR statement with the text screen (SCREEN 0) but when you use the VGA high-resolution screen SCREEN 12 only the foreground number can be specified because there is a different statement (PALETTE) which is used for colours.

Number	Colour
0	Black
1	Blue
2	Green
3	Cyan
4	Red
5	Magenta
6	Brown
7	White
8	Grey
9	Light Blue
10	Light Green
11	Light Cyan
12	Light Red
13	Light Magenta
14	Yellow
15	Bright white

Figure 20.2. The numbers used to code the screen colours. For monochrome monitors, the colours translate to shades of grey but, unfortunately, with no simple relationship between the number and the shade.

In addition, there are some additional factors about the COLOR statement used with SCREEN 0. You can add 16 to your choice of foreground colour number to make the characters flash – try COLOR 23,0,0. If, after placing some characters on the screen you change back with COLOR 7,0,0, the flashing will continue for the characters that were made to flash until the screen is cleared. You are also limited to using colours 0 to 7 for background, and if you omit a border number then it remains unchanged.

With that in mind, take a look at the program of Figure 20.3. It starts by calling up the text screen, using SCREEN 0 . This is then followed by a COLOR statement, and CLS to ensure that the screen background is established.

```
SCREEN 0
COLOR 0, 4, 5
CLS
FOR N% = 0 TO 15
  COLOR N%, 4, 5
  PRINT CHR$(N% + 65);
NEXT
```

Figure 20.3. A program which illustrates the colour numbers for SCREEN 0.

The next part is a loop, which uses numbers 0 to 15. These are the colour numbers, and they are used to set the foreground colour on each pass through the loop. In the following line we print characters. Because we have used PRINT CHR$(N%+65), these will be the letters of the alphabet, because ASCII code 65 is the code for 'A'. What you will find unexpected is the different colour of each letter. Run this, and just look at it.

Using PALETTE

You will very often find colour graphics card described as supplying hundreds or even thousands of colours. This does not mean that all of the colours (if you could distinguish them from each other) could be available in a drawing, only that you have a large selection to choose from. The word *Palette* is used to describe the selection of colours that is available at one time.

To take a very simple example, suppose that you are using a colour monitor in a screen mode that allows only two colours, one for foreground and one for background. You could nevertheless use 16 colours – as long as you only used two at a time. You might in one drawing use blue for background and yellow for foreground, but in another drawing use red as background and green as foreground. The two colours that you use constitute a Palette. You choose the colours that you draw with from the Palette and, before you draw, you can fill your Palette with the colours that you want it to contain, specifying them by number.

This is most easily illustrated using a screen mode of only a few colours or shades, such as SCREEN 10. In this mode, you can keep 4 colours, numbered 0 to 3 in the Palette, and you can choose from a colour number range of 0 to 8. The statement:

```
PALETTE 1,4
```

would make colour number 1 in the palette be equivalent to colour number 4 that you can select from.

The main use of PALETTE is to allow fast colour changes. If, for example, you have drawn a box and filled it with colour 2 (see later), then by using a PALETTE statement which reassigns colour 2 in the Palette, you can change the colour of the filling.

PSET graphics

BASIC offers one way of producing graphics that is based on specifying whether a specified point on the screen should be in background or foreground colour. These points are high-resolution in the sense that they use very small blocks, or, to give them their proper name, *pixels*. The pixels of the SCREEN 12 are, in fact, the smallest units that we can place on to the VGA graphics screen. We can place up to 640 pixels across the screen, and up to 480 down the screen, a total of 307200.

This assumes that you are using all of the VGA screen. As we shall see later, it is possible to use a window section of the screen, so that the number of pixels that fits in the window is considerably less.

QBASIC does not provide for Super VGA (SVGA) screen displays.

The key instructions now are PSET and PRESET. PSET has to be followed by at least two numbers within brackets, and its effect is to make a pixel appear in a selected place. By adding another number, outside the brackets, we can also select a colour. If this colour code is omitted the pixel will appear in normal foreground colour – whatever that has been selected to be.

The position of the pixel is specified by two numbers. The first of these, called the x coordinate, is the number of units across from the left hand side of the screen. The VGA screen, using SCREEN 12, is divided into 640 units across and 480 down. We can use numbers 0 to 639 to control the position across the screen (the x-position) and numbers 0 to 479 to control the position down the screen (the y-position). The lefthand side of the screen is denoted by x=0 and the top by y=0. These are very tiny pixels, as you can see from the program in Figure 20.4. This sets SCREEN 12, so that no colours are used.

```
SCREEN 12: CLS
FOR N% = 0 TO 630 STEP 15
  PSET (N%, 100)
NEXT
FOR N% = 0 TO 630 STEP 2
  PSET (N%, 120)
NEXT
```

Figure 20.4. Pixel size illustrated for SCREEN 12, using PSET.

In the second line a loop starts which prints pixels in a line across the screen. By choosing 100 as the y-number, we can make this line appear about one fifth of the way down the screen. Using N% for the x-number allows us to PSET a number of positions, 15 units apart. The distance apart is measured from the lefthand side of each pixel. The second loop shows the effect of using STEP 2. The pixels appear almost joined, and the line of pixels takes slightly longer to draw, though in both cases the drawing is very fast.

The effect of PRESET is, as you might guess, to reset the pixel, changing it to the background colour so that it disappears. This is mainly used to make pixels appear to move, and we'll look at that point later on. It's time for another example. The main use of PSET and PRESET is in drawing graphs, so that's what we'll illustrate. Figure 20.5 shows a graph drawing program. It draws several graphs at the same time, using different colours. Because the pixels of the high-resolution screen are so small, however, it's not easy to see the dots, and since all the dots are in the same colour, you can't easily distinguish the graphs.

```
SCREEN 12: CLS
FOR X% = 0 TO 635
  PSET (X%, 100 + SIN(.1 * X%) * 90)
  PSET (X%, 100 + SIN(.1 * X%) ^ 2 * 90)
  PSET (X%, 100 + SIN(.1 * X%) ^ 3 * 90)
NEXT
```

Figure 20.5. Graph drawing using PSET with SCREEN 12.

The second line starts the loop which makes use of all the permitted values of X%. The graph shapes are achieved by using the SIN function, with one used as it is, one squared, and one cubed. The multiplying factors are put in to make the shape fill a reasonable amount of the screen in the Y direction. The sine or sine cubed of an angle cannot have a value less than -1 or more than +1, so we have to 'amplify' it a bit by multiplying by 90. The square cannot have a value of more than +1 or less than 0. The value of X has to be multiplied by .1 to make the range of angles suitable. Remember that QBASIC does not use angles in units of degrees. Instead, it uses the more natural unit, the radian which is about 57 degrees.

The separation of the graphs is easier if you plot in three colours, using SCREEN 12, as shown in Figure 20.6. The range of X numbers has had to be altered, and the use of a colour number in the PSET statements, following a comma, causes the drawing to be in colour.

```
SCREEN 12: CLS
FOR X% = 0 TO 635
  PSET (X%, 100 + SIN(.1 * X%) * 90), 7
  PSET (X%, 100 + SIN(.1 * X%) ^ 2 * 90), 9
  PSET (X%, 100 + SIN(.1 * X%) ^ 3 * 90), 15
NEXT
```

Figure 20.6. Using SCREEN 12 for a graph drawing program so that the three graphs appear in different colours. The separation is reasonable even in monochrome.

Sometimes, instead of specifying exact position on the screen by means of x and y numbers, you just want to specify the *shift* or *displacement* of a number of pixels. You can do this by using STEP immediately following PSET or PRESET, meaning that the x and y values will be measured from the current cursor position (whatever that is).

Lines, boxes, circles and paints!

PSET and PRESET can have their uses, however, if you want to use a few pixels. It would be hard work to design a program which used PSET and PRESET to draw lines. Fortunately, BASIC allows you to draw lines, boxes and circles without having to resort to any special effort thanks to the LINE and CIRCLE commands.

The LINE command, used at full power, can be quite a lot to take in, so we'll start very simply. Try the program in Figure 20.7. This draws a diagonal line, using the small sized pixels that you should have become used to in SCREEN 12.

```
SCREEN 12: CLS
LINE (10, 10)-(240, 180), 15
```

Figure 20.7. Using the LINE statement to draw a diagonal line with colour number 15.

The LINE command is followed by at least two sets of numbers. The first pair, in brackets, are the x and y numbers for the starting point of the line. By using X=10 and Y=10, we have chosen a position very near the left hand side and the top of the screen. After the second bracket, there must be a hyphen sign (-). This is followed by the finishing point of the line, in another set of brackets. This uses numbers X=240 and Y=180 to ensure that this point is near the bottom of the screen and at the right hand side. The result is a diagonal line from top left to bottom right. How about drawing yourself a line from top right to bottom left?

note The length and slope of the line will be different for different SCREEN numbers that provide different resolution values.

Now take a deep breath, because there are a lot of extras that can be tacked on to this command. Special Offer Number One is that once you have drawn one line, you can make the LINE commands simpler. Suppose that you want to draw another line which starts where the first one left off. You don't have to type the starting position all over again, simply omit the first bracket. Figure 20.8 shows what is needed, with LINE -(10,150) causing another line to join on to the end of the first one.

```
SCREEN 12: CLS
LINE (10, 10)-(600, 180)
LINE -(10, 150)
```

Figure 20.8. Adding one line to the end of another, using a LINE statement with no starting coordinate numbers.

This extension to LINE is particularly useful if you want to draw squares and for random patterns it's essential. Just try Figure 20.9, which draws a starter line, and then uses a loop in which random numbers are used to place the finishing point of the next lines. You'll see, incidentally, just how fast BASIC draws these lines when you run this one. You could exhibit these at the Hayward Gallery and make your fortune if they weren't so well drawn.

```
SCREEN 12: COLOR 0: CLS
LINE (20, 20)-(150, 150), 10
FOR N% = 1 TO 50
  X% = RND * 639: Y% = RND * 479
  LINE -(X%, Y%), 10
NEXT
```

Figure 20.9. A random line program for aspiring abstract artists.

note -(X%, Y%) is used to draw the new line from the end-point of the previous line. This is not mentioned in the on-screen Help pages.

The next one is quite an astonishment. Try the program in Figure 20.10, in which the letter B has been added after the rest of the LINE command. The effect is to draw a box – hence the letter 'B'. When you want to draw a box in this way, you must either use the colour number, or the correct number of commas, then the B.

```
SCREEN 12
COLOR 0
CLS
LINE (30, 30)-(210, 140), 14, B
```

Figure 20.10. Using the B subcommand in LINE to create a box. The first coordinate pair is the top left hand corner, the other is the bottom right hand corner.

You cannot place the B immediately following the last bracket, because this will not be taken as a box command when it is in the place where the computer expects to find a colour command. If you do not use a colour number, retain the comma. The two points in the LINE command form the opposite corners of the box, so you always get neatly rectangular boxes when you use this command. If any of the sides looks bent, it's time to get your monitor serviced.

Figure 20.11 shows something of the speed of this command. It chooses two sets of X and Y numbers at random, and then draws a box in a random colour. The colour has been selected by using N% MOD 4, the remainder after N% has been divided by four, and this will, of course, make some boxes be drawn in colour 0, which is black. A better method would be to use 1+(N% MOD 3) to eliminate the possibility of this number coming out at 0.

```
SCREEN 12
COLOR 0
CLS
RANDOMIZE TIMER
FOR N% = 1 TO 10
  X% = RND * 255: Y% = RND * 199
  X1% = RND * 255: Y1% = RND * 199
  LINE (X%, Y%)-(X1%, Y1%), (N% MOD 4) + 10, B
NEXT
```

Figure 20.11. Random boxes for students of abstract sculpture.

No, we haven't finished, because there is yet another twist to LINE. Take a look at the simple program in Figure 20.12. This draws two boxes, using LINE in the way that you have seen earlier, but with 'F' added to the B. You don't need any commas or other dividers here, just the F at the end.

```
SCREEN 12
COLOR 0
CLS
LINE (10, 10)-(100, 100), 2, BF
LINE (150, 20)-(250, 190), 3, BF
```

Figure 20.12. Filling a closed box with colour, using the F subcommand following B.

The effect of the F is to fill the rectangle with colour. The colour used is the colour that you have specified in the LINE command, which is palette colours 2 and 3. You'll see from the example that more than one box can be drawn and filled in this way.

Qnote You can subsequently use a PALETTE statement to change the colour in the box without needing to redraw the box.

There is one final number that can be added, following another comma, to the LINE statement. This will determine whether a line is solid or dotted, and the number must be an integer. Determining this number, however, is quite another matter, because the number that are used must be in the range –32768 to +32767, and there is no simple relationship between the number and the pattern until you express the number in binary.

In fact, the best way of using this number is as a hexadecimal number, See Appendix C. To use a hex number requires the number to be preceded by &H as a signal to QBASIC that this is a hex number, and some useful patterns are:

```
&HFF00 dashes
&HAAAA fine dots
&HF6F6 dot dash
```

The pattern number can be used for lines or boxes, but not for fill patterns.

Moving in better circles

Drawing straight lines and boxes is useful, but being able to draw circles greatly extends our artistic range. QBASIC as you might expect by now, has a very useful CIRCLE instruction. As usual, we'll keep it simple for starters. CIRCLE has to be followed by a pair of coordinate numbers, in brackets, and then by another number outside the brackets. As usual, commas separate the numbers. The coordinate numbers are of the centre of the circle. The number that follows the brackets is the radius of the circle. In case you've forgotten, that's the distance from the centre to the outside. It's measured in screen units, these 640 by 480 units that we work within all the time for a VGA screen. If you want to show the whole of a circle on the screen, the largest number that you can use for the radius is 239, assuming that the centre of the circle is the centre of the screen. Following the radius number we can have another number, the colour number for the circle.

After that introduction, take a look at Figure 20.13. The first line sets up the familiar SCREEN 12 condition, and the loop that starts in the following line causes a set of circles to be drawn.

```
SCREEN 12
FOR N% = 10 TO 200 STEP 20
  CIRCLE (320, 240), N%, 13
NEXT
```

Figure 20.13. The CIRCLE statement, which produces circles of excellent shape.

On my monitor, the largest circles were no more than a millimetre out. We're not finished with circles, though. What you know of BASIC so far might lead you to believe that there could just be more to this CIRCLE command. There is. Try Figure 20.14, which shows how you can draw part-circles. Angles have to be specified in radians.

```
SCREEN 12
COLOR 0
CIRCLE (127, 96), 80, 14, 0, 3.14
```

Figure 20.14. Drawing partial circles (arcs) with an extended CIRCLE statement.

The key to this is the provision of start and stop numbers. The number 0 is taken as the 3 o'clock position on the screen, and the circle is drawn, going anti-clockwise from this position. The end-point is specified by the second number. I have made this 3.14, which is the value of PI. Using this number gives a semicircle (because Pi radians is 180°), and for other parts of a circle, just use the appropriate fraction.

Don't square it, squash it!

BASIC also allows you to draw shapes which are ellipses, squashed circles. The re-shaping of a circle is done by adding yet another number to the circle instruction. If this number is 1, then we simply get a circle. If this extra number is less than 1, however, we get an ellipse which is wider than it is high. If the extra number is greater than one, the ellipse is higher than it is wide. We can even make ellipses which are stretched out so much that they look like straight lines. This gives you unparalleled power to create all sorts of curved shapes. One of the features of the CIRCLE command is that it allows the use of numbers which take the cursor beyond the screen area, so that what you see on the screen is only part of a drawing.

Take a look at Figure 20.15, used to illustrate the ellipses that we can create. The range of the number that we can use, following the radius number (don't forget the comma) is 0 to 255, but the range that I have illustrated here is the most useful part.

```
SCREEN 12
COLOR 0
FOR E = 1 TO .1 STEP -.1
  CIRCLE (320, 240), 100, 14, , , E
NEXT
FOR N = 1 TO 3000
NEXT
CLS
FOR E = 1 TO 3 STEP .2
  CIRCLE (320, 240), 80, 15, , , E
NEXT
```

Figure 20.15. Creating elliptical shapes by adding yet another number in the CIRCLE statement. Note that where quantities are missed out, such as the part-circle numbers in this example, the commas must be inserted.

The only problem with this command is that it comes after the 'start and finish' commands which we use to draw a part-circle. If you want a complete ellipse, you won't want to use these numbers. We can get round this, as the program indicates, by omitting the start and finish numbers, but putting in their commas. It makes the command look rather odd, but it works. Notice how the circles are drawn starting from the two horizontal ends.

Meantime, there's another command to look at. Figure 20.16 demonstrates another amazing feature of this BASIC, the PAINT instruction. This will fill a space with colour, providing that you have enclosed the space with lines.

```
SCREEN 12
COLOR 0
CIRCLE (320, 240), 88, 14
CIRCLE (320, 240), 30, 14
PAINT (350, 290), 5, 14
```

Figure 20.16. Using the PAINT statement to fill a closed space with colour.

The CIRCLE statements draw two circles, one within the other. The PAINT instruction then fills with colour the space between the circles. PAINT needs the usual pair of coordinate numbers following it, in brackets. You have to choose these numbers so that they will act as a starting point for the painting operation. They must, therefore be somewhere inside the area that you want to paint. You may get odd things happening if you select a point on the edge of the area that you want to paint. You will certainly not get what you want if you pick a point which is outside the area you want to paint. Following the starting point, we've used two other numbers. The first is the number of the colour that we want to use for painting and the second is the colour of the boundary where you want to stop painting. If you omit the boundary colour you will find paint all over the screen, and trouble will also be inevitable if there is a gap in your boundary that allows the paint to leak out.

POINT the way!

There's another command which fits along with PSET and PRESET which provides a chance to show PRESET in action. The command is POINT, and it's a way of reporting what's going on. POINT gives you the colour of a pixel. It has to be followed by the usual X and Y location numbers, and you can find what it does by using something like PRINT POINT(X,Y) or A=POINT(X,Y). What is printed or assigned to A by these commands will be a number between 0 and 15. It is the colour number for the pixel, so that you can tell whether the pixel is at background or at foreground colour.

note Another option of POINT allows it to report the x or y coordinate of the pixel.

That description makes it sound quite straightforward, but it's not quite as simple as it seems, as the program in Figure 20.17 will illustrate. The program sets a black background, and draws two vertical lines. A dot is placed at the top left hand side, and it moves across the screen. This is done by using PSET (X%,Y%), 14.

```
SCREEN 12
COLOR 0
CLS
FOR Y% = 0 TO 199
  PSET (10, Y%), 14
NEXT
FOR Y% = 0 TO 199
  PSET (254, Y%), 14
NEXT
K% = 1: x% = 11: Y% = 1
DO WHILE Y% < 199
  PSET (x%, Y%), 14
  IF POINT(x% + K%, Y%) <> 0 THEN K% = -K%: Y% = Y% + 1
  FOR x = 1 TO 10: NEXT
  PRESET (x%, Y%)
  x% = x% + K%i$i
  IF Y% = 199 THEN END
LOOP
```

Figure 20.17. Using POINT to detect a boundary.

The future position of the dot is tested by using POINT, and if this point is background, the point is PRESET, the value of X% is increased, and the new point is PSET. When the wall is found from POINT, then the variable K% is made negative, so that X%+K% will have the effect of subtracting 1 instead of adding 1. This causes the point to move left rather than right. At the same time, Y%=Y%+1 has the effect of moving the point one step down. The POINT function tests to find if the next position will be background, and if it is not, you have reached the wall. The PRESET(X%,Y%) will erase the previous dot position so that the movement of the dot does not leave a line behind it.

In this example, of course, there was no need to use POINT, because we knew exactly where the walls were. In maze games, however, the walls are drawn at random, and you can't put their X and Y numbers so easily into a POINT command. It's then that POINT really comes into its own. Another reason for using POINT is that if you have two objects moving on the screen, it's easier to detect any kind of collision (object to object or object to background) with POINT. Just one POINT test will detect any type of collision, but if you were testing values of X% and Y%, you might have to use a lot of tests.

New windows

All of the statements and functions noted in this Chapter have made use of the screen coordinate system in which 0,0 is the top left-hand corner and 639,479 is the bottom right hand corner. This is not always the most convenient of number sets to work with, and you can use a WINDOW statement to change the numbers that are used. You might, for example, want to work with numbers 0 to 100 for both X and Y.

The WINDOW statement must follow a SCREEN statement so that the correct video mode is being used. The line:

```
WINDOW SCREEN (0,0)-(100,100)
```

will make the coordinates 0 to 100 as required. If the word SCREEN is omitted, the coordinates 0,0 refer to the bottom left hand corner and 100,100 to the top right hand corner, the normal co-ordinate arrangement for graph paper.

The use of WINDOWS does not, as you might expect, allow you to create screen Windows, for which the appropriate statement is VIEW, see Chapter 21.

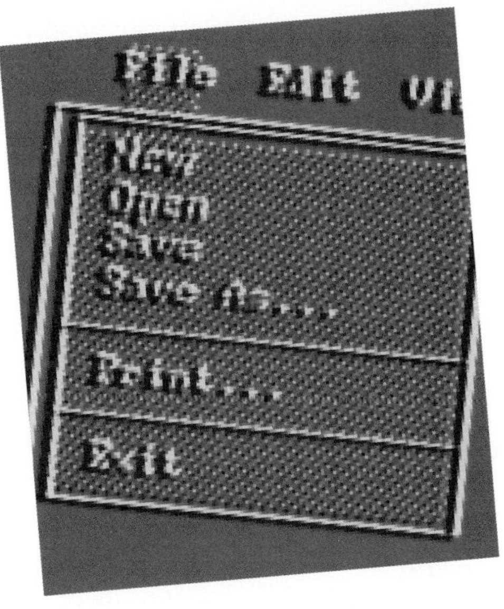

Graphics 2

Computer drawing

The ability for drawing lines and circles is just the start of the graphics capabilities of QBASIC. We're going to look at another way of drawing now, one which uses the instruction word DRAW. DRAW has to be followed by a string variable name, like DRAW A$ or DRAW GR$, and it's what you put into this string variable that decides what is drawn. Figure 21.1 shows a list of the letters that can be used, each of which can be followed by an integer number or variable (or a pair of coordinates in some cases).

Letter	Effect
U	Upward movement
D	Downward movement
L	Move to left
R	Move to right
E	Move up and right
F	Move down and right
G	Move down and left
H	Move up and left
M	Move to point whose x,y coordinates follow
	The following letters can precede any movement letter:
B	Blank, leave no trace when moving
N	Move but return to start after movement
	The following set effects rather than movement:
A	Set angle in multiple of 90 degrees.
TA	Turn angle, followed by angle in degrees, range -360 to +360
C	Colour - followed by colour number (0 to 15)
S	Set scale factor 1 - 255 (4 is normal scale)
P	Set paint fill and border colours (two numbers needed)

Figure 21.1. The letter subcommands for the DRAW statement.

What you have to do is to chart your drawing in terms of a starting point, then as up, down, left, right, or diagonal movements. The amount of each movement can be small, just one pixel, so that it's possible to make very detailed patterns in this way when you use SCREEN 12. You can also move to a new starting point without drawing a line. The very considerable advantage of using DRAW is that a complete pattern can be put on to the screen by just one simple instruction like DRAW G$. Now to the nitty-gritty. Figure 21.2 illustrates just how we go about creating a drawing in this way.

```
SCREEN 12
CLS
GR$ = "bm20,180;u100r20d100r20u100r20d100"
DRAW GR$
```

Figure 21.2. A simple DRAW string illustrated.

In the third line, a string is defined. It's a funny looking sort of string which consists of command letters and numbers. The command letters are the letters of the draw commands, and the numbers are the pixel units of screen size. As you know by now, these are 0 to 639 in the x direction, and 0 to 479 in the y direction for SCREEN 12. The string starts with BM. B means blank and it's used to ensure that no line is drawn, and M means move. The letter M has to be followed by two numbers, which are the x and y coordinates for the place where you want the drawing to start. I have chosen a point near the bottom left hand side of the screen.

Following the BM step, you might need to indicate what colour you want for your drawing, but this is not necessary for a SCREEN 12 production (it would be done by using the letter C, followed by the colour number). The next parts are movements - 100 up, 20 right, 100 down, 20 right and so on. The string ends with a quote mark as usual.

All we need to draw this is the command DRAW GR$. It's delightfully simple, but a very fast and powerful way of creating a drawing. It's particularly easy to make repetitive drawings in this way, because we can include a sort of subroutine. This is called a *substring*, and Figure 21.3 shows how it is used. What it amounts to is that you can define a string which is part of a pattern, then *execute* this substring inside the main string.

```
SCREEN 12
COLOR 0
CLS
SB$ = "u100r20d100r20"
XS$ = ""
FOR N% = 1 TO 5
  XS$ = XS$ + SB$
NEXT
GR$ = "bm20,180;c14X" + VARPTR$(XS$)
DRAW GR
```

Figure 21.3. Using a substring within a DRAW string.

In this case, I have illustrated only the substring being used. The calling command is X (eXecute), and it must end the normal part of the string within quotes. The substring name is used as an argument for the VARPTR$ statement in a part of the string that must not be enclosed in quotes.

note VARPTR$ is considered further in Chapter 22. It locates the position of the string in the memory so that it can be used.

If you are converting old GW-BASIC programs to use with QBASIC, you will have to alter any DRAW or PLAY (see Chapter 23) statements that use the X-command.

In this example, I have used SB$ to contain a simple up, across, down, across, set of instructions. The loop then packs five of these patterns into a longer string, and the GR$ assignment is made. The result is five sets of the pattern on the screen.

Now for a much more elaborate drawing, in Figure 21.4, that makes use of all of the commands so far. The screen conditions are set up in the usual way, and the following lines then define the strings. M$ is the main string, and it starts with BM40,20.

```
REM More substrings.
SCREEN 12
COLOR 0
CLS
C$ = "U2LU2LU2LU2L2U2L5U2R30D2L5D2L2D2LD2LD2LD2L"
D$ = "U5LU5LU2LU3L2U2L4U3L4UL2DL4D3L4D2L2D3LD2LD5LD5"
M$ = "BM40,20;C14D10R10D60L10U5D20U5R200U60L10U10;X"
 + VARPTR$(C$) + "D10L60;X" + VARPTR$(D$) +
 "L50U20L60"
REM Above is all one line
DRAW M$
FOR X% = 100 TO 200 STEP 50
CIRCLE (X%, 100), 20, 14: NEXT
LINE (100, 110)-(200, 110), 14
```

Figure 21.4. A more elaborate drawing which demonstrates the speed and simplicity of this method.

Two substrings are used. In this example, C$ is the chimney, and D$ is the dome. Using C$ and D$ in the VARPTR$ parts of the main string therefore draws these details in the correct places. If you aren't pleased with these places, it's easy to move position. All you have to do is to alter the place where the substring is called. Incidentally, I typed this with the CAPS LOCK pressed, because in the graphics strings, a capital L is less likely to be confused with the number 1 than a small l. You can use either, because the machine is not confused by the difference between them.

I have used semicolons after BM40,20, and before and after each substring. The semicolon must be used after the string ($) sign, but it doesn't have to be used in the other positions. I put in the extra semicolons just to make it easier to read the items in the string by marking out the positions of the substrings. The main body of the drawing is then carried out at an astonishing speed by DRAW M$ in line 60. The next point in this example is that you can mix the familiar LINE and CIRCLE commands along with the DRAW. The CIRCLE commands are used for drawing the driving wheels, because there is nothing in a DRAW string that can do this. The LINE could have been replaced by a DRAW, but it's easier to use LINE in this case, because it needs only one instruction.

Now for some more DRAW magic. As well as the up, down left and right commands, there are letters which indicate diagonal directions. These are illustrated in use in Figure 21.5.

```
SCREEN 12
COLOR 0
CLS
DM$ = "C14G10H10E10F10"
FOR N% = 1 TO 10
  P% = INT(RND * 220 + 20)
  Q% = INT(RND * 150 + 20)
  PSET (P%, Q%)
  DRAW DM$
NEXT
```

Figure 21.5. A set of diamond patterns to illustrate the use of diagonal drawing.

This uses a string which draws a diamond pattern, and then chooses ten randomly selected places on the screen. Now you have to be careful here as to how you get to these places . Using LOCATE works only for the instructions of the text screen, like PRINT, but does not move the DRAW position. The command that you have to use is PSET (or PRESET). By picking P% and Q% values at random, followed by PSET (P%,Q%), the invisible graphics cursor is in the correct place to draw the diamond pattern. You might think that you could use "BM P%,Q%" for this, but you can't. You are not allowed to use variable names inside a graphics string, except in ways that use the VARPTR$ function as noted earlier. The BM command is not one of the commands that can make use of variables.

Artistic creations

The DRAW command is a very useful way of making straight line drawings with less effort than is needed by LINE. You can use the LINE commands as well, and all the varieties of CIRCLE, along with box fill and PAINT to create any shape you want. What we have to look at now is how to plan these shapes. Trying to make a program that creates shapes on the screen is difficult enough, without planning it's almost impossible. The planning must start, as always, on paper – preferably with a piece of graph paper.

You will have to start with a pad of graph paper. It should be of A4 size and scaled in centimetres and millimetres. In addition, you need a pad of tracing paper. These items are not cheap, but they will last you for a long time. The principle is to mark out on the graph paper the coordinate numbers for your graphics screen, place the tracing paper over the graph paper, and then to make drawings on to the tracing paper. Because the tracing paper is transparent, you can see through it to the grid of coordinates underneath, and you can read off the values. Strictly speaking, you should use scales of 0 to 319 or 639 and 0 to 199, but its unusual to have to draw right to the edges of the screen, and using 10 to 310/630 and 10 to 190 is much more convenient – it fits the paper better.

You count each square on the graph paper as having sides of ten pixels, and diagonals also of ten pixels. That point about the diagonals is very important, because it saves a lot of awkward calculations or measurements. You draw your patterns on the paper, remembering that you can use up, down, left and right. When it comes to diagonals, remember that these must be 45 degree diagonals. This makes some shapes look distorted, and if the distortion is unacceptable, then you will have to use LINE instructions for these parts. When you make the drawing, you will make life a lot easier if you keep to simple dimensions, like multiples of five and ten. It is a lot more difficult to follow a pattern that goes U13L27D17R29 and so on! Working with the tracing paper over the graph paper makes it much easier to see what you are doing, and check your measurements.

The next step, once the drawing is to your satisfaction, is to obtain any distances and coordinates that you need. If you are using LINE and CIRCLE, you will need to read the x and y coordinates of points such as the start and end of a line or the centre of a circle. These are easily read from the graph paper underneath the tracing paper. DRAW graphics are just as easy – you simply count sides of squares or complete diagonals as ten pixels each, and then write the numbers against the lines. It helps if you write the letters like U,D,G,H and so on as well. You can then program directly from this. Programming is made easier if you program a section at a time, and join the strings up for final drawing.

Shrink, grow and turn

The possibilities for creating drawings with the DRAW instruction are made even greater by the options of altering both the size and the angle of patterns. These actions are carried out by using the letters S (for scale) and A (for angle) within the DRAW string. We can also add these instruction letters to a string, and we can put numbers in along with them by using STR$(number). BASIC allows another way of putting variables into these DRAW strings. If you have a variable such as J%, which carries a value, then you can put something like S=J%; into the string. The semicolon is essential and you will get an error message if you omit it. The effects which can be produced with this scale command are spectacular – most other machines could do these actions only with a lot of very complicated programming.

Try the program of Figure 21.6 now. This starts off as a simple piece of programming that draws a box. After the delay, though, things start to happen.

```
SCREEN 12
COLOR 0
CLS
G$ = "U50R50D50L50"
DRAW "BM10,450C14" + G$
FOR N = 1 TO 3000: NEXT
FOR J% = 1 TO 50
  CLS
  DRAW "c14BM10,450S" + STR$(J%) + G$
NEXT
```

Figure 21.6. The use of the scaling subcommand which allows you to shrink or expand your drawings. This allows you, for example, to display a drawing on the whole screen, then to shrink it to one corner.

The fancy business starts with the loop that uses variable J%. The range of the counter J% is 1 to 50, and you can use up to 255. This figure of 255 is the whole of the permitted range for the scale instruction, which uses the letter S. The scale which is used for drawing is one eighth of the number which follows 'S'. For example, if you use S2, then the drawing is 2/8, which is 1/4 size. Using S16 would make the drawing 16/8, which is double size.

This letter S has been put into the DRAW instruction so that the pattern is drawn with a different scale number each time. Watch these scale effects carefully. They are very easy to use, but the effects may not be exactly what you want. One point is that the start which is given by the BM part of the command is one edge of the square. The square will always start at this edge and grow from that point. The other problem occurs if the pattern grows too much, because this can take some of the boundaries beyond the screen edges. Some careful planning, with graph paper and tracing paper, is needed when you start to work with these 'Incredible Hulk' graphics!

Take a quick look now at a small change which makes a big difference. The program is in Figure 21.7, and starts with items that should be familiar territory to you now.

```
SCREEN 12
COLOR 0
CLS
G$ = "BU5L10F5G5R20H5E5L10"
DRAW "BM140,80c14" + G$
FOR N = 1 TO 2000: NEXT
FOR J% = 1 TO 60
  CLS
  DRAW "c14BM140,80s" + STR$(J%) + G$
  FOR Z = 1 TO 1000: NEXT
NEXT
```

Figure 21.7. A scale-changing program adapted so that the centre of the shape remains in the same point.

Variable G$ carries a short and simple string for a shape. Notice that this shape has no defined starting point, and it starts with a blank move upwards. The reason, as you'll see later, is to make the starting point in the centre of the shape. When we expand the shape, the expansion is always around the starting point. If this now is the centre, then the centre of the shape stays put. In the previous example, because the starting point was at a corner the shape expanded from that corner outwards. The line that draws this shape has a starting point added at 140,80 using the + sign to join the strings.

Angle antics

The use of the command letter S to make the drawing take different scales is a splendid feature of this BASIC, but there is another command letter that we can use. This time it's A, and its effect is to alter the angle at which a shape is seen. With A0, the shape is shown just as it has been drawn. With A1, the shape is turned through 90 degrees anticlockwise. Using A2 makes the shape turn through 180 degrees, and A3 makes it turn through 270 degrees. The number which is used with A must not exceed 3, otherwise the program will stop with the 'Illegal function call' error message.

```
SCREEN 12
COLOR 0
CLS
G$ = "C14BU5L10D10R20H5E5L10"
DRAW "C14BM140,80S8A0" + G$: FOR N = 1 TO 2000: NEXT: CLS
FOR J% = 0 TO 3
   DRAW "C14BM140,80a" + STR$(J%) + G$
   FOR Z = 1 TO 1000: NEXT
   CLS
NEXT
```

Figure 21.8. The angle subcommand letter A will allow a shape to be rotated by multiples of 90 degrees.

Figure 21.8 shows an example of this command in action. The shape is drawn, using 'S8A0' to make sure that its size and angle are unaffected by any previous program that was running. It is then rotated by using values of J% ranging from 0 to 3, with the value put into the graphics string in the same way as before, using STR$.

Multiple shapes

Now take a look at Figure 21.9. It illustrates how a number of shapes can be easily joined up. The key to this is the use of the + or - signs along with M or BM. Adding the sign + to a BM or M instruction causes a movement of as many spaces as you specify.

```
SCREEN 12
COLOR 0
CLS
DRAW "C14BM10,80"
G$ = "C14BU5L10F5G5R20H5E5L10"
FOR X% = 1 TO 8
DRAW "BM" + "+" + STR$(20) + ",5" + G$
FOR N = 1 TO 2000: NEXT
NEXT
```

Figure 21.9. Shifting shapes with the + or - subcommands.

This is an important difference. BM 10,10, for example, means move to position X+10, Y+10. If we use BM +10,+10, we mean a move of ten places left and ten places up from where the last piece of drawing finished. Note the contradiction here. You would normally expect BM+10 to mean that the X position number was increased by 10, so causing movement to the right. It works exactly the opposite way round, and so does the Y position number. Similarly, BM-10,-10 would mean a move of ten places right and ten places down.

The tricky bit here is adding the + or - signs to the string, and two methods are demonstrated. The + sign which is enclosed by quotes is the one that is put into the string, the others are there only to provide the joining action. The method that uses STR$(20) is more useful when the quantity that is being added is a variable value. The method that uses ",5" is more suitable when the value is a fixed and known number.

Even all that doesn't exhaust the graphics possibilities of BASIC, because we haven't looked at PUT and GET for recording and replaying graphics patterns in the form of arrays, nor at the principle of making 'invisible' drawings that can be put on to the screen with a single command. Lack of space is the problem here, and to do justice to the formidable capabilities of BASIC graphics would take a book devoted entirely to that subject. I hope that this Chapter, however, will allow you to make considerable use of the excellent graphics capabilities of this combination of machine and software.

Save and load

A screen image, or any other stored number of bytes, can be saved to a file by using BSAVE, and the same set of bytes can be restored by using BLOAD. These statements are not as straightforward as you might expect, however. BSAVE saves the number of bytes you specify to a named file (creating a file of the name you specify) subject to an upper limit of 65535 bytes. The starting number of the bytes can also be specified. BLOAD recovers these bytes from the named file.

The trouble is that you might not know what bytes you were saving. If you have not used any DEF SEG statement, the 64K segment that is being used is the current data segment, but if you want to save an image you need to save the video memory. Similarly, it would be pointless to load back data for an image into the data segment – it must be placed in the video memory.

The way that different graphics boards use video memory, makes the use of BSAVE and BLOAD quite difficult unless you want the actions to work on just one type of display. Since most users of PCs nowadays have the VGA type of board, it is reasonable to tailor BLOAD and BSAVE to this type.

The important point is that careless use of BLOAD with an incorrect segment address causes the machine to lock up. It is better to ignore these statements unless you know that they work correctly on your machine, for example if they appear in a program that runs correctly. The same applies to the PCOPY statement which copies screen data from one video page to another

Using screen windows

A screen window is a piece of screen which behaves as an independent entity, so that you could, in theory, have two windows, one bearing words and the other showing graphics. In practice, the use of screen windows with QBASIC is more often used for items such as keeping a title or a set of reminders in view while another part of the screen is used for changing items. When screen windows are in use, a CLS can be applied to clear one window but will leave other windows unaffected.

The main keyword for screen windows is VIEW. VIEW requires you to state what rectangular area, as described by coordinate numbers, is to be used. Programming with VIEW is hard work, because the VIEW statement has to be used each time a window is to be changed – some versions of BASIC have allowed each window to be created and then referred to by a reference number. Figure 21.10 shows two windows being created on a VGA screen. The SCREEN statement must precede VIEW – otherwise you will get an error message.

```
CLS
SCREEN 12
VIEW SCREEN (100, 100)-(1, 1), , 15
CIRCLE (50, 50), 20
VIEW SCREEN (300, 300)-(150, 150), , 15
LINE (160, 160)-(220, 220), , B
```

Figure 21.10. Two windows with different shapes. The outline of the windows has been indicated by using a border line.

The VIEW SCREEN statement uses SCREEN to make the coordinates follow the familiar pattern of 0,0 being the top lefthand corner and 639, 479 being the bottom righthand corner of the whole screen. This means that when you are, for example, drawing the box in the second window, the coordinates do not start at 0,0 again. By omitting the word SCREEN, coordinates will be relative to the top left hand corner of the window rather than the top left-hand corner of the screen, Figure 21.11.

note SCREEN is used in a different sense in the VIEW PRINT statement, Chapter 14.

```
CLS
SCREEN 12
VIEW (1, 1)-(100, 100), , 15
CIRCLE (50, 50), 15
VIEW (200, 200)-(400, 400), , 15
LINE (10, 10)-(180, 180), , B
```

Figure 21.11. By omitting the keyword SCREEN, the co-ordinates in each window are relative to the top left-hand corner of that window, rather than to the top left-hand corner of the screen.

If you want to switch back to the whole screen, use VIEW with nothing following it.

One other function relevant to VIEW use is PMAP, which allows you to translate the co-ordinates from window co-ordinate number to whole screen co-ordinate numbers. PMAP is followed, in brackets, by the co-ordinate you want to translate and, separated by a comma, the translation that is required, using the codes:

```
0 ..............from X in main screen
1 ..............from Y in main screen
2 ..............from X in window
3 ..............from Y in window
```

For example x% = PMAP (50,2) finds the x co-ordinate on the main screen that corresponds to an x co-ordinate of 50 inside the currently used window.

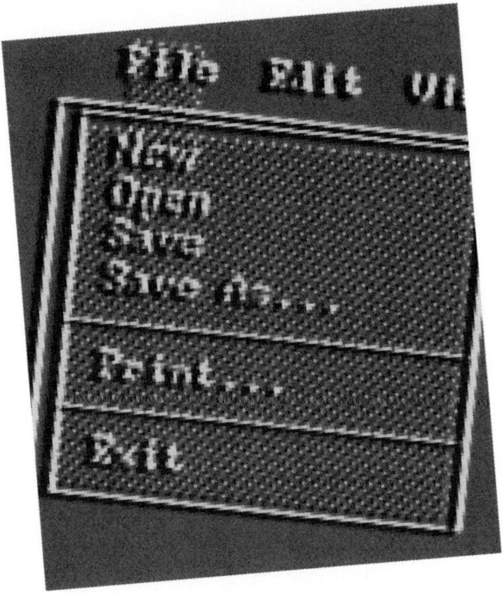

Events

Interrupting the machine

An event in QBASIC, is an action that can be detected by way of the interrupt system of the computer. The normal action of the microprocessor is to carry out its actions in sequence, following a program which is written as a set of number-codes stored in the memory – as all programs are. While you are running QBASIC, for example, the microprocessor is working on the commands of the QBASIC interpreter program, some of which will be concerned with running a program written in BASIC, others with controlling screen, printer, disk drives and all the rest.

The action of the microprocessor can be interrupted by electrical signals delivered to one of its connections, and when this happens a set of new actions is started:

1. The command that is being executed is completed.
2. The internal memory of the microprocessor is copied to part of the main memory called the stack.
3. A routine called the interrupt service routine runs.
4. When the interrupt service routine is finished, the data that the microprocessor was using is returned from the stack.
5. The microprocessor resumes its program.

The *interrupt service routine* is another piece of code whose starting position in the memory is notified at the same time as the interrupt occurs.

A good example to look at is the action of the keyboard. There are two ways in which a keyboard can be made to work with a microprocessor. One is that the microprocessor continually checks the keyboard, working in a loop rather like the INKEY$ action. This is called *polling*, and it is very inefficient because so much of the activity of the microprocessor is being used whether it is needed or not – at normal typing speeds, the microprocessor could have got through several million actions in the time between pressing one key and the next.

The better alternative is an interrupt-driven keyboard. The microprocessor gets on with its work, ignoring the keyboard, until a key is pressed. This creates an interrupt, and the interrupt service routine attends to reading the keyboard and making sense of whatever key has been pressed. In this scheme, no time is wasted because the keyboard is only checked when a key has been pressed. At microprocessor speeds, there is plenty of time to do all of the work when a key has been pressed.

The pressing of a key on the keyboard is an *event*, and the normal action of the system is that this event creates an interrupt signal. When you run QBASIC (and many other programs), the interrupts from the keyboard, other than from the Ctrl-Break keys, are ignored at times. Obviously they are not ignored while you are editing, otherwise you could not type in a program, but they are ignored while one of your own programs written in QBASIC is running. If you want keys other than Ctrl-Break to cause some effect then you have the choice of using polling or interrupt methods. The polling methods make use of keywords such as INPUT or INKEY$, making the program wait. *Event-trapping*, by contrast, uses the interrupt system so that pressing a key at any point in the program will make something happen. What that something is depends on you, because QBASIC allows you to write your own routines for each of these event traps.

The starting keyword for all event programming is ON, followed by the type of event that is to be trapped. Some of these events will be of little concern to most PC users because they rely on hardware such as light-pens or joysticks that are not normally part of the equipment of a PC. These are briefly noted later in this Chapter. By far the most important of all event traps is the ON ERROR GOTO type of trap, which was illustrated in Chapter 18 but without detailed explanation. Running close behind this one are ON KEY and ON TIMER, so that these three deserve close attention.

Error trapping

At several stages in this book we have come across the idea of mugtrapping, checking data that has been entered at the keyboard to see if it makes sense or not. Mugtrapping is normally carried out by using lines such as:

```
IF LEN(A$)=0 THEN
GOSUB Correctit
```

or their equivalent, and you need a separate type of mugtrap for each possible error. This can be fairly tedious, and it usually turns out that there is one other error that you haven't spotted. In addition, there are actions that generate errors which stop the program, like trying to work with a disk file that doesn't exist because you are using the wrong floppy disk or in the wrong hard disk directory. QBASIC is one of the versions of BASIC that offers you mugtrapping statements that can intercept such errors. The main one is ON ERROR which can be used with GOTO (but *not* with GOSUB or CALL).

Figure 22.1 gives a very artificial example – a real-life example would involve too much typing. In this example, the length of a word is measured, and the number inverted (divided into 1). This is impossible if the length is zero, and the ON ERROR GOTO is designed to trap this. You could get a zero entry, for example, by pressing ENTER without having pressed any other keys.

```
ON ERROR GOTO sortit
PRINT "Type a word, please"
INPUT a$
L% = LEN(a$)
PRINT 1 / L%
PRINT "END"
END
sortit:
PRINT "Word has no letters!"
RESUME NEXT
```

Figure 22.1. Using ON ERROR GOTO to trap an error message and take appropriate action.

Normally, when this happens, you get an error message and the program stops. The great value of using ON ERROR GOTO is that the program does not stop when an error is found, instead it goes to the subroutine. In this example, the subroutine at label sortit prints a message, then resumes on the next instruction, the one following the division which caused the error. As you can see, the RESUME NEXT is as important as the ON ERROR GOTO, because if the RESUME NEXT is omitted you get an error message (No RESUME) unless the END statement is put in place of RESUME NEXT.

Another option is shown in Figure 22.2. This uses a label name for the start of the program, and the RESUME statement takes the execution back to this point.

```
ON ERROR GOTO sortit
starter:
PRINT "Type a word, please"
INPUT a$
L% = LEN(a$)
PRINT 1 / L%
PRINT "END"    END
sortit:
PRINT "Word has no letters!"
RESUME starter
```

Figure 22.2. Another option of RESUME is to go to a label position in the program.

This allows the user another chance at the entry, and is more likely to be useful in a program where some sort of input is needed if the program is to run. It also avoids the problems that an inexperienced user would face when a program ends unexpectedly.

Normally, this type of error is avoided by testing the value of LEN(A$), but there are actions which cannot be tested and it is for these that the ON ERROR type of statement is useful. Do not use ON ERROR to compensate for badly thought out programming.

The use of ON ERROR GOTO is delightfully simple at this level, but it's something that calls for experience. If your program still contains things like syntax errors, these also will cause the error subroutine to run, and this can make the program look rather baffling as it suddenly goes to another line or ends. Always omit, or precede with REM, any ON ERROR GOTO line until you have tested the program sufficiently to remove all syntax errors; in fact, all errors other than the ones you are trying to trap. You can also make the error-handling point out errors other than the ones that you are particularly looking for, as we shall see.

If RESUME is used alone, with no label name (or line number) or NEXT statement, the program resumes at the stage that caused trouble. This is not always useful, because if the error cannot be corrected in the error routine lines (like a 'disk full' error on a floppy drive) then you get an endless loop. Used alone, however, RESUME can be very useful as a way of inserting a default value, as Figure 22.3 illustrates.

Once again, this sort of error example would be programmed by other ways, but the idea of altering a value and then resuming can be very useful if you cannot be sure what circumstances would create the error.

```
ON ERROR GOTO sortit
PRINT "Type a word, please"
INPUT a$
L% = LEN(a$)
PRINT 1 / L%
PRINT "END"
END
sortit:
PRINT "Word has no letters!"
PRINT "Default used"
L% = 1
RESUME
```

Figure 22.3. Using RESUME alone as a way of placing a default value instead of a faulty one.

ON ERROR GOTO actions are particularly useful when disk files are being dealt with, because you cannot be sure what a disk file contains, or if a filename exists. Note that QBASIC has no way of checking that a filename exists, which was the reason for the use of ON ERROR GOTO in Chapter 18.

Figure 22.4 shows another example in which an error routine makes a change in the output.

```
CLS
ON ERROR GOTO sortit
FOR N% = 1 TO 5
  READ X
  Y$ = STR$(SQR(X))
printit:
  PRINT "Number"; X; "; square root is "; Y$
NEXT
DATA 5,4,3,-2,2
END

sortit:
Y$ = STR$(SQR(ABS(X))) + "j"
RESUME printit
```

Figure 22.4. Another example of a value being changed in the ON ERROR routine so that an answer can be printed.

When the error routine is triggered by the SQR functions encountering a negative number, the action is to generate a different version of Y$ in which the j indicates that a square root of a negative number has been used – j is the mathematical symbol for the square root of -1. This quantity is in normal terms impossible, but if it is interpreted as a length whose direction is at right angles to other lengths it can be very useful.

There is an important difference between QBASIC and some earlier types in the way that repeated errors are detected. Older BASIC versions often used ON ERROR GOTO in a one-shot way, so that once an error had triggered the ON ERROR GOTO routine, no other error could do so until the routine was rearmed by using another ON ERROR line in the routine itself. This is not needed in QBASIC, as Figure 22.5 illustrates.

```
CLS
ON ERROR GOTO sortit
FOR N% = -5 TO 5
  PRINT LOG(N%)
NEXT
END
sortit:
PRINT "There is an error"
RESUME NEXT
```

Figure 22.5. A routine which generates a set of errors, but which will run normally when correct data is fed in.

In this example, the negative numbers cause an error in the LOG function, but the ON ERROR GOTO ensures that the program does not stop. Instead, the error message generated by the routine is printed and the action resumes where it left off (because RESUME is used alone, with no NEXT or label name). There is no need to rearm the routine.

As has been mentioned, ON ERROR GOTO can be a source of trouble if it is triggered by any other sort of error, because normally you are using it to work on some specific error type. Though the Editor will catch syntax errors before they do any harm, it is possible for other errors to occur which cause the wrong response.

Figure 22.6 shows this type of mistake in a simplified example. This causes an endless loop, which you have to escape by using Ctrl-Break.

```
CLS
ON ERROR GOTO sortit
FOR N% = 1 TO 5
  READ j%
  PRINT SQR(j%)
NEXT
END
DATA 5,-6,4,this,10
sortit:
j% = ABS(j%)
RESUME
REM This will cause an endless loop - use Ctrl-Break
```

Figure 22.6. The dangers of using ON ERROR for one particular type of error when others may be lurking.

The error routine is intended to trap and deal with the problem of a negative number in a square root function, but the data line (which might be read from a disk and is therefore not so easily checked) contains a string quantity. This generates an error because a string quantity cannot be read into an integer variable. Because this is an error, however, it triggers the ON ERROR GOTO action and, because it is not dealt with, the RESUME statement carries out the same line action again. There is no end to this, so that Ctrl-Break has to be used.

This is bad planning, because you should have anticipated that there could be other errors. The way out is to use the error routine to test for the errors that may occur, so that you use the trap for the correct one. This is not as straightforward as it might appear because the most recent error is stored in a variable called ERR which only the QBASIC interpreter can alter. Figure 22.7 shows what can happen.

```
REM Problems here!
CLS
ON ERROR GOTO sortit
FOR N% = 1 TO 5
  READ j%
  PRINT SQR(j%)
fromhere:
NEXT
END
DATA 5,-6,4,this,10
sortit:
IF ERR = 5 THEN
  j% = ABS(j%)
  RESUME
END IF
RESUME fromhere
```

Figure 22.7. The danger of testing for a single error but not for others.

In this example, the error number of 5 is used for an Illegal Function Call such as the square root of a negative number. The sortit routine contains a test for this, corrects the number and uses RESUME, all within the IF block of statements. This deals with the item -6 in the data list.

As far as the string is concerned, the test for ERR=5 fails, so that the RESUME fromhere part is executed. This skips the printing, so ignoring the string. What is not so obvious is that this also ignores the last DATA entry of 10. This happens because ERR holds the value of the last error encountered. In this program, the error caused by the string is a Syntax error, ERR 2, so that ERR has the value of 2 when this item is read. ERR retains this value, however, so that when the last item is read the presence of the error code causes the ON ERROR GOTO to operate, and the retained value of ERR causes the print action to be skipped.

note: This does not occur for the ERR 5 action, and seems to be peculiar to a Syntax error of this type. The only way out in this example is to change the program so that strings are read and converted to numbers. Figure 22.8 shows this done.

```
REM Much better!
CLS
ON ERROR GOTO sortit
FOR N% = 1 TO 5
  READ j$
  j% = VAL(j$)
  PRINT SQR(j%)
fromhere:
NEXT
END
DATA 5,-6,4,this,10

sortit:
IF ERR = 5 THEN
  j% = ABS(j%)
  RESUME
END IF
RESUME fromhere
```

Figure 22.8. A modified program is preferable to endless efforts to get around the Syntax Error trap!

note There is another variable, ERL, which is present in QBASIC only for compatibility with earlier programs. This holds the line number of the line in which the error occurred, but since QBASIC lines are not normally numbered its use is limited. It also holds line labels but, if the error happens in a line that is not labelled, the label name taken is the most recently used one which might be a long way from the error. ERL should be regarded as a survivor from the past rather than something to use nowadays. Figure 22.9 shows the list of standard error numbers.

Code	Message	Code	Message
1	NEXT without FOR	37	Argument-count mismatch
2	Syntax error	38	Array not defined
3	RETURN without GOSUB	40	Variable required
4	Out of DATA	50	FIELD overflow
5	Illegal function call	51	Internal error
6	Overflow	52	Bad file name or number
7	Out of memory	53	File not found
8	Label not defined	54	Bad file mode
9	Subscript out of range	55	File already open
10	Duplicate definition	56	FIELD statement active
11	Division by zero	57	Device I/O error
12	Illegal in direct mode	58	File already exists
13	Type mismatch	59	Bad record length
14	Out of string space	61	Disk full
16	String formula too complex	62	Input past end of file
17	Cannot continue	63	Bad record number
18	Function not defined	64	Bad file name
19	No RESUME	67	Too many files
20	RESUME without error	68	Device unavailable
24	Device timeout	69	Communication-buffer overflow
25	Device fault	70	Permission denied
26	FOR without NEXT	71	Disk not ready
27	Out of paper	72	Disk-media error
29	WHILE without WEND	73	Feature unavailable
30	WEND without WHILE	74	Rename across disks
33	Duplicate label	75	Path/File access error
35	Subprogram not defined	76	Path not found

Figure 22.9. A full list of error codes and the messages they normally place on the screen.

There is another command word, ERROR, which can be used to make an ON ERROR GOSUB execute, and which is very useful for testing the effect of error trapping. You may, for example, want to find out how your program might react to a floppy disk being full, not something that you can easily cause during testing. ERROR can be used with the error numbers that are listed above, which are the QBASIC error numbers, making the program's error trapping respond as if one of the standard errors had occurred. This use of ERROR is indicated in Figure 22.10, in which the routine in the procedure detects when you run out of DATA, something that you could easily do while working with a program.

```
CLS
ON ERROR GOTO sortit
FOR n% = 1 TO 10
  READ j%
  PRINT j%
endloop:
NEXT
backhere:
REM disables on error
PRINT "The next message has been forced by the ERROR command"
ON ERROR GOTO 0
ERROR 61
END
DATA 1,2,3,4,5,6,
sortit:
IF ERR = 4 THEN RESUME endloop
RESUME backhere
```

Figure 22.10. Using an artificial error, and ON ERROR GOTO 0.

The artificial error in this example is invoked by using ERROR 61, the Disk full error, but in this program such an error would normally be handled by the ON ERROR GOTO sortit routine. So as to show what is going on, the line:

```
ON ERROR GOTO 0
```

has been included. This has the effect of ending the ON ERROR action, so that when the ERROR 61 is used, the normal error message is delivered. You would probably want to write a routine that asked for a disk change, and resumed the disk action when a key was pressed in indicate that the disk replacement had been done.

Programmed keys

Any key can be used to create an event when it is pressed, but for many purposes the function keys F1 to F10 are best suited to this use. The statement that is used is ON KEY GOSUB. This event trapping action cannot take place unless the action has been enabled by using a KEY statement such as KEY 1. When such trapping is in use, pressing the key which is specified allows a subroutine to run. Note that the statement format is ON KEY(1) GOSUB and not ON KEY(1) GOTO. Figure 22.11 shows an example of the F1 key being used to deliver a message while a program is working on a long loop.

```
CLS
KEY(1) ON
ON KEY(1) GOSUB message
FOR n% = 1 TO 200
  PRINT n%
  FOR j = 1 TO 500: NEXT
NEXT
END
message:
CLS
LOCATE 5, 10: PRINT "Your program is still working"
FOR k = 1 TO 5000: NEXT
CLS
RETURN
```

Figure 22.11. KEY(1) being used to deliver a message at any point in a program, interrupting a loop action in this example.

The KEY(1) ON statement ensures that key event trapping is enabled, and you can disable it by using KEY(1) OFF – once again, you would use the key number that you needed. The use of ON and OFF allows you to confine where key trapping is used – you might, for example, enable trapping during a long loop but not in other parts of a program. Another option is KEY(1) STOP which suspends key trapping. If a key has been pressed during the time when KEY () STOP is in operation, there will be no action until the program comes to a KEY () ON statement.

Any key can be used for this trap action – you are not confined to the Function keys – see Figure 22.12

1-10	Function keys F1-F10.
11	Cursor Up key.*
12	Cursor Left key.*
13	Cursor Arrow key.*
14	Cursor Down key.*
15-25	User-defined keys.
30, 31	Function keys F11 and F12.

(* Cursor keys on numeric keypad only)

0 can be used in the form KEY(0) ON, KEY(0) OFF, and KEY(0) STOP to mean all of the keys listed.

Figure 22.12. The key reference numbers that can be used in the KEY statement. Do not confuse these with key scan codes, later.

The important point to remember is that the cursor key codes refer to the cursor keys on the numeric keypad only, not the usual set of cursor keys that lie between the main key set and the numeric keypad on a standard 101/102 key keyboard.

The numbers 15 to 25 are reserved for user-defined keys, meaning that any key or key combination can be defined as having one of these numbers. This action allows you to use any key on the keyboard, including the separate set of cursor keys, providing you know how to assign a user-defined number to these keys. Such an assignment is made by using the KEY command followed by a list of characters that carry key codes, and for this you need a list of keycodes. These are not the same as the ASCII codes that the keys normally provide. Figure 22.13 shows these codes.

If, for example, you wanted to make the code for user-defined key 15 respond to the spacebar, you would program this as:

```
KEY (15), CHR%(0) + CHR$(57)
ON KEY(15) GOSUB routine
```

since the spacebar uses code 57 in the list above. This allows you to interrupt your program by pressing the spacebar.

The first CHR$ setting is for the keyboard state. A key can be struck by itself or along with either SHIFT key, the Ctrl key, Alt, Numlock, or Caps Lock. In addition, the 101/102 key type of keyboard found on modern machines contains keys that do not exist on the older types. A set of codes is therefore used for keyboard state as follows:

Value	Key
0	No special keys
1 to 3	Either Shift key
4	Ctrl key
8	Alt key
32	NumLock key
64	Caps Lock key
128	Extended keys on a 101/102-key keyboard

You can specify more than one state by adding numbers. For example, since most PC/AT keyboards start up by default with the Num Lock key on, the NumLock code of 32 can be added to any other key you want to use

This also allows the four cursor keys on the 101/102 key set to be used, because these need the extended keyboard code of 128. If the Num Lock is set as a default, we need to add 32, so that for the up-cursor key (code 72 for the one on the number keypad) we would use:

```
KEY (15), CHR$(128+32) + CHR$(72)
```

note The first CHR$ number is for the state of the keyboard and the second is for the key scan code.

Key	Code	Key	Code	Key	Code
Esc	1	A	30	Caps Lock	58
! or 1	2	S	31	F1	59
@ or 2	3	D	32	F2	60
# or 3	4	F	33	F3	61
$ or 4	5	G	34	F4	62
% or 5	6	H	35	F5	63
^ or 6	7	J	36	F6	64
& or 7	8	K	37	F7	65
* or 8	9	L	38	F8	66
(or 9	10	: or ;	39	F9	67
) or 0	11	" or '	40	F10	68
_ or -	12	~ or `	41	F11	133
+ or =	13	Left Shift	42	F12	134
Bksp	14	| or \	43	NumLock	69
Tab	15	Z	44	Scroll Lock	70
Q	16	X	45	Home or 7	71
W	17	C	46	Up or 8	72
E	18	V	47	PgUp or 9	73
R	19	B	48	Gray -	74
T	20	N	49	Left or 4	75
Y	21	M	50	Centre or 5	76
U	22	< or ,	51	Right or 6	77
I	23	> or .	52	Gray +	78
O	24	? or /	53	End or 1	79
P	25	Right Shift	54	Down or 2	80
{ or [	26	Prt Sc or *	55	PgDn or 3	81
} or]	27	Alt	56	Ins or 0	82
Enter	28	Spacebar	57	Del or .	83
Ctrl	29				

Figure 22.13. The key scan codes for the PC keyboard.

Other F-key actions

Each of these keys can be assigned to a word or phrase, because if you have used function keys to perform actions in your program by way of the ON KEY statement it is useful to have a way of remembering what they do. Suppose, for example, that you have programmed the machine so that pressing F1 will clear the screen and display a menu. You can be reminded of this by using statements that assigns short words or phrases (up to 15 characters) and display the function key assignments.

For example, try the short program of Figure 22.14.

```
CLS
KEY 1, "Menu" + CHR$(13)
KEY ON
FOR N = 1 TO 10000: NEXT
REM Prevents Press any key to continue message
```

Figure 22.14. The method of assigning a function key with a message and displaying it at the foot of the screen.

A slightly different syntax is used, with no brackets around the key number. If you use brackets for this type of assignment, the Editor will remind you with an error message.

The TIMER event

Another event trigger makes use of the timing action that is built into any PC machine. The keyword for this action is TIMER, and the syntax follows very closely the previous examples, so that no timing is used until TIMER ON is executed, following which ON TIMER (5) GOSUB routine will active the routine each 5 seconds. You can use any number of seconds in brackets ranging from 1 to 86400 (24 hours). Figure 22.15 shows an example which prints the time by using the function TIME$.

One point to note is that the timekeeping of PC machines is not to quartz watch standards, though the quartz crystal that determines the timing of the microprocessor is of a very high standard of precision. The reason for the discrepancy is that the clock time is derived from the crystal pulses by way of software, and the software is subject to interrupts. Each interrupt may be brief, but it makes a difference in the time, and over a few days this become noticeable, particularly if you use a mouse or other device that generates a lot of interrupts.

- The SLEEP 0 statement, which normally waits for any key to be pressed, also releases when any trapped event comes along.

```
CLS
ON TIMER(10) GOSUB looktime
TIMER ON
PRINT
FOR n% = 1 TO 100
  PRINT "Count is "; n%
  FOR j = 1 TO 3000: NEXT
NEXT
END

looktime:
col% = POS(0)
row% = CSRLIN
LOCATE 1, 70
PRINT TIME$
LOCATE row%, col%
RETURN
```

Figure 22.15. Illustrating ON TIMER as used to print the time at intervals.

Other ON statements

There are two ON statements which are of very little importance to most PC users. ON PEN GOSUB, along with the inevitable PEN ON, PEN OFF and PEN STOP, are used to allow the action of a light pen to interrupt a program. Since few PC machines are equipped for a light pen, we'll ignore this one because so few users could try out an example. The same applies to ON STRIG (with STRIG ON, STRIG OFF and STRIG STOP) which allows a joystick to interrupt the PC. The ON STRIG statement can take as its argument a number which is 0, 2, 4 or 6, depending on which of two joysticks is activated and which trigger on the joystick. Once again, so few PCs are equipped with this (games) hardware that there is little point in describing it further.

The joystick is also needed for the STICK function, which returns a number for the X or Y coordinate of the joystick, with an integer 0 to 3 used to select which of two joysticks is read, and whether the X or Y coordinate is being read.

ON COM, with COM ON, COM OFF, and COM STOP is used to interrupt a program when a message of any kind is received at a serial port. The routine that is called to deal with an interrupt must use OPEN COM to read the codes from the serial port into memory or to a disk file, and this type of programming is not for newcomers to QBASIC (it is not generally available in other versions of BASIC).

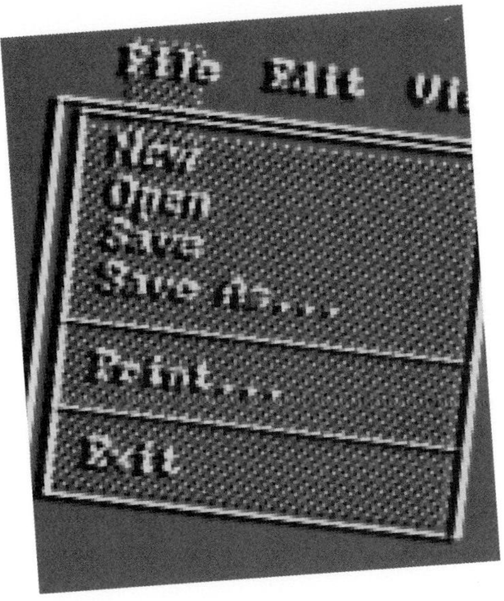

Sound on the PC

Sounds unlimited

The ability to produce sound is an important feature of all modern computers, but the use of sound is less important on a machine that is intended for serious use. The sound of the PC computer comes from a small built-in loudspeaker and the hardware of the sound system is very simple, mainly aimed at providing a noise to attract the attention of the user. Plug-in sound cards are available for the PC machine, but their use is beyond the scope of this book. However, QBASIC does allow you a number of different ways of creating sound effects, whether you want just a reminder, a melody or a noise, using only the normal PC equipment.

What we call sound is the result of rapid changes of the pressure of the air round our ears. Everything that generates a sound does so by altering the air pressure – Figure 23.1 shows how the skin of a drum does this.

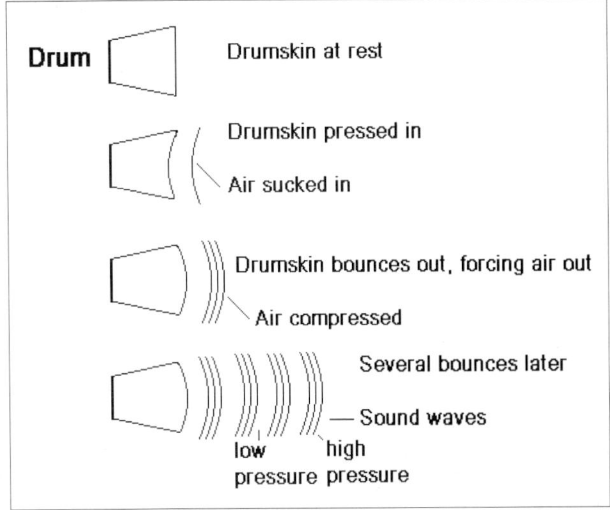

Figure 23.1. How a drumskin produces sound by alternately compressing and decompressing air.

All other musical instruments also rely on the principle of something which vibrates and pushes the air around. However, air pressure is invisible and we don't notice these pressure changes unless they are fairly fast – they are measured in cycles per second, or *Hertz*. A cycle of any wave is a set of changes, first in one direction then the other, and then back to normal, as illustrated in Figure 23.2. The reason that we talk about a *soundwave* is because the shape of this graph is of wave shape.

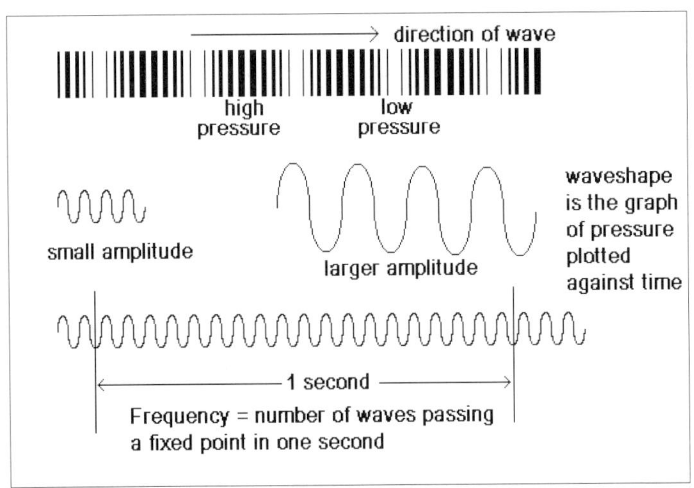

Figure 23.2. Sound waveforms that show how the pressure of the air changes during the time of a sound. The amount of change determines the loudness of the sound, and the rate of change determines the pitch of the note.

The frequency of a sound is its number of Hertz – the number of cycles of changing air pressure per second. If this amount is less than about 20 Hertz we can't hear it though it can still have disturbing effects. We can hear the effect of pressure waves in the air at frequencies above 20 Hertz up to about 15000 Hertz. The frequency of the waves corresponds to what we sense as the *pitch* of a note. A low frequency of 80 to 120 Hertz corresponds to a bass note. One of 400 or above corresponds to a treble note. Human ears are not sensitive to sounds whose frequency is above 20000 Hertz (20 kilohertz) but many animals can hear sounds in this range.

The amount of pressure change determines what we call the loudness of a note. This is measured in terms of *amplitude,* which is the maximum change of pressure of the air from its normal value. For complete control over the generation of sound, we need to be able to specify the amplitude, frequency, shape of wave and also the way that the amplitude of the note changes during the time when it sounds.

QBASIC has three main sound instructions, BEEP, SOUND and PLAY. Of these three instructions, BEEP is a simple instruction, and the notes from it have fixed pitch and amplitude. If you have a PC which incorporates a volume control of your monitor you can have this sound as loud or as soft as the circuits of the machine permit. The SOUND instruction is a much more complicated one, though it needs only two numbers following it. What makes it more complicated is that several SOUND instructions are needed to set up one sound, and it's designed mainly to produce sound effects that can't be produced by the other commands. We'll keep SOUND until later, and concentrate on the other two for the moment, starting with BEEP.

BEEP doesn't have to be followed by numbers, it simply causes a short sound, the same as the one which you hear along with an error message. Figure 23.3 illustrates how you might use BEEP.

```
CLS : PRINT "message coming..."
FOR N = 1 TO 2500: NEXT
PRINT "Hey, you, operator..."
FOR N = 1 TO 10: BEEP: NEXT
```

Figure 23.3. Using the BEEP statement to produce a sound of fixed pitch and duration. Some versions of BASIC offer no more than this.

There is a message appearing on the screen, and you want to make sure that the user looks at it. A long beep is produced by using a loop of ten beeps, and it makes a noise which is quite an effective attention getter unless you are using a machine with a volume control that is turned down.

You shall have music...

The BEEP instruction is very useful for its purpose, but BASIC has a lot more in store for you. A lot of computers are not really suited to working with music, because they require all of the instructions to be in number form. If you read music, or can work with sheet music, this is the last thing that you want. The ideal method of programming music would be to work with the named notes of music – and this is what the PLAY instruction of BASIC does. It might appear to be the obvious thing to do, but very few versions of BASIC for the PC do it, and some permit no more than a beep!

However, if you have no experience of music this may seem rather puzzling to you. How do we go about writing down music? For each note, we have to specify what the note is (its pitch), how loud it is to be and for how long it is to be played. In written music, this is done by using a type of chart of lines and spaces for the pitch, and different shapes of markings (notes) for the duration. Loudness is indicated by using letters such as f (loud) and p (soft). More than one letter can be used, so that ff means very loud, and pp means very soft. Each sound is indicated by a note, a shape on the chart, and the shape of the note gives some information about the duration of the note. In addition to this, each piece of music starts with some advice about the speed at which the notes are to be played.

What these speed settings decide is how many unit notes are played in a minute. The unit note is the *crochet*, so if a piece of music is marked at a speed of 60 (pretty slow), then there will be 60 crochets played per minute, one each second. A more normal rate would be 120, two notes per second.

The durations of all the other notes are decided in comparison to the crochet. For example, the minim sounds for twice as long. The crochets and other timed notes are indicated by the shapes of the written notes, as Figure 23.4 shows. In addition, symbols are used to indicate silences in the music, and these are based on the same idea of a unit duration of silence, and others which are twice, four times, half etc. These silence marks are also shown in Figure 23.4.

Note symbol	Time	Name	L No.	Rest	R No.
♩	1/8	Demisemiquaver	L64		
♩	1/4	Semiquaver	L32	𝄿	R32
♩	1/2	Quaver	L16	𝄾	R16
♩	1	Crotchet	L8	𝄽	R8
𝅗𝅥	2	Minim	L4	𝄼	R4
𝅝	4	Semibreve	L2	𝄻	R2

Figure 23.4. The note and rest symbols of written music. These are used to indicate the time of each note and each silence (or pause). The length numbers of QBASIC are also shown.

The pitch of a note is indicated in written music by placing it on to a kind of musical map which is called a staff (one staff, two staves) as shown in Figure 23.5. Piano music uses two of these staves, each consisting of five lines and four spaces.

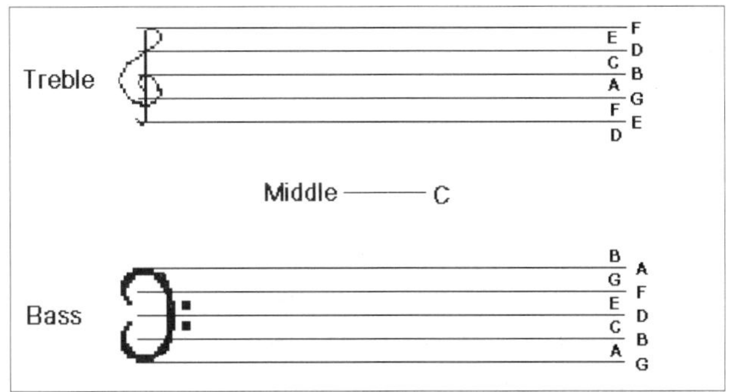

Figure 23.5. The staves, showing treble and bass staff as for a piano. This is a type of map for musical notes. The position of a note on this map indicates the pitch of the note.

In addition to this representation of notes by position on staves, we also use the letters of the alphabet from A to G to name the notes.

The piano is still the most familiar type of musical instrument, and its keyboard is set out so as to make it very easy to play one particular series of notes, called the *scale of C Major.* The scale starts on a note that is called Middle C, and ends on a note that is also called C, but which is the eighth note above middle C. A group of eight notes like this is called an 'octave', so that the note you end with in this scale is the C which is one octave above Middle C.

Most music in the Western hemisphere is based on this group of eight notes, so we use only the first seven letters of the alphabet in naming them. The eighth note is the end of one octave and the start of the next, so that it bears the same name. The scientific basis of all this is that if you take Middle C, and find the frequency of the sound of this note, then the C which is the next octave above Middle C has precisely double the frequency value of Middle C. The C below Middle C has half the frequency of Middle C, and so on. That's why the Ancient Greeks always thought that music was a branch of mathematics. Come to think of it, the way that the times of notes are related to each other in multiples of 2 corresponds exactly with the way that the computer deals with number values. Perhaps the Ancient Greeks were right.

The appearance of these keys on the piano keyboard is illustrated in Figure 23.6. Middle C is at the centre of the keyboard, and we move right for the higher notes, left for the lower ones. One of the complications of music, however, is that the frequencies of the notes of a scale are not evenly spaced out. The normal full spacing is called a *tone* and the smaller spacing a semitone. Each scale contains five tones and two semitones. In written music, Middle C appears midway between the treble and bass staves.

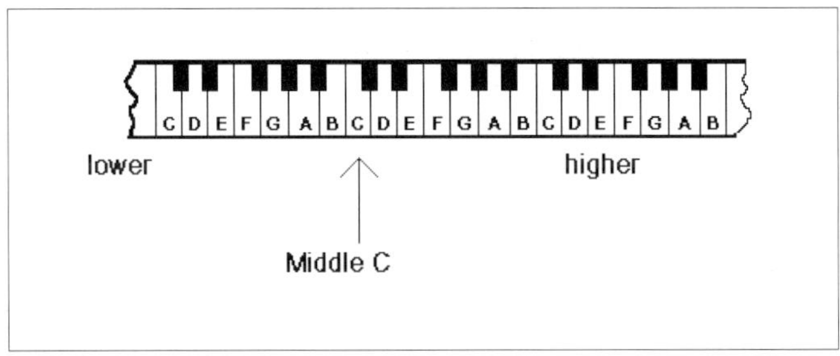

Figure 23.6. Part of the piano keyboard, showing Middle C. There is only one semitone between B and C and between E and F in the straightforward scale of C Major, starting with Middle C and ending with the C above it.

The important instruction for playing music with BASIC on your PC computer is the PLAY instruction. Like DRAW, PLAY has to be followed by a string name. The string then contains all the information that is needed to produce the music. The notes are specified simply by their names, as used in music. These are the letters A to G, and we also use the signs + and -. The + sign or # sign means a semitone higher than the note indicated by the letter, so that A+ or A# is a semitone above A, the note a musician would call *A sharp*. Similarly, A- would mean a semitone below A, or *A flat*.

In addition to the letter names of the notes, we can use other control letters to indicate the octave, length, tempo and pauses. The octave is denoted by the letter O, and it has to be followed by a number whose range is 0 to 7. If you don't specify any 'O' value, the computer sets itself to O4, which is the range of notes above Middle C. O0 means the lowest range of BASIC computer notes; O7 gives the highest, and O3 contains Middle C. This means that BASIC can play eight octaves of notes – more than the range of any ordinary musical instrument.

One odd weakness in this system is that there is no provision for altering the relative volume of notes though this is provided in some other varieties of BASIC that use almost identical instructions. We can, of course, still set the volume control to suit our own tastes. The letter L controls the length of all note codes that follow it, and has to be followed by a number in the range 1 to 255 (though the useable range is 1 to 16). This number does not behave in the way you might expect, because the low numbers give the long notes, and the high numbers give the short notes. Figure 23.4 shows how these length numbers and also the pause numbers relate to the marked length of musical notes on sheet music. The pause or rest is a silent interval, and uses the letter P. It follows the same number scheme as note length. If you don't specify any other values, the computer uses L4 and P4.

Time now for some illustrations, starting with Figure 23.7. This begins by defining a string A$. It consists of the notes that start at Middle C. Middle C on the QBASIC PLAY system is the first note in octave number 3, so by starting with O3 and C, the first note that we get is Middle C.

```
A$ = "O3CDEFGABO4C"
PLAY A$
```

Figure 23.7. Defining and playing a string of music subcommand letters.

The other notes have been written in sequence, but we need to put O4 before the next C, If we don't, then we'll get Middle C again instead of the C above. The scale uses the default values of volume and speed (tempo).

This is a simple scale, but it's a good piece of music to illustrate what can be done with this BASIC command. Try Fig.23.8 now, to see what we can do to alter the way in which this scale can be played and the effect of the length L.

```
A$ = "T120L4O3CDEFL16GABO4L2C"
PLAY A$: 'hear how it sounds
PLAY "MN" + A$: 'Normal
PLAY "MS" + A$: 'Staccato
PLAY "ML" + A$: 'Legato
```

Figure 23.8. Using MN, MS and ML to play the same note sequence in different styles.

The first thing that you have to know at this point is that T means *tempo,* and it controls the number of crochets per minute – this in turn controls the speed of playing the string. The setting of tempo is 120 by default. The range of T is a curious one, 32 to 255. The fastest tempo is obtained by using 32, the slowest by using 255. In the example, we have used the ordinary tempo, 120, but changed the length of note settings.

The reason for having separate tempo and length control letters is that you can get the tune sounding right by using L to select the length of notes, and then use T right at the start to set whatever tempo you like, If you want to speed things up, use a low value for T, if you want a funeral march, use a high value. You can even write the string without a T, and then add it in later by a command like:

PLAY "T100"+A$.

The length of a note can also be specified by using a number following the note, like C4 or A3, rather than the clumsier L4C or L2A. This allows you to use L to set the length of most of the notes and deal with any notes of different length by tacking a length number following them. In addition, you can lengthen a note by 50% by typing a dot following the letter, such as C. or A. which corresponds to the notation used in written music.

The specification of timing and note length, however, does not tell us how the notes are played. You can play a set of notes in many different ways, depending on the spaces that you put between the notes. Rather than require you to put in these spaces for yourself, BASIC allows you to specify with three control codes, MN, MS and ML. MN means 'Music Normal', and plays the music string that follows it using short spaces between notes. MS means 'Music Staccato', and plays the notes as short bursts with longer pauses. ML means 'Music Legato', in which there are no pauses and each note runs smoothly into the next. The terms *staccato* and *legato* are standard musical names for these effects, which are demonstrated in Figure 23.8.

Figure 23.9 shows an example of a tune written using the PLAY instruction. Points to watch for here are the use of # for sharp notes, and the use of a dot following a note letter. When you use, for example, C., then this note will play for one and a half times as long as C with no dot.

```
M$="03L4CC02B803C8D02A.G.FFE8F8G4D2E2L6F#GA.03D202L4
G03CCC1602B.A8G4"
PLAY "T90" + M$
```

Figure 23.9 A tune written for the PLAY instruction (stand to attention, please) and using a tempo number that is inserted when the tune is played.

The dot is used in written music in the same way, so that being able to do this with BASIC as well makes it all the easier to transfer written music to the form of PLAY strings. Incidentally, you have the choice of playing music strings of up to 32 notes either as foreground or background. If you pick foreground (which is a default anyhow, but can be commanded by starting your string with MF) then nothing can be done in BASIC until the music has finished. If you want the music as background, you start the string with MB, and the music plays away while the program moves on. This is possible only if the length of the music string is fairly short, however.

note These MUSIC strings can be long and, unless you make use of substrings (see later) you have to type them in one line. This is awkward if you want to print out a program, because the Editor will not print the characters that extend beyond the normal line length of the printer. If you want to print music strings, load the program into a wordprocessor and then print.

The use of PLAY follows so closely the pattern set by DRAW that you would expect to be able to use substrings in much the same way. The letter X is used to mean 'Execute a substring', and it has to be followed in the same way by using VARPTR$(substring). You could, for example, use:

```
PLAY A$ + "X" + VARPTR(B$) + "X" + VARPTR(C$)
```

to play three music strings in order. The X commands could be incorporated into the preceding strings, left as they are, or added to so that they changed tempo or whatever.

The use of substrings is particularly suitable when a set of notes is repeated often – want to try Beethoven's Fifth?

One last point on PLAY is that you can make items like the T number into variables, so that you can alter them more easily. Figure 23.10 illustrates this by using the music lines from the previous example.

```
CLS
DO
   PRINT "What tempo would you like (1 to 255. 0 to end) ";
   INPUT TEMPO%
   IF TEMPO% = 0 THEN END
   PRINT "playing....": GOSUB playit
LOOP
END

playit:
M$ =
"O3L4CCO2B8O3C8DO2A.G.FFE8F8G4D2E2L6F#GA.O3D2O2L4GO3CCC16O2B.A8G4"
PLAY "T=" + VARPTR$(TEMPO%) + M$
RETURN
```

Figure 23.10. Using a variable within a string to control tempo. Note how the value of the variable has to be entered.

In the PLAY line, using the "T=" + VARPTR$(TEMPO%) uses, as a value of T, whatever number has been input for TEMPO% earlier. For simplicity no testing has been used other than to stop the loop, but you would normally check the input number to ensure that it was in the correct range.

Sounds unlimited

We now need to take a look at the third sound instructions of BASIC, using the SOUND command word. SOUND is an instruction word which is used in a simple way, with just two numbers following SOUND. The first number in the SOUND command is a frequency number. The values that can be used here range from 37 to 32767, but the highest numbers are for the benefit of bats only and you won't hear them. The second number is a duration number for which a count of 18 plays the sound for one second. If you use zero for this number no sound is produced which can be a useful way of getting a silence.

Since the first number in a SOUND instruction is a frequency number, the effect of a change of number becomes less as the frequency increases. This is because an octave in sound corresponds to a doubling of frequency. For example, if we take the lowest note of frequency 37, then the octave above is obtained using 74. If you take the treble note whose frequency is 5000, then an octave above this needs 10000. In one case, the octave change used just 37 steps, in the other 5000.

This is made clear in the example of Figure 23.11, which uses the SOUND instruction in a loop, playing notes by using the frequency numbers in the loop. Because the loop uses steps of 1, the frequencies change rapidly at first, but by the time you get to around Middle C, the notes change very slowly, and in the upper ranges it seems to take forever – use Ctrl-Break when it becomes unbearable.

```
FOR N% = 37 TO 10000
SOUND N%, 1: NEXT
```

Figure 23.11. A very long duration loop which shows the range of the SOUND statement.

The main use for SOUND is in creating effects which would be tedious using PLAY. As an example, lend an ear to the example in Figure 23.12. This produces a warbling note by using two SOUND instructions in a loop, with the duration of each note as short as can be used.

```
FOR N% = 1 TO 36
SOUND 264, 1
SOUND 330, 1
NEXT
```

Figure 23.12. Creating a warbling note with SOUND.

This is not short enough to convince anyone that the notes are being sounded together, however, but if you want to simulate telephone noises it could be useful. It can also at times be handy to know that you can produce a note of precisely controlled frequency. For example, SOUND 440,90 gives you five seconds of standard orchestral A (is there an oboe player in the house?) and allows you to dispense with tuning forks if you happen to use them.

PLAY events

In Chapter 20 we looked at the events that use statements such as ON ERROR or ON TIMER. There is also the ON PLAY statement, which performs similar actions for the playing of music strings. The statement is in the form:

```
ON PLAY(5) GOSUB routine
```

and its effect in this example is to run the subroutine when there are five notes left in the music string.

As for other event traps, this one has to be enabled by using PLAY ON, and can be disabled by using PLAY OFF. If PLAY STOP is used, this disables the action until a subsequent PLAY ON, so that the subroutine will then run if it has been triggered during the time of the PLAY STOP action. The number of notes that can be used in the ON PLAY statement is in the range 1 to 32.

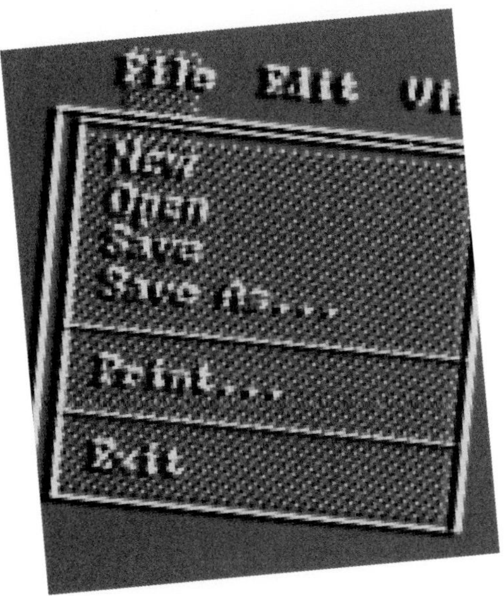

System Interactions

The QBASIC interpreter is a program which runs on the PC allowing you to edit and run your own programs. As it runs, the QBASIC interpreter makes use of the MS-DOS operating system which has to be present to allow the QBASIC interpreter to be used. It also makes use of the memory of the PC machine directly.

All of these actions can be lumped together under the heading of *System Interactions* to which we can add some statements that cannot be placed under any other heading, such as those which allow one program to load and run another. Of the others, the simplest are the MS-DOS interactions. These are FILES CD, MD, DR, KILL and NAME used as QBASIC commands.

There is no space in this book to deal with MS-DOS commands, directory structure or paths in detail. If you need information on this subject, consult any good book dealing with MS-DOS, such as Newnes MS-DOS Pocket Book (published by Butterworth-Heinemann).

FILES is the QBASIC equivalent of the DOS DIR command, allowing you to see a directory listing. If you use FILES as an Immediate window command, you can see a list of the directory that contains QBASIC. Using the direct command:

```
FILES ("A:")
```

produces a directory listing for the floppy disk in the A: drive. Note that the drive designation is A: rather than just A, and that this must be surrounded by quotes. Figure 24.1 shows an example of FILES being used in a program.

```
CLS
current$ = "C:\": 'directory that contains QBASIC
parent$ = "..": 'next directory closer to root
floppy$ = "A:": 'floppy drive
FILES (current$)
FILES (parent$)
FILES (floppy$)
END
```

Figure 24.1. A short program demonstrating FILES in use.

NOTE that you can use wild card descriptions, such as:

```
FILES ("*.BAS")
```

which only lists those files which have the BAS extension or:

```
FILES ("TE?T.DOC)
```

which finds files named TEXT.DOC, TEST.DOC, TENT.DOC, TEUT.DOC and so on. The asterisk can take the place of any set of characters; the question mark can take the place of any single character. These wildcards are used exactly as they are in MS-DOS.

If you use FILES with a description that does not correspond with any available drive or directory, there will be an error (error 53) of 'File not Found'. This can be useful if you are incorporating an error trap (Chapter 22) because file actions are the main area of use for error trapping.

note For that reason, the error numbers associated with errors in file and directory manipulation are shown for each statement below.

The use of FILES can be very handy in a program in which files are read, but you need to be able to specify and check the directory that is used. By having a FILES statement in a DO loop, followed by an INKEY$ waiting loop, you can check if the directory is the one you want and signify acceptance with 'Y' or use 'N' to activate a routine which will change directory and return you to the start of the loop for another FILES action.

The three main commands for directory manipulation are CHDIR, MKDIR and RMDIR – note that you *cannot* abbreviate these to CD, MD and RD as is done in MS-DOS. Each of them needs a specifier in the form of a string such as:

```
CHDIR "C:\BASIC\NEWWORK"
```

with the name of the directory in quotes, or as an assigned string variable.

CHDIR is used to change from one directory to another. For example, while you are using QBASIC, the current directory will normally be the one in which the QBASIC files are stored – this might be C:\BASIC, for example. By using the statement or direct command:

```
CHDIR "C:\TEMP\BASFILES"
```

you will change the current directory to the one specified – if such a directory has previously been created. If this directory does not exist, error number 76 is generated, corresponding to the message 'Path not found'. You would normally use CHDIR in a program to make a directory containing data files into the current directory.

MKDIR creates a new directory, which branches from the current directory that you are using. For example, if you are currently using C:\BASIC and you place in a program or as an Immediate command:

```
MKDIR "BASFILES"
```

you create a directory whose path is C:\BASIC\BASFILES. This does not make this the current directory – for that you need CHDIR. RMDIR used with a name always creates a directory on the hard disk if there is space, and if you specify a name of more than the allowed maximum, (eight characters of main name, optionally another three as an extension separated by a dot) the MKDIR statement uses the first part of the name you supply up to the maximum permitted. If you try to create a directory on a disk that is already full, an error message of the Disk Full (number 61) variety is created.

You should always specify the full path for a MKDIR statement if you do not want the new directory to branch from the current directory. This normally requires you to use a command of the form:

```
MKDIR "C:\TEMPS\OLDBAS"
```

which requires you to specify intermediate directories. If you specify an intermediate directory incorrectly, this also leads to a Path not found error, number 76.

The RMDIR statement or Immediate command removes a directory, and there are two important restrictions which prevents this from executing:

1. RMDIR cannot remove a directory which contains files – use KILL statements to remove files first.
2. RMDIR cannot remove the current directory – it must be executed from another directory which is not a branch from the current directory.

For example, if you use the statement:

```
RMDIR "C:\TEMP"
```

for a directory that contains files, you get the Path/File access error message, error code 75. Attempt to remove the current directory and you get the 'Path not found' error, number 76. These might not be the messages you expect, so that it is useful to know what you need to trap.

With the CHDIR, MKDIR and RMDIR statements used for manipulating directories, we are left with the statements that work on files. These are KILL and NAME, used respectively to delete and to rename a file.

KILL takes the form:

```
KILL "FIG2_27.BAS" or KILL K$
```

with the name of the file contained in quotes or in the form of a string variable. Obviously a file can be deleted only if it exists, so that the use of KILL with a filename that does not correspond to a file is an error with the message 'File not found' – number 53.

KILL can be used with the wildcards ? and * which allow more than one file to be killed with a single statement. This requires some care, because using:

```
KILL "*.*"
```

deletes every file in a directory. You must be quite certain before you use such a command that:

1. You are in the directory that contains files you want to delete.
2. You really want to delete all of the files.

For these reasons you should always use a FILES statement along with a waiting loop before any KILL "*.*" type of statement.

If there are no files in the current directory or in the directory specified in the KILL statement, the error message is 'File not found' – error code 53.

The NAME statement is used to rename a file, and its syntax is:

```
NAME "oldfile" AS "newfile"
```

or

```
NAME A$ AS B$
```

A string is used for each filename as usual. Note the order of *old* AS *new*, because if you rename in the wrong order an error message is the better of the options that you can expect. If 'oldfile' does not exist, you get the 'File not found' message.

Wildcards cannot be used in a NAME statement, though they can be used to a limited extent in the corresponding MS-DOS RENAME. If you try to use a wildcard you will get the 'Bad file name' message, number 64.

Machine level interactions.

QBASIC provides a few statements that directly affect the memory of the computer. One of these, VARPTR$, has already been used in connection with DRAW and PLAY strings, and the others are PEEK, POKE, FRE and CLEAR.

The POKE statement should be used only if you are very clear about what you are doing, or are following expert advice. Careless use of a POKE statement can lock the machine up so that you have to reboot, or it can result in deleting files or causing incorrect operation of essential components such as the disk system until the machine is switched off and re-started. Treat this statement with the utmost caution if you are experimenting for yourself.

The VARPTR and VARPTR$ statements are used to find out where a variable quantity is stored in the memory of the machine. The only difference between the commands is that VARPTR returns a number and VARPTR$ returns a string.

In Figure 24.2 a number is assigned to a variable, and the VARPTR statement prints the number that is returned. What this number happens to be depends on how the memory of your machine is being used at the time and is not necessarily the same as the number another user will obtain. For that reason it is important to try these for yourself. Numbers returned from VARPTR in this chapter are for illustration only.

```
CLS
a%=292
PRINT VARPTR(a%)
```

Figure 24.2. Using VARPTR to return a memory location number for an integer.

In this example, running the program on my machine produced the number 32020, and we now have to look at what this means.

Memory in the PC machine is divided into segments, each of 64K, which use memory address numbers of 0 to 65535. The data for a QBASIC program is normally held in one segment and, when VARPTR is used, the number it returns is the memory address number for that segment. There is a statement, DEF SEG, that changes the segment, but you should not attempt to use this unless you know a lot about the memory organisation of the PC. The segments also use reference numbers of 0 to 65535, though this does not imply that you can have this number of 64K segments.

What we need to know now is what exactly is stored at the address that VARPTR produces, and this involves the use of the PEEK statement. PEEK is followed by a memory address number, in brackets, and the effect of PRINT

PEEK(address) is to print the code number that is stored at the address. Figure 24.3 shows the contents of two address numbers being printed for the integer variable.

```
CLS
a% = 293
x% = VARPTR(a%)
FOR n% = 0 TO 1
  PRINT PEEK(x% + n%)
NEXT
Results: 37 and 1
```

Figure 24.3. Using PEEK to find what is stored at the VARPTR position and the following position.

The numbers that are printed are 37 and 1 – the coded version of 293. The way that this is worked out hinges on the fact that each memory address can store a number in the range 0 to 255. For an integer number, two bytes are used, one containing the integer divided by 256, the other containing the remainder. In this way, for the range of an integer, no number will exceed 255.

The numbers are then stored in the order of low byte, high byte, so that the first number here, the 37, is the remainder, and the second number, 1, is the number of 256's. The number stored is 1 x 256 + 37, which is 293.

The storage of a string is rather different. When the program is altered to find a string, as in Figure 24.4, the output from VARPTR consists of two numbers. The first is the length of the string, and the second is the start of its location.

```
CLS
a$ = "This is a string"
x% = VARPTR(a$)
FOR n% = 0 TO 3
  PRINT PEEK(x% + n%)
NEXT
```

Figure 24.4. Using VARPTR on a string variable.

In this example, when tried on my computer, the numbers that were printed were 16 0 78 125. The first pair, 16 and 0, indicates 0 x 256 + 16, 16 characters in this string. The second pair, 78 and 125 means 125 x 256 + 78, which is 32078, and this is the address in memory where the string of ASCII codes are found. By PEEKing at this set of address numbers, we can find the ASCII codes and, by using CHR$, check that this is the string we are looking for. Figure 24.5 shows this done by assembling the VARPTR address numbers into an address and PEEKing the set of 16 locations.

```
CLS
a$ = "This is a string"
x% = VARPTR(a$)
a% = PEEK(x% + 2) + 256 *
(PEEK(x% + 3))
FOR n% = 0 TO 15
PRINT CHR$(PEEK(a% + n%));
NEXT
```

Figure 24.5. Reading the bytes of a string from their location in memory as revealed by VARPTR.

note There is an important difference between a string and a number in this respect. When VARPTR is applied to a number variable, it gives the location of the first of the bytes that make up the number. When VARPTR is used on a string variable, it yields the length of the string and the memory address numbers, not the string itself. This is a way of allowing predictable handling of variables, because it allows the details of any string to be stored in four bytes.

The PEEK function reads the contents of memory, but the POKE statement changes these contents, using the address number and the new content number for each byte. No harm can be done by reading, but writing to memory always carries the risk that some vital piece of memory will be altered. In fact, using POKE on a data segment carries less risk, because it only alters the data that a program is using, but does not interfere with the operating system in the way that a POKE to other segments might. Figure 24.6 shows an example in which the string of the previous example has its letters progressively changed.

```
CLS
a$ = "This is a string"
x% = VARPTR(a$)
a% = PEEK(x% + 2) + 256 * (PEEK(x% + 3))
FOR n% = 0 TO 15
POKE a% + n%, 65
PRINT a$
NEXT
```

Figure 24.6. A program to find a string location and alter it by POKEing the code for the letter A.

When this runs, you can see the letters of the string being replaced, one after the other, by ASCII code 65, which is the letter A. This is not exactly useful, but it illustrates the action of POKE and its syntax using a comma to separate the address number from the data number.

POKE actions can be used to carry out operations which are impossible to do in any other way, and the Help page for POKE illustrates this as applied to altering the status of the CAPS LOCK key. The action depends on using segment 0 and loading in a byte, each of whose bits performs some keyboard alteration. The actions are illustrated in Figure 24.7.

```
REM Make sure all indicator lights are out.
DEF SEG = 0
keystat% = PEEK(1047)         'Read keyboard status.
d% = 1
FOR n% = 0 TO 7
  POKE 1047, keystat% XOR d%
  PRINT "Bit"; n%; "is now reversed"
  GOSUB waitnow
  d% = 2 * d%
NEXT
END

waitnow:
a$ = INPUT$(1)
RETURN
```

Figure 24.7. Investigating the effect of reversing keyboard byte bits.

The program is started with all keyboard lights out – this usually means that you must press the Num Lock key, because this is usually on by default when a PC machine starts up. When you run the program, each bit in the byte is reversed in turn, using XOR. The basis of this is that 0 XOR 1 is 1 and 1 XOR 1 is 0. By using the number 1, the bit in the first position is reversed, because in binary, 1 is 00000001. Using 2 (00000010 in binary) checks the bit in this position, and the next number is 4 – doubling the test number each time.

Running this program reveals that bits 0 to 3 have no noticeable effect, but 4 to 7 affect the keyboard indicators, turning each one on and off in turn, with 128 turning all lights off if they started in that state. This poke provides a form of control over the keyboard that you cannot achieve with any normal QBASIC statement.

FRE, ERASE and CLEAR

FRE and CLEAR are two memory-related actions that are not normally required. FRE is used to check the amount of memory space used for arrays, for the stack portion of memory and for strings. Using:

```
PRINT FRE(-1)
```

shows the maximum size of array (not string array) that can be created. The value is in bytes, and is typically around 151000 if no arrays are being used. With:

```
PRINT FRE(-2)
```

you can see how much of the stack remains – expect a small value here, probably around 136. Using:

```
PRINT FRE("")
```

shows how much string space is left after making the maximum amount of space available. A typical figure is 29800.

note This last use also clears out string space, removing any string characters that are not allocated to a variable name. When a string is deleted, the variable name for the string has its four bytes altered, but the string characters that were in the memory are not deleted until FRE ("") is used.

All of these FRE statements would normally be used in program routines of the type:

```
IF FRE ("") < 100 GOSUB warning
```

so that a warning could be delivered about memory being in short supply.

The ERASE statement is used to clear out array space. Its effect on a dynamic array is to free the memory that was used by an array, and make this space available. If the array name is to be used again, it needs to be dimensioned again using either DIM or REDIM. For an array that has been declared as STATIC, ERASE clears the elements, making each number in a number array equal to zero, and each string in a string array a blank string.

CLEAR is a drastic statement used to tidy up after a program. Any open file is closed and buffers released, variables are cleared and arrays set to zero or blanks, and the stack is reset. An option is to change the size of the stack. For stack alteration, use:

```
CLEAR ,, 1000
```

which, in this example, clears and sets the stack to 1000 bytes. By using CLEAR alone, the stack is unaffected. Note that the two commas must be included (for parameters that are no longer used).

Odds and ends

The statements and functions below are ones which are seldom used and which, like POKE, require some care in their use.

CALL ABSOLUTE allows you to start a machine code routine from within BASIC. Obviously to use it requires knowledge of machine code programming. You must also know the starting address of the machine code bytes, relative to the start of the segment that is used, and this starting address is used as the argument for CALL ABSOLUTE. In the example that is shown in the HELP page for CALL ABSOLUTE, the VARPTR functions is used to find the address for the machine code bytes (which are a call to the MS-DOS print-screen action).

ENVIRON and ENVIRON$ are concerned with the MS-DOS environment variables such as PATH or PROMPT. ENVIRON in the form ENVIRON = NEWDATA allows a change to be made to an environment variable of MS-DOS, and ENVIRON$ allows the existing value of the specified environment variable to be read as a string.

INP and OUT are port functions that make use of the port addresses of the PC. To make use of these functions you need to know what addresses are designated for the ports, and the action of each, so that a detailed knowledge of the design of the machine is necessary.

IOCTL and IOCTL$ are concerned with device driver software, such as that for the hard or floppy disk drives. To use these two you need to know the device reference number and what information can be sent to it (using IOCTL) or read from it (using IOCTL$).

SYSTEM shuts down both a QBASIC program and QBASIC itself, and returns directly to MS-DOS. In normal use, you would want to return to the QBASIC interpreter so as to run another BASIC program.

WAIT is used to suspend program action until some pattern of bits is read from a port, so that you need to know port address numbers and what bit patterns to expect.

Calling other programs

When you run a program, the RUN action (whether called from the QBASIC interpreter using the Shift-F5 key, selected from the menu, or used because of a RUN statement in an existing program) deletes whatever program is in the memory at the time when the command is executed.

A form of command that is more flexible is CHAIN, which allows one program to load and run another, keeping all the variable values of the previous program intact if you want to do so. Figure 24.8 shows a simple example. Type the listing of (b) and save it, using a filename of "second" Now type and save the listing in (a). With the main program section in the memory, run and watch the screen. You will see the values of '6.667 example' appear on the screen from the main program, and then '13,334 New example' caused by the running of the second program, into which the variable values a and b$ have been passed.

```
(a)
REM Main program
COMMON a, b$
CLS
a = 6.667
b$ = "Example"
PRINT a, b$; " exist in main program"
SLEEP 5
CHAIN "SECOND.BAS"
END

(b)
REM Second program
COMMON a, b$
x = 2 * aC$ = "New " + b$
PRINT C$, x; " in second program"
END
```

Figure 24.8. Using CHAIN along with COMMON definitions to allow one program to run another.

The variable passing in this example has used COMMON in both programs to describe the variables that will be passed on. If this is omitted, the second program erases all the variables used in the first.

A very common use of this type of action is the use of overlays. In this system, a main program calls in a number of routines that are used as needs be, each in turn calling back the main program.

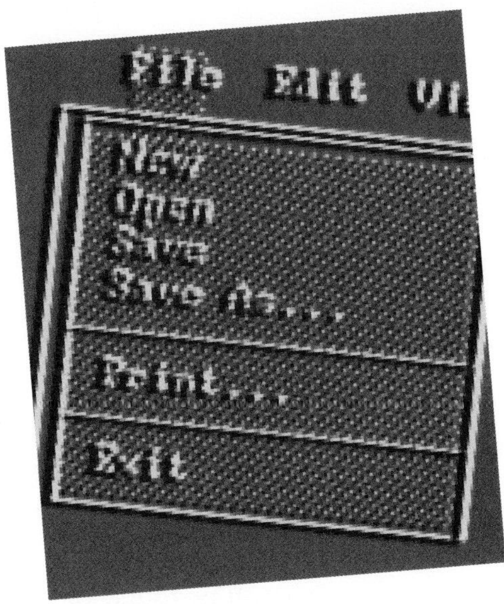

Appendices

A: Standard Form of Number

Standard form is a method of writing and working with numbers that are either very large or very small. The principle is that only a limited amount of the digits in a number are ever really significant. For example, if a poll calls for 10,000 people to be questioned it does not really matter very much if the number happens to be 9,990 or 10.010. Taking another example, a number like 0.000000126842314 might just as well be written as 0.000000127 unless there is some special need to use more than three significant figures. In most cases, measurements on which we base figures cannot be much more precise than one part in a thousand, and most are little better than one part in a hundred.

To see why standard form is used, consider the number 1,000,000. If you wanted to multiply this by 1.5 you would not go through the stages of saying 'one point five times zero is zero, one point five times zero is zero..' and so on, until you got the 1.5 x 1 = 1.5. You would simply say that one point five times a million is 1.5 million. This is what standard form is all about. Each number, in standard form, consists of two parts. One part is a number that is between 1 and 10 which will use as many significant figures as needed. If you settled for three figures following the decimal point, for example, you might use numbers like 1.776, 5.204, 9.917 and so on. The second part of the number is a power of ten. This is just a way of writing the zeros of the number and showing whether the number is greater than or less than unity. For use with calculators and computers, the multiplier 10 is written as E1 (one zero), 100 as E2 (two zeros), 1000 as E3 and so on. Fractions are written with a negative sign and a number that is one more than the number of zeros. Thus the multiplier 0.01 is written as E-2, 0.001 as E-3 and 0.0001 as E-4. As an example of the compete form, a number 1.617E3 is the equivalent of 1,617 and 4.116E-3 is the standard form of 0.004116.

note The exponent is often written in textbooks as a power of ten, so that what we type as E3 is 10^3, and what we type as E-3 is 10^{-3}.

To put a number into standard form

1. Shift the decimal point until the number lies between 1 and 10. Count the number of places shifted and whether the shift is to the left or to the right.
2. Write down the number that you now have and chop off or round off all digits beyond the limit you have decided on – two or three decimal places usually.
3. Write down the E and if you have shifted the decimal point to the right, add a minus sign.
4. Follow this with the number of places that you had to shift the decimal point.

Examples:

1,814,519,371,402 to use four places of decimals. Shift the point 12 places left, and write down the figures 1.8145E12.

0.000 000 000 141 536 to use three places of decimals. Shift the point ten places right and chop to get 1.415, so that the result is 1.415E-10.

Converting back from standard form

1. If the sign following the E is negative, then the point is moved left, otherwise it is moved to the right.
2. Move the point, filling with zeros where there are no figures.

Examples:

3. 124E8 Move eight places right to get 312,400,000
4. 198E-4 Move four places left, inserting zeros to get 0.000 419 8

Appendices

B:Converting GW-BASIC Programs

Programs written in GW-BASIC will convert very easily to QBASIC, and many will run with absolutely no changes, and this also applies to BASICA which is virtually identical to GW-BASIC. Both of these, however, can save their program files in two different formats and only the ASCII format provides a program listing that can be used in QBASIC. This is by far the only important difference, because other differences are minor.

note If all of your GW-BASIC programs are recorded in coded form you must read each one into the GW-BASIC interpreter and save it to another directory as an ASCII file.

BASICA programs that deal with mathematical work in serial or random access files may use a different number format in their data files. By starting QBASIC using QBASIC /MBF you can read such files, automatically converting to the number format used in QBASIC, without modifying the program.

BASICA programs that include machine code sections will include a CALL statement. Change each of these to CALL ABSOLUTE to run on QBASIC. Note that statements like CALL, SUB, END SUB, END FOR and many others do not occur in GW-BASIC, and it is much harder work to convert each GOSUB to a CALL form. This is why QBASIC contains both the older forms and the more modern forms of these actions.

Other points you need to watch are:

1. The use of BLOAD and BSAVE in QBASIC is likely to cause problems.
2. Any CHAIN statement in GW or BASICA must be edited if it contains a line number or a MERGE. Use COMMON for variables that must be used by both programs (in place of MERGE action).
3. If a BASICA or GW program contains statements other than REM before a COMMON or a DECLARE line, shift these elsewhere. QBASIC cannot work with any statement preceding these lines.
4. Watch for a variable that has changed type, usually by over-riding a DEFINT, DEFSNG, DEFDBL, DEFSTR type of statement. QBASIC does not allow a variable to change type after it has been used.
5. BASICA and GW use only dynamic arrays. In QBASIC you can choose dynamic or static arrays.
6. Both GW and BASICA can use DRAW and PLAY strings in which the X command is followed immediately by another string. In QBASIC you must make use of the VARPTR$ statement, see Chapter 21. Note that Turbo-BASIC also uses the VARPTR form.
7. When file inputs are read in a loop, using EOF to find the end of the file, QBASIC needs the EOF test at the end of the loop; BASICA and GW-BASIC normally use a WHILE..WEND loop that is tested at the start.
8. GW and BASICA programs sometimes make use of field variables obtained by using GET after files have been closed. In QBASIC, closing the file zeros these variables.
9. Unsupported keywords of GW and BASICA cannot be used in QBASIC

AUTO	**CONT**	**DEF USR**	**DELETE**	**EDIT**	**LIST**	**SAVE**
LLIST	**LOAD**	**MERGE**	**MOTOR**	**NEW**	**RENUM**	**USR**

Any program in which these keywords appear (an unusual one) should be checked carefully and some re-writing may be needed.

10. Line numbers are optional in QBASIC. They can be removed from a GW/BASICA program by using the program REMLINE.BAS that is packaged with QBASIC. Place the program you want to convert in the same directory as QBASIC and REMLINE.BAS and run REMLINE.BAS. Any line numbers that remain afterwards are being used purely as labels.

Programs written for Borland's Turbo-BASIC need less work, most will run without changes, but there are a few keywords (seldom encountered) which are not supported by QBASIC.

Programs written in Microsoft QuickBASIC will run in QBASIC with no changes.

Programs written in Locomotive BASIC-2 can usually run after some editing.

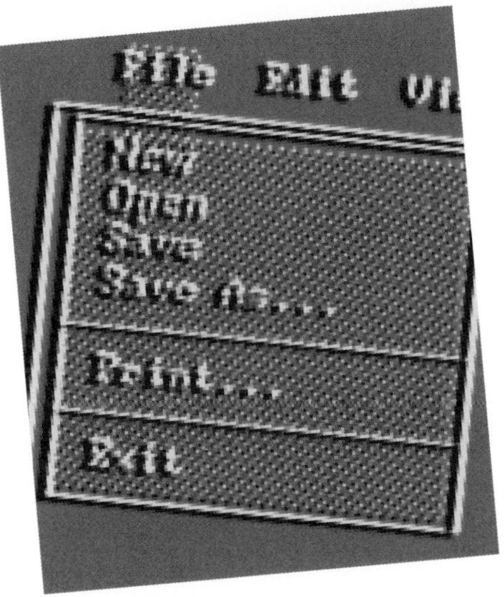

Appendices C: Binary and Hex

Binary code is the form of number code used within the computer. Its digits are 0 or 1 only, so that any number in binary form will consist of more digits than the equivalent in normal (denary) scale. The methods used for writing positive integers are identical to those used for ordinary numbers, where the number following 9 is written as 10, meaning one ten and one zero. In binary, the number following 1 is 10, meaning a two and a zero, and this is followed by 11, meaning a two and a one, three.

To convert a binary number to denary, start at the right hand side and look for the 1's in the number. A 1 at the right hand side counts as 1, in the next position is counts as 2, in the next as 4, then as 8 and so on, with each place to the left meaning a doubling of value. For example, the binary number 1011 is 1 + 2 + 0 + 8 = 11 in denary.

Your main encounter with binary is in creating dot-dash lines for the LINE statement, where a binary number such as:

1010101010101010

will create a finely dotted line and

1111000011110000

will create a dashed line. The main problem is to convert these binary numbers into a form that you can type into a LINE statement, and using Hex code is by far the easiest method.

The hex scale

Hexadecimal means scale of sixteen, and the reason that it is used so extensively is that it is naturally suited to representing binary bytes. Four bits, half of a byte, will represent numbers which lie in the range 0 to 15 in our ordinary number scale. This is the range of one hex digit

Binary	Hex	Binary	Hex	Binary	Hex	Binary	Hex
0000	0	0100	4	1000	8	1100	C
0001	1	0101	5	1001	9	1101	D
0010	2	0110	6	1010	A	1110	E
0011	3	0111	7	1011	B	1111	F

Since we don't have symbols for digits higher than 9, we have to use the letters A,B,C,D,E, and F to supplement the digits 0 to 9 in the hex scale. The advantage is that a byte can be represented by a two-digit number, and an integer by a four-digit number. Converting between binary and hex is much simpler than converting between binary and denary, using the table above, because a binary number can be split into four-digit groups (starting the right hand side) and each set of four binary digits converted to hex using the table above. The final hex number is written with the &H prefix if it is to be used in the QBASIC LINE statement.

Now the great value of hex code is how closely it corresponds to binary code. If you look at the hex-binary table above you can see that &H9 is 1001 in binary and &HF is 1111. The hex number &H9F is therefore just 10011111 in binary – you simply write down the binary digits that correspond to the hex digits. Taking another example, the hex byte &HB8 is 10111000, because &HB is 1011 and &H8 is 1000. The conversion in the opposite direction is just as easy – you group the binary digits in fours, starting at the least significant (right-hand) side of the number, and then convert each group into its corresponding hex digit.

For example, the number for dotted lines that in binary is 1010101010101010 is grouped as 1010 1010 1010 1010 and in hex this is &HAAAA. The binary number 1111000011110000 similarly translates to &HF0F0, so that it becomes relatively painless to write down the binary pattern for a dot/dash line and convert to hex. This is considerably easier than using denary numbers, because a lot of these binary patterns correspond to negative integer values, and the conversion is nowhere near so simple.

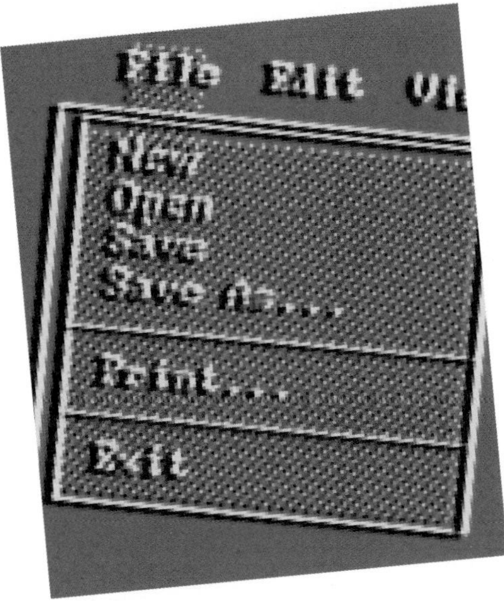

Appendices

D: Bruce Smith Books for your PC

Bruce Smith Books are dedicated to producing quality personal computer publications which are both comprehensive and easy to read. Our PC titles are written by some of the best known names in the marvellous world of personal computing. Below you will find details of all our currently available books for the PC owner.

Brief details of these books are given below. If you would like a free copy of our catalogue and to be placed on our mailing list then phone or write to the address below. As a small, dedicated publisher, we are able to respond flexibly to customers' needs so if you would like to see a book from us on a subject that we don't cover then please call to let us know. Equally if you have an area of expertise in a personal computer related field and you'd like to produce a book then talk to us about becoming an author.

Our mailing list is used exclusively to inform readers of forthcoming Bruce Smith Books publications along with special introductory offers.

Bruce Smith Books,

PO Box 382,

St. Albans, Herts, AL2 3JD

Telephone: (0923) 894355

Fax: (0923) 894366

Note that we offer a 24-hour telephone answer system so that you can place your order direct by 'phone at a time to suit yourself. When ordering by 'phone please:

- Speak clearly and slowly
- Leave your name and full address and contact phone number
- Give your credit card number and expiry date
- Spell out any unusual names

Note that we do not charge for P&P in the UK and endeavour to dispatch all books within 24-hours.

Buying at your Bookshop

All our books can be obtained via your local bookshops – this includes WH Smiths which will be keeping a stock of some of our titles, just enquire at their counter. If you wish to order via your local High Street bookshop you will need to supply the book name, author, publisher, price and ISBN number.

Overseas Orders

Please add £3 per book (Europe) or £6 per book (outside Europe) to cover postage and packing. Pay by sterling cheque or by Access, Visa or Mastercard. Post, fax or phone your order to us.

Bookshop and Dealer Enquiries

Our distributor is Computer Bookshops Limited who keep a good stock of all our titles. Call their Customer Services Department for advice and best terms on 021-706-1188.

Compatibility

We endeavour to ensure that all our personal computer books are up to date and pertinent to all current releases of the relevant software.

QBASIC

Our 700-page plus dual volume set covers QBASIC in its entirety, no stone left unturned. While *QBASIC Beginners* is a complete tutorial for novice users, assuming no previous programming experience, *QBASIC A to Z Reference* is for both beginners and experts alike. *A to Z Reference* is a detailed and comprehensive command by command analysis for reference while working with QBASIC. Both books cover QBASIC 1.0 as the major release and are completely compatible with QBASIC revision 1.1.

The information contained in the two volumes is complementary so you need have no hesitation in purchasing both volumes to provide you with the complete guide to QBASIC.

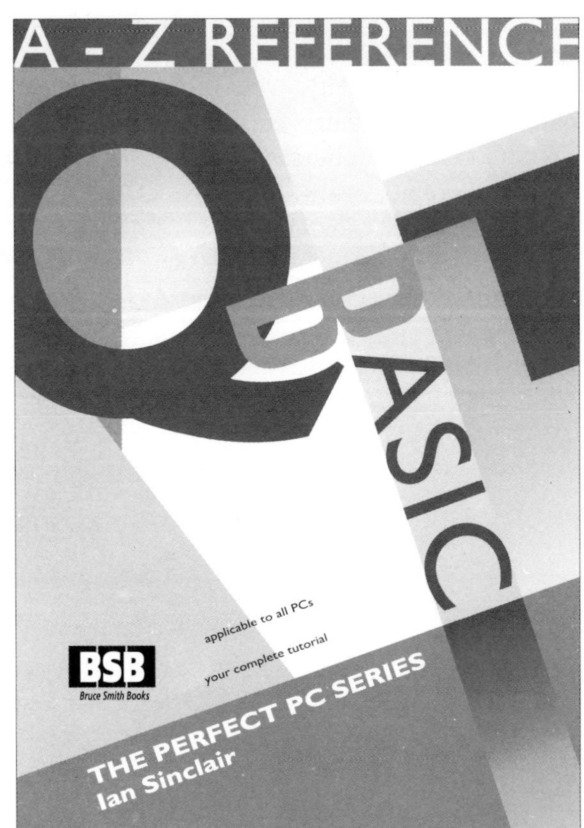

QBASIC A to Z Reference

QBASIC A to Z Reference is the companion volume to *QBASIC Beginners*. It complements the beginners tutorial and is designed to sit beside your PC to act as a reference and advisor while you are programming in QBASIC. Each command is given with a run-down on type, typical syntax, action, options, arguments and restrictions. Associated commands are given and QBASIC code examples listed with full explanation and ideas on further use.

The aim is that information is easy to reach and understand and the pertinent coded examples are particularly useful as a reminder of how things should work. Programmers converting from another version of BASIC will find QBASIC very accomodating and this guide advises on commands which are included for compatibility and for potentially useful alternatives available in the modernised version.

QBASIC A to Z Reference

by Ian Sinclair

ISBN: 1-873308-22-1, price £17.95, approx 416 pages.

APPEND

Type: Statement

Typical syntax: OPEN filename FOR APPEND AS number

Action: Allows new data to be appended to an existing sequential file rather than replacing the existing data, as is done when OUTPUT is used in place of APPEND.

Options: None

Argument(s): None

Restrictions: Used only in an OPEN statement following FOR. APPEND is applicable to sequential files only.

Example:

```
OPEN "Cats" FOR APPEND AS #5
PRINT #5, A$
REM will add the data in A$ to the existing data in
REM the CATS file.
```

Associated with: BINARY, INPUT, NAME, OPEN, OUTPUT, PRINT, WRITE

Points to note:
APPEND can be used even if a file has not been created. Its action is then the same as that of OPEN, creating the file and writing the data. It is therefore better to use APPEND for opening a serial file for writing unless you specifically want any file of the same name to be deleted. Use NAME to rename an old file if OPEN is used with the same name - this allows a new file to be opened with the old file retained as a BAK file.

Example pages from QBASIC A to Z Reference – your companion guide

AS

Type: Statement

Typical syntax: DIM name AS type
name AS type
OPEN filename FOR filetype AS number
FIELD number AS variable
NAME oldfilename AS newfilename

Action: Nominates a name or number to be used with the preceding statement.

Options: None

Argument(s): Depend on context:
Variable type in declarations
Element in TYPE statement
File number in OPEN statement
Field name in FIELD statement
File name in NAME statement

Restrictions: Can be used only in association with DIM, FIELD, NAME, OPEN, TYPE statements.

Examples:

```
DECLARE varnam AS INTEGER        ' declares type for variable name
TYPE datacard
  Surname AS STRING * 20         'declares fixed-length strings
  Forename AS STRING * 12        ' in the variable type
END TYPE
OPEN "myfile" FOR INPUT AS #1    'establishes file reference number
FIELD #2, 25 AS person$          'establishes field size
NAME "oldfile" AS "newfile"      'establishes new name for file
```

Associated with: COMMON, DECLARE, DEF FN, DIM, REDIM, FIELD, FUNCTION, NAME, OPEN, SHARED, STATIC, SUB, TYPE

Points to note:
Because of the large variety of statements in which AS can be used it is easy to provide the wrong form of argument.

QBASIC Book

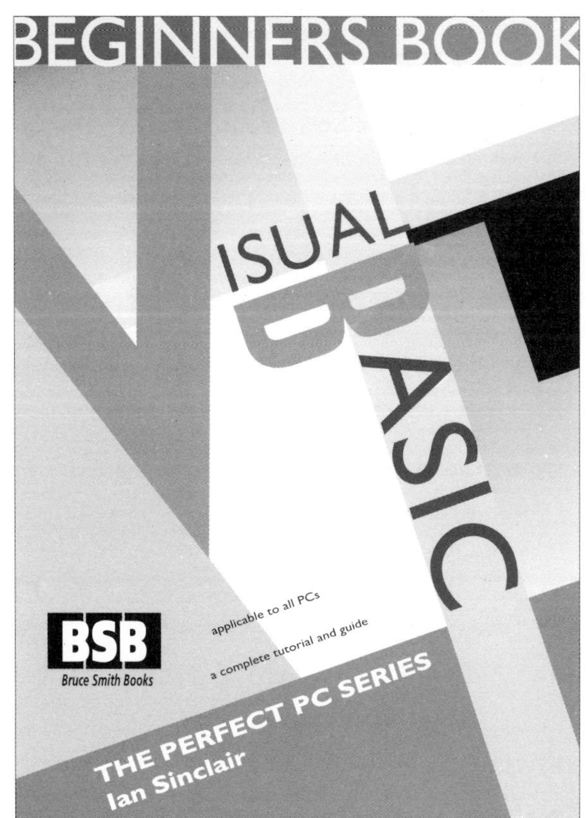

Visual Basic Beginners

Visual Basic has captured the imagination of programmers looking for an accessible and productive way to create their code. This tutorial guide starts from scratch with how to use the tools provided by Visual Basic with lots of shortcuts and hints, and a few warnings about limitations.

The advent of Windows 3.0 and 3.1 has made previous versions of BASIC look decidedly old-fashioned. By following this book step by step you will be able to create programs that make full use of all that is built into Windows, without the need to write vast numbers of lines of code.

You'll find plenty of help and lots of worked examples to practice with and use as the basis of your own programs. If you are starting out with Visual Basic or coming to it new from another version then this Beginners guide is an essential purchase. If you have some Visual Basic experience then you'll appreciate the hints and tips, advice on design and structure and the later chapters on more advanced programming.

Visual BASIC Beginners

by Ian Sinclair

ISBN: 1-873308-23-X, price £17.95, approx 416 pages.

WordPerfect 6.0 for DOS

WordPerfect 6.0 is a new departure for the best-selling wordprocessor and here's a new type of book for beginners to the program. Wordprocessing skills are part of the modern office and business environment and Stephen Copestake's helpful style will get you up to speed on WordPerfect in an enjoyable way.

As well as describing the features of WordPerfect in an easy to understand manner, the author teaches you how to achieve results. Step by step instructions guide you towards professional-looking documents and you learn through doing on the way. Screen shots are used liberally to illustrate the step by step tutorial and to further clarify the instructive text. If you use WordPerfect 6.0 then choose this book to get the most from your investment.

WordPerfect 6.0 for DOS

by Stephen Copestake

ISBN: 1-873308-25-6, price £TBA, approx 416 pages.

Corel Draw 4.0 Practical Projects

Overwhelmed by everything that Corel Draw 4.0 has to offer? When you've come down to Earth, try our volume of practical projects to help you to publish in print and on screen.

Stephen Copestake introduces the whys and wherefores of the Corel suite but he doesn't leave you to it. Instead you have here an ideas book and a practical guide to creating objects such as newsletters, slides, flyers, maps, advertisements, magazines, posters, forms and much much more. Don't get bogged down in the fonts and clipart, focus on results with *Corel Draw 4.0 Practical Projects.*

Corel Draw 4.0 Practical Projects

by Stephen Copestake

ISBN: 1-873308-26-4, price £TBA, approx 320 pages.

Established in 1990 as a publisher dedicated to producing computer-related books in the UK, Bruce Smith Books has expanded its range at a steady pace ever since. We've gained a reputation for technical excellence, coupled with a an easy to read informal style which makes reading a pleasure.

Our authors are experienced writers and journalists – often well-known names – working full-time in the personal computer field, which means that your book is as thoroughly researched and up to date as it can be. Their full-time involvement means that our writers are in touch with you, the reader, and the requirements you have expressed.

PC Perfect, Ace for Amiga

Also available from Bruce Smith Books is a range of titles for the Commodore Amiga – graphics workstation and home computer both. If you use an Amiga for work or play then we have some interesting reading for you.

Titles Currently Available

- Mastering Amiga Beginners
- Mastering Amiga AMOS
- Mastering Amiga C
- Mastering Amiga Printers
- Mastering Amiga System
- Mastering Amiga Assembler
- Mastering Amiga ARexx
- Amiga A1200 Insider Guide
- Amiga Gamer's Guide
- Mastering Amiga Workbench 3*
- Mastering AmigaDOS3 Volume 1*

*These titles available autumn 1993. Other version 3.0 and A1200 specific books are planned so get yourself on our mailing list for further information.

Other titles which relate to Amigas with AmigaDOS and Workbench prior to version 3.0 are:

- Amiga A600 Insider Guide
- Mastering Amiga Workbench2
- Mastering AmigaDOS2 Vol. 1
- Mastering AmigaDOS2 Vol. 2

New publications and their contents are subject to change without notice.

E&OE.

Here's what the press have said about some of our previous books for personal computers:

"If you're a complete beginner or unsure of a few areas, this book is an amazingly informative read." Amiga Format on Volume One of Mastering AmigaDOS

"As a reference book it's very useful. So far as I know there isn't any similar book...If you need to know how every AmigaDOS command works get this book...it is a definitive reference" Amiga Format on Volume Two of Mastering AmigaDOS.

We reserve the right to change specifications. E&OE.

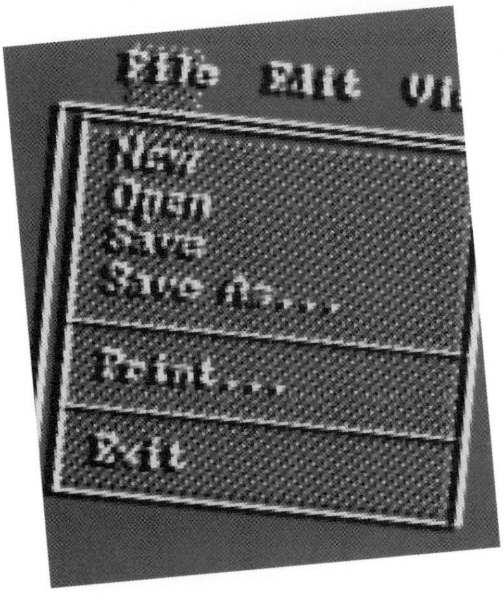

Index

C

D

E

F

G

H

I

J

K

L

M

N

O

P

Q

R

S

T

U

V

W

X

Notes